Shadow Worlds

Shadow Worlds

A History of the Occult
and Esoteric in New Zealand

Andrew Paul Wood

MASSEY UNIVERSITY PRESS

For Fiona Pardington
Διπλοῦν ὁρῶσιν οἱ μαθόντες γράμματα

Contents

	Introduction	13
1.	The not-so-secret doctrine	29
2.	Children of the Golden Dawn	77
3.	The Empire Sentinels	107
4.	The Golden Dawn: A coda	115
5.	Rudolf Steiner and Anthroposophy	129
6.	Gomorrah on the Avon	141
7.	Bumps in the night	155
8.	The women of the Beast	221
9.	In science's robe	247
10.	The Age of Aquarius	271
11.	Witchcraft and neopaganism	295
12.	The Rosy Cross and the OTO	321
13.	The Devil rides out	341
	Epilogue	363
	Notes	368
	About the author	412
	Acknowledgements	413
	Index	414

For the scientific method can teach us nothing else beyond how facts are related to, and conditioned by, each other. The aspiration toward such objective knowledge belongs to the highest of which man is capable, and you will certainly not suspect me of wishing to belittle the achievements and the heroic efforts of man in this sphere. Yet it is equally clear that knowledge of what *is* does not open the door directly to what *should be*. One can have the clearest and most complete knowledge of *is*, and yet not be able to deduct from that what should be the *goal* of our human aspirations. Objective knowledge provides us with powerful instruments for the achievements of certain ends, but the ultimate goal itself and the longing to reach it must come from another source. And it is hardly necessary to argue for the view that our existence and our activity acquire meaning only by the setting up of such a goal and of corresponding values. The knowledge of truth as such is wonderful, but it is so little capable of acting as a guide that it cannot prove even the justification and the value of the aspiration toward that very knowledge of truth. Here we face, therefore, the limits of the purely rational conception of our existence.

— ALBERT EINSTEIN, 'SCIENCE AND RELIGION', AN ADDRESS DELIVERED AT THE PRINCETON THEOLOGICAL SEMINARY ON 19 MAY 1939

But memetics possesses the very fault for which it purports to be a remedy: it is a spell with which the scientistic mind seeks to conjure away the things that pose a threat to it — which is also how we should view scientism in general. Scientism involves the use of scientific forms and categories in order to give the appearance of science to unscientific ways of thinking. It is a form of magic, a bid to reassemble the complex matter of human life, at the magician's command, in a shape over which he can exert control. It is an attempt to *subdue* what it does not understand.

— ROGER SCRUTON, 'SCIENTISM IN THE ARTS AND HUMANITIES: WHY ART IS MORE THAN MATTER AND MEME', *THE NEW ATLANTIS*, AUTUMN 2013

Introduction

Philosophy is odious and obscure,
Both law and physic are for petty wits;
Theology is basest of the three,
Unpleasant, harsh, contemptible and vile.
'Tis magic, magic that has ravished me.
— CHRISTOPHER MARLOWE, *THE TRAGICAL HISTORY OF THE LIFE AND DEATH OF DOCTOR FAUSTUS*, I. I, 1604

The occult and the magical are very much part of the everyday world. Even if you don't check your horoscope regularly, you probably know your zodiacal star sign. At some point you may have had your palm read or your cards done. You've probably seen a clairvoyant on television or know someone who says they saw a ghost. You may have experimented with a Ouija board, have a four-leaf-clover or own lucky underwear. You may throw salt over your shoulder when you spill it. You may have participated in a formal religious ceremony or read a self-help book. I do not mean magic in the sense of conjuring tricks, but for an excellent history of that in Aotearoa, consult Bernard Reid's *Conjurors, Cardsharps and Conmen*.[1]

The magical takes many forms, from the ability of marketing and public relations experts to change how millions of people experience reality, and thoroughly ridiculous politicians rising to the highest office through the proliferation of memes on the internet, to someone you know shifting consensual reality on its axis by changing their pronouns. Around 75 per cent of adults in the Western world have some belief in magic or the paranormal. A survey of 35,000 Americans carried out by the Pew Research Forum in 2007 revealed that 79 per cent believed in miracles in the Old Testament sense. In the 2011 UK census, out of the total population of 63.2 million, 56,620 people identified as pagans, 11,766 as Wiccans, and 1276 described their faith as 'witchcraft'.[2]

By comparison, in the 2018 New Zealand census, out of the total population of 4.7 million people, 19,434 people identified their religious affiliation as 'Spiritualism or New Age' and 6453 people identified with Māori belief systems other than Rātana or Ringatū. In 2021, All Black Ethan de Groot had his elbow tattooed with a *vegvísir*, an ancient Icelandic runestave — sometimes inaccurately called a 'Viking compass' — that is supposed to protect the wearer while travelling, particularly in bad weather.[3] That's not to say that he is some kind of magician, but rather that he clearly felt some sort of symbolic attraction to a magical talisman.

Before we can tackle the particulars of the unique and fascinating history of the Western occult, esoteric and magical in Aotearoa New Zealand, we must first tackle the fraught subject of definitions for terminology — or rather, what I intend by definition.

The term 'occulture' was a neologism coined in the late twentieth century in the Industrial Music scene by Genesis P-Orridge,[4] and later taken up by scholar of religion Christopher Partridge, in an academic sense, to describe the influential counterculture of esoterism, magic, parapsychology and the occult, which, largely ignored by the mainstream, has had a major influence on moulding Western modernist identity. Partridge describes it as 'the new spiritual environment in the West; the reservoir feeding new spiritual springs; the soil in which new spiritualities are growing'.[5]

☦

The emergence and rapid evolution of a 'modern' occulture over the past 200 years or so is, in part, a response to the trajectory of multiple strands of philosophy that developed out of the work of Immanuel Kant in the 1780s and 1790s, particularly in Germany, as to the nature of the relationship between thought and being. These arguments carried on through the nineteenth century and into the twentieth. Arthur Schopenhauer (1788–1860), for example, believed that the world exists only as an idea and was susceptible to the human will. This idea becomes important as a kind of metaphysics of magic.

Martin Heidegger (1889–1976), deeply unfashionable these days because of his enthusiasm for Nazism, determined (in more convoluted terms than I care to go into here) that being was defined by time and death — or, to paraphrase Nietzsche, who put it rather more succinctly, the meaning of life is that it ends — and that being is defined by the social relationship of a community's way of life.

In a similar vein, sociologist and philosopher Max Weber (1864–1920) warned of the 'disenchantment' of the world by modernity, that is science, technology, bureaucracy, capitalism, and the decline of traditional religion and folk culture.[6] Essentially modernity was draining the colour, ritual and magic out of life, and as it turns out colour, ritual and magic are important to a healthy sense of human identity. Weber's theory of disenchantment (*Entzauberung*) is an important concept here. Weber saw in modernity a society based on the desacralised pursuit of rational goals without any appreciation of the mystical and the mysterious, and on valuing scientific explanation over belief.[7]

In the second half of the twentieth century, the Anglo-Czech philosopher Ernest Gellner (1925–1995) argued that an unexpressed desire for 're-enchantment' manifested itself variously in forms that considered themselves rational and naturalistic: psychoanalysis, analytical philosophy, Marxism, ethnomethodology and phenomenology.[8]

American philosopher and social scientist Jason Josephson Storm argues that Weber has been misrepresented because he was well aware of the existence of occult and esoteric movements, but this position implies that Weber saw them as something authentic and organic — something of which I am unconvinced.[9] Arguably those occult and esoteric movements are all responses to a desire for re-enchantment that Gellner would have recognised. For with the exponentially accelerating modernisation of the nineteenth century, orthodox religion lost authority to science and new spiritualities emerged.[10]

☦

It all distils to a yearning for spiritual experience. Writing in the early decades of the twentieth century, the German theologian Rudolf Otto (1869–1937) described the essence of the spiritual experience as an encounter with the overwhelming, compelling and ineffably numinous.[11] That's a tall order when science is culturally ascendant and bent on describing and rationalising everything in the universe. To an extent it could be sublimated into the sublime wonder of the natural world. This was the age in which X-rays, radio waves, early atomic physics and diesel engines first made an appearance, leading to a yearning for the numinous beyond all this rational positivism, and a turn to the romantic and subversive. At times even the science could seem magical.

In 1846 the historian George Grote (1794–1871) observed that the science of his day understood the physical world as 'lifeless and impersonal aggregate, slavishly obedient to the rules of which it has no consciousness, and destitute of all sympathy with the men who suffer or profit by it'.[12] This was a strictly materialistic view of an arbitrary universe with little room for human abstractions such as love, justice or religion. By the 1890s, science in the form of anthropology was turning its analytical lenses upon what archaeologist Chris Gosden describes as magic as part of a 'triple helix', with science and religion threading through culture, rather than magic being some primitive precursor of religion. Religion can be slippery, though, and easily confused with magic when it comes to things like animism, totemism and fetish-worship, yet it distinguishes itself from magic by its tendency to moral precepts and the expansive development of an afterlife and an eschatology.[13]

In the late Victorian and early Edwardian period, two anthropologists emerge whose understanding of magic would colour all later responses to it: founder of cultural anthropology Sir Edward Burnett Tylor (1832–1917), and the social anthropologist and folklorist Sir James George Frazer (1854–1941).

Tylor saw anthropology as an 'emancipatory science' for rooting out the superstitious, primitive worldviews that warped Western rationalism. Frazer — whose ideas, despite often being crude projections based on dubious information, were widely popularised in his 13-volume work *The Golden Bough* (1890–1915) — saw human civilisation as an evolution away from the magic of fertility cults to the power of nature represented by the gods, and eventually science.

For Frazer, magic was an attempt to directly control nature; religion was an attempt to intercede with God or gods; and science sought to understand the world in exclusively naturalistic terms. Frazer divided magic into two principles: 'contagion', where magical properties and influence were transferred by proximity or contact; and 'sympathy', where influence could be conveyed by using something that resembled what the magic user wanted to influence, like affecting like.

The Victorian occult, which is where the story of the New Zealand occult begins, is very much of the aesthetic of its time. Seeking distraction from late nineteenth-century industrialism and social problems, the Victorian age saw the enormous popularity of mock-medievalism in the form of the gothic revival architecture, Pre-Raphaelite paintings, and Arts and Crafts-style decoration. It makes sense that other practices consigned to the Middle Ages in the popular consciousness might likewise be resuscitated, including magic. An obsession with the gothic seems to go hand-in-hand with the rediscovery of magic.[14]

The Victorians who colonised Māori Aotearoa had reinvented the gothic. New Zealand cities are full of stunning examples of gothic revival architecture — or were, prior to the machinations of developers in Auckland and the earthquakes in Christchurch. In the late nineteenth century, a substantial body of gothic fiction was set in imperial contexts — Rudyard Kipling's short story 'At the End of the Passage' (1890) and Joseph Conrad's novel *Heart of Darkness* (1899), for example — tending to focus on white colonial encounters with terrifying indigenous experiences.[15]

At the same time, we find a bewildering array of occult groups and movements taking root in antipodean soil among the neo-gothic piles, influenced by a lot of complex feelings about colonialism and the indigenous, and culminating in the splendid final phase of the Stella Matutina magical order in Havelock North (Chapters 2 and 4). By comparison, the magical, occult and esoteric activities of the twentieth-century New Age look a little dumbed-down and ignoble.[16]

☥

These islands at the end of the Earth, where the light of the dawn first touched each day, must have seemed deeply appealing to nonconformists. A very early example of this attitude was Robert Pemberton (1788?–1879), one of the last of the Owenite sect in England, whose utopian plans for a collectivised commune in New Zealand were outlined in his book *The Happy Colony* (1854). Efforts were made to establish a colony in Taranaki, where children were to be raised communally and educated in spiritual perfectibility, but nothing ever came of it.[17]

Worldwide in the nineteenth and twentieth centuries, even within Christianity itself, old and new beliefs struggled with each other, and novel syntheses emerged. These included Christian Science, the Church of the Latter-day Saints (Mormonism), the Jehovah's Witnesses, the syncretic movements of Theosophy and Spiritualism, and a host of secretive occult and esoteric societies. Within the High Anglican Church, a desire for renewal resulted in Tractarianism, otherwise known as the Oxford Movement, which eventually led to Anglo-Catholicism, of which Lytton Strachey writes, tongue deep in cheek, in *Eminent Victorians* (1918):

> Some of the divines of the seventeenth century had, perhaps, been vouchsafed glimpses of the truth; but they were glimpses and nothing more. No, the waters of the true Faith had dived underground at the Reformation, and they were waiting for the wand of [Cardinal John Henry Newman (1801–1890)] to strike the rock before they should burst forth once more into the light of day.[18]

A similar yearning for spiritual supernaturalism was to be found in the decadent and symbolist movements of fin-de-siècle France. The French writer Jean Lorrain (1855–1906) bemoaned in his short story 'Lanterne magique' (1900) the dissection of fantasy by psychiatrists, and witches' sabbats driven from cemetery cypress groves by the electric lights and whitewashed corridors of hospitals.[19] J.-K. Huysmans (1848–1907), author of the infamous novels of the decadence, the outré aesthetic *À rebours* (1884) and the satanically-themed *Là-Bas* (1891), likewise confessed that his interest in the occult came from a need to be compensated for the squalor of daily modern life.[20]

Perhaps, then, it is better to speak of 'occultures' rather than a single global occulture, as each version tends to acquire a regional flavour, including in New Zealand. The surprising thing is the degree to which these ideas have had an influence on culture, society and modernity. It is not the purpose of this book to answer any epistemological or metaphysical questions about the reality of occult beliefs or the supernatural. Yet most Victorian occultists and magical practitioners regarded themselves as only a slightly spicier flavour of Christian. Many saw their esoteric pursuits as entirely consistent with, and therefore unproblematic for, their profession of High Church Anglicanism.

This was not an attitude shared by mainstream New Zealand, and we see, circa 1900, vigorous, even vitriolic resistance from the churches to Theosophy and Spiritualism. In 1933 we find a lengthy *Auckland Star* column warning of the dangers of the occult:

> But observation would lead one to assert that urbanites are not a whit more enlightened than the people of the soil; an Aucklander returned from a visit to Great Britain tells of the flocking crowds

of Londoners to various halls and 'temples' to listen on Sunday nights to lectures on the occult; and here in Auckland one learns of a large number of apostles (chiefly women) of various cults; that there is something much more serious and sinister afoot than the silly tea-cup reading and fortune-telling by cards, with which we are all familiar, is only too evident; even in these days of stress and strain there are still many so little touched by the realities of life that they can retain the puerile mind which makes for belief in fantastic fatalism . . .[21]

The same article, by 'M. B. Soljak' (teacher, political activist, feminist and journalist Miriam Soljak, 1879–1971), likewise warns of the rise of the occult in Nazi Germany, and goes on to say:

The publicity given in the cables a short while ago to the Brocken scene in the Austrian Alps, made some of us scornfully pitiful for the ignorance of a populace which could believe that magic could enable a beautiful maiden to induce a he-goat to turn into a handsome youth; — but if the next few years bring about an increase of the recent swing to superstition — the signs of which are all round us — we may expect to see similar scenes enacted among the snows of Egmont [Taranaki] or Ruapehu, or even on our own Mount Eden.[22]

It behoves us, also, to acknowledge the postmodern erosion of the authority of scientific positivism and 'progress'. These days we tend to accept the validity of a far broader range of forms of knowledge that don't fit into the usual hierarchy.[23] This inclusivity hasn't been without pushback, as in 2021, when, in response to a government review of the secondary school curriculum, seven University of Auckland professors and emeriti professors published a letter in the *New Zealand Listener* titled 'In Defence of Science', claiming that the inclusion of mātauranga Māori (ancestral Māori knowledge) in the science curriculum 'falls far short of what can be defined as science itself'.[24] This resulted in considerable controversy.

And yet the welfare of Māori, and social reform more generally, was often a prominent component of many early occult and esoteric movements in Aotearoa. German historian Anna Lux points out that 'science' is 'not only determined in the arena of scientific practice, but also in the public'.[25]

Likewise there is a certain amount of truth in philosopher, psychologist, sociologist and polymath Theodor Adorno's assertion that 'semi-erudite' occultists were, and likely are, 'driven by the narcissistic wish to prove superior to the plain people', but were 'not in a position to carry through complicated and detached intellectual operations'.[26] We should, however, recall that Adorno was viewing the subject through the lens of a Holocaust survivor looking at the popularity of occultism and superstition in Nazi Germany with justifiable hostility.

Yet one might wonder if we should be so quick to dismiss beliefs that have lasted many thousands of years. We run up against French Enlightenment philosopher and mathematician Blaise Pascal's distinction between mathematical reason and the sort of *intuitive* reason that allows us to perceive space or understand one plus one equals two without recourse to theory.[27]

Nor should we pretend that occultism is incompatible with modernity or fall into the dialectical trap of assuming occult thought is irrational.[28] Rather, it follows a consistent, if circular, logic of its own, as does theology, and modern neuroscience seems to show that the brain processes evidence differently in either a 'scientific' or a 'religious' framework.[29] A belief in the occult or magical, therefore, isn't necessarily the product of ignorance or delusion.

Drawing on philosopher Charles Taylor's notion of a 'social imaginary', Eric Kurlander raises the concept of a 'supernatural imaginary' or 'how people imagine their social existence, how they integrate with others, and the deeper normative ideas that influence these expectations'. The social imaginary 'is shared by a whole society or large group; theory is expressed in theoretical terms while imaginary is described by images and legends; the imaginary is the common understanding that creates possible commonplace actions and a sense of legitimacy that is shared among all'.[30]

The social imaginary cannot be expressed as doctrine or theory because it is entirely indefinite and unlimited. Taylor sees the *social* imaginary emerging from post-Enlightenment disenchantment, but Kurlander frames the *supernatural* imaginary as the transfer in the nineteenth and twentieth centuries of supernatural thinking and authority from Christianity to occultism.[31]

Of course, there had been many occult revivals before the late nineteenth century; indeed, the occult had never really gone away even at the heights of its most fervent persecution, but its rabid expansion and diversification in that later period is remarkable. It could not have happened without, as Christine Ferguson and Andrew Radford observe of Britain, *infrastructure,* 'a rich and robust public sphere of institutions, gathering places, performance venues' to provide a public platform.[32] This revival was unprecedentedly open in discussion and consumption — that which the philosopher Jürgen Habermas called the 'public sphere'.[33] And New Zealand's flourishing development was contemporary with, and part and parcel of, the Victorian age.

This openness continues into the twenty-first century, and in Aotearoa has expanded to include many Māori traditional understandings, detected in the granting of legal personhood and associated human rights to Te Urewera National Park,[34] the Whanganui River,[35] and soon Taranaki National Park.[36] Although this animistic way of looking at the landscape is very much rooted in a Māori worldview, its adoption into an otherwise materialistic and literal Western legal structure suggests a certain degree of intellectual flexibility on the part of the Crown.

‡

Occulture, as I understand the concept, is primarily a Western phenomenon, and while this book will talk about Māori who were interested in these Western traditions and ideas, and the many occasions where these movements appropriate from Māori tikanga and Māoritanga, it is not my intention to attempt to colonise Māori traditions any further than they already have been.

With the possible exceptions of the Māori prophetic movements and their Christian syncretism, Māori traditional medicine and reverence for the spirit world would have been regarded by the likes of Renaissance Swiss alchemist and physician Paracelsus (Philippus Aureolus Theophrastus

Bombastus von Hohenheim, 1493–1541) as no more sinister than the natural magic of stones and herbs condoned by the Catholic Church of his day. In any event, those things need to be written about by Māori.

By the same token, while I am absolutely certain that when they came to the goldfields of Otago in the 1860s some Chinese gold prospectors brought with them *feng shui*, a knowledge of the properties of the five elements — wood, fire, metal, water, earth — and the flow of energy (*qi*) that links all things, and probably the *I Ching* as well, I am going to try to restrict myself to Western esoteric traditions.

With a nod to the British historian Eric Hobsbawm, New Zealand culture in the long nineteenth century leading up to the First World War tended to be a highly organised and international affair. There were, of course, the folkloric natural magics brought by settlers from the more rural parts of the British Isles; hence we occasionally find, in common with the other British colonies, deposits of items of clothing, single shoes and knives hidden away in the walls and floors of old buildings to ward off or deflect evil and misfortune. Aside from these, however, the most influential esoteric movements were established ones primarily from Britain.

The first of these was undoubtedly Freemasonry, with the first Masonic meeting in New Zealand being held in 1837 by the captain of a French whaling ship, the *Comte de Paris*, and the first lodge being founded in 1842. At the time there was considerable debate as to whether Freemasonry in Aotearoa should be allied to the British or the French lodges.[37] By the end of the nineteenth century, however, the grand fraternal order was well on its way to becoming a community service club in exotic drag, its mysteries taking a back seat to mutual security and public good deeds.[38]

But what defines the esoteric? Essentially a whole web of concepts of mystically understood (anagogic) ideas and attitudes are drawn together by the gravitational pull of Renaissance-era Hermeticism, a highly influential school of esoteric thought in the early modern period, consisting of a syncretic quasi-religious philosophy derived from the purported writings of the mythical Hermes Trismegistus as translated into Latin by Marsilio Ficino (1433–1499). Surprisingly it can even be found discussed in early twentieth century New Zealand newspapers.[39]

The broader esoteric tradition is a Western development, incubated within a Christian culture, and includes alchemy, the Christian and post-Christian variants on Kabbalah,[40] Paracelsianism (alchemical medicine), Theosophy (a mystical form of Christianity developed by Jakob Böhme in the seventeenth century and unrelated to the Theosophical Society of Chapter 1), Bavarian Illuminism, Rosicrucianism (which we will look at more closely in Chapter 12), and various forms of occultism.

They are all loosely compatible, believing in a system of correspondences that link this world with another, that these correspondences are united in nature in a cosmic order, that the creative imagination through ritual or invocation can connect to this other world, with a desire to transcend this world's limitations, that wisdom to do so can be found in a synthesis of historical traditions, and that this knowledge can be transmitted, leading to *gnosis*.[41]

So, what is gnosis? It is the Greek word for 'knowledge', and generally refers to a personal, inner revelation about the true nature of the universe in which the human is part of the divine essence but kept in darkness and ignorance by a material world created for that purpose. As a concept it occurs across many ancient philosophies and some religions. In New Zealand, its most pure form may be found preserved among the Iraqi community of Mandaeans in Auckland, the Naqshbandi Sufi and Gurdjieff-inflected Gnostic Society founded in Auckland by Shaikh Abdullah Isa Neil Dougan (1918–1987) in 1986, and in barely recognisable form in Scientology, but in general Gnostics believe in an evil material universe created by a demiurge to ensnare souls and prevent them realising their intrinsic divinity.[42]

This demiurge, inherited from Platonic thought, goes by various names — Yaldabaoth, Saklas, Samael, Nebro, Leontoeides and Achamoth among them. The last, Achamoth, is a feminine version, a fallen Sophia or Gnostic wisdom, and was used as a sociological allegory by New Zealand writer M. K. Joseph in his speculative novel *The Time of Achamoth* (1977). In a broader neopagan or neo-shamanic worldview, gnosis can be transitory and doesn't necessarily bring coherent clarity, but may speak through archetypes and metaphors during an altered state of consciousness and communication with another realm and entities. These entities can take many, often culturally determined forms: embodied and disembodied, animal, vegetal, nature spirits, gods, angels, demons, elementals, devas, the land itself, fairies, DMT clockwork elves, aliens and many others. It is a non-rational or a-rational form of knowledge, but not an irrational one.

‡

The first actively esoteric group with a fully unique cosmology to establish in New Zealand was the international Theosophical Society, followed in short order by that bastion of the Western occult tradition, the Order of the Golden Dawn — or at least some of its offshoots. Spiritualism — communicating through the veil to the spirits of the departed by means of séances, mediumship and other techniques — was not an organisation per se, but was a loosely consistent global mass movement which also featured strongly in Victorian life. As can be imagined, there were also a fair number of charlatans, for which our exemplar case study is the Temple of Truth (see Chapter 6), which so scandalised Christchurch in the final decade of the nineteenth century.

In the twentieth century, esoteric and occult movements continued to find adherents in Aotearoa, but increasingly they had to appeal to a pragmatic, materialistic and technologically minded society. The UFO phenomena were assimilated into the mix. The first homegrown examples of occulture begin to emerge at this time, spurred on into the 1970s by the late arrival in Aotearoa of the Summer of Love. In the 1980s, variants of the libertarian Satanism, kicked off by the American Anton LaVey a generation earlier, stirred interest in the 'Me Generation'. Wicca and various flavours of Wicca and neopaganism arrived, practised by individuals and communities.

This leads us to magic, and the famous difficulty in trying to define it.[43] In its broadest sense, magic is the use of ritual or will to manipulate natural and supernatural forces. In the Western tradition this can be loosely grouped in a self-explanatory and moralistic way: the right-hand path of light and good, or white magic; the left-hand path of the material realm, often linked with negativity and black magic (though of course such positions are subjective); and natural magic, the magic inherent in natural phenomena, often intricately linked with folk magic and Wicca. Magic can also be, again loosely, divided between the instrumentalised (often lumped together as 'witchcraft') and the ceremonial, abstract high magic of groups such as the Golden Dawn.

My own view is that magic or magical thinking overlaps intensely with creativity and imagination. Arthur Schopenhauer says repeatedly throughout *The World as Will and Idea* (1819) that the universe only exists as a representation or thought-image in an individual's mind rather than being a true perception of an outer reality.[44] An analogous concept is Robert Anton Wilson's 'Chapel Perilous', borrowing from Arthurian legend — the point where you cannot determine whether you have experienced something supernatural or entirely of your own imagination, and therefore you may continue in life either deeply paranoid or entirely agnostic.[45]

Fantasy and comic-book author and ritual magician Alan Moore once had the important realisation that his manipulation of words and images were the equivalent of a magical manipulation of reality, and that the only place he could be sure magic and the gods existed was in his own infinite imagination.[46] In other words, his will. Magic is, perhaps, something that lies at the intersection of these concepts.

This book primarily deals with the nineteenth and twentieth centuries, despite several of these groups and beliefs still being active. At the point in time that the internet becomes omnipresent, the idea of secretive esoteric groups, successive lineages and initiation into mysteries becomes largely redundant as occult practices become almost exclusively DIY affairs with little social stigma attached to them. By the millennium, any bored, disenfranchised soul with too many candles and a penchant for table arrangements might call themselves a Wiccan without having the faintest clue who Gerald Gardner and Doreen Valiente, the founders of the Wiccan movement, were.

In the New Age section of any bookshop you will find popular books on inviting the fairies into your home; previous generations, rather more sensibly, endeavoured at great lengths to keep them out. Occulture merges with pop culture to the point that sustaining the methodology of this book becomes difficult. That, and you have to set limits somewhere or where will it end?

I do not pretend this to be a comprehensive or exhaustive history of the subject — an undertaking of that sort would take many years of research and extend to multiple volumes. Sometimes you will be astonished at the well-known figures of our history who rub up against occulture — as former US Vice President Dan Quayle said of Rasputin, 'people that are really very weird can get into sensitive positions and have a tremendous impact on history'.[47] What I hope this book will do is give a taste of the parallel universe of the unexpected, the strange, and the high weird that exists just beneath the New Zealand story you thought you knew.

Chapter 1.
The not-so-secret doctrine

As when with downcast eyes we muse and brood,
And ebb into a former life, or seem
To lapse far back in some confused dream
To states of mystical similitude . . .

— ALFRED, LORD TENNYSON, 'TO ___, "AS WHEN WITH DOWNCAST EYES" ', 1872

Excluding Freemasonry, the earliest esoteric group to gain traction and influence in nineteenth-century New Zealand was the Theosophical Society. As American religion historian Robert Ellwood acknowledged in his landmark 1993 study of alternative spirituality in Aotearoa, *Islands of the Dawn*, no other unconventional spiritual movement in the Anglosphere has had the persuasive, and often indirect, penetration and influence that Theosophy had, and in New Zealand it was supreme in terms of membership, influence and stability. Until after the Second World War, Theosophy and Spiritualism stood alone as alternative creeds among Pākehā, and the new alternatives spawned in the 1960s owe much to the successes of the Theosophical Society.[1]

Theosophy offered a heady cocktail of spiritualism, reincarnation, lost continents and Eastern metaphysics attractively packaged for Western tastes. Its reach was international, and connected industrialists, politicians, social reformers and avant-garde artists attracted to its promise of something that transcended Victorian rational materialism and Protestant morality.

The Society was formed in New York City — the 'new world' appropriately enough — in 1875 by Madame Helena Petrovna Blavatsky (1831–1891). This Russian — descended from minor nobility, unprepossessingly moon-faced and portly, extraordinarily charismatic, and rapaciously partial to material comforts and other people's money — had emigrated to the United States in 1873. Her formidable hypnotic stare is at once evident in photographs, which in combination with her forthright personality and aristocratic manners quickly attracted followers.

Blavatsky claimed to have visited Tibet in 1849 and to have made telepathic contact with a group of hidden ascended mystics known as the 'Indian Masters' in the vicinity of Tashi Lhunpo. It seems unlikely that Blavatsky did in fact visit Tibet — even Sylvia Cranston's earnest 1993 biography hedges its bets. For one thing, none of the many travellers to the region, nor indeed the Tibetans themselves, had ever heard of these Indian Masters. Additionally, Blavatsky's descriptions of Tibet are few, and her explanations of Tibetan cultural and belief are trivial where not outright erroneous.[2]

But Blavatsky's claim did play to a discernible psychological urge

Helena Petrovna Blavatsky, minor Russian noble, devotee of Indian Masters and founder of the Theosophical Society.

among her compatriots. In the nineteenth and twentieth centuries, a significant number of Russians felt drawn to their Asiatic heritage as a way of distinguishing a more authentic Russian identity from the Western European influences introduced by Tsar Peter the Great in the eighteenth century. In the final decades of tsardom, Russian intellectual life readily embraced the fringe.

Russian artists and writers had forged their own Symbolist movement, distinct from that in the West, and boundaries between the separate realms of science and religion softened, so that by the early 1900s the latest advances in Russian mathematics, particularly the study of infinity, were being influenced by the heretical *Imiaslavie* or 'Name worshipping' sect of the Orthodox Church.

The sect was known for its obsessive worship of the name of the mystical God as God itself.[3] Theosophical conventions about higher spiritual dimensions and the so-called 'Fourth Way' promulgated by the mystics P. D. Ouspensky (1878–1947) and George Gurdjieff (d.1949) — we will encounter them in Chapter 8 — were inspired by developments in mathematics and pangeometry made by Nikolai Lobachevsky (1792–1856) at Kazan University in Russian Tartarstan.[4]

Another widespread underground heretical sect was the flagellant and reputedly sin-to-be-saved (autoerotic asphyxiation was said to feature) the *Khlysty*, which arose in the seventeenth century and was finally stamped out in the Soviet period. Radical politics simmered, and Lenin would embrace revolutionary socialist politics following his brother's 1886 execution. Notoriously randy peasant mystic Grigori Rasputin would become a major figure at the Romanov court in 1905.

Less known is that before Rasputin, the French occultist Gérard Encausse (1865–1916), better known as 'Papus', held similar sway over Nicholas II and Tsarina Alexandra, visiting Russia in 1901, 1905 and 1906, and prophesying that the Tsar would rule as long as Papus lived. Nicholas held out a further 141 days.[5] Russian minds at the time were, clearly, wide open.

Blavatsky may not have visited Tibet, at least in the flesh, but Tibet had come to her. Buddhism had been an officially recognised religion in Russia since the incorporation of Siberia in the seventeenth century. Blavatsky's father, Peter von Hahn, was the government-appointed guardian of the Kalmyks, descendants of Oirat Mongols who had migrated to Astrakhan and the Volga steppe around the same time. The Kalmyks followed the Gelugpa school of Vajrayana, the esoteric/tantric Buddhism of Tibet. Hinduism had been present in Russia since the annexation of Astrakhan in 1556.

In the 1720s, shortly before his death, Tsar Peter the Great passed a law, at the request of Hindu Khatri and Marwari traders who had come via Persia, protecting their religion — the first such law protecting an alien religion in Russia. Those traders had stayed and naturalised. When Blavatsky and her mother accompanied her father on his posting to Astrakhan and Saratov in the late 1830s, they would certainly have gained some first-hand knowledge of both religions.[6]

As she developed her belief system during the 1870s, Blavatsky also threw into her pot the popular writings of French occultist Éliphas Lévi, and the turgid and often virulently white-supremacist proto-speculative fiction of the novelist Edward Bulwer-Lytton, son of Robert Bulwer-Lytton, First Earl of Lytton, who was Viceroy of India when Blavatsky later made her first pilgrimage there in 1880.[7] She was also deeply interested in Spiritualism, the heartland of which was in the United States, attracting her attention to the New World.

At an 1873 séance conducted by the internationally celebrated brother mediums William and Horatio Eddy, of Chittenden in rural Vermont, Blavatsky met Colonel Henry Steel Olcott (1832–1907), a former American military officer, journalist, lawyer, and one of the founding members of the New York Conference of Spiritualists. Beetle-browed and with an enormous white beard, Olcott had fought in the American Civil War, and under the auspices of the US Naval Department had assisted in the investigation of the assassination of President Abraham Lincoln.[8]

Olcott was particularly interested in 'psychology, hypnotism, psychometry, and mesmerism'.[9] Blavatsky convinced him of the existence of her invisible Tibetan Masters and their doctrines, and together they officially founded the Theosophical Society — from the Greek roots *theo* meaning 'divine', and *sophia* meaning 'wisdom' — with Olcott its first president and financial backer.

Colonel Henry Steel Olcott, military officer, journalist, lawyer and co-founder of the Theosophical Society.

‡

The basic tenets of Theosophy were attractive and straightforward: to foster a universal brotherhood of humanity without discrimination of creed, gender, caste or race; to encourage the study of comparative religion, philosophy and science; and to investigate the mysterious laws of nature and the mystical powers latent in humanity. Theosophy promotes harmony and altruism, and believes in karma, reincarnation, and entities and realities beyond our own. Recognising that Spiritualism alone was an insufficient foundation on which to establish itself, the Theosophical Society appropriated the doctrines and Orientalist trappings of Hinduism and Buddhism. This hybrid combination of Western Enlightenment and Eastern mysticism flourished in the fertile soil of late nineteenth-century Romanticism. To further the connection with the ancient belief systems of the East, the Society relocated its international headquarters to Adyar in Madras (now Chennai), India, in 1882.

Theosophy is striking in its cosmology and mythos, the things from which its present-day day members tend to distance themselves. In essence, borrowing the idea of *Maya* or Indra's net of illusion from Hinduism, our perceived reality is merely an emanation of a greater reality. In Theosophical teachings, the solar system, and every other planetary system in the universe, is ruled over by a godlike solar 'Logos', which commands seven planetary spirits or ministers. Each planet possesses two astral bodies, two mental bodies, and two spiritual bodies superposed in space, and evolution ascends and descends between these bodies from mineral to vegetable to animal to human, to superhuman and to spirit.

According to Blavatsky's two-volume book *The Secret Doctrine* (1888), humanity over time has existed as seven 'root races', each of which divided into seven sub-races. The first root race was of pure spirit and dwelt on a continent referred to as the 'Imperishable Sacred Land', which presumably transcended to another plane. The second root race were the Hyperboreans, also of spirit, who lived in a land near the North Pole in a period when it had a temperate climate. The third root race were the inhabitants of the continent of Lemuria, which sank, leaving behind Australia and Rapa Nui (Easter Island). These beings were vaguely reptilian, hermaphroditic, and possessed a second pair of eyes in the backs of their heads and four arms.[10]

At some point, beings of flame from the planet Venus descended to Earth to assist in the evolution of the Lemurians, eventually taking up benign residence in their bodies, causing fully physical bodies to develop and the sexes to diverge. They thus became the fourth root race, the Atlanteans, who more closely resembled humans and who had advanced technology and telepathic powers. Some equate the Atlanteans with the giants of mythology and Nephilim of the Bible. Others claim that they grew decadent and mated with beasts, producing the great apes. Their abuse of their great power and science lead to the sinking of Atlantis, but not before some escaped to found the civilisations of Egypt and Mesoamerica.

The fifth root race were the Aryans, essentially the Indo-European peoples, and this race was destined to be replaced by a sixth with the coming of Lord Maitreya, a messianic figure from Mahayana Buddhism. Eventually humanity would evolve into a seventh root race and transcend the material world altogether. On a more individual level in this epic science-fictional mythos, the purpose of human life is to break free from the karmic cycle of reincarnation and emancipate the soul.[11]

‡

Not surprisingly, Theosophy proved popular in Britain, given India was very much the prize jewel in Queen Victoria's imperial crown. As they wrestled with their own conflicting cultural mix of rational materialism and the limitations of modern Christianity, Victorians became fascinated by Eastern spiritualism, with its emphasis on karma, samsara (reincarnation) and nirvana, and its more relaxed attitudes to sexuality. Nor did Theosophy require one to give up one's customary creed and convert to another.

The movement spread through the Empire via the agency of 'wealthy international travellers with an interest in the occult and esotericism'.[12] New Zealand in the 1890s was no exception, and had the added attractions of being closer to India and being home to Māori culture. From the 1870s onwards the English poet, Spiritualist, Egyptologist and Theosophist Gerald Massey (1828–1907), putting one in mind of Casaubon in George Eliot's *Middlemarch*, attempted to link Māori spiritual beliefs to

Egyptian lore and Jewish Kabbalah in his epic comparative studies of world mythology.[13]

Although the colonial undertones are obvious to us today, at the time such sentiments reflected a sympathy, mingled with romanticism and even envy, regarding indigenous peoples. A typical attitude is that of the British Theosophist Alfred Percy Sinnett (1840–1921), who wrote in 1883: 'The bigotry of modern civilization . . . is to blame if the European races are at this moment more generally ignorant of the extent to which psychological [our psychical] research has been carried, than the Egyptian population of the past, or the people of India in the present day.'[14]

Four prominent Theosophical leaders travelled to New Zealand on lecture tours in the late nineteenth century: Isabel Cooper-Oakley in 1893, the second International President Annie Besant in 1894 and 1908, Blavatsky's close friend Countess Constance Wachtmeister in 1895–96, and Colonel Olcott in 1897.[15] In the 1920s and 1930s the New Zealand Section of the Society sent delegates to conventions in Adyar,[16] and Adyar leaders came to New Zealand,[17] attracting large audiences. As the historian Tony Ballantyne has written:

> In New Zealand, India loomed large in the spiritual and intellectual lives of Pākehā colonists who, like their counterparts in Europe and North America, saw India as a source of intellectual and spiritual revivification. While this new Oriental Renaissance was a transnational affair . . . it found particularly fertile soil in New Zealand, where heterodox religious practices and alternative forms of spirituality enjoyed popularity and power that were unsurpassed in the Anglophone world . . . The Theosophical Society was the primary institutional site for this kind of engagement with Asia.[18]

The first New Zealand member of the Theosophical Society was Augustine King, who joined on a visit to London in 1879. Beyond apparently being from Auckland, little is known about him, but upon his return to New Zealand he was the first Theosophist in the southern hemisphere. Thomas de Renzy Condell, a schoolmaster in Dunedin, and Mr and Mrs James Cox of Auckland became members in 1883. Cox, whose house, 'Wentworth', was located on Ponsonby Road, was a psychometrist who performed psychic medical readings by holding or touching an object relevant to the patient.[19] Olcott wrote of Cox: 'He had such a reputation as a psychometrist principally by the way of distinguishing disease that he made a good living by practicing the profession, constantly going between Auckland and Sydney to see his patients.'[20]

The fabulously named, Canadian-born Edward Toronto Sturdy (1860–1957), described by Colonel Olcott as the 'Father of Theosophy in New Zealand',[21] joined by post in 1885 from Woodville in Hawke's Bay. After meeting Olcott in Rajputana and Blavatsky in London, he returned to New Zealand and founded the Wellington Lodge in 1888. This, the first lodge in New Zealand, was dissolved when Sturdy returned to London to join Blavatsky's 'inner group'.[22]

Sturdy had arrived in New Zealand at age 19, settling at Woodville, which was then largely pristine bush, with an independent income. He made his living as a livestock agent. There amid 'the solitude and beauty of the mountains and forests' he read books on Theosophy and Buddhism, the Hindu *Vedanta*, the novels of Thomas Hardy, and the two volumes of German philosopher Arthur Schopenhauer's *The World as Will and Idea*.

Many of these books were purchased by mail order from the Australian spiritualist W. H. Terry.[23] It was through reading an eighteenth-century translation of the *Bhagavad Gita* that Sturdy found his way fully to Theosophy, and not long after he set off on an epic voyage taking in Adyar, London, New York and San Francisco, meeting with many of the prominent leaders of the movement. Upon his return to New Zealand, he moved to Wellington to gather like-minded people.[24]

Sturdy's Wellington circle included some very influential people: Prime Minister Sir Harry Atkinson (1831–1892) — a prominent Freemason who was known for political and philosophical faddism[25] — and his wife, Annie; the country's most senior rabbi, Herman van Staveren (1849–1930) and his wife, Miriam; the licensed te reo Māori interpreter and tohunga Henry Matthew Stowell (Ngāpuhi, 1855–1944); and Edward Tregear (1846–1931), public servant and scholar.[26]

Tregear's controversial book *The Aryan Maori*, published in 1885, argued that te reo was an Indo-European language and that Māori and

Europeans shared an Aryan origin. This was certainly not out of step with Theosophical ideas.[27] Europeans and Brahmin Indians were both Aryan in this system, which is where Tregear's theory would also place Māori. As Emma Hunt, general secretary of the New Zealand Section in the mid-1940s, put it: 'In outlook [Māori] represent the East and the West; the Maori has an inborn tendency to religion and philosophy, while the European turns outward to conquer the worlds of form.'[28]

The Australian-based Theosophist Charles Leadbeater (a founding bishop of the Liberal Catholic Church, a mystical sister organisation to Theosophy) saw a new sub-race emerging in Australasia that would fuse the rational and the intuitive, and usher in the next human age. Aside from the esoteric metaphysics, this was also consistent with the social Darwinism and eugenics theories prevalent at the time, although Blavatsky was at pains to emphasise the egalitarian nature of the Society.[29] Tregear was also responsible for the 1895 novel *Hedged with Divinities*, in which the protagonist is put into an induced coma for three years by a Māori tohunga after a near-fatal wounding by a stingray, and awakes in a world where all of the other males have been wiped out by a plague.[30]

‡

At the time there was little easily accessible Theosophical material for groups to study — the main texts available being Alfred Sinnett's *Esoteric Buddhism* (1883) and Blavatsky's *Isis Unveiled* (1877) and *The Key to Theosophy* (1889). By the mid-twentieth century, however, New Zealand's four main cities and some of the larger provincial centres each had their own Theosophical lodges, though many of these did not survive the outbreak of the First World War. The Wellington Lodge regrouped in 1894 and remains active. Dunedin launched in 1893 and likewise remains active.

In 1895 both Woodville and Pahiatua founded lodges, but these only lasted a decade. The still-active Whanganui and Napier lodges formed in 1903, the Napier Lodge changing its name to the Hawke's Bay Branch in 2012 to accommodate members from the closed Hastings lodge (founded 1913). Christchurch's Kashmir Lodge opened in 1905 and exists today as the Canterbury Study Group. Invercargill and Gisborne started lodges

Edward Robert Tregear, New Zealand public servant and scholar, prominent social reformer and labour progressive, and proponent of the 'Aryan Māori' theory.

the following year, although the former is now a Study Centre (a smaller private group rather than the public outreach-tasked lodges), and the latter, gaining a new charter in 1951, has since disbanded.

The Motueka and Nelson lodges were founded in 1907, with Nelson reforming — gaining members and renewing its charter — in 1922, folding in 1924, reforming again in 1955 and finally closing in 2011. In 1908, the Dannevirke (until 1914) and Cambridge (until 1924) lodges began, with the Hamilton Lodge becoming active at about this time. Dannevirke is now a Study Centre. The Hāwera and Palmerston North lodges started in 1911 and are both currently active. Little can be ascertained about the Tīmaru branch except that it was founded in 1912.

The Stratford (1916–42) and still-active New Plymouth lodges began in 1916. Whangārei and Ōamaru initiated their lodges in 1918, and both remain active, although the Ōamaru branch disbanded and reformed in 2002. The Waipukurau Lodge lasted from 1919 to 1933. The Tauranga Lodge, based at Mount Maunganui, began in 1947, Rotorua in 1949, Kerikeri (a Study Centre since 2012) in 1954 and Arundale in Tauranga in 1957. The most recent is the Ōrewa Lodge which opened in 1964 and re-formed in 2002.

At its height, in around 1922 the official Theosophical Society membership sat at around 1299, or 1 in 1000 New Zealanders. In strictly numerical terms, its membership peak was in 1987 when it had 1671 members, or 1 in 2000 New Zealanders.[31] Today, at last count, the Society has around 13 lodges — more commonly called 'branches' — five Study Centres and around 800 or so members in Aotearoa.

Theosophy does not observe ritual or ceremony as such, and the format of meetings varies from group to group. Many choose to open and close with brief meditations, attunements or affirmations. There are no clergy, and meetings are led by democratically chosen officials. There are no cult objects or symbols of veneration, but a general respect is observed for all creeds. Meetings consist of discussions, presentations, the study of a set topic, or workshops. This does not hold, however, for Theosophy-adjacent organisations such as the Liberal Catholic Church, which observes rituals that incorporate High Anglicanism and Freemasonry.

‡

Auckland, which has largely remained the centre of Theosophical activity in New Zealand, has had multiple lodges at various times: Waitematā was established around 1896, and the H.P.B. (for Helena Petrovna Blavatsky) Lodge launched in 1903 on Auckland's Queen Street, and remains the movement's chief national base in its current Epsom premises. The other Auckland lodges were Ōnehunga (1904–20), Northcote (1910–14), and Vasanta House (1920–22).

The movement took root in the city over six months between September 1891 and March 1892, when 16 new members joined the Society, among them some prominent people in the city. William Henry Draffin (1857–1938) had just completed a year as headmaster at the Newton East public evening school and had taken a position as second master at the public primary school in Wellesley Street. His wife, Sarah (1858–1908), was described by Colonel Olcott as 'having suddenly blossomed out as an eloquent platform speaker after having passed through a severe illness'.[32]

Other founding members were the artist and photographer Samuel Stuart (1855–1920), a keen yachtie, amateur mathematician, astronomer, and dabbler in astrology, although he baulked at Theosophy's more esoteric teachings,[33] and Margaret Lilian Edger (1862–1941), daughter of the well-known Swedenborgian Reverend Samuel Edger,[34] and a leading suffragette. She was the second official female member of the Theosophical Society in New Zealand after her sister Kate Milligan Edger (1857–1935). They were also the first two women in New Zealand to gain university degrees. Lilian Edger went on to start her own secondary school and became first general secretary of the New Zealand Section, but Olcott, recognising her talents as a lecturer, convinced her to take a role at the Society's global headquarters in Adyar, assisting Annie Besant.[35] She was replaced as general secretary by Dr Charles W. Sanders, a homeopathic practitioner who maintained extensive correspondence throughout the colony.[36]

As Ellwood observes, the sixth and final volume of Olcott's *Old Diary Leaves*, covering the years from 1896 to 1898, are full of Miss Edger — not so much in breathless word-portraits such as he once penned of Blavatsky, Edger being a more pragmatic character and the colonel being

Lilian Edger, the first woman in New Zealand (along with her sister Kate) to gain a university degree, teacher, writer and Theosophist.

much older and no doubt exhausted — but perhaps enough to suggest more tender feelings. He wrote of observing her at a fancy-dress ball *en voyage* back to India: 'I confess that I was pleased with her dissipation for it showed that there was the usual quota of human nature beneath the shell of collegiate enamel.'[37]

This enthusiastic coterie formed the Auckland Lodge that became chartered on 24 March 1892, with Draffin as president. They are first recorded sharing rooms with the newly formed New Zealand Section of the Society, the national body, on the second floor of the no-longer-standing Colonial Mutual Life Insurance Building in Queen Street, near the Customs Street corner. Here, there was a small lecture hall, and study classes met each Tuesday. Regular Sunday lectures took place in an unidentified 500-seat hall (either the Choral Hall, now part of the University of Auckland, or perhaps St Andrew's Church Hall) in Lower Symonds Street. According to the 1901 census there were 189 Theosophists in Aotearoa, and the lion's share of those were in Auckland.

‡

The other chief location of Theosophical activity in Auckland was the Hemus family home at 203–209 Ponsonby Road. Charles Hemus (1849–1925), a photographer, was married to Gertrude Evangeline, sister of Margaret and Kate Edger. Eventually this large house became a communal dwelling for the metaphysically like-minded, and it was here that Theosophists visiting from abroad were accommodated. This pleasant association did not last, however, and towards the end of 1902 trouble arose between members of the Auckland Lodge.[38] The exact nature of the disagreement has not been recorded.[39]

Perhaps it was the not uncommon tensions that can arise between the esoteric disciples and the more practical members of such groups. Whatever its nature, the resulting schism could not be resolved, and a group of members — including the general secretary, the homeopath Dr Charles Sanders and the Draffins — decamped to form the H.P.B. Lodge in February the following year. Stuart remained with the Auckland Lodge, which dwindled away, shedding members, before eventually handing back its charter in 1924.

The H.P.B. Lodge first rented rooms in the Strand Arcade, and then later in His Majesty's Arcade. In early 1906, the New Zealand Section moved to the Auckland City Council chambers, only to lose many precious archives in a fire shortly thereafter. After that, the Section and the H.P.B. Lodge both moved to 351 Queen Street, now the site of University of Auckland buildings, occupying the entire building and setting up a printing press in its basement. At the time this top part of Queen Street, near the intersection with Karangahape Road, was far from salubrious.

Perhaps taking their cue from the tranquil and orderly environment of Theosophy's Adyar headquarters, both the H.P.B. Lodge and the New Zealand Section embarked on a programme of meditation and concentrated thought to improve the local squalor. No doubt they credited this activity with the development of Myers Park across the road shortly afterward.[40]

Both organisations remained at this address until the opening of a new building further along the road at 371 Queen Street. The lodge had acquired the land in 1921 for £4000, and a building was designed by Auckland architect and member of the Society Henry F. Robinson, and constructed by the Craig Brothers for £9982. The brick structure was a far greater building project than anything hitherto attempted by the Society in New Zealand, being built in monumental Edwardian baroque style after the manner of similar public buildings associated with Freemasonry and nonconformist churches.[41]

The façade consisted of a shallow portico with a large triumphal arch of an entrance flanked with robust Doric pilasters and engaged columns on the ground floor. The loggia on the first floor featured a playfully mannerist distribution of graceful Ionic columns and pediment. The Tuscan being traditionally seen as rustic, and the Ionic style being airy and feminine with the narrowest columns, the effect is suggestive of a passage in Blavatsky's *The Secret Doctrine* (1888): 'Father-Mother spin a web whose upper end is fastened to Spirit (Purusha) — the light of the one Darkness — and the lower one to Matter (Prakriti) its (the Spirit's) shadowy end; and this web is the Universe spun out of two substances made in one, which is Svabhavat [the essential nature of the universe].'[42]

Membership of the H.P.B. Lodge grew rapidly from 70 in 1905 to 400 by 1918. By 1949 membership exceeded 500 souls, making it one of the largest Theosophical lodges in the entire Society worldwide at that time.

✢

In the second half of the twentieth century, the most important figure in Auckland Theosophy — and in New Zealand as a whole — was Geoffrey Hodson (1886–1983). Hodson was born in Lincolnshire, England, and was of the same eccentric strain of mystic Englishman as the poet William Blake, experiencing visions in childhood. He served in the British Army as an officer and tank commander during the First World War, subsequently becoming an anti-war activist. When not conducting his professional role in the YMCA secretariat, he travelled throughout Lincolnshire, recording the county's fairy lore.

Like Sherlock Holmes' creator Arthur Conan-Doyle, who admired his work, Hodson was taken in by the 1917–21 Cottingley Fairy hoax, perpetrated by two young girls, Elsie Wright (1901–1988) and Frances Griffiths (1907–1986). These two young cousins lived in Cottingley, near Bradford in England, and took photographs they claimed to be of fairies, but which were in fact paper cut-outs traced from the 1914 *Princess Mary's Gift Book*, and, appropriately enough, photographed with a Box Brownie (more on this incident in Chapter 7).

While holidaying in Sheepscombe, Hodson claimed to have been contacted by an angel and to have received its teachings. In 1937 he and his wife, Jane, travelled to South Africa, and then later to Australia, where Jane's multiple sclerosis finally paralysed her. As the president of the Blavatsky Lodge in Sydney, in 1940 Holden was invited by the New Zealand Section to tour the four main centres, and he stayed on, becoming founder and president of the New Zealand Vegetarian Society in 1943, and being elected president of the Council of Combined Animal Welfare Organisations of New Zealand in 1944. In these roles he campaigned for the introduction into all New Zealand abattoirs of the 'humane killer' or stun gun.[43] Jane eventually succumbed to her condition and died in 1962.[44] Apart from brief periods spent in India and the United States and on international speaking tours, he remained in Auckland for the rest of his life, publishing some 50 books on spiritual and Theosophical subjects.

The most famous member of the Auckland Theosophical Society in the 1940s, however, was none other than Edmund Hillary (1919–2008).

In 1955, two years after his conquest of Everest, Hillary was no longer a member, but remained a friend of the Society. That year, he spoke at the Theosophical Convention about his friendship with the Theosophist, broadcaster and social justice advocate Brian Dunningham, who did much to revive the organisation in the 1950s and 1960s, as well as his respect for Hodson, and religious practice in the Himalayas.[45]

Mountaineering has long been an esoteric allegory for spiritual ascent.[46] Indeed, the author and Theosophist Edward Douglas Fawcett was even better known as a climber of mountains.[47] Infamous British magician Aleister Crowley was a keen mountaineer, and a member of both Oscar Eckenstein's K2 expedition in 1902 and Jules Jacot-Guillarmod's 1905 climb of Kachenjunga.[48] Hillary was also a devotee of Herbert Sutcliffe's Radiant Living movement, which had its roots in Theosophy (see Chapter 9).[49]

The H.P.B. Lodge property was eventually sold in 1994 and a new building erected on Warborough Avenue in the suburb of Epsom, on a section divided from the headquarters' Vasanta House property. In 1997 the old lodge building on Queen Street became the White House night club, which since the early 2000s has been an 'Adult Entertainment Centre' — a cabaret venue and bordello.[50]

☦

As we have seen, the Wellington Lodge was New Zealand's first, acquiring famous and influential adherents, a pattern that continued nationally into the twentieth century. The community and religious worker Emma Jane Richmond, who had been president of the Christchurch Lodge, became a member of the Wellington Lodge when she moved there in 1900; and Henry Mason (1885–1975), monetary reformer, attorney general (1935), minister of education (1940–47), native minister (1943–46) and minister of justice in two Labour governments (1935–49 and 1957–60), became a prominent member.

The Wellington hall, which still exists, was built in 1918 on Marion Street, Te Aro, and is unusual among the metropolitan lodges in apparently not being designed by an architect; rather the builders probably worked from a standard hall plan. The façade, which is not structural, resembles a small, simplified Doric temple with four pilasters. The Society's motto — 'There is no religion higher than truth' — was inscribed on the tympanum of the pediment, as was its emblem, a Star of David (wisdom) containing an Egyptian *ankh* (life), surrounded by an *ouroboros* (a snake biting its own tail, symbolising eternity). Where the snake's mouth and tail meet at the top, there is a counter-clockwise swastika — an ancient Eurasian symbol before Germany's Nazi Party got a hold of it — above which is the Devanagari character ॐ, the Hindu AUM, the syllable representing the universe and the ultimate reality.

The front of the building's most striking feature, however, are two round porthole-like windows, which are perhaps symbolic of the sun or eternity. Conceivably these windows, which resemble eyes in a face, might represent the divine gaze, or imply that the Society's symbol on the pediment was the pineal 'third eye', important to Theosophical ideas, the seat of psychic power, recalling the passage in James Joyce's *Ulysses*: 'Lotus ladies tend them i' the eyes, their pineal glands aglow. Filled with his god, he thrones, Buddh under plantain. Gulfer of souls, engulfer. Hesouls, shesouls, shoals of souls.'[51] The Wellington Lodge operated from this venue for over 80 years.

The Wellington Lodge sporadically attracted the politically influential, and in the mid-twentieth century this was once again realised in Henry Mason. There had been past attempts by the Society to align itself with the New Zealand Labour Party. In 1911, Harry H. Banks, president of the Auckland branch, wrote to Michael Joseph Savage — then secretary of the first iteration of the New Zealand Labour Party — suggesting that the shared aims of Theosophy and Socialism were not incompatible and that perhaps some sort of joint committee of combined forces should be created. Savage, friendly but politely firm, replied that the proposed relationship was impossible under the party constitution.[52] Such a relationship, however, is not as unimaginable as it might first appear; there is a close relationship between Labour and the Rātana church, an entity likewise inspired by a visionary and prophetic movement.

Mason and his wife, Dulcia, were both intellectuals, vegetarians and teetotallers. He was a champion of daylight saving, decimal currency

Henry Mason, cabinet minister, decimal currency and daylight saving champion and Theosophist.

reform, and the humane treatment of conscientious objectors — a number of prominent pacifists worldwide have been Theosophists or associated with the Society — and was drawn to Theosophy through his wife. Dulcia was also a staunch believer in Social Credit, a theory also discussed in Theosophical circles of the time.

Dulcia was a leading figure in the Theosophical Women's Association (TWA, founded in 1940), a group dedicated to exalting womanhood and the 'World-Mother, who, as a mighty archangel, focuses the spiritual forces on the maternal nature of God', with various mother goddesses from Isis and Parvati to Papatūānuku called to witness. The TWA also dedicated itself to the evolution of a 'distinctive culture for New Zealand' and finding solutions to social problems 'in the light of Theosophy'. This group was particularly energetic in the 1940s and 1950s, excited by the promise of Princess Elizabeth, future queen.[53]

‡

On 13 May 1894, a Theosophy meeting was held at the house of clothing manufacturer William Denne Meers with the purpose of forming a Christchurch Lodge. According to *The London Gazette*, Meers had been a Berkshire draper and furniture dealer, but his business went bankrupt in 1879.[54] Presumably he chose a fresh start in the colonies, hence we find him in Christchurch 15 years later. As a result of this meeting, a lodge was established the following month, on 28 April. Meers believed himself guided by the spirit of a twelfth-century Franciscan monk — quite an accomplishment, given that order wasn't founded until the thirteenth century — and was also a prominent agitator for the Spiritualist cause in Dunedin and Christchurch.[55]

For a city founded as a colony of the Church of England, late Victorian Christchurch was peculiarly receptive to religious nonconformism. As Colonel Olcott describes in detail in his account of his visit to the city on his 1897 tour, Christchurch was then dealing with the aftermath of the charlatan and bigamist Arthur Worthington and his Temple of Truth[56] (see Chapter 6). Indian culture was also relatively visible. At the time, Christchurch had one of the largest Indian populations in New Zealand, simply on the basis that John Cracroft Wilson, a former magistrate and Thuggee hunter of the Indian Civil Service, and a New Zealand politician, had emigrated from the subcontinent in 1859 with a large retinue of Indian staff. The Christchurch suburb of Cashmere is named after Wilson's sheep run in the Port Hills, which he named after the region of Kashmir where he was posted.[57] Wilson's ghost is said to vigorously haunt the Old Stone House that still stands in Cashmere.[58] Emigrating Punjabi Sikhs from 1890 onward may also have contributed to Cantabrian curiosity about the East.

Not having any formal premises, the Christchurch Society initially met at the Tuam Street Opera House, but a month after Olcott's visit it moved to Lichfield Street, opposite Bennett's corner, and in mid-1900 relocated to Hobbs' Buildings in Cathedral Square. Following the 2010 and 2011 Canterbury earthquakes the buildings were demolished as unsafe and the site is now occupied by state-of-the-art Tūranga, the city's new central public library. By then the Society was long-gone: in 1906 it had moved again, this time to Worcester Street opposite the Federal Club, and then in 1910 it took rooms in Manchester Chambers. By this point, it had become clear that a permanent location held in Society ownership was required.

One of the chief benefactors of this project was Thomas Edmonds (1858–1932), the wealthy baking powder manufacturer. Edmonds had already contributed to the construction of several public buildings in Christchurch, including the Cambridge Terrace Band Rotunda by the Avon River and Radiant Hall, built on Kilmore Street in Spanish Mission style with a Moorish twist. Radiant Hall was a meeting place for the Radiant Health movement (an earlier and unrelated movement to Radiant Living, which we will encounter in Chapter 9) — an alternative health group specialising in the study and practise of Christian psychology, diet and solar plexus breathing, in which Edmonds was also interested. The building would eventually become the Repertory Theatre.[59]

Although Edmonds was not himself an official member of the Theosophical Society, his daughter Beatrice was a frequent attendee of meetings, and when fundraising began in 1925 he offered his assistance.[60] Aside from his daughter's interest and his generosity in general to public building projects, perhaps Edmonds' munificence also had something to do with a perceived symbolic identification with the Society. Edmonds and

Thomas Edmonds, baking powder magnate and Christchurch Theosophical Society benefactor.

his wife, Jane, regularly attended meetings with their daughter and were supporters of Theosophy's goals.[61]

Although Edmonds' relationship to Theosophy was at a remove, and his distinctive branding was already in use by 1879, 15 years before the first Christchurch meeting, it is impossible not to look at the company's iconic 'rising sun' logo and famous 'Sure to Rise' trademark and not see connections to Theosophical symbolism. The official company tradition is that the idea for this slogan came from Edmonds' response when a customer expressed uncertainty about the quality of his baking powder compared to her usual brand. Edmonds is said to have replied: 'It is sure to rise, Madam.'[62]

The imagery of the rising sun, however, also has a prominent place in Theosophy. At its most basic level, it represents the rise of a new age and renewal from the East. Blavatsky wrote of the 'Sun of Truth',[63] an image which probably derives from the Gāyatrī Mantra in the *Rig Veda*, where the sun is referred to as a source of divine enlightenment.[64] More esoterically, for Theosophists the rising sun represents the universe emerging into the plane of objectivity from the hidden plane of subjectivity. Blavatsky writes: 'The Hindoos [*sic*] call such alternations the "Days and Nights of Brahma," or the time of *Manvantara* and that of *Pralaya* (dissolution). The Westerns may call them Universal Days and Nights if they prefer. During the latter (the nights) *All is in All;* every atom is resolved into one Homogeneity.'[65] Perhaps Edmonds considered it a good omen, having recently constructed his new Woolston factory and gardens with its Art Deco revisioning of the rising sun in 1922.

‡

The Society chose prominent Christchurch architect Cecil Wood (1878–1947) to design its new premises at 267 Cambridge Terrace in the central city. Unlike the designers of other Theosophical halls, Wood eschewed the vocabulary of Classical temples for a neo-Georgian one — a style he had popularised since 1922. Constructed from brick, and rectangular in form, the building's sparse street frontage was enlivened by the use of multi-paned windows and quoins. Diverging slightly from neo-Georgian, the front entrance was pure Edwardian baroque — an open pediment containing the Society's emblem on a mantled cartouche and the word THEOSOPHY, supported by Tuscan Doric order columns. Some members of the Society were critical of the design for looking too much like a domestic house.[66] Budget limitations forced Wood to use corrugated iron for the roof and the rear exterior walls.

The building contained the typical library, kitchen and lecture hall, and a chapel,[67] and was dedicated on 25 July 1926, at precisely 4.43 p.m. — the moment the Buddha supposedly began his first sermon at the deer park at Sarnath in Benares (Varanasi), at the hour of the full moon, outlining the Four Noble Truths of Buddhist thought.[68] The Society used the hall until it was damaged in the 2011 Canterbury earthquake and demolished the following year. The Christchurch branch of the Society now meets at the Canterbury Workers' Educational Association building in Gloucester Street.

Theosophy was also likely responsible for one of the strangest paintings ever produced in the Garden City. Daisy Osborn (1888–1957) is a relatively obscure figure in the annals of New Zealand art. An only child, she enrolled at the Canterbury College School of Art in 1906 and went on to become a part-time teacher there.[69] In 1930, Osborn exhibited *Lo, These Are Parts of His Ways* at the Canterbury Society of Arts' annual exhibition.[70] The painting, whose current location is unknown, depicts a young, boyish Christ crucified with a kneeling Virgin beside him. In the background, a number of Christchurch churches, religious buildings and some notable secular structures are arranged in a row: the Durham Street Methodist Church, Victoria Street Clock Tower, Canterbury College School of Art, the Cathedral of the Blessed Sacrament, the Bridge of Remembrance, St Paul's Presbyterian Church, ChristChurch Anglican Cathedral, the Government Building in Cathedral Square and the Edmonds Band Rotunda. Many of these buildings were lost to the 2010 and 2011 earthquakes.

The image is broken up like a stained-glass window by a map of the streets of Christchurch rotated with west to the top, the horizontal crosspiece of the Cross — the *patibulum* — aligned with Colombo Street and the vertical post — the *stipes* — aligned against Worcester Street, centred exactly on the inner city as framed by the four main avenues.

It is tempting to recall James K. Baxter's interpretation of the Cross, where the vertical represents the relationship between humanity and God, and the horizontal as communal human love and *caritas*.[71] One may observe that the base of the Cross rests at the corner of Tancred and Worcester Streets in the suburb of Linwood, where Osborn grew up.

The title is a quotation of Job 26:14, a text that also appears above the front porch of Canterbury Museum, carved there by Claudius Brassington (1873–1945) in 1896. This may reference the apocryphal story that the museum (representing science) and Christchurch Cathedral were positioned in line of sight at opposite ends of Worcester Street so that neither would forget the authority of the other, or, more diplomatically, 'linkage of religion and science which was the aim of the Museum's founders'.[72] Such a linkage is also an important part of Theosophical thought.

The cathedral, the central axis of the city, representing Osborn's nominally Anglican faith, is located at Christ's heart chakra, and the museum at the top of the Cross.[73] Christ's head, tilted at an awkward angle, and the Third Eye chakra overlap with another Anglican church, St Michael and All Angels. Mary's head overlaps the Catholic Basilica of the Blessed Sacrament, and the strange, curved line around it, resembling both halo and rising sun, directly connects to the dome of the Basilica in the row of buildings. The Avon River meanders through the image and around the Cross in a way suggestive of the Brazen Serpent (Numbers 21: 4–9) made by Moses at God's command to protect the Israelites from the fiery serpents sent to punish them for speaking against Him and Moses.

In art this is usually depicted on a cross-like structure, to which Christ compares himself in the New Testament: 'And as Moses lifted up the serpent in the wilderness, even so must the Son of man be lifted up' (John 3:14–16). Blavatsky says of it in *The Secret Doctrine*:

> The Protestants try to show that the allegory of the Brazen Serpent and of the 'fiery serpents' has a direct reference to the mystery of Christ and Crucifixion; but it has a far nearer relation, in truth, *to the mystery of generation*, when dissociated from the egg with the central germ, or the *circle with its central point*. The *brazen Serpent*

Christchurch artist Daisy Osborn's Theosophy-inspired painting *Lo, These Are Parts of His Ways*.

had no such holy meaning as that; nor was it, in fact, glorified above the *'fiery serpents' for the bite of which it was only a natural remedy.* The symbological meaning of the word 'brazen' being the feminine principle, and that of fiery, or 'gold,' the male one.[74]

Blavatsky also goes on to state that the Brazen Serpent is Jehovah, the chief of the fiery serpents, and the *kundalini*, the dormant potential force running through the spine between the chakras that makes ascension possible when awakened.[75]

‡

The Dunedin Lodge was formed in 1893 and its charter signed by Colonel Olcott that year. Eighteen members were recorded in 1896, and numbers slowly grew to 39 by the century's end. The Dunedin Lodge's early history is one of the most well explored of all the New Zealand lodges thanks to a very thorough Honours dissertation by Alison Yvonne Atkinson in 1978.[76] Although not quite as illustrious as the Wellington group, as Robert Ellwood surmises the Dunedin membership was likely more representative of the typical 'rank-and-file' Theosophist of the time — professional, middle-class, social, intellectually curious, well-read, and predominantly British immigrants, who would rather stay home reading challenging texts than go to the pub.[77] Unlike Freemasonry, it also admitted women, making it something that families could do together.

For all that Dunedin was a sophisticated and prosperous university town and attracted a high-minded and cultured elite, Theosophy had a fraught reception in Scots Presbyterian Dunedin that was far more intense than the more muted responses in other centres. It is likely this was in no small part due to being caught in the wake of the fierce debate over Spiritualism and Rationalism that had gripped predominantly Presbyterian communities in the preceding two decades.[78] The local papers kept readers abreast of the Theosophical Society's doings: in 1896 Dunedin's *Evening Star* ran an error-riddled and imaginative 'exposé' column by a Reverend C. Watt of London,[79] and the *Otago Daily Times* reported extensively on Annie Besant's 1894 and 1908 tours.

The Dunedin-based Presbyterian *Christian Outlook* disapproved of the Society, and from his pulpit throughout the 1890s its editor, the influential and vocal religious leader, social reformer and author of the anti-capitalist sermon 'The Sin of Cheapness', the Reverend Rutherford Waddell (1850–1932), vigorously condemned what he declared to be heresy.[80]

This response was not unusual. When the prominent international Theosophist and Blavatsky intimate Countess Wachtmeister, visiting in 1896, was mocked by the Reverend Robert Wood in Masterton, local Society members responded with a letter to the *Wairarapa Daily Times*, describing Wood — and no doubt with the likes of Waddell in mind as well — as 'an incarnation of one of the monks that tore the quivering flesh of Hypatia!'[81] Hypatia, the female, fourth-century neoplatonist philosopher and mathematician of Roman Egypt, was a well-known figure in the British Empire at the time, her life and martyrdom at the hands of a mob of Christians being memorably portrayed in Charles Kingsley's popular 1853 novel of the same name.[82]

Similar sentiments could be found in other New Zealand newspapers throughout the 1890s, but they took on a particular edge in Dunedin. A local pharmacist, James Neil (1881–1931), went so far as to publish a pamphlet in 1901 provocatively titled *Spiritualism and Theosophy: Twain Brothers of the Anti-Christ*, which condemned Theosophy's synthesis of the Bible with Eastern spiritual texts (although of course the Bible is itself an Eastern spiritual text) and reducing 'Jesus to the level of man' and 'the Bible to the level of other books'.[83] No doubt they felt threatened by the large audiences attracted to Theosophical lectures in the city. As far as many Presbyterians were concerned, heresy and apostasy stalked the Octagon, and the morality of the colony was at stake. In reality the average Theosophical gathering was about as exciting as a Quaker meeting.

‡

The local branch developed against this background. According to tradition, the formation of the lodge was sparked by a chance meeting in 1892, on the train from Sawyers Bay to Dunedin, of Augustus William

Maurais (1858–1926), a proofreader and son of a bookseller, and Grant Farquhar (1828–1916), a wealthy partner in the Sawyers Bay tannery factory, when Maurais observed the latter reading a Theosophy text. Unbeknownst to either, elsewhere in Dunedin, Robert Pairman (1859–1939), a ship's draughtsman, and his wife, Susannah (1864–1946), were also studying Theosophical publications.

Robert was a hard-drinking, gambling Scotsman who eventually settled down when he met Susannah, daughter of prominent Dunedin publisher and Theosophist John Stone (1839–1897). A meeting was convened in 1892 at the Rothsay, West Harbour, house of prosperous Scottish draper Thomas Ross (1855–1943), attended by Susannah's sister, schoolteacher Louisa Stone (1860–1920), the English-born Quaker and homeopathic pharmacist John Oddie (b.1864), and another pharmacist, Frank Allan (d.1921).[84]

Also present were a handful of Spiritualists, including William Rough (whom we shall meet later), who were dismissive and felt that Theosophy had nothing more to teach them. Maurais, who was mostly interested in the Wisdom Tradition aspects of Theosophy, fell out with the Spiritualist contingent and the Spiritualists were not invited to the 1893 meeting to establish the lodge.[85] This was probably for the best, for (as we shall see in Chapter 7) Spiritualism was a formidable power in Dunedin in its own right and might easily have dominated the group, as well as the tendency in the minds of some to conflate the two.

While Theosophy possesses characteristics that are distinctly Spiritualism-adjacent, any such confusion was swiftly rejected, as we find in a letter to the editor of Dunedin's *Evening Star* in 1894 written by a Theosophist under the nom de plume 'Altiora Peto' — Latin for 'I seek higher things'. Refuting an anti-Theosophy letter to the editor in a previous issue, the correspondent writes:

> He has, I have no doubt, unwittingly confounded Theosophy with Spiritualism when he refers to 'that state of Theosophical bliss (minus the gauze and phosphorus).' Theosophy has received more opposition from the spiritualists than from any other body, because it denounces as wrong and dangerous the intercourse with 'spirits'.[86]

The Dunedin Lodge remained small until the First World War, but retained a prominence in Dunedin cultural and intellectual life, popularising the concepts of karma and reincarnation, vegetarianism and astrology. Lectures by visiting Society leaders further helped build numbers. In the first half of the twentieth century the Dunedin lodge was guided by the women of the Inglis and Pollard families. Pollard matriarch Sarah Rosetta Pollard (1873–1957) served as lodge president. Her equally dedicated daughters Cecilia Pollard and Truda Burrell also served in this role at different times. Rose Pollard was the lodge's secretary and treasurer for many years.

Agnes Inglis (b.1911), who lived into the 1980s, was a member of the Society along with her father, John, her mother and her sisters, and avidly embraced the more mystical and esoteric aspects of Theosophy epitomised by the invisible Ascended Masters. Public speaking is a central feature of Theosophy, and Agnes was trained in elocution from a young age as a member of the Lodge's Order of the Round Table. Extremely well read in the occult, and widely believed possessed of psychic powers, Agnes was the Dunedin Lodge's long-serving general secretary and librarian, as well as a member of the Lotus Circle, the lodge's equivalent of a Sunday School.

The Inglis family's interest in Theosophy began when Agnes was a child, as a way of seeking meaning and comfort after the death in infancy of Agnes's sister Annie. Agnes believed herself to have been visited by a Master at that time and later in life — including being saved by one of the Masters when a bookshelf in the lodge library fell on her — and it was understood within the family that when Agnes's sister Alexandrina 'Lex' Inglis was born in 1903, she was a reincarnation of Annie.[87]

From 1914 the Dunedin Lodge operated from leased rooms in Downing Street, then moved to a freehold Victorian house with a witch's hat turret in High Street in 1945 after the Downing Street landlords doubled the rent. The lodge, ever dangling close to penury, remained at this striking address for the next 61 years. Then, in 2006 — the Ascended Masters' wisdom in matters of property speculation and New Zealand's real estate bubble notwithstanding — the Dunedin chapter sold the High Street property, solving a number of financial difficulties, and rented a room in the old RSA building on Moray Place.

236 High Street, Dunedin, the premises of the local branch of the Theosophical Society from 1945 to 2006.

OTAGO DAILY TIMES

This venue was owned by a life member of the Society, Margaret van der Vis, who started the chapter's meditation group. It was sold when she moved into a retirement village in 2009. The chapter rented again in the Upstart Building on Water Street, before finally buying the former Fitzroy Hotel in Caversham in 2015.[88]

‡

In 1895, in the Andhra Pradesh town of Madanapalle, 250 kilometres inland from Adyar and with conspicuous lack of accompanying stellar phenomena, wise men or virgins, a child was born to a Telagu-speaking Brahmin family who would dramatically shake Theosophy to its foundations. Jiddu Krishnamurti's (d.1986) father was an administrator for the British, and his mother died when he was 10. At the time of his birth Madanapalle was part of Madras, and when the boy's father moved his family to Adyar, he was 'discovered' by the prominent Theosophical occultist Charles Leadbeater (1854–1934), who, with Annie Besant's blessing, declared Krishnamurti the future 'World Teacher', avatar of Lord Maitreya (the future Buddha) and reincarnation of Jesus Christ. Given that the vast majority of Society adherents were nominally Christian, this revelation was deeply troubling for many members around the world.

Previously, Theosophy had offered no significant challenges to the established churches of mainstream Christianity. At worst, they recast Christian dogma as the literalisation of the allegorical and Jesus as an avatar and teacher among many others, equivalent to Buddha rather than the literal unique Son of God. They were no more of a threat than atheism. The term 'Christ' in Theosophy merely meant the divinity indwelling in all human beings.[89] This hijacking of the Second Coming, then, was beyond the pale, and caused much friction within the Society.

Leadbeater and Besant supervised Krishnamurti's education in Adyar, England and Ojai in California. In 1911 the Order of the Star in the East was formed as a vehicle for his coming. In 1912 Krishnamurti's father, citing Leadbeater's rumoured pederastic predilections, attempted and failed to regain custody of the son he had surrendered to the Society. Even the most publicly infamous magician of the day, the debauched 'Great Beast' himself,

Aleister Crowley (discussed more thoroughly in Chapter 8), expressed his concern about Leadbeater's grip on the young man with characteristic venom:

> About Krishnamurti: There is no objection on my part to paederasty as such. This is a totally different matter. It is the question of the following practice, which I class as black magical because it is unnecessary, uneconomical from the magical standpoint, and likely to arouse highly undesirable forces as being in opposition to the Law of Thelema.[90]

Krishnamurti grew into a handsome and charismatic young man and became a *cause célèbre* in fashionable globetrotting circles.

Things were no different in New Zealand. In the year Leadbeater discovered Krishnamurti, the Reverend C. W. Scott-Moncrieff was ordered by the Anglican Bishop of Auckland to resign as warden of St John's Theological College and return to England because he had joined the Theosophical Society.[91] Back in London, Scott-Moncrieff was entirely unrepentant, joining and swiftly ascending in the ranks of the Order of the Star in the East, promoting its teachings as a form of esoteric Christianity and a natural extension of the Second Coming, all while retaining his status as a member of the Anglican clergy.[92] The more cynical might argue that Theosophy and the Church of England were actually quite similar in that neither required you to believe in anything at all.

Back in New Zealand the Order flourished, headed by the Dunedin schoolteacher and poet David William Murray Burn (1862–1951), whose main legacy to posterity is the screeds of verse he contributed to the *Otago Daily Times* over the years under the pen name 'Marsyas', his composing of hymns, and his propensity for hiking around the hills of St Clair in plus-twos and a skullcap. He was also president of the New Zealand and India League, and in that capacity echoed Besant's urging for India to be liberated and granted Dominion status.[93]

☦

Then in 1929 it all stopped abruptly when, in front of an estimated audience of 3000 (including Besant) in Ommen, the Netherlands, Krishnamurti dissolved the Order. The star had set. Krishnamurti distanced himself from Theosophy and all other such esoteric groups, choosing his own reclusive spiritual path.[94] This had a depressive effect on many in the Society, particularly the younger members who had anticipated this much-yearned-for dawning.[95] By coincidence, this was the same year a correspondent for the *New Zealand Herald* in London sent back a report on an exhibition of the Seven and Five group of artists, and the work of two New Zealand expats, Frances Hodgkins and Len Lye, noting of the latter's work:

> Mr. Len Lye of Christchurch, has advanced ideas of art expression. He is showing in the same exhibition patterns for two shawls, a curtain fabric, and a scarf. All these form and colour schemes are very much on the lines of what the Theosophist knows as thought forms. They certainly have their attractiveness.[96]

Krishnamurti himself visited New Zealand on a lecture tour in 1934 that coincided with a similar visit by Irish playwright George Bernard Shaw. As Robert Ellwood notes, they did not meet while in New Zealand, although Shaw had been a close friend of Besant before she joined the Society and she and Shaw both crossed paths occasionally later in London. Both, however, bear the ignominy of being barred from being broadcast by New Zealand radio that year — Shaw for his proto-communism and Krishnamurti, rather more ambiguously (likely for fear of offending conservative Christian listeners), for being 'too objectionable'.[97]

While in New Zealand, Krishnamurti explained that he had dissolved the Order of the Star in the East because it had become a cult of personality and an end in itself rather than the means to transcend to something greater.[98]

None of this would have come to pass were it not for Leadbeater, who had briefly been an Anglican curate before he joined the Theosophical Society in 1883, and the following 51 years of his life were tumultuous ones for Theosophy. At the same time, however, Theosophy was at its most

Annie Besant, British socialist, Theosophist, Co-Freemason, women's rights activist and educationist.

influential on Western society. As an occultist, Leadbeater took Blavatsky's more fragmentary and abstract ideas and created a whole cosmology out of them. He was Besant's closest associate, and, as Ellwood notes, his enemies called him her 'Svengali'. Together they brought about what may be regarded as the second generation of the Theosophical Society. From 1907 to 1933 Leadbeater was the Society's international president,[99] and his books were, and remain, Theosophical bestsellers, inspiring many to join the Society.

Nowhere was his impact felt more keenly than in Australia after he moved to Sydney in 1914. This move conveniently placed some distance between himself and the events of 1906–09, when Leadbeater was forced to resign from the Society — he was reinstated three years later — under accusations of improper relations with the circle of young men and boys with whom he surrounded himself under the auspices of training them in the mysteries of Theosophy.

‡

Besant's judgement of character would again be called into question when the Society's secretary general in the United Sates, Alex Fullerton, whom Besant had declared to be a 'Theosophical Worthy', was arrested in 1910 for sending inappropriate letters to a 16-year-old boy.[100] Something of Leadbeater's preferences could have been intuited from the 1924 book he co-wrote with Besant, *The Lives of Alcyone*, in which the former used his clairvoyant powers to examine his own and others' former lives, leading to the rather startling revelation that in a previous life he had been married to both Krishna and his brothers in another incarnation, and that, in an earlier existence, Christ had been married to Julius Caesar.

This was publicly ridiculed in an anonymous verse that ran 'In the Lives, in the Lives, / I've had all sorts of husbands and wives'.[101] Even more alarming was Leadbeater's rumoured teaching of masturbatory practices to the boys and his assertion that 'The closest man can come to a sublime spiritual experience is orgasm,'[102] which, while in keeping with the tantric left-hand path of Hinduism and Buddhism, seems entirely inappropriate coming from an educator of young men.

Mary Lutyens, Krishnamurti's biographer, visited Sydney in the 1920s and offered the vivid description of Leadbeater 'prancing down the wharf like a great lion . . . hatless and in a long purple cloak, holding on to the arm of a very good-looking blond boy of about fifteen. This was Theodore St John, an Australian boy of great charm and sweetness, who was Leadbeater's current favourite and who slept in his room.'[103] St John (1908–1931) was the English-born son of the artist and Theosophist Theodora St John, and died tragically young in a motorcycle accident.

Within the international movement, a quasi-independent fiefdom developed around Leadbeater, and naturally that influence was felt across the Tasman in New Zealand. His book, developed out of a series of four lectures delivered in Sydney in 1915, *Australia and New Zealand: The Home of a New Sub-Race*, proved popular with Theosophists in both countries. It pressed all the right buttons — the precursors of the coming Sixth Root Race would be born of the rugged independence and isolation of the Antipodes, reincarnated from the souls of the Anzac 'glorious war dead'.

To further this end, he exhorted the leadership of both countries to improve the living conditions of indigenous populations, but he also embraced the White Australia policy on the grounds that while a certain amount of mixing between Anglo-Saxon and Celt was healthy, other sub-races could not contribute to the new race. Aboriginal Australians, as the direct descendants of the Lemurians, were to be excluded, although Māori may have been more acceptable, being widely regarded as a higher type.[104]

Then in 1916 Leadbeater was ordained to the Liberal Catholic Church (LCC), an independent esoteric church not in communion with Rome or the Pope, and quickly became its supreme bishop. The LCC was aligned to the Theosophical Society and shared a number of its teachings and members, but under Leadbeater it took on an increasingly occult hue and pursued ritual magic. The relationship was a controversial one. For an older generation of Theosophists who had joined the Society when the emphasis was on the secular study of Eastern philosophy, this shift, combined with the various rumours about Leadbeater's conduct (the Sydney constabulary investigated him for homosexuality in 1917), caused tensions to run high.

In 1922 Leadbeater took up residence in a large Federation Queen

Charles Leadbeater, former Anglican priest, influential member of the Theosophical Society, Co-Freemason and co-initiator of the Liberal Catholic Church.

Anne-style house and estate known as The Manor in the suburb of Mossman with the inevitable retinue of boys, and the police resumed their investigations of the bishop's proclivities. The Australian press covered the allegations with lurid headlines such as 'Where Leadbeater Bishes' and 'Leadbeater: A Swish Bish with the Boys',[105] playing on 'bish' being Australian slang for 'blunder'. The investigation unfortunately coincided with a visit to Sydney by Krishnamurti and his brother, who were interrogated by detectives.[106]

No sufficiently compelling evidence of Leadbeater's improprieties ever emerged, although Sydney's *Truth* newspaper, for which Leadbeater was a favourite target, continued to make scandalous allusions about his conduct until 1926, when one of Leadbeater's supporters, wealthy manufacturing jeweller Gustav Kollerstrom — father of Oscar Kollerstrom (described by *Truth* as the 21-year-old in whom 'the old man [Leadbeater] discovered a "great soul"') — initiated a lawsuit against *Truth* for £10,000 in damages.

When *Truth* announced it would call Leadbeater as a witness and produce documents from the police investigation, Kollerstrom attempted to withdraw the suit, but *Truth* refused to allow him to. When the case finally came to court, Kollerstrom's solicitors did not present a case and he was ordered to pay the newspaper full costs. Leadbeater, as so often happened when the law was involved, claimed to be too 'ill' to attend.[107]

These events were undoubtably being followed in New Zealand, not least in the pages of *Truth*'s New Zealand edition, and in both countries there was a sharp decline in Society membership, by as much as 18 per cent in New Zealand between 1921 and 1926 according to census figures.[108] Leadbeater died in 1934, a year after Besant, drawing this particular chapter of the Theosophical Society to a close. Membership slowly recovered afterwards.

‡

The exceptional receptivity to Theosophy in late nineteenth-century New Zealand no doubt has much to do with the colony's view of itself as a beacon of progress and as a 'better Britain', something to which the New Zealand Section seemed to be attuned. In 1904 the Section's chief periodical published a letter by a British Theosophist visitor to New Zealand, which stated: 'I was in New Zealand as the 19th passed to the 20th century, and then I became convinced of what a very progressive country New Zealand really is.' This is not quite the compliment it sounds, given that he goes on to say 'the strength of a nation lies in its mediocrity, the mediocrity of all round strength...'[109]

Ellwood makes the connection to a 1903 inclusion in *Theosophy in New Zealand* of Besant's lecture-pamphlet 'Theosophy and Imperialism', in which the reviewer indignantly retorts that 'there is no need to preach imperialism to the New Zealander; he is in every fibre an Imperialist, having grasped the idea of Greater Britain, he scarce knows when or how, but grasping it strongly and vitally as becomes his race'.[110]

Theosophy also had an influence on the pacifist movement, and it would be remiss if a discussion of Theosophy in Aotearoa did not mention Beeville. This curious community was based at Orini, between Taupiri and Morrinsville in Waikato, and centred on two brothers, Ray Hansen (1910–1985) and Dan Hansen (1918–2006), and their several sister-wives. Beeville, established in 1933, was agriculturally self-sufficient and financed itself, as its name suggests, by selling high-quality honey. The inhabitants of Beeville were vegetarian pacifists, lived communally and advocated free love. They mainly came to public attention in the 1940s because of their wartime conscientious objection, which led to puritan interest in the community's unconventional marital arrangements in the 1950s.[111]

Beeville was a loosely anarchist settlement whose inhabitants frequently came into conflict with the government over the payment of taxes.[112] The Hansen family had emigrated to Aotearoa from Denmark in the 1880s, and Ray, at age 18, joined the Hamilton branch of the Theosophical Society, followed by his six brothers. Ray was also something of a poet, corresponding with the Theosophist poet David Burn in Otago. These Theosophical connections also led to Ray's involvement in the early 1930s with the Social Credit movement, for which he enthusiastically campaigned.[113]

Through Theosophy, Ray met and married his wife, Olive, but then in 1937 another woman, Anne Sanders, joined the *ménage*. It seems Anne was suffering personal problems that led to her being welcomed into the home, and apparently Olive was agreeable to the arrangement. Olive would have 10 children by Ray, and Anne four. In 1955 both women were 51 years old, and both were described by *Truth* as 'charming and intelligent women', and it was said that the family lived together harmoniously.[114]

By then, Beeville was flourishing beyond the original troika. There was Ray's brother Dan, who arrived in 1944 to set up a welding workshop,[115] and his wife, Edith. They had met near the end of the war, chauffeuring visitors to a camp for objectors, when Edith came to see her brother. Dan was rendered paraplegic by an accident, and because he was unable to father children, Edith, by arrangement, was impregnated by one of Ray's sons.

The Hansens had nearly 20 offspring, and their subsequent spouses and children lived at Beeville. The community also attracted a handful of non-family. Of these non-family members, one ex-convict who arrived in 1948 caused considerable friction. He was a naturist conman, argumentative and not sharing of the pacifist ethos. Beeville's lack of clear hierarchy and consensus decision-making made it difficult to decide what to do about him, but he left of his own accord shortly before the media became interested in the settlement.[116]

Beeville's spiritual culture began as orthodoxly Theosophical, but eventually pivoted to the teachings of Krishnamurti. They remained, however, in good fellowship with the Theosophical community, and a number of glowing articles about Beeville's friendly, smiling children, carrot juice and soy flour appeared in the pages of the *Young Theosophist* in the late 1950s:

> Twenty-three people live on the farm and the smaller section, enjoying communal life because they believe that this is the right way to live in order to develop initiative and co-operation in the individual. They do not aim to separate themselves from society, but rather to integrate with it.
>
> There are no rules and no programme and they face difficulties as they arise. Each individual strives to pull his or her weight for the sake of the community. There are not any wages, all cheques being made out to the community account from which two members are authorised to draw. Thus each member needs only to ask for money

to meet his or her requirements. Decisions involving large sums of money require the unanimous consent of the members, but this seldom causes difficulty.[117]

Letters from the 1970s indicate cordial relations between Ray and Olive Hansen, the Theosophical Society in Ōrewa, and the Theosophical Society convention, and Ellwood reports hints of a brief flirtation with Scientology around this time, but beyond that the final chapters of Beeville are opaque. Ans Westra took a photograph of a young man picking apples at Beeville in around 1971.[118] Ray Hansen donated his papers to the Alexander Turnbull Library in Wellington in 1984 and 1985, and retired to Whangamatā, still, presumably, on good terms with the Theosophical Society. That seems to have been the end of Beeville.[119]

‡

If Beeville can be said to have had a persuasive influence on pacifism in Aotearoa, the Society proper had a considerable impact on the country's animal welfare. Much of the Theosophical Society's work in New Zealand was accomplished through the Theosophical Order of Service. The New Zealand branch of this component of the Society was founded in 1908, and went through a number of incarnations, being revived in the 1950s and 1960s by Brian Dunningham with a focus on animal welfare; and with Geoffrey Hodson it was successful in campaigning for reforms that would guarantee the humane slaughter of animals in the nation's abattoirs, and the outlawing of hare coursing, captive pigeon shooting and vivisection. This was all enshrined in the Animals Protection Act 1960.[120]

The Order of Service's largest single impact on New Zealand, however, was in the progressive reform of education via the British-based New Education Fellowship (NEF), which was active in New Zealand in the 1930s and 1940s. Its members included such prominent educationalists as Crawford Somerset, A. E. Campbell and Clarence Beeby, and it was influential in education policy and curriculum development for the compulsory education sector.[121]

What is less known, however, but has been explored in detail by Sue

Middleton of the University of Waikato, is the influence of Theosophy on its development through its founder Beatrice Ensor, a prominent Theosophist, and that NEF influence in New Zealand, India and England from the late nineteenth century was facilitated by international Theosophical networks.[122]

As we have seen, a number of members of the lodges were schoolteachers and principals or established their own schools, but they were also parents and politicians. The New Zealand branch of NEF was closely connected to the Theosophical Vasanta Garden preparatory school, established in Auckland in 1919. 'Vasanta' is Sanskrit for 'spring', but also a transliteration of Besant. The Vasanta School, which closed in 1960, was heavily influenced by the theories of Dr Maria Montessori (1870–1952), who had joined the Society some time in the 1930s. Montessori had been invited to lecture on education at Aditya, India, in 1938, but shortly after her arrival the following year, found herself exiled there for the duration of the Second World War.[123]

Theosophy had a considerable impact on Montessori's vision of universal and child-centric education. At the time of writing, in New Zealand there are nearly 200 Montessori early learning centres, 17 state or state-integrated schools with Montessori primary classes, four private Montessori primary schools and three Montessori high schools.[124]

There is also a Theosophical influence, albeit an indirect one, on New Zealand education through the country's 11 Steiner Waldorf schools.[125] The German philosopher, esotericist and social reformer Rudolf Steiner (1861–1925) had been a deeply involved member of the Theosophical Society in the early 1900s, but was dissatisfied with its emphasis on Eastern religion and wanted to concentrate more on Christianity and natural science. The Krishnamurti incident was the final straw, and Steiner split from Theosophy in 1912 to form his own Anthroposophy movement, taking a good many disgruntled Theosophists with him.

The name was a deliberate jab at Theosophy, translating roughly as Human Wisdom as opposed to Divine Wisdom. Despite the split, Steiner retained an abiding interest in Theosophical ideas and developments.[126] In recent years, New Zealand's Steiner schools have moved to distance themselves from Steiner's misrepresented racial beliefs, which were largely inherited from Theosophy's theories about root races.[127] (Anthroposophy will be examined in Chapter 5.)

Today, the Theosophical Society in New Zealand, while perhaps not as crusadingly vibrant as a century ago, nor with the high membership levels evident in the 1980s, is by no means quiescent, nor are its energies spent. Its influence on all the esoteric movements to emerge or establish in Aotearoa since the nineteenth century is inarguable, and few forms of homegrown alternative spirituality have managed to emerge in the modern period without at least some taint of Theosophical mystagogy.

Chapter 2.

Children of the Golden Dawn

And what rough beast, its hour come round at last, Slouches towards Bethlehem to be born?

— W. B. YEATS, 'THE SECOND COMING', 1920

As we saw in the previous chapter's discussion of the Theosophical Society, throughout the Empire many Victorian Britons were turning to the occult and esoteric as a viable alternative to scientific, rationalist materialism and the prescriptive, conventional religions that had long since lost their miraculous edge or monopoly on the supernatural. As historian of Western esotericism Christopher McIntosh has written of the nineteenth-century French occult revival:

> A person who has strong faith rooted in an accepted religion tradition will, in a sense, be inoculated against outlandish beliefs. The sceptic, on the other hand, weakens his defences by denying a fundamental part of his nature, namely the need for religion belief; thus he is an easy prey for the self-appointed prophet or messiah with some colourful new cult to offer.[1]

While some preferred to contemplate the mystical philosophies of distant Imperial possessions, others were drawn to the fading traces of Western traditions of ritual magic. It was thus that on 12 February 1888, three British Freemasons with enormous beards — William Robert Woodman (1828–1891), William Wynn Westcott (1848–1925) and Samuel Liddell MacGregor Mathers (1854–1918) — signed the pledges that brought into being the Hermetic Order of the Golden Dawn, *Ordo Hermeticus Aurorae Aureae*. Woodman, a medical doctor, had volunteered as a surgeon during Napoleon III's 1851 coup d'état. He served as a police surgeon in the London suburb of Stoke Newington and was a keen horticulturalist, but died before the Golden Dawn officially opened its doors.

Westcott was also a medical doctor, and was deputy coroner for North-East London and Central Middlesex from 1881 to 1918. Mathers, by far the least establishment and most theatrical of the three, eked out a living as an impoverished translator, but managed to secure a position in 1888 as assistant librarian to Frederick Horniman, an obscenely rich tea importer and founder of the Horniman Museum in London.

The Golden Dawn would rise to become the pre-eminent Hermetic and magical society of the nineteenth century, recruiting a healthy membership through notices published in the Theosophical journal *Lucifer* and by word of mouth. Woodman and another early member, Robert Wentworth Little (1840–1878), had also both been members of the esoteric study group Societas Rosicruciana in Anglia (SRIA), an English Rosicrucian esoteric Christian group founded in the mid-1860s for Grand Lodge Master Masons. Mathers had the most showman to him; the 'MacGregor' was entirely a pseudo-Jacobite affectation as Mathers wasn't even Scottish.[2]

The allure of the Order lay in its promise of initiation in the use of natural magic to deepen the connection between the individual being and the spiritual realm. Although the Golden Dawn was ostensibly a secretive order, paradoxically it was also very fashionable, attracting many celebrity members from the artistic, dramatic and literary spheres, and it made a huge impact in popularising the occult in the public imagination. As with Theosophy, Fabianism, Logical Positivism, the Temperance Society and the Working Men's Educational Union, the Golden Dawn tapped into the Victorian thirst for self-improvement.

Not unlike early psychiatry (both Jung and Freud were fascinated by the occult),[3] the aim was spiritual purification and perfection.[4] Order member and Irish activist Maude Gonne — she who so besotted Yeats — described the membership as the 'very essence of middle-class dullness'.[5] Because many of the early members came from Theosophy, unlike Freemasonry, the Golden Dawn admitted women and gained much of its early social momentum from women members, despite most of the membership being male. These co-Masonic relationships are relatively common among occult groups.

Structurally the Golden Dawn based itself on Freemasonry, adopting that organisation's structure of initiatory degrees, but following the SRIA system of an outer, public order, an inner order, and then the Secret Chiefs, who served a similar function to Theosophy's Ascended Masters, though Egyptian this time rather than Tibetan. The Golden Dawn also embraced ancient Egyptian religion, the Kabbalah, esoteric Christianity, paganism, neoplatonic theurgy, alchemical allegory, the surviving grimoires (magicians' manuals) of the Renaissance, and the Elizabethan Enochian magic of Dr John Dee.

For the Order, magic was the use of methodical ritual to inspire altered mental states of imaginative intensity to initiate change in consciousness

Samuel Liddell MacGregor Mathers, co-founder of the Golden Dawn, keeper of its rituals, decider of initiates and conferrer of degrees, in the regalia of that order.

and the physical world in accordance with the universal will.[6] Tarot scholar Mary Greer describes this will as 'the consciously focused intention of one's highest, divine, or God-like Self, charged by a desire that was purified of all ego-content and actualized through an imagination that used all the senses but was untainted by material illusion'.[7] When members invoked gods and spirits, the purpose was not worship but rather spiritual development. Mesmerism, hypnotism and mediumship, as practised by spiritualists, were strongly discouraged.[8]

☦

The basis of the Golden Dawn's belief system was what are known today as the 'Cipher Manuscripts', whose authenticity, as member and Order scholar Arthur E. Waite (1857–1942) — co-creator of the ubiquitous Rider–Waite–Smith tarot deck — observed, has been doubted nearly since the Order's inception.[9] Supposedly and variously, these encrypted documents were discovered among the papers of the nineteenth-century Freemason and occultist Frederick Hockley, or they came from a Hungarian count named Apponyi, or they were found in a second-hand bookstall and passed to British occultist Kenneth Mackenzie, an honorary magus of the SRIA and eventual founding member of the Order. Mackenzie in turn gave the papers to Mathers. Waite dated the papers to the 1870s,[10] making it likely Mackenzie had forged them. Mathers stated near the end of his life that William Westcott had forged the manuscripts, and at one point it was suggested (it is unclear by whom) that the novelist Edward Bulwer-Lytton had written them.[11]

Written from right to left and encoded in a fifteenth-century Trithemius cipher, once decoded by Westcott the documents gave the outline of a ceremonial and symbolic structure for ritual magic. Conveniently they also contained the address of Anna Sprengel of Nuremberg, purportedly one of the shadowy Rosicrucians, whom Westcott supposedly contacted in pursuit of authentic rituals and mysteries.[12]

Sprengel intimated herself to be the countess of Landsfeldt, the illegitimate daughter of King Ludwig I of Bavaria and dancer-cum-political revolutionary Lola Montez, and a point of contact with the ascended

William Wynn Westcott, medical doctor, coroner and co-founder of the Golden Dawn order, in Rosicrucian regalia.

masters known as the 'Invisible Chiefs' who held the world's arcane knowledge. As it turns out, Sprengel and her husband Theo Horos were a couple of con artists with their own occult racket going on in France, and were given a colourful backstory by Mathers to make his own rituals and writings look more believable. Theo was a notorious seducer and rapist, and the pair's later-revealed actions did much to tarnish the reputation of the Golden Dawn as the supposed source of occult knowledge and documents authenticating an official Rosicrucian lineage for the group.[13]

☦

At this point the general reader will be, quite rightly, wondering who the Rosicrucians are. The SRIA arose as a spiritual and cultural movement, and quite likely a hoax, in seventeenth-century Europe. Like the Bavarian Illuminati, the more famous Enlightenment secret society founded in 1776 to oppose superstition, religious control and abuse of state power, Rosicrucianism was supposed to be enormously influential on world affairs. As with modern-day conspiracy theories, there was a lot of speculation about who was a member, and a lot of celebrity intellectuals such as Benjamin Franklin and Victor Hugo liked to give the impression that they were for notoriety, although there is no concrete evidence such a group ever actually existed. The name comes from their symbol, a cross superimposed on a rose, a symbol of great antiquity in mystical Christianity.

Most of the evidence for Rosicrucianism's existence consists of three anonymous manifestos that appeared between 1614 and 1617, drawing on Kabbalah, mystical Christianity, Hermeticism, alchemy garnished with a dabble of Sufism and Zoroastrianism, and promising a universal renewal and reformation of humanity. According to the first of these manifestos, the *Fama Fraternitatis Rosae Crucis* or *Fame of the Rosy Cross Brotherhood* (1614), a likely allegorical German physician, philosopher and mystic known as Father Christian Rosenkreuz, allegedly born in 1378 and who died aged 106 years, gathered around him a small group of thinkers to spread around the world the mystical knowledge he had gained in the Middle East. Upon his death, his body was secretly hidden in an underground vault along with an encyclopaedic archive of secret sciences and wisdom, only to be rediscovered, as he had prophesised, by a brother Rosicrucian 120 years later.

By the Enlightenment, Rosicrucianism was thoroughly entangled with Freemasonry, which together became important foundation stones of the Western esoteric tradition.[14] As embroidered in various esoteric legendaria, the Rosicrucians, if they were ever flesh and blood, had taken on saint-like or even semi-divine status. Rosicrucianism is, in turn, built on an even older tradition, Hermeticism, which emerged in late antiquity and is based on the writings of an Egyptian, Hermes Trismegistus ('Thrice-Greatest Hermes'), who is likely mythological, if not outright fictitious, and derived from the Ptolemaic syncretisation of the Greek god Hermes with the Egyptian god Thoth.[15]

‡

The mysterious Fräulein Sprengel 'responded' to Mathers, chartering the first Golden Temple — the Isis-Urania Temple in London in 1888 — and conferring upon Westcott, Mathers and Woodman the honorary grades of *Adeptus Exemptus*. The Isis-Urania Temple was quickly followed by the Osiris Temple in the seaside resort of Weston-super-Mare, the Horus Temple in industrial Bradford in Yorkshire, the Amen-Ra Temple in Edinburgh, and the Ahathoor Temple in Paris. In 1892, Westcott stepped back from management of the Order, leaving Mathers, who was by now the only original founding member, in a leadership role.

From Paris, Mathers appointed Florence Farr (1860–1917) as the Chief Adept in England. Farr, a feminist and West End actress, was a friend of Kelmscott designer William Morris's daughter May and had posed for Edward Burne-Jones' painting *The Golden Stairs* (1880, Tate Britain, London), as well as having affairs with both the poet W. B. Yeats and the playwright George Bernard Shaw. Farr was the first of the Order's celebrity members, and, as with Lisa Marie Presley and Scientology, through her connections many more followed at the height of the Golden Dawn's popularity in the 1890s.

At its peak it had hundreds of members, including Farr, Gonne, Yeats, author Arthur Machen, co-founder of the Fabian Society and children's author Edith Nesbit, authors Algernon Blackwood, Arthur Conan Doyle (inventor of Sherlock Holmes), Sax Rohmer (creator of Fu Manchu) and Bram Stoker (author of *Dracula*), artists Henrietta and Henry Paget, and others.

It was also at this point that Farr and the other British Temples began challenging Mathers' authority as head of the Order, keeper of rituals, decider of initiates and conferrer of degrees. The final insult was Mathers' initiation into the inner order in 1898 of the already infamous Aleister Crowley, flamboyant bisexual, drug-taker, debaucher of women and sex magician. Farr resigned, and three months later the British Temples expelled Mathers from the Order.

Let us pause to consider the size of the egos involved, the carefully cultivated neuroses, the rivalries and the spleen. Within the year the Golden Dawn disintegrated. Waite took control of the Isis-Urania Temple, which survived until 1914 and became the Hermetic Society of the Morgenröthe (from the Old English for 'Red Dawn'), before itself splitting in two. Those who were most interested in Christian Mysticism, led by Waite, formed the Independent and Rectified Rite of the Golden Dawn, and later the Fellowship of the Rosy Cross. Those from the Morgenröthe group, who were more interested in occultism, formed the group Stella Matutina (Morning Star), which had the lion's share of remaining members, including the poet W. B. Yeats, who remained a member for 20 years. In 1903 the group was based at the Amoun Temple under the leadership of British doctor, Freemason and Bahá'í Robert Felkin (1853–1926). Mathers founded his own Alpha et Omega Order, or A.O., in 1900. Crowley formed his own order, the Argenteum Astrum ('Silver Star') or A∴A∴ in 1907.[16]

‡

Robert Felkin was born in Beeston, Nottinghamshire, to a well-known family of lacemakers. While still a student at Wolverhampton Grammar School, he met the explorer David Livingstone, who inspired the young Felkin to become a missionary in Africa. In 1876 he began studying medicine at Edinburgh, taking time out in 1878 to join a Church Missionary Society mission to Central Africa. On this mission, he met Major-General

Robert William Felkin, missionary, medical doctor and founder of the Stella Matutina order and the Smaragdum Thalasses Temple (Whare Rā) in Havelock North.

Charles Gordon, the hero of Khartoum during the Mahdi revolt in 1884, documented a number of indigenous African medical practices, including his observation of a Caesarean section, served as royal physician to King Muteesa of Buganda in modern-day Uganda — a turnaround from the king having initially ordered his execution — and agitated against slavery in Zanzibar, a primary centre for that vile trade. Felkin's non-magical claims to fame lie mainly in his writings on tropical medicine, including his research on the geographical distribution of the Guinea worm parasite, and multiple books on Uganda, Egypt and Sudan.

Felkin remained in Africa for two years.[17] He completed his medical degree at Marburg, Germany, in 1885, and for a while practised in Edinburgh. Here, Felkin and his wife Mary joined a Bible study circle, some of the members of which were Theosophists. Robert and Mary joined the Edinburgh Theosophical Society in 1886, and then in 1894, seeking something with more ritual attached, joined the Golden Dawn Amen-Ra Temple (not to be confused with the later Amoun Temple, although they are both merely variants on the same name, Amun-Re, the Egyptian sun god).

Mary Felkin died in 1903, two years or so after her husband had established the Amoun Temple and the year the Golden Dawn itself finally imploded. The world-weary and deeply distressed Felkin went on retreat at the Anglo-Catholic Community of the Resurrection in Mirfield, West Yorkshire. The Mirfield community was dedicated to the contemplation of the mystery of Christ's Resurrection, and was politically active with a strong vein of Christian socialism, while also dabbling in Rosicrucian-inflected esoteric strands of Christianity.

By 1902 the Mirfield Fathers had a strong missionary presence in South Africa and what was then still Rhodesia, and perhaps that held some appeal for Felkin, given his experiences. Here he met the priest Father Fitzgerald, who would later be a key player in bringing Felkin to New Zealand.

Felkin's spiritual quest did not end in Mirfield. In 1907 he was initiated into Freemasonry and the Societas Rosicruciana in Anglia, officiated by William Westcott. He attained high rank in both organisations, although he does not seem to have been particularly interested in their work, being largely directed by messages from the 'sun masters' — entities of the by now familiar Ascended Master/Invisible Chief type. The first of these, Ara Ben Shemesh, an 'Arab Teacher', 'the Chaldean', lived in a 'Temple in the Desert' inhabited by the 'Sons of Fire'. The second, Sri Parananda, he encountered astrally in the steam of the baths at a spa in Bad Pyrmont, Germany, and more prosaically in the flesh in the lounge of the Carlton Hotel in London.[18]

Meantime, in New Zealand, in the prosperous Hawke's Bay town of Havelock North, population around 1000, a peculiar brew of Quakers, Theosophists, Anglicans and adherents of Radiant Living were developing a receptive climate into which Felkin would drop: the Havelock Work. Much of what we know of the nature and history of the Havelock Work comes from an article written by John von Dadelszen (1913–1988) for the Havelock North *Te Mata Times* in 1983.[19] Von Dadelszen served variously as president of the Hawke's Bay District Law Society in 1965 and 1966, and as both a councillor (from 1952) and mayor of Havelock North (1958–1959), chancellor of the Diocese of Waiapu, Hastings coroner, and a director of various Hawke's Bay newspaper companies. He was senior chief of the Smaragdum Thalasses Temple after 1962.[20]

According to von Dadelszen, the Work began in 1907 when the Australian Reginald Gardiner and his Canadian wife, Ruth, came to live in Havelock (the 'North' wasn't added until 1910 to distinguish it from the Marlborough town of Havelock in the South Island). Gardiner's brother was already resident there as the Anglican vicar, and would also become involved in the Work. Gardiner started out in the import–export business, but, in the year that Havelock became Havelock North, he became first chairman of directors of the company that published the *Hawke's Bay Tribune*. He and Ruth built a fine house called 'Stadacona' in what is now Keirunga Gardens, named after the sixteenth-century St Lawrence Iroquoian village in Québec.

In 1908 a meeting was held in Frinley, near Hastings, called by the Gardiners and attended by over 100 people, a curious mix of Anglicans, Quakers and Theosophists. The Havelock Work had begun. It was the first of many years of activity characterised by Shakespeare and Dickens readings, carving, Morris dancing lessons and festivals, climaxing in the Old Village Fête of 1911 presided over by a pantomime King Arthur and his court. In language reminiscent of both Theosophy and the Golden

Dawn, the first issue of the literary magazine *The Forerunner* tells us: 'As each proves true to his own special Ray, he will speed for his Birth-star in the vast horizon and revolving in the fire-mist of his own special hue, will unite with the others and form a vortex of glowing whiteness which will be Beaconlight to attract the seekers after love and truth and beauty.'[21]

The Work turned to the tarot and Kabbalah, but it remained staunchly Christian, specifically High Anglican, in outlook and tone, if of a mystical and esoteric flavour.[22] The members of the Work sought to purify themselves in worthiness for the secrets promised in Luke 8:10 that lesser Christians, 'seeing they might not see, and hearing they might not understand'. The Work grew in numbers and eventually became the Society of the Southern Cross, their simple rites becoming increasingly complex Golden Dawn rituals.[23]

The general aesthetic of the movement was Edwardian, the violet twilight of Pre-Raphaelite high romanticism, and Ye Olde Merrie Englande. The Work had a similar pageantry to the first series of Glastonbury festivals (1914–26) launched by socialist English composer Rutland Boughton (1878–1960) as a kind of utopian 'English Bayreuth',[24] and Dion Fortune's Glastonbury workings of around the same time.[25] The Havelock Work's *The Forerunner*, of William Morris-style design, ceased publication with the outbreak of the First World War in 1914. The war also brought to a rude halt the broader atmosphere of the time: optimism, *völkisch* nostalgia, liberal Anglicanism and Evelyn Underhill-esque mysticism had until then been in the air. As the novelist J. B. Priestly described it:

> [The Edwardian age] was moving in many different directions. It was opening out, not hurrying one way. What it was opening *from*, so leaving behind, was the decaying hulk of middle-class Victorian belief, thought, feeling, taste, customs, habits. It might be reaching out not to Wells' scientific Utopia but towards India and Theosophy, Irish peasants and leprechauns, Catholicism and the distributive state, Merrie England and the guilds, a quiet life and a new closeness to Nature, Free Love or no Love but plenty of social service. Where it moved at all, the age — as we say now — was wide open.[26]

Yet this may be too swift a leap in judgement to apply to what was going on in Havelock, for in many ways its social order remained strictly Victorian well into the early twentieth century, one anonymous villager reporting to local historian Matthew Wright in 1996:

> There was never a really Edwardian period. Victorianism really held its grip on society until after the First World War. It was not until the 1920s when you had shorter skirts for women and Oxford bags at universities, clothing styles began to change and a lot of habits, morals and so on . . . we've seen one of the greatest revolutions since the industrial revolution in our own lifetime.[27]

The removed and out-of-time atmosphere of the place, and the culture of patronage and patriarchy, enabled the husbanding of unusual philosophies received from the late Victorian mystical revival — some more discreetly clandestine than others. The Havelock Work could really only have come about in that sort of environment. The name carries with it echoes of the 'Great Work' of alchemy, the apotheosis of the soul for which the transmutation of base metals into gold was merely a metaphor often taken too literally.

‡

The Southern Cross Society and the Work both believed that the Eastern emphasis of Theosophy was unsuitable for Westerners, and that the Church had lost its way in shedding Christ's supposed esoteric teachings around achieving mystical heightened states and reincarnation. In 1910, the Mirfield Fathers of the Community of the Resurrection had sent a mission to New Zealand, and Father Fitzgerald, who had previous contact with a member, agreed to direct their spiritual instruction from Britain, later recommending that Robert Felkin go there in person. In 1912 Felkin, his second wife Harriot (often misspelled as Harriet in the literature), and his daughter by Mary, Ethelwyn (Ethel for short), were invited to Havelock North by the Society of the Southern Cross.

Harriot was just 10 years older than Ethel. A dedicated occultist herself, she had met Felkin while working for him as a maid. When Felkin had

Harriot Felkin, occultist, wife of Robert Felkin and later leader of the Smaragdum Thalasses Temple (Whare Rā).

PHOTOGRAPH BY HUBERT LOVELL-SMITH, HAWKE'S BAY DIGITAL ARCHIVES TRUST

first arrived in New Zealand in 1912, on what was intended as only a short visit, he and Harriot recorded their responses to the land and people, later published in 'A Wayfaring Man', a lightly fictionalised memoir published from 1936 to 1949 in the Society of the Southern Cross's journal *The Lantern*. Their observations are disappointingly banal — they are surprised at the large amounts of tea consumed, the cabbage trees remind them of Egyptian dom palms, the locals are helpful, friendly and generous, the native bush doesn't compare favourably with picturesque English woods, and so on. At Rotorua, through clairvoyantly attuned eyes, they marvelled at deformed and primordial elementals in the geothermal regions unlike the orderly dryads and fairies they were used to.[28]

Finding disciples eager for enlightenment in Havelock, in 1912 Felkin founded the Smaragdum Thalasses (classical Greek for 'Emerald Seas') Temple of the Stella Matutina order.[29] 'We claim to bring to you,' Felkin announced in his first address, 'the Message of Western Occultism as descended from the Middle Ages and a part of the very fascinating message which during the past 30–35 years has come from the East to the West. The message which we bring is this — firstly, that in the Catholic or Christian Church, as in every great religion that the world has ever known, there is an Esoteric as well as Exoteric side. We want to try to set forth this Esoteric teaching which has been ignored for so very long.'[30] With key acolytes now in place and raising funds to prepare the way, the Felkins returned to England, handed the leadership of the Amoun Temple to others and settled their household affairs.

Strangely oblivious to the unfolding political landscape in Europe, the Felkins decided to return to Germany in 1913 in search of the Rosicrucians. On this trip the Felkins built a relationship with Rudolf Steiner in Stuttgart, and were informed by their mysterious Rosicrucian contacts that Christian Rosenkreutz was preparing for his resurrection in 1926, or 1933, or perhaps 1935.[31] Unfortunately, another prophesy, while more precise, proved a little off-beam, with uncomfortable consequences: Felkin's 'Arab', Ara Ben Shemesh, had correctly prophesied war, but he was less on the ball regarding kick-off time. When war broke out a year earlier than foreseen, in 1914, Robert Felkin found himself trapped in Germany, which no doubt caused a great strain on his health and mind.

In 'A Wayfaring Man', Harriot Felkin pulls no punches. Her husband's health was beset with alcoholism, malaria and other tropical diseases contracted in Africa, and he was under great strain what with running the Order and opening new temples.

Given all this, risking German U-boats in 1916, at the peak of the First World War, to voyage by ship to tranquil New Zealand may well have seemed an opportunity worth taking. Presumably they had some influential support to travel across the Pacific as civilians in wartime.[32] There was also the certainty of a firm offer from Havelock: the locals had been impressed with Felkin, and within a year of meeting him had formalised plans to bring him back.

John Chambers (1854–1946) and his brother Mason Chambers (1860–1948), scions of a wealthy Quaker farming family, put up the money for both New Zealand voyages of the Felkin family, and provided the land for a temple building for Smaragdum Thalassa and the Felkins' home in Havelock.[33] From all accounts John Chambers was the very model of a conservative Victorian pastoralist patriarch,[34] a milieu that does not, at first, sound like fertile ground for something as exotic as an occult sect. But then the 1913 Whare Rā trust deed, bearing the signatures of both Reginald Gardiner and both Chambers brothers, makes far from sensational reading, describing the group as being created for:

> the purposes of instituting, carrying on or developing such scientific, religious, charitable and similar work as the trustees shall in this discretion deem expedient and also for the purpose of aiding and assisting the carrying out or developing of literary work in all its branches and crafts, work and similar or analogous work of which the trustees may in their absolute discretion approve or for such one or more or all of the above purposes as the trustees may from time to time determine...[35]

Things were moving quickly, and the Chambers and Gardiner engaged renowned New Zealand architect James Chapman-Taylor (1878–1958) to design a temple for the new order. The building was designed in Chapman-Taylor's signature Arts and Crafts, Jaco-Tudorbethan cottage style, with small-paned windows, plain roughcast concrete walls with steel reinforcing, and a high, gabled roof of 10-centimetre-thick concrete and Marseilles tiles. It was constructed over the top of a large underground ceremonial area (the vault) built into the slope of the hill with massive concrete roof beams. (On the matter of Chapman-Taylor's tendency to build for the ages, it is worth noting that most of his builds in the area, including the vault, survived the 1931 earthquake intact.)

‡

The vault was completed in around 1913, with the rest of the house following in 1915.[36] It was one of the first such concrete houses in the district, and evidently Chapman-Taylor was relatively new to the material. Harriot Felkin later recalled: 'Unluckily for us the year of our arrival proved to be one of the rare wet seasons . . . the house which had stood empty for eighteen months before our arrival had not been waterproofed . . . [as] the architect had not realised that concrete is porous. The south walls leaked, and of course so long as it rained nothing could be done . . .'[37]

Only a few subtle design oddities, such as the T-shaped window in the upper storey suggesting a Tau cross, indicate anything unusual. The building came to be known commonly as 'Whare Rā', te reo Māori for 'House of the Sun' — no doubt Felkin was amused and intrigued by the fact that the Māori and Egyptian sun gods shared the same name. As historian of alternative religion Timothy Worrad notes, Harriot Felkin had a fascination with Māori names, quoting 'A Wayfaring Man':

> I think we were all thankful when we caught our first glimpse of Aotearoa, the Great White Cloud, which is the Māori name for New Zealand, and a much better name than ours. I wonder why we have such a passion for changing beautiful native names into commonplace English ones. Think of Mt. Cook for instance, instead of Aorangi, Cloud Piercer.[38]

Why indeed? This insight into the colonial agenda aside, the Temple boasted some Māori members, albeit in a Christian context. One such member, allegedly, was the Right Reverend Bishop Wiremu Nētana Pānapa (1898–1970, Ngāti Ruanui, Ngāti Whātua, Te Rarawa and Ngāti Kahu), second bishop of Aotearoa — a fact not usually mentioned in his biography.[39]

Smaragdum Thalassa also tried to integrate itself into the whakapapa of the landscape with a pseudo-legend, of Felkin's invention, that Te Mata Peak, visually dominating all of Hawke's Bay, was where local Māori trained in white healing magic.[40] The actual Māori tradition is that Te Mata is the prostrate body of the tohunga Rongokako, grandfather of Kahungunu and ancestor of all Ngāti Kahungunu associated with the waka *Tākitimu*. European settlers independently noticed the similarity and called the mountain the 'Sleeping Giant'.[41] Other than that, there does not seem to have been an attempt to appropriate or assimilate Māori traditional beliefs into the magical workings of the Temple.

Leading an esoteric order was not going to provide a source of income, and Felkin enjoyed almost immediate authority in the Havelock North community as its first medical doctor in permanent residence, not least during the horrific influenza epidemic of 1918. He headed the town committee set up to control the infection, and was apparently phenomenally successful in doing so as there were no deaths from the virus there.[42] One wonders, however, what the more conventional citizens of the town made of the secretive behaviour around Whare Rā and the rituals in the hexagonal chamber beneath the building.

This 'Vault of the Adepti' was painted with colourful grids and adorned with Hebrew letters and magical, astrological and alchemical symbols. Occult author Nick Farrell relates a story that Felkin made the builders swear an oath of silence, with the inevitable result that the entire town soon knew the details.[43] The mother of one of the later Whare Rā chiefs, Betty Jones, herself a high-ranking member, suffered from dementia and would ask random strangers on the street if they were attending that night's ceremony.[44]

The vault, attached to an underground temple, was reserved for the use of the higher-degree Second Order. Its design was based on an earlier design by Mathers, intended to represent the tomb of Christian Rosenkreutz, mythical founder of the Rosicrucians.[45] The secret entrance

The 'Vault of the Adepti' inside the Smaragdum Thalasses Temple (Whare Rā), Havelock North.

to the subterranean parts of Whare Rā was hidden in a wardrobe, and one popular story states that this was the inspiration for the magical portal to Narnia in C. S. Lewis's *The Lion, the Witch, and the Wardrobe* (1950), and that Felkin had told his friend Arthur Waite about it, who passed it on to the theologian and novelist Charles Williams, a member of Waite's Golden Dawn successor order, who was a close friend of Lewis.[46] One cannot regard some of these earnest scholars of the esoteric tradition and not be slightly reminded of how Jadis, the future White Witch of Narnia, describes Uncle Andrew in *The Magician's Nephew* (1955): 'a little peddling magician who works by rules and books' with 'no real magic in [his] blood or heart'.[47]

That might be a little unfair, though it is worth comparing the staid and straightlaced adepts of Havelock North with their more flamboyant Golden Dawn counterparts in the UK. In London in 1896, Florence Farr, the actress who had been mistress to both George Bernard Shaw and W. B. Yeats, sought to summon Taphthartharath, the spirit of the planet Mercury, by boiling a pickled snake in a magical 'hell broth'.

This was done in the company of Allan Bennett, Farr's assistant magus in the operation, an electrical engineer by non-magical trade, credited with formally introducing Buddhism to English society and establishing it institutionally. Bennett also reportedly once paralysed a mocking Theosophist for 14 hours with his 'magical blasting rod' (one suspects surreptitious electrical or magnetic trickery was involved). Such rods (also known as the 'lightning rod', rod of Moses, or the '*verge foudroyante*' in the 1821 French grimoire *Le dragon rouge*) — basically a specialised magic wand — it must be said were normally a thing reserved for conjured spirits in Solomonic magic rather than recalcitrant Theosophists.[48] It is to Felkin's credit that he was able to transition between both cultures.

Not that it would have mattered much if any of the town's inhabitants *had* objected (and some did), as most of the town's leading personages were members of the Temple. Membership of Whare Rā is reputed to have included members of Parliament and two governors-general.[49] In 1978 there was a weekend-long bonfire when the Temple was dissolved and most of the Whare Rā documentation and paraphernalia was burned, making it difficult to determine everyone involved, but Nick Farrell names one of the governors-general as John, Earl Jellicoe GCB,

OM, GCVO, SGM, DL (1859–1935), former Lord Admiral of the Royal British Navy.

Jellicoe was governor-general of New Zealand from 1920 to 1924, a senior Freemason, and a fervent British Israelite — a group that believed that events in the Old Testament actually took place in the British Isles rather than the Holy Land, and that King George V was a literal descendent of Moses via King David. Another alleged member was a hero of the Great War, Andrew Hamilton Russell (1868–1960), who led the New Zealand Mounted Rifles Brigade, and commanded the Anzac evacuation from Gallipoli and the New Zealand Division on the Western Front in 1917 and 1918.[50]

☦

Local historian S. W. Grant informs us: 'Naturally, the Village being a place where gossip was, and is, rife, dark rumours circulated about secret meetings held underground at the Felkin residence, titillating the imaginations of the good, credulous people of Havelock.'[51] People could hardly have missed the red stockings that female members were obliged to wear. There is some reason to believe that the rites practised at Whare Rā were not those Felkin created for the Stella Matutina order, but rather the pure form of the original Golden Dawn order rites; Whare Rā having essentially split from the Order in London, though it retained good relations with the Hermes Temple in Bristol, and a good number of members from there ended up emigrating to Havelock North.[52]

New members, having first been furtively assessed for suitability by the Felkins, were initiated into the Order by a ceremonial ritual of symbolic death and rebirth. One initiate, Francis 'Frank' Salt, has left us an evocative picture of what the ritual was like upon stepping through the wardrobe in 1936:

> On being led by the hand, blindfolded and wondering, into what felt like a large hall — incense was very strong—, I had a sudden feeling — 'I have come home'. It was very silent, until clear voices spoke, then there was movement... in the total darkness. The atmosphere was very intense, one felt almost as if in outer space, with spiritual

forces flickering about one. A sense of deep reverence — even awe — as one was led many short distances. It was an 'other worldly' experience, as if being part of a heavenly host among the stars. I was asked to take a solemn obligation, which I did very sincerely, as a personal consecration to the Divine Science. Halfway down the stairs, where the candidate was required to await further instructions, was a landing, known as 'the Cave', lined with hessian curtains on which Egyptian figures were worked in light blue. After an interval of time the candidate was met by two Temple officers dressed in robes and Egyptian headdresses, blindfolded by one of them, and then led into the Temple where the ceremony of initiation began.[53]

Like all Golden Dawn-derived rituals, the initiation from the rank of Neophyte to Zelator, and thus entry to the lowest sphere of the Sephiroth or Kabbalah Tree of Life, was complex, involved and wordy, peppered with Latin, Hebrew and Enochian, the language of the angels, invoking the Egyptian gods representing the hidden forces of the universe. The Sephiroth, depending on the variety of Kabbalah observed, was the ideal representation of the universe, a bridge between the mortal and the divine, or the body of God itself. Imagine one of those pyramids of champagne glasses at aspirational weddings, where the sparkling wine is poured in the top and flows down to fill all the glasses. In this case the champagne — the divine power — never stops flowing and each glass is a different quality of the Godhead.

By means of a thorough understanding of the mysteries of the aura and the Kabbalah, meditating on ancient symbols, astral travel to higher dimensions and engaging the transcendent beings who dwell there, initiates might move through the Sephiroth, and free themselves from terrestrial mortal dross and the Karmic wheel of reincarnation to eventually become ascended beings themselves, or at least spiritually purified. All of this took place within the context of Christianity, in its mystical and esoteric form, and was the synthesis of all religions and spiritual traditions.

The initiate was required to spend a night sealed alone in the symbolic tomb of the vault with the intention of astral travelling to the Masters. The first four ranks — Zelator, Theoricus, Practicus and Philosophus — the outer order, represented the four elements: Earth, Air, Water and Fire. The ranks of the second, inner order — Adeptus Minor, Adeptus Major and Adeptus Exemptus — represented a deepening of understanding. The aspirant to any grade was tutored on the metaphysical symbolism involved, and then had to pass a written examination and a practical to receive admission. Most never reached the third order, Magister Templi, Magus, and finally the exalted Ipsissimus, the top of the Tree of Life.[54] The rite for initiation to Adeptus Major begins thus:

> Chief Adept and Second Adept (in unison): 'Benedictus Dominus Deus Noster.' [Blessed be our Lord God.]
> All: 'Qui Dedit Noble Hoc Signue.' [He who has given this noble sign] All touch Rosy Cross on breast.
> Chief Adept: 'Very Honoured Adepti Majores, assist me to open the Vault of the Adepti in the exalted Grade of Geburah [the fifth sephirah] in the Sephiroth Excellent Prince of the Horizon [Horus], see that all present have been admitted to the Mystery.'
> Second Adept: 'Very Honoured Fratres et Sorores give the sign.'
> Chief Adept: 'Noble Lord of Eventide [Horus] what is the word?'
> Third Adept: 'Elohim Gebur [the fifth Name of God as the punisher of sin].'
> Chief Adept: 'Grant us Thy strength, O Lord. Excellent Prince of the Horizon what is the mystic number formed therefrom?'
> Second Adept: 'The number is Twenty.'
> Chief Adept: 'Noble Lord of Eventide what is the signification thereof?'
> Third Adept: 'It is the Union of the Enochian Tablets and the Kerubic [Cherubic, of the Cherubim] Emblems.'
> Chief Adept: 'The Lord is my strength and my song.'
> Second Adept: 'He is also become my salvation.'
> Chief Adept: 'In the strength of Elohim Gebur, let us with tranquil minds and recollected hearts enter into the Valley of the Shadow [death/the grave/the Underworld].'
> Second Adept: 'Thou wilt keep him in perfect peace whose mind is stayed on Thee.'

> Third Adept: 'The night cometh and also the day: if ye will return, return ye.' (Turn down light in Vault) 'O Death, where is thy sting?'
> Second Adept. 'O Grave, where is thy victory?'
> Chief Adept and Second: 'Thanks be to God which giveth us the Victory.'[55]

As one might expect, this all required a lot of highly specialised maintenance, most of which was beyond the upper-middle-class Felkins, who were not the most practical of people. The linen robes creased and required regular starching. Ivy and rainwater would invade the sanctity of the Vault, leading to frequent emergency calls to help bail it out, and possums had a habit of crawling into its ventilation shafts, getting stuck and pungently shuffling off their mortal coils.[56]

These practical failings stand in sharp contrast with the way Felkin ran the Order, as Golden Dawn revivalist Pat Zalewski relates:

> During the ten years Felkin lived at Whare Rā he ran the temple like a military operation. Classes were held on week nights for Outer Order members in which esoteric philosophy and ritual were taught. On weekends he held classes for Inner Order members to hone their knowledge to a fine point. These included ritual, Enochian pronunciation and meditative exercises in the vault. By 1926, the year of Felkin's death, the Inner Order had grown to over 100 members, with an unspecified number in the Outer Order. The Inner Order group was an extremely wealthy one and had members in many of the key local bodies throughout the Havelock North and Hastings area and collectively wielded a tremendous amount of power...[57]

As recounted above, when Felkin died in 1926 the inner order alone reportedly had a hundred members, and the outer order around 200, consisting of some of the most important people in Hawke's Bay.[58] Felkin was buried in Havelock North cemetery, facing Whare Rā, in the cloak, mantle and purple cross of a Knight of the Arthurian Ordo Tabulae Rotundae (the Order of the Table Round or OTR), which he had also founded, and which, according to the SRIA in Napier, still exists today.[59]

Felkin was clearly an intelligent, complex and gifted man. And unlike Mathers there is no reason to doubt his earnest belief in the esoteric system he had established at the bottom of the Pacific. Meanwhile, back in the United Kingdom, the much-degraded Amoun Temple in London had closed in 1919. By then practice there had degenerated into mediumship and an obsession with astral travel. Two of its members developed a mental health condition described at the time as schizophrenia; one, a clergyman, later died in a mental hospital.[60]

Felkin was survived by two adult sons, Samuel and Laurence; Harriot, now aged 53, who continued to lead the Temple; and Ethel, who doted on her stepmother. The sons had remained in Britain. Samuel served in the First World War, after which he was posted to Berlin to work for the Reparations Committee. In the Second World War, he was promoted to flight lieutenant and placed in charge of the Air Intelligence section AI1(K), and later became the Chief Interrogation Officer at Trent Park POW facility north of London. After that conflict he was awarded an OBE, MBE, American Legion of Merit, and the Belgian Order of Chevalier with Swords.[61] Laurence led a quieter life as an English school inspector, and from 1903 was the husband of the novelist Ellen Thorneycroft Fowler.[62]

Although Felkin had already introduced Anthroposophy's ideas about colour therapy into the rituals at an early stage, under Harriot's leadership a distinct Anthroposophical influence, which took its cue from a more relaxed post-war age with less patience for elaborate ritual, entered the Order, particularly biodynamic gardening. This may be the reason German botanist and Anthroposophist Alfred Meebold (1863–1952) made Havelock North his home from 1945 until his death. Whare Rā could still assert some political influence as late as 1959 when Harriot — then aged 85 — and a number of the old guard came forth to successfully petition for a referendum against the fluoridation of the local water supply.[63]

Harriot Felkin and Reg Gardiner, one of the last of the senior chiefs, both died in 1959. Without that continuity of leadership the Temple began losing its way. Ethel died three years later, and was succeeded by John von Dadelszen; she and Harriot were both buried with Felkin. A report from a meeting in 1960 reveals the writing on the wall: 'I think we have all, at times, had that same feeling that when [Harriot Felkin] our keystone left us, the Order would go crashing about our ears . . . such a happening is quite unthinkable.'[64]

With the death of the last of the Felkin women, members began leaving in numbers.[65] Farrell relates that the sanctum of the vault itself began being used for magical rituals that Harriot would never have allowed had she been alive. According to former member Barbara Nairn, some of the initiates were using the space to experiment with Mathers' and Crowley's *The Goetia*, a 1904 version of the mid-seventeenth-century grimoire *Clavicula Salomonis Regis* or *The Lesser Key of Solomon*, which purports to give control over spirits of a decidedly unclean character.[66] This was not entirely forbidden by Whare Rā protocols, as stated in the Pentacle Ritual: 'Also revile not evil spirits, but remember that the Archangel Michael, of whom St. Jude speaketh, when contending with Satan durst not bring a railing accusation against him, but said: — "the Lord rebuke thee".'[67]

Farrell quotes another former member: 'After my initiation I stood in the door of the vault with my crook and staff. There was such a strong feeling that "this is all an abomination" that I had the urge to destroy the entire vault. I never went back to that vault ever again.' Will Chesterman, the leader of the Builders of Adytum (BOTA) in New Zealand (discussed in Chapter 4), considered buying Whare Rā after the Temple's closure, but on visiting it felt something 'really horrible about the place'.

Whare Rā was eventually sold to a Roman Catholic family, who thought they were merely getting a Chapman-Taylor-designed heritage house, unsealed a door to find the vault in their basement, and were so plagued by supernatural happenings that they had an exorcism performed.[68] More recent inhabitants seem to have experienced nothing out of the ordinary, however.[69]

☦

Without the vision of the Felkins, leadership cracks began to show. The largest clique was loyal to Jack Taylor, the most magically adept of the senior members, who held the rank of Adeptus Exemptus. He was not inclined to fall into line if he didn't agree with something, and was profoundly upset that he wasn't made a chief when one of the incumbents, a fed-up Archie

Shaw, quit. Taylor was also rather more enthusiastic about the OTR, which put him at odds with the other two major players, John von Dadelszen and Frank Salt.

Von Dadelszen and his wife were observant Christians and committed to reforming the order along those lines, and, not being able to work with Taylor, appointed Betty Jones to replace Shaw. Things rapidly began going the way of the British temples, and there was a showdown between the OTR and Smaragdum Thalasses, which concluded when von Dadelszen handed over some never-performed Adeptus Minor rituals on the condition that Taylor and the OTR cleared off.[70]

By the mid-1970s, Betty Jones, who had moved into Whare Rā to undertake restoration, was, like her mother before her, succumbing to dementia. Other members reported a loss in psychic connection with their invisible masters. In 1978, von Dadelszen unilaterally decided to end the Temple, and on 24 August 1978, to the consternation of the remaining members, a letter from the three Chiefs of the Order, written by von Dadelszen, was circulated to the membership and published in *The Lantern*:

> Dear Fratres and Sorores,
> This letter is addressed to all members of the Order of S.T., including members of the Second Order.
> It is with great great regret that we write to inform you that the temple is closing and there will be no Vernal Equinox ceremony. Those of you who have been present at recent Equinox ceremonies will surely have been aware, not only of the lack of numbers, but also the lack of power in the temple. Those who have read their annual reports can scarcely have failed to notice that no new members have been admitted since 1975. Indeed, there have been no grade ceremonies at all for the last two years or more . . .[71]

The proceeds were invested in the New Age centre Tauhara, in Taupō. The Taupō Borough Council eventually acquired the best part of the property for a reservoir, and the following year the rest was sold and the present site purchased overlooking Acacia Bay.[72] Thus did the oldest-surviving successor chapter of the Esoteric Order of the Golden Dawn come to an end.

Chapter 3.

The Empire Sentinels

Don't try to be paranormal until you know what's normal.

— TERRY PRATCHETT, *LORDS AND LADIES*, 1992

In the second half of the nineteenth century, as predominantly agricultural societies transitioned into industrial, organised societies, and migration from country to city increased in developed nations, a growing sense of dislocation resulted in a flourishing of social clubs and groups. Unsurprisingly, many of these were aimed at the population's youth, who, it was feared, were growing louche and dissolute. 'O tempora, o mores!' — 'Oh, the times! Oh, the customs!' — as Cicero had complained two millennia previously.

The new century dawned on dozens of such groups, often of martial or religious character, promoting practical skills, physical activity, a love of nature, and upright living. The best-known of these is Lord Robert Baden-Powell's Scout (1908) and Girl Guides (1910) movements. In the United States there were Ernest Thompson Seton's Woodcraft Indians (1902) and Daniel Carter Beard's Sons of Daniel Boone (1905). Germany had the *Jugendbewegung* or 'youth movement' (1896).

The influence of Baden-Powell (1857–1941) was particularly pervasive, and groups affiliated to, or modelled on, his Scouts sprang up throughout the British Empire and in other countries. Baden-Powell was a veteran of the British colonial wars in South Africa; during the 1899 Boer siege at Mafeking, massively outnumbered, as the colonel in charge, he was forced to mobilise young boys as uniformed messengers, orderlies and lookouts. Mafeking stood, and Baden-Powell returned to Britain in 1903 a hero.

He also returned to find that the manual he had created for those young boys at Mafeking, *Aids to Scouting*, had somehow preceded him home and was being widely disseminated among British youth in bootleg versions. His response was typically Victorian, and, updating what was born of pragmatism and adversity into something suitable for civilian life with Victorian notions of duty, patriotism and decorum, within a few years there were Scout troops throughout England.

Around 6500 New Zealanders also served in the South African Wars between 1880 and 1902, including one close to Baden-Powell: Major David Cossgrove (1852–1920). A Scottish-born Presbyterian, Cossgrove had migrated to Aotearoa with his family as a child in 1859 and settled in North Canterbury. He had trained and become a schoolteacher before volunteering to serve in South Africa in 1900, at 48 years old, being well

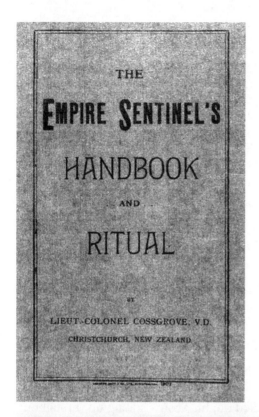

LEFT: The Empire Sentinel's Handbook.

BELOW: Major David Cossgrove, Boer War veteran, schoolmaster, founder of the Empire Sentinels and First Dominion Chief Scout of New Zealand, and his wife Selina.

over the age of active service. On his return, now headmaster of the former native school at Tuahiwi marae near Kaiapoi, and inspired by Baden-Powell's ideas, he set about organising Scouts in Aotearoa, resulting in 36 troops by the end of 1908. Baden-Powell confirmed Cossgrove as Dominion Chief Scout in 1910.[1]

Shortly thereafter, Cossgrove established his own movement for older boys, which he named the 'Empire Sentinels'. But whereas the Scouts drew on Rudyard Kipling's *The Jungle Book* (1894), the Empire Sentinels had quite another flavour indeed. Sentinels were organised into four 'Towers' for the four cardinal directions, and a system of three degrees through which Sentinels might progress based on religious duty, patriotism, work and sacrifice. They were initiated into each degree in a ritual called a 'Watch', with secret knocks, passwords, halters and blindfolds, and use of the phrase 'So Mote it Be'.[2] The latter phrase also finds its way into Wiccan ritual.

The officers of the Sentinels' opening and closing ceremonies were: the Chief Sentinel, whose symbol was a pole surmounted by an arrowhead, presumably representing the North Star; the Sentinel of the South, supporting a pole surmounted by a cross bearing four stars, representing the Southern Cross; the Sentinel of the East, carrying a pole topped by a representation of the rising sun; and the Sentinel of the West, with a pole supporting the same of the setting sun. There were also an Inner Guard with a halberd, an Outer Guard with a pike, and Watchmen with poles tied with white ribbons.[3]

‡

The reader has already likely detected a blatantly Masonic influence in this, yet it does not appear that Cossgrove was himself a Freemason.[4] Curiously, Baden-Powell does not seem to have been a Freemason either, but this may simply have been propaganda after the fact to spare the blushes of Roman Catholic Scouts. In New Zealand, however, until 1953 the governor-general fulfilled the role of both Grand Master of New Zealand's Masonic Grand Lodge and Dominion Chief Scout.[5] The stated missions of the two organisations — to serve God, family, humanity and country — also overlap, the Scout Promise and the Masonic Obligation being very similar. A formal understanding has existed between the two international fraternal organisations since 1952, and there exist a handful of Masonic-affiliated Scout groups worldwide.[6]

The non-Masonic references to four watchtowers in the cardinal directions strongly resemble the Golden Dawn ritual known as the 'Opening by Watchtower': a preliminary to purifying the ritual space by calling on the angelic guardians of the four directions, developed by Mathers from the Elizabethan angel magic of Dr John Dee. In the Golden Dawn ritual the directions are represented by: a central altar, bearing the ritual Tablet of Union, a rose, and the magician's ceremonial wand and dagger; the altar of fire to the south; the altar of water to the west; the altar of air to the east; and the altar of earth to the north — each with a ritual invocation of the appropriate guardian to keep the space pure and protect it from unclean powers.[7] Similar ceremonies can be found in most formal magical ritual sects and practices.

However, Cossgrove does not seem to have been the magical type, unlike disaffected scoutmaster John Hargrave (1894–1982), who founded the British Kibbo Kift movement in 1920. Intended as a demilitarised version of the Scouts, Kibbo Kift was replete with bizarre costumes and esoteric ceremonies in Anglo-Saxon and Esperanto drawn from Theosophy and the Golden Dawn. Its leaders had titles like 'Blue Falcon' and 'Deathwatch', and its mission was to free Western youth from the industrialised prison of modernity.[8]

Cossgrove was nothing like that: aside from the usual 'Maoriland' romantic animism and folk themes flavouring his Fairy Scouts for girls, his evident love of nature, and an apparent membership in the Oddfellows, there is nothing unusual about him. His role in the Scouts, however, would place him in regular contact with high-ranking Freemasons, who in turn were in close contact with Dr Felkin in Havelock North, and other facets of the Western esoteric tradition.

Yet even in more mainstream scouting there are nods towards the occult. For example, we find in *The American Boys' Book of Signs, Signals, and Symbols*, the 1918 offering of Daniel Carter Beard — founder of the Sons of Daniel Boone, which later merged with the Boy Scouts of America

— a perplexing chapter titled 'Numerals of the Magic: Ancient System of Secret Numbers'. It begins:

> You know that in ancient times religion, astronomy, medicine, and magic were all mixed up so that it was difficult to tell the beginning of one and the ending of the other and to-day the Gypsies, hoboes, free masons, astronomers, scientists, almanacs, and physicians still use some of the old magical emblems. So there is no reason why the boys of to-day should be debarred from using such of the signs as may suit their games or occupations and we will crib for them the table of numerals from old John Angleus, the astrologer. He learned them from the learned Jew, Even Ezra, and Even Ezra learned them from the ancient Egyptian sorcerers, so the story goes; but the reader may learn them from this book.[9]

It does not appear that Cossgrove's Empire Sentinels survived his taking up of an official role within the Scouts, and information about the group is scarce. Nevertheless, it seems highly unlikely that beyond the suggestive ceremonial trappings there was anything more occult going on than within the Rudyard Kipling-inspired ceremonies of the Scouts. In the end, Cossgrove's Sentinels and other groups simply could not compete in popularity and acceptability with the mainstream Scouting movement, and were eventually abandoned once Cossgrove, failing to beat 'em, joined 'em. One, however, cannot help but wonder where his inspiration came from.

Chapter 4.

The Golden Dawn: A coda

We heard him say, 'I will destroy this temple made with hands, and in three days I will build another, not made with hands.'

— MARK 14:58

In 1922, American occultist Paul Foster Case (1884–1954) was expelled from the third iteration of the Golden Dawn successor Alpha et Omega and decided to create his own order, which he named the Builders of the Adytum (BOTA). An 'adytum' is the Greek term for the innermost sanctuary of a temple. Case was born in Fairport, New York. His father was the Fairport librarian and deacon of the local Congregational Church. His mother began teaching him music from a young age, and he quickly progressed from playing the church organ to becoming a talented violinist and orchestra conductor, with his musicianship earning him an honorary doctorate.

Case's first experience of altered consciousness took the form of regular bouts of what we would now call 'lucid dreaming', and he wrote of these to Rudyard Kipling, who encouraged him to explore this and other ineffable phenomena.[1] Aside from music, the gangly youth dabbled in amateur stage magic, for a time struggling along in vaudeville, and was fascinated by playing cards. When architect, publisher, Theosophist and mystic Claude Bragdon (1866–1946) asked him what he thought the origins of the playing card suits were and introduced him to the tarot, Case dedicated himself to the interpretation of its symbolic secrets.[2]

Guided by an inner voice which he identified as one of the 'Masters of Wisdom', Case joined the Thoth-Hermes Temple of the Golden Dawn in New York, rising to the rank of Praemonstrator of the Hermetic Order in the United States.[3] The Thoth-Hermes Temple was under the leadership of Samuel Mathers, and it would be taken over by the Alpha et Omega order. Case's interest in the tarot eventually led to his expulsion from Alpha et Omega, his publications on the tarot resulting in accusations of revealing the Order's secrets to the public. In 1929 Case founded a small group of his own, the School of Ageless Wisdom, before moving to Los Angeles and starting BOTA in 1938.

The chief distinction between BOTA and the direct successor orders of the Golden Dawn was that it rejected the latter's obsession with evocational magic and psychism, preferring to concentrate on esoteric wisdom and spiritual growth. BOTA was based on using its own tarot — a 'corrected' version of the ubiquitous Rider–Waite–Smith deck — as a teaching tool, by means of symbolic learning and dramatic re-enactment.[4]

Case's approach to understanding the tarot was more psychological than symbolic. As occult historian Mitch Horowitz describes it:

> He taught that by meditating on a certain image, you could embody its virtues, such as the gentle power of the mistress on the Strength card or the self-control of the angel on the Temperance card. 'We become what we contemplate,' he later wrote. 'Contemplate these pictures in your spare moments, and they will alter your whole life in no time.'[5]

Case's big breakthrough, however, was his creation of well-organised and comprehensive mail-order tutorials, which became enormously popular and widely circulated. As Horowitz puts it: 'He became the Charles Atlas of home-study occultism, and his BOTA lessons commanded a following that has continued to the present day.'[6]

In 1943 Case took on as a pupil an enthusiastic young woman by the name of Ann Davies (1912–1975). She came from a New York Jewish family, and, after a troubled childhood, had passed through various phases of spiritual rebellion — atheism, agnosticism, Buddhism, yoga — until meeting Case and taking him as her spiritual teacher. The charismatic Davies inherited Case's role as prolocutor general of the Order on his death in 1954.

The flavour of BOTA's teaching is a mixture of the positive-thinking doctrine of nineteenth-century New Thought churches (groups that believed in positive visualisation to bring about one's desires), Kabbalah and Gnosticism, loosely structured after the Golden Dawn and the Masonic 'blue lodge' system. BOTA instructs that the world is the ritual of God, and all life a ritual act leading to evolution through reorganisation, with the consciousness of God the Creator suffusing all things.[7]

Davies visited New Zealand in 1963 on a lecture tour, and, as Robert Ellwood puts it, '[b]y all accounts the aureate pond of New Zealand occultism was greatly roiled by the imposing guest'.[8] This was for Davies, in no uncertain terms, a power play for who would gain control of Smagardum Thalasses' considerable Havelock holdings, and which esoteric organisation would emerge supreme in Aotearoa. Other groups feared they might be next, or at the very least lose members to this shiny

Paul Foster Case, American occultist and founder of the Builders of the Adytum.

new entrant on the scene. In fact, she had been invited to New Zealand by Jack Taylor in the hope of amalgamation and continuing the survival of the temple.[9] New Zealand's Theosophists and Anthroposophists were similarly riled, albeit to a lesser degree. It was also about this time that a number of Whare Rā members abortively set up a new temple, Io-Ana (cod te reo Māori for 'the cave of God') under the auspices of the Cromlech Temple, an esoteric group contemporaneous with the Golden Dawn but with a mystical Christian focus rather than the latter's syncretic approach.[10]

About then Dr Albert Richard Riedel (1911–1984), a Paracelsian alchemist better known as Frater Albertus, arrived in Havelock North from Salt Lake City and began asserting his own influence over Whare Rā.[11] Both Taylor and the leadership of BOTA regarded Riedel as a troublemaker, but he maintained a respectable following in Havelock North before eventually relocating to Australia.[12]

‡

Regardless of these currents, BOTA emerged as the strongest contender to take on the mantle and membership of Smaragdum Thalasses and Whare Rā. In the words of the official BOTA narrative:

> Fifty years ago, our Beloved Soror in L.V.X., the Rev. Ann Davies brought the spiritual impetus of Builders of the Adytum to New Zealand. In her own words she stated that the Master R. had spent many years preparing the way for the Ageless Wisdom teachings, through the vehicle of BOTA, to be brought to New Zealand. This was to bring about the development of the linkage in New Zealand for the balancing of certain forces necessary as required by the Inner School. New Zealand is geographically situated so it is relatively the same distance from the equator as California. This balance was required for the linkage to take place.[13]

Davies claimed to have received communications from a higher sphere that she was to gather some 'lost sheep of British descent from somewhere south into the fold'.[14] Nick Farrell, occult historian and practitioner, and thus not entirely disinterested chronicler, suggests that Davies saw that BOTA would gain legitimacy if it assimilated Whare Rā, and that she and tour organiser, Temple member Alastair Wallace, had an eye on the potential income from the Taupō property.[15] A summit between Whare Rā members and Davies and her BOTA contingent, yang and yin, was held at the Napier Hotel in 1963 to discuss terms. Pat Zalewski, a solo BOTA follower whom we shall meet shortly, wrote about the meeting in his 2016 book *Secret Inner Order Rituals of the Golden Dawn*. Citing accounts by the Whare Rā participants who were in attendance, and who described Davies' 'movie star' entrance, he also recorded Jack Taylor's memory of the event:

> During the meeting my wife got very worried, as it was clear to me and others that Anne [*sic*] Davies was claiming the adeptship of this entire planet. I then noticed one of the younger members get up and rush outside. Since I thought he was ill, and at the insistence of my wife who thought that Anne [*sic*] Davies' persuasiveness might corrupt some of these younger people, I followed him out to his car where he was bent over. When he turned around I found he was bent over all right, with laughter; he said he could not see Anne [*sic*] Davies' performance being topped by anyone.[16]

Nick Farrell identifies this younger member as Ron Raison, Temple member and gardener at Whare Rā, and a leading figure in the Order of the Table Round in the 1990s. Farrell also claims that Davies' presentation was made all the more comical by her being rather the worse the wear from imbibing too much Dutch courage.[17] Davies made two further visits to Aotearoa, in 1965 and 1969.[18] Sufficient converts were made for a branch of BOTA to be created in Auckland under the leadership of Alastair Wallace.

Farrell makes the claim that Wallace was a Lothario whose womanising held him back from advancing in grades at Whare Rā, and with whom Davies had become infatuated.[19] Indeed, many of the New Zealand BOTA members had relocated from Whare Rā once it became defunct. This in itself is interesting, as it was clear by this time that the highly theatrical Davies was asserting herself as the rightful leader of the Golden Dawn, and while Dr Dee's Enochian workings were held in high esteem at Whare Rā, they were anathema to BOTA as fearsomely dangerous.[20]

On her final visit, Davies was given a civic welcome by the mayor of Lower Hutt, Percy Dowse,[21] at the Little Theatre on Queen Street.[22] One cannot help but note that this seems oddly out of character for that pragmatic politician, who was responsible for so much of Lower Hutt's modern development. However, Dowse was heavily involved with a wide range of community groups, including churches and religious organisations, so it may simply be the case that this was his habit when such groups contacted him about visiting dignitaries.[23] Three public talks were advertised in the *Hutt News*, promoting the 'World Revered Mystic' and the 'Authoritative Voice of Esoteric Wisdom' Dr Ann Davies.[24]

On Wallace's death, authority for BOTA passed to William Chesterman (1917–2003), a personage of considerable intelligence, attention to detail (attributed to his astrological natal chart having the Sun in Virgo)[25] and business acumen, under whom BOTA thrived in New Zealand. Chesterman, who at the time was also the president of the New Thought non-denominational church Higher Thought New Zealand, had been a member of Whare Rā as an acquaintance of Chapman-Taylor the architect. On the death of Ann Davies he was called to Los Angeles to run the organisation.

‡

Unlike the Smagardum Thalasses, BOTA does not consider itself magical in the sense of affecting change through occult means, but it can certainly be considered magically-adjacent. Nick Farrell attributes much of its approach to the American New Thought movement.[26] Researcher John Latham describes BOTA as 'a Right Hand path tradition and Thelemic traditions as Left Hand path', which is to say transcendental and of the light rather than about personal gratification and emphasis on the individual will.[27]

That said, Case cribbed much of BOTA ritual from Alpha et Omega via Aleister Crowley's book *The Equinox* (1909).[28] The aversion to talk of sex magic — the channelling of sexual energy to magical ends — is curious given that in the 1920s Case himself began exploring the concept. Indeed,

The Builders of the Adytum advertisement for Ann Davies' tour in March 1969.

it was his refusal of asceticism that caused him to be asked to resign from Alpha et Omega and found BOTA in the first place, remarking: 'I have no desire to be a "teacher and pioneer in this Purgatorial World". Guidance seems to have removed me from the high place to which I have never really aspired. The relief is great.'[29]

Three BOTA temples were founded in New Zealand. The largest and most magnificent of these is the Higher Thought Temple at 1 Union Street in the Auckland CBD. It was originally designed by Devonport architect Henry F. Robinson in 1927 for Chesterman's Higher Thought Centre in a stripped-back Classical style in brick, with some Streamline elements, and was built the following year. It came into BOTA possession in the 1970s, complete with a fully operational George Croft organ. This was followed by the temple in Naenae, Lower Hutt — an elegantly simple white building, formerly a Brethren Every Boys' Rally Hall — and in 1981, the Dunedin temple in the quasi-rural Otago harbour setting of Strawberry Lane between Sawyers Bay and Roseneath, established by two members of the Auckland temple.

Incorporated in California and still headquartered in Los Angeles, BOTA has branches throughout the United States, Europe, the Ivory Coast in Africa, Latin America, Australia and New Zealand, and is easily one of the largest groups of its type extant. The New Zealand branch of BOTA has always been an important part of the administration of the overall organisation.[30] BOTA is still in operation, with around 3000 adherents worldwide being reported in 1991.[31] Present numbers are not known, but the New Zealand chapter remains active with a website, although the Auckland temple was sold in 2014 due to diminishing adherents.[32]

BOTA describes itself as a mystery school seeking to gain higher consciousness analogous to Buddhist Enlightenment or Gnostic illumination, through esoteric theory and practice: 'These teachings and practical secrets constitute what is known as AGELESS WISDOM.'[33] It has an analogous system of ranks to that of the Stella Matutina, up to Adeptus Minor. While the magical aspect of the curriculum is played down by some of its adherents, BOTA does observe monthly Khabbalic 'Pronaos' services. *Pronaos* is the Greek term for the portico of a temple.

The Pronaos ceremony proper is exclusive to initiates only, who are sworn to secrecy, although parts are occasionally open to the public. Three of these lead the initiate to Melkoth, the bottom sphere of the Tree of Life. Another of these takes place at the equinoxes, when previous ceremonial officers stand down and new ones are installed. There is also the shorter Shekinah (Glory of the Divine Presence) ceremony created by Ann Davies independently of the ceremonial laid out by Case. These rituals act as a kind of psychodrama that aids aspirants in internalising the symbolism of Ageless Wisdom, but their nature is a closely guarded secret. We may speculate that some sort of ritual enactment of Tarot archetypes is involved. Some informants observe a similarity with Alpha et Omega ceremonial.[34]

As a curious sidenote, the musical twelfth episode of the third season of joint US–New Zealand television production *Xena: Warrior Princess*, 'The Bitter Suite' (first broadcast in 1998), was heavily inspired in costume and sets by the BOTA tarot, with additional material from other decks, and features narration taken from Case's *The Book of Tokens* (1934), a volume of meditations on the tarot.[35]

It is tempting to wonder if this episode — the first in the trend for television shows having a musical episode — was not somehow inspired by a BOTA Pronaos ceremony, or even some far-fetched scheme by a rebel BOTA faction to covertly implant the seeds of Ageless Wisdom in a worldwide audience of millions.

Alas not. Rob Tapert, *Xena* producer and largely responsible for the episode, had the idea of using the tarot as the basis for telling the story of Xena and her companion Gabrielle falling out and reconciling in a magical musical land called Illusia. He says:

> I had a girlfriend who had various books of Tarot and I would always look through them and try to sort the meaning of the cards. I read Foster's *Book of Tokens* and always loved the poetry of portions of it. But much of the deeper meaning went over my head. I also enjoyed the 'historical religious' interconnections to the Torah and Jewish mysticism. It was all an interesting weave but ultimately is just scholarly fun. The writers and I knew we were building this giant rift between Xena and Gabrielle and we would need to resolve it. Music is the glue that fixes the human heart and soul and I pitched

the writers a musical set against the backdrop of the figures in the deck of tarot. They thought it mad but liked the ambition. Then it all kind of fell into place.[36]

☦

A more recent attempt to start a Golden Dawn order in Wellington in the early 1980s, and the briefest, is worthy of mention here. Patrick 'Pat' Zalewski was born in Brisbane in 1948, and at age 18 set out on his own to travel the wilds of Papua New Guinea, trekking up the Sepik and Fly rivers and wreck-diving in the mid-1960s. A colourful character, Zalewski took up martial arts, obtaining his brown belt in karate in 1965, and training in Tai Chi and Qi Gong in Hong Kong and Macau in 1968.

He spent time in Thailand, and in Sri Lanka and India, where he studied Tantric yoga, before moving on to Nepal. In Thailand he rather foolishly attempted the martial art Muay Thai: 'Errol Flynn's son Sean (who later went missing in Laos) got me in the ring with a Thai Boxer and I got creamed. He ran around Bangkok getting ice packs for me after the match.' Zalewski returned to Australia the following year and earned his black belt in karate in Cairns.[37]

In 1970, Zalewski relocated to New Zealand and studied Radionics, an alternative therapy developed by the American Albert Abrams (1863–1924) that is supposed to work through the operations of electromagnetic energy on the chakras and psycho-spiritual 'subtle body'. Zalewski founded three karate clubs in Wellington, and represented New Zealand at the IAKF World Karate Championships in Los Angeles. It was about this time that he was introduced to the writings of the Golden Dawn. Eventually, in 1979, he contacted various former members of the by now defunct Smaragdum Thalasses Temple, and with his then-wife Chris Zalewski, and Jack Taylor of the former Whare Rā, founded the Thoth-Hermes Temple in Wellington in 1981.[38]

The Temple was visited in 1983 by occultist Israel Regardie (1907–1985),[39] a member of the Societas Rosicruciana in America who had been initiated into Stella Matutina in England. He had also been Aleister Crowley's personal secretary in the 1920s. During his time in

Stella Matutina, Regardie grew disillusioned with the squabbling and title-gathering, and, fearing that it all might be lost if the Order fell, he published secret Golden Dawn material he had sworn a vow on initiation to protect. This was seen as an enormous betrayal by many in the occult community and Regardie was widely vilified.[40]

Ironically, Regardie's publications would prove a primary reference to relaunching the Golden Dawn, and his blessing anointed the Thoth-Hermes Temple with considerable authenticity. As Zalewski put it: 'At Thoth-Hermes we fully understood Regardie's predicament and we were of the opinion that the important thing was not to restrict the [Golden Dawn] teaching to a few, but to try to foster its beliefs to all those who would listen.'[41] Zalewski did, however, find himself in conflict with Golden Dawn traditionalists, such as the now very elderly former members of Whare Rā, who clung to a Christian framing for their rituals, whereas he saw them through the lens of his Eastern Tantra and Yantric training.[42]

By 1995 Zalewski had moved from Wellington to Hastings and the Thoth-Hermes Temple was closed, having initiated three people in the advanced degree Adeptus Exemptus, the highest level of the second, inner order. He eventually moved back to Australia, where he founded the Second Thoth-Hermes Temple.[43]

In terms of ritual, the Thoth-Hermes Temple ceremonies and ranks are identical to those of Stella Matutina, with the exclusion of three ranks of the third order, these being regarded by Zalewski and Regardie as more or less redundant. Given the Thoth-Hermes Temple's relative lack of influence on the broader occulture or mainstream of Aotearoa, that is probably all we need to say about it.

Undoubtedly there are solo practitioners of Golden Dawn rites still in New Zealand, working from Regardie's and Zalewski's books and others. There are fragmentary online references to an Osiris Temple of Stella Matutina in New Zealand some time around 2009, including a now-defunct website. Perhaps, in time, there will be another temple drawing on those traditions in Aotearoa, but any claims to be a direct successor group to the original Golden Dawn will be increasingly tenuous and homoeopathically dilute.

Chapter 5.
Rudolf Steiner and Anthroposophy

There slumber in every human being faculties by means of which he can acquire for himself a knowledge of higher worlds. Mystics, Gnostics, Theosophists — all speak of a world of soul and spirit which for them is just as real as the world we see with our physical eyes and touch with our physical hands.

— RUDOLF STEINER, *KNOWLEDGE OF THE HIGHER WORLDS AND ITS ATTAINMENT*, 1914

We have already briefly looked at Anthroposophy in connection with Theosophy and education, but given its rationalising philosophy it would seem germane to examine it in more detail in the context of this chapter. Rudolf Steiner's Anthroposophy contains within it many vestiges of its Theosophical origins — the existence of an objective, intelligible spiritual world accessible to human comprehension — but it rejects most of the Eastern mysticism and is primarily organised around ideas from German folk culture, German philosophy, Rosicrucianism and other European esoteric traditions, Steiner's take on Christianity, and his own spiritual innovations. Steiner's version of the spiritual realm is one that can be investigated and understood by rational mythologies that parallel the way scientists investigate the material universe.

Like Theosophy, Anthroposophy describes human consciousness as a process of evolution through reincarnation following the laws of karma, but, contrary to Theosophy, sees all life as a devolution from a perfect spiritual archetype, with humans as the least specialised animal being the least devolved.[1] The universe, and this evolutionary process taking place within it, are controlled by a hierarchy of spiritual forces variously governing successive ages. Loosely and crudely speaking — the theology is incredibly complicated — in the present age (beginning in 1879 after a celestial war between good and evil) the dominant forces of good are Christ (the present spiritually harmonising force), the Archangel Michael (the messenger of the Christ being, creativity and inspiration in assertive opposition to negative forces), who stand in opposition to the predominantly (though not exclusively) negative forces of Lucifer (pride, passion and the delusion of divinity, but also creativity and spirituality) and Ahriman (materialism and unfeeling intellectualism, but also intellectuality and technology).[2]

Steiner and Anthroposophy's influence can be found in a broad swathe of areas, notably Steiner Waldorf schools, biodynamic agriculture, alternative medicine, special needs education and services, the arts, architecture and socially responsible finance initiatives, among others. The movement's headquarters are the Goetheanum in Dornach, in the Swiss canton of Solothurn.

The Goetheanum is a gigantic building designed by Steiner along expressionistic and organic lines as a synthesis (a *Gesamtkunstwerk*) of

Rudolf Steiner, philosopher, educationist and founder of Anthroposophy.

Ada Wells, teacher, suffragist, activist and Anthroposophist.

artistic, sensory and spiritual principles, and named after the German poet, polymath, scientist and statesman Johann Wolfgang von Goethe (1749–1832). Steiner based much of his philosophy of Goethe's idea that sufficiently developed imaginative power is capable of synthesising the outer appearance of a thing and a concept of its inner nature.

Steiner elaborated on this by asserting that this imaginative power could be turned back on itself so that the thinker would simultaneously perceive their natural-outer-material and supernatural-inner-spiritual nature. This is the basis of the Steiner Waldorf model of education.[3] The present Goetheanum was completed in 1928, replacing the previous 1920 building which burned down in 1923.

‡

Garth Talbott contends that the first Anthroposophist in New Zealand was Ada Wells (née Pike, 1863–1933). Raised Plymouth Brethren in an English immigrant family in Christchurch, Wells later became an Anglican but was drawn to Theosophy. When her father died of tuberculosis in 1877, her mother Maria was left widowed and pregnant with her ninth child and obliged to support her family as a massage therapist — an occupation that two of her sons and two of her daughters, including Wells, would take up.

Wells was an intelligent young woman, and at high school was awarded a scholarship to attend Canterbury College in 1881, where she partially completed a BA and became a teacher. She taught at Christchurch Girls' High School until 1884 and her marriage to Harry Wells, a musician and church organist. It wasn't a happy match — Harry was a drinker, prone to temper and unable to maintain steady employment. Accordingly, Ada, like her mother before her, had to support her family as a massage therapist.[4]

By the late 1880s Ada Wells was heavily involved in the women's suffrage movement as an organiser and campaigner. While many suffragettes retired from the fight after winning the vote for women in 1893, Wells recognised that it was only a first step for political equality and became a prominent activist for free kindergartens, universal secondary education, reform of local government, charitable aid, prisons, and the repeal of the 1869 Contagious Diseases Act. Around this time Wells joined forces with the eccentric Canterbury University science professor Alexander Bickerton and founded the Canterbury Women's Institute, over which she presided for many years.

Among many achievements, Wells was the first national secretary of the National Council of Women of New Zealand, helped lead the formation of the Canterbury Children's Aid Society, was elected to the Ashburton and North Canterbury United Charitable Aid Board (much to the chagrin and animosity of the male members), was involved in the Prison-Gate Mission to rehabilitate former convicts, and was a member of the National Peace Council of New Zealand providing support to conscientious objectors in the First World War. She is perhaps best known as the first woman to be elected to the Christchurch City Council, in 1917, on a Labour ticket.[5]

It is possible to see a strong Theosophical influence in Wells's political activism. In a 1901 Whanganui lecture on education to the National Council of Women's sixth conference, she made consistent reference to the role of great teachers, often unrecognised in their time, to evolving society, naming Old Testament prophets, Christ, Plato and the New England transcendentalist philosophers among them.[6] During a visit to Leipzig the following year, Wells heard Steiner lecture and was immediately converted to his ideas.

This trip came about because Wells's two oldest daughters, having inherited their father's musical abilities, were both gifted talents, and their mother, determined to develop their talent and give them every opportunity, took the eldest daughter, Christabel ('Chris'), to Leipzig to enrol in the School of Music there.[7] At this stage Steiner had not yet broken with Theosophy, having recently been appointed general secretary of the German Section of the Theosophical Society, and it was as a Theosophist that Wells would have attended his lectures. Wells returned to Leipzig with her second-eldest daughter, Alma ('Cos'), in 1904.[8]

‡

In Wellington, Anthroposophy established in more organised fashion under the leadership of Emma Richmond (née Parris, 1845–1921). Raised a broad-church Anglican, she was the daughter of school administrator and prominent New Plymouth politician Robert Parris (1816–1904),[9] and in 1868 married the Unitarian widower Henry Richmond, of the prominent Atkinson-Richmond dynasty of public figures.[10] Like Wells, Richmond was politically active, becoming the first woman elected to the Taranaki Education Board in 1886, chairing the Ladies' Visiting Committee for New Plymouth Hospital from 1886, being the first woman elected to the Taranaki Hospital Board, and campaigning against corporal punishment for girls and for the better treatment of women in prisons.[11]

Various Atkinsons and Richmonds were active in Theosophy, and so it is likely that this is how Emma Richmond was introduced to the movement. Henry Richmond died in 1890, and in 1893 Emma moved to Christchurch. There, alarmingly, it seems she fell in with conman, bigamist, seducer and cult leader Arthur Worthington (we will meet him in Chapter 6) as the 1893 Electoral Roll lists her place of residence as the Temple of Truth on Madras Street, and her occupation as 'Universal Service'.[12]

This period was mercifully short-lived, and the following year she joined the Christchurch branch of the Theosophical Society, becoming its president by 1897.[13] Around 1900 Richmond moved to Wellington, serving as president of the Wellington branch of the Theosophical Society for three years. She was elected president of the national body's sixth annual convention in 1901.[14]

In 1904 Richmond and her daughter Beatrice travelled to London, where they first encountered Anthroposophy and Steiner's ideas, and arranged for translations of Steiner's lectures and books to be sent back to Wellington. On her return, Richmond continued to receive Anthroposophical publications for distribution around Aotearoa.

In 1914, Richmond moved to Havelock North to be with her daughter Rachel and son-in-law Bernard Crompton-Smith, helping them to set up St George's Preparatory School in Duart House, the old McLean mansion, in 1915. The Crompton-Smiths had both studied Anthroposophy in Germany prior to the First World War, and they ran the school in the Steiner model.[15] When Richmond died in 1921, the Crompton-Smiths took over the national leadership of the movement, and for a while Havelock North became one of Anthroposophy's most important centres outside of Germany.

Although Steiner himself never visited the village, a number of prominent Anthroposophists did. I have already mentioned Steiner's close associate Alfred Meebold in connection with Whare Rā. Other important Anthroposophists who moved to Havelock North included Ruth Nelson (1894–1977), her sister Gwen (1897–1973), and Nelson's life partner, Ōamaru-born Ethel Edwina (Edna) Burbury (1890–1978). The Nelson girls had been born into a wealthy and influential family in Hawke's Bay, enabling them to travel to Europe and pursue their interests.

The girls attended the Woodford House school, where Anthroposophist Mabel Hodge was headmistress. Later they went to the Canterbury School of Fine Art in Christchurch, Ruth to study sculpture and Gwen landscape painting. Increasingly interested in Anthroposophy, while travelling overseas Ruth would even meet Steiner in person.

Nelson and Burbury, quaintly known in the village as 'the Ladies', became committed Anthroposophists, building the house they named 'Taruna' (the bonds of friendship and kinship), which served as a key venue for Anthroposophy summer conferences and study groups. The two women would also establish the Taikura Rudolf Steiner School in Hastings. Relatively late in life Gwen married a fellow Anthroposophist, Henry Malden, and began creating paintings on Anthroposophic themes. She established the natural pharmaceutical company Weleda in the early 1950s, supplied by a medicinal garden across the road from Taruna. In 1946 the sisters jointly acquired Kereru Station, west of Hastings in the Ruahine Ranges, which was eventually put into a charitable trust to fund various philanthropic ventures.[16]

‡

When Ada Wells's mother died in 1905, Ada inherited the family's large house on Office Road in the Christchurch suburb of Merivale. From here she continued her political activism, provided massage therapy, and with her daughters studied Anthroposophy. Her daughter Chris was appointed the official Christchurch representative of the Anthroposophical Society by the Crompton-Smiths.[17] Wells urged her children to continue their Anthroposophical studies after she died. Chris married Christchurch lawyer Ron Twyneham, later divorcing, and maintained a small Anthroposophy study group of around 10 people in Merivale throughout the 1950s and 1960s. Cos married another Anthroposophist, William Reynolds Carey, general manager of the Kaiapoi Woollen Mills, and held monthly meetings in their home in the Christchurch suburb of Cashmere. The work of the two sisters laid the groundwork for the expansion of Anthroposophy in Christchurch and the establishment of a second Steiner disability health and education provider, Hōhepa South, in the mid-1960s.[18]

It wasn't until 1933 that the Anthroposophical Society of New Zealand was established, with the approval of the General Anthroposophical Society in Dornach, Switzerland. The Easter Conference of 1936, held in Wellington, brought together 50 of New Zealand's 119 Anthroposophists. The newly appointed society secretary, Henry Malden of Wellington, summed up the state of Anthroposophy in the country thus:

> Anthroposophy has been in New Zealand now approximately 21 years; it has reached its majority, and, having grown up, reached the age of discretion. The Easter Conference of 1936, one may perhaps say, marks the starting of a definite epoch in the life of the Anthroposophical Society in New Zealand. It is now standing firmly on its own feet. Our ideas and concepts about such matters have been gradually oriented in a new direction, and, with the proper spirit engendered throughout the Society in New Zealand, there is no reason why the future should not be faced with optimism. With elasticity and mobility in organisation, with as little organisation as possible, and with no thought of autocratic 'authorities', Anthroposophy in New Zealand should continue to grow and prosper and be able to meet the changing conditions as they arise.[19]

During the Second World War, Anthroposophy went into something of a hiatus. The society dramatically reduced its public activities, no doubt conscious that its strong German connections were a huge liability for its members. On the other hand, membership had increased considerably with the influx of European Anthroposophist refugees who had fled Nazi persecution. As if in anticipation of the Allied victory, it awoke from its dormancy with a flourish in a festival at Taruna over the 1944–45

Christmas period. The festival was to commemorate 21 years since the re-founding of the Anthroposophical Society in Germany and the laying of the foundation stone of Steiner's Goetheanum in 1923.

Havelock North really hadn't seen anything like it since The Work's fête in 1911, attended by around 90 Anthroposophists, approximately half the total number in the country.[20] It was celebrated with a reading of one of Steiner's Christmas lectures and his 'Inaugural Lecture', and, in the words of one of the attendees, the European refugee Ernst Reizenstein, who is perhaps better known as the breadmaker who introduced European-style wholegrain breads to New Zealand in 1941, and, in particular, Vogel's, in the early 1950s:

> ... [the] central impulse of Anthroposophy suddenly awoke. The room faded away. There were women and men united in pure thinking, forgetting themselves but listening openly to the words of Rudolf Steiner inspired by the Christ-impulse through Michael [the Archangel]. The words entered into us, they reached the hearts and united them. I find I can only express this in saying: Michael was near. Indeed Anthroposophy is living anew.[21]

The New Zealand Society renewed its subscription to the parent organisation in Dornach and fully paid its arrears,[22] and the society's main newsletter, the *New Zealand News Sheet*, was revived. Nelson and Burbury continued living at Taruna until Nelson's death in 1977, Burbury going into care and dying a year later.[23] Havelock North remained the centre of Anthroposophical activity in Aotearoa until 1963, with a smaller but influential nexus at York Bay on Wellington Harbour centring on Hal Atkinson (1895–1975), another of the sprawling extended Richmond-Atkinson clan.[24]

‡

Since Anthroposophy's first stirrings in Aotearoa with Ada Wells and Emma Richmond, one of the driving calls of the movement was in education. For the rest of the twentieth century much of its energies were put into promoting Steiner's system of education. It was resolved in 1936 that a

Steiner school should be established in New Zealand when Nelson, Burbury and Jean Stuart-Menteath (1898–1983) visited the Waldorf School in Stuttgart. This ambition came to fruition in 1950, when Nelson, Burbury and Hugh Chambers (1888–1952), of the aforementioned Havelock Chambers family, formed a trust and established Queenswood School in Hastings with Stuart-Menteath as headmistress. Chambers owned the land, part of his family's Tauroa Station in Havelock North. Queenswood was the only such Steiner Waldorf School in Aotearoa until another school opened in Christchurch in 1975, and a kindergarten in Auckland in 1978.[25]

At a general meeting at Taruna in 1959 it was agreed that the society should incorporate as a charitable trust. A combination of the substantial subscriptions to the mother organisation in Dornach and the costs of maintaining the *News Sheet* were taking a serious toll on the society's financial situation.[26] Incorporation subsequently took place in 1963. This marked a changing of the guard in New Zealand Anthroposophy. Then general secretary Henry Malden's health was failing, and he resigned at the 1963 AGM. The role was taken up by Brian Butler, with the full support of the regional groups and Dornach. Butler proved an excellent choice.

Born in Dunedin in 1919, his passion for music as a chorister at that city's St Paul's Anglican Cathedral, as well as a talent for the cello, lead him into contact with Anthroposophy through a local pianist, who introduced him to Alfred Meebold on one of his botanising trips to the South Island. Butler worked at a Dunedin radio station as a programmer and announcer, as an arts and crafts teacher, and as an organiser for the YMCA. He married Olive Lovelock, sister of the Olympian runner Jack Lovelock, and eventually became an Anthroposophist in 1941, unable to serve during the war due to a knee injury and repulsed by the wartime militancy of the Dean of St Paul's in Dunedin, the Very Reverend George Craig Cruickshank (1881–1951).[27]

Butler remained general secretary of the society until 1992, and with his excellent communications skills, more modern views and familiarity with other parts of the country, revitalised New Zealand Anthroposophy. As the century progressed, much of the energy in the core Anthroposophy movement dissipated into more practical Steiner-based daughter movements that were less interested in the beliefs of Anthroposophy than in the benefits of things such as Waldorf schools and biodynamic agriculture.

Chapter 6.

Gomorrah on the Avon

The thyrsus-bearers are many, but the mystics few.

— PLATO, *PHAEDO*, 69C, 5 BCE

Among the many genuine seekers after mysteries in these pages it behoves us to consider the case of an absolute mountebank and charlatan. Upright, Anglican *fin de siècle* Christchurch seems an unlikely place for a licentious cult to take a firm grip, however briefly, on a significant chunk of the populace. Nonetheless it did, and the huge scandal it caused cast a pall over many other esoteric, occult, nonconformist and free-thinking groups in Aotearoa. In the 1890s the Temple of Truth scandal was known as far afield as Australia and the United States, yet, strangely, it has now been almost completely forgotten.

Arthur Bently Worthington (1847–1917) is hard to trace before his arrival in Christchurch in 1890. His real name was Samuel Oakley Crawford, and he sported a host of other aliases. He was born in Saugerties, New York state, in the United States. He served in the American Civil War and was apparently ordained a Methodist minister in 1867. Worthington was a bigamist and a conman. His first marriage to Josephine Ericsson Moore in New York City in 1868 was, we may presume, out of some genuine affection.

In 1870 he was imprisoned for fraud, and when he was released in 1873 he fled town, abandoning his wife, and embarking on a spree of swindling. His modus operandi was to go from state to state, adopting a dizzying array of false identities, passing himself off in various professions including lawyer, banker and medical doctor, attaching himself to rich women, deceiving them out of their fortunes, and abandoning them for the next town and the next mark. Worthington is known to have had at least eight bigamous marriages after Josephine, and to have fathered three children.[1]

In 1889 Worthington bailed out of his latest marriage in Grand Forks, in the Dakota Territory (not yet split into the future states of North and South Dakota), and headed for New York City again. There he joined, as a faith-healer, the relatively new religious sect of Christian Science, which had been established in 1879 by Mary Baker Eddy (1821–1910), and soon seduced the editor of the group's international journal and close friend of Baker Eddy, Mary Plunkett, going through a widely reported 'spiritual' marriage.

There was a small problem in that Plunkett was already married, but with surprising magnanimity her husband John Plunkett stepped aside. However, following the outcry from his co-religionists, he dug

Arthur Bently Worthington, bigamist, conman and Temple of Truth founder.

THE WEEKLY PRESS PHOTOGRAPH, BISHOP COLLECTION, CANTERBURY MUSEUM, 1923.53.115

into Worthington's past and uncovered his history of blaggardry and deception. Worthington confessed all, and promptly did what he always did — skipped town, this time with Mary Plunkett and her two children in tow. And this time he decided to head as far away from his past as he could possibly get — New Zealand — and along the way Mary Plunkett became Mary Worthington, and eventually 'Sister Magdala'.[2]

Like Simon Magus and his Helena entering Rome, the Worthingtons arrived in Christchurch in January 1890 and immediately made an impression. According to the *Bismarck Weekly Tribune* of North Dakota in 1889, Arthur was tall, distinguished, charming and handsome, with a military bearing, fluent patter and 'steel-blue grayish and expressive eyes', and Mary was 'decidedly attractive'.[3]

It wasn't long before the Worthingtons began drawing well-heeled Cantabrians all too willing to be parted from their worldly possessions to join what Arthur proclaimed was a new religion. Progress was swift, and by August 1892 the believers had built the Temple of Truth on Madras Street, overlooking Latimer Square. It was an imposing building in the classical style, with matching side towers and a striking portico, though rather fittingly this was all hollow wood sprayed with sand and painted to look like marble. Designed by architect W. A. P. Clarkson, the edifice cost £5200 to build.[4] The irascible journalist, poet, lawyer and Supreme Court judge O. T. J. Alpers (1867–1927), who, like many Cantabrians had attended a meeting out of curiosity, described the décor:

> The interior decoration was exceedingly crude and ugly, but no doubt impressive to the members of the congregation. The splendours of Jerusalem and Chicago were happily mingled. There were suggestions of Solomon's temple, and the triangles and set squares and compasses in massive gilt, with here and there a swastika, were suggestive to me of the symbolism of Freemasonry.[5]

It's not entirely clear how large the congregation — known as the 'Students of Truth' — was, but at its height it was estimated at at least 2000 people, with the Temple seating 1000, and clearly they had deep pockets. Next door the believers built a palatial 12-room home for the Worthingtons. Then came a regular publication, and the following year a branch in Auckland.[6]

There is some evidence, in the form of a letter to the editor of the *Lyttelton Times*, that Worthington's Students of Truth, at least the women, were affiliated to an American interdenominational Christian charitable organisation known as the Order of the King's Daughters (with the addition of 'and Sons' to include men after 1891), which was based in New York City. This may have been a slightly different arrangement to the women who became members of Worthington's notorious Society of the Blue Veil, which was rumoured to function as his personal harem.

‡

But this was Christchurch, founded as a settlement of the Church of England in 1840, and it was not long before, confronted with the spectre of 'Worthingtonism', the city's established sects found themselves united in common cause. Although outwardly Worthington preached abstinence and celibacy, rumours abounded of the promotion of free love and orgies at Temple services. Arthur, it was said, had the townswomen in thrall, and Mary, apparently trying to create her own powerbase in the group in competition with her 'husband', had her own circle of male favourites. 'Marriage vows under [Worthington's] teachings have lost their divine sacredness, and wives are leaving their husbands and husbands their wives,' reported the *Oamaru Mail*, the *Bay of Plenty Times*, the *Poverty Bay Herald*, and the *Temuka Leader*.[7]

Reading between the clutched pearls of the newspapers and secondhand reports of the sect's published material (now vanishingly rare), we may guess that this was conducted under the guise of 'spiritual marriages' recognised by 'spiritual law' that transcended those laws recognised by the state, and that this seemed to form a substantial part of Worthington's 'sexological' (a term he coined) science.[8] As one anonymous correspondent to the editor of the *Oxford Observer* put it:

> Sir, — I have read and tried to understand Worthington's Pamphlet *Talk to men* and have come to the conclusion that he did not intend that I or anybody else should understand him, because once the veil

The Temple of Truth, Latimer Square, Christchurch, in 1894.

of mystery with which he is clever enough to surround himself is penetrated and with which a portion and unfortunately a very large portion of the public are ever ready to be humbugged the profits accruing from his mental legerdemain would inevitably cease. There is one thing that strikes me very clearly in reading this Pamphlet of arrant nonsense and that is that Worthington is advancing his interests on the same lines that Joe Smith [presumably Joseph Smith (1805–1844), the founder of Mormonism] did viz by pandering to the morbid tastes and lascivious desires of converts. Worthington's and Joe Smith's spiritual marriages are just on a par, only Worthington puts the matter a little stronger by telling us that when we have come to understand it, we have reached the realization of a sublime and mighty truth. Faith I should think so, if we could believe that the Creator would condescend to change a natural law to a spiritual one because Worthington says 'When this truth is announced, when it is known, when it is lived, it will win the world.' But he lost sight of the fact that when his doctrine is carried out to the full, there will be no world to win, unless the process of recuperation goes on, on the Darwinian process by manufacturing men out of monkeys. Yours &c.[9]

One newspaper report of a Students of Truth lecture explained that Worthington distinguished between 'the Creator referred to in the first chapter of Genesis and the Creator of the second chapter; between the man *created*, and the man formed of the dust of the ground'. Worthington claimed that the first chapter 'is the record of thought subjective' and the second 'the perfecting as real of the ideal man, world and existence'.[10] This suggests Worthington had a passing familiarity with some version of the teachings of the Kabbalah. The report goes on to say:

> The main articles of faith with the Student of Truth are belief in the possibilities of humanity; negation of the theory of original sin; disbelief in a personal devil, in heaven and hell as commonly understood. Such a creed has one ennobling feature, in that it fosters universal brotherly love, and such love is a fundamental principle of the Church of Truth.[11]

A typical Worthington sermon might begin with a burning lamp placed on a table beside him on the stage. 'Brethren,' he would begin, as remembered by Alpers nearly 40 years later, 'you think you see a lamp before me on the table. You think that lamp is an actual, concrete, permanent lamp. You are wrong. The only actual, real, and eternal thing is the concept of that lamp in your minds and mine.' Then he would elaborate on Platonic idealism and Berkeleyan immaterialism, substance, matter, form and spirit, before dashing the lamp to the floor and proclaiming merely the symbolic concept of a lamp, not its reality.[12]

Elsewhere Worthington's faith was described as 'Pantheism'[13] — the belief, popularised in the United States by Whitman, Emmerson and Thoreau, that nature is identical with divinity, and that the totality of the universe constitutes an all-encompassing, immanent God. Another source describes his teachings as containing 'elements of spiritualism, faith-healing, and Unitarianism, into which was infused germs of the Pythagorean belief in the transmigration of souls'.[14]

‡

In 1893 the Reverend John Hosking (1860–1919) of St Asaph Free Methodist Church took it upon himself to write to the American newspapers enquiring about the Worthingtons, who were only too happy to provide the assiduous clergyman with a litany of criminality and matrimonial irregularity. Hosking's digging revealed five marriages prior to Mary. There was Josephine, Worthington's first and only non-bigamous union in New York City; a Miss Groot in Albany, New York; Lizzie Cowell, a widow in Troy, Michigan; Joy Winfield in Chicago; and May Barlow in Xenia, Ohio — though they would not be the last. The pamphlet Hosking subsequently produced, revealing all, was extensively reported in *Truth* and other papers, but Worthington brazenly denied the allegations.[15]

Hosking had some form as a champion of faith. In 1891 the Freethought activist and scientific secularist William Whitehouse Collins (1853–1923) had challenged any Christian minister in Christchurch to publicly debate him on the utility of God, and Hosking rose to meet him on the platform in the Tuam Street Hall. Both men were experienced debaters and the

Mary Worthington, aka 'Sister Magdala', accomplice and later spurned wife.

event made quite an impression on the Christchurch public.[16]

Despite the maelstrom Hosking stirred up in 1893, most of Arthur Worthington's followers remained loyal as the storm broke around him. But the same could not be said of Mary. Her money had run out and her rivalry chaffed her husband, and so Arthur threw her out, exiling her to Sydney on a stipend. By mid-1893 she was telling her story to anyone who would listen, resulting in a regular flow of exposés in the press. Mary returned to Christchurch after Worthington skipped town in 1895, when he could no longer avoid his creditors among the congregation, but she grew increasingly depressed and eventually in her despair drowned herself in an ornamental fountain in the grounds of the Temple in 1901.[17]

It was said of Worthington that he could 'shed copious crocodile tears and bleed freely from his lungs, whenever the occasion required', and that he was 'one of sin's most miserable slaves, one of Satan's most degraded vessels, and one of hell's most legitimate victims'.[18] Scandal followed on scandal. The *South Canterbury Times* reported in 1893 that Worthington:

> was seen at 10.30 one evening proceeding to the house of a lady, and a guard was kept over the house by three students [of Truth]. Worthington was watched through a window and was seen to leave at 2.30 next morning. He excused himself by stating that he and the lady were engaged in literary work, and that he was revising proofs.[19]

Even then, miraculously, Worthington maintained a loyal following, and by March 1894, following a police investigation, the New Zealand government made a desperate attempt to persuade the United States to extradite him. Washington, prudently, felt that Worthington was far less of a nuisance if he stayed in New Zealand. Worthington's luck, however, was beginning to run out. In early 1895, growing suspicion within his congregation of around 2000 people had forced Worthington to buy the temple building from its trustees, leaving him in a dire financial situation. 'To forecast the result of an inquiry instituted by a Sanhedrin of enchanted donkeys is not easy,' printed one newspaper, 'but anyhow they are inquiring, and up to latest advices seem to be the right track.'[20]

The flock was less willing to open their wallets, especially when Worthington decided to 'marry' 29-year-old 'spinster' Evelyn Maud Jordan in August.[21] The government refused the marriage licence and they eloped. More followers deserted, others pressed for debt and by November were threatening to sue. In December 1895 Worthington fled New Zealand on the pretext of returning to the United States to gather funds, but in March 1896 it was learned that he was hiding out in Hobart, Tasmania, setting up a new Temple of Truth with no intention of returning.[22]

☦

True to form, though, Worthington's Tasmanian scams were soon detected, and fleeing the attention of the law and the wrath of Hobartians he came skulking back to Christchurch at the end of 1897. He then attempted a comeback with an advertised programme of Sunday lectures at the Oddfellows Hall on Lichfield Street. The Christchurch public was not having it, and angrily gathered in a febrile crowd outside the hall to protest, requiring police reinforcements that were barely able to maintain order. Around 6000 people came together threatening violence for the third lecture, and the Riot Act had to be read by Mayor Charles Louisson. But by now Worthington was merely a pathetic figure in the public view, too discredited to be a threat to anyone. He tried for two years to revive the movement, but by mid-1899 he had once more fled to Australia and would never return to Aotearoa.

Nevertheless, it seemed he could not turn from his old ways. In 1902, in Melbourne, he was imprisoned for seven years for attempting to con a wealthy French widow, a Madame Miranda May de la Juveny, under the pretext that he was the reincarnated Egyptian god Osiris and that she was his immortal, reborn Isis, and that together, he intimated on pieces of pink parchment accompanied with a curiously graven metal pyramid, they would create a lodge of the Rosy Cross and usher in a new age. As Alpers puts it: 'Having once persuaded her that she was indeed the All-Mother, spouse of the many-eyed God, he had but to tell her that the High Gods of Egypt practised community of goods, to induce her to transfer her banking account.'[23]

Juveny eventually became wise to the deception, though Worthington insinuated in court that 'she bought my embraces with all her property'. Evelyn, the woman he had attempted to marry in Christchurch and his latest consort, now alone in the world and with few prospects, returned to New Zealand with their four children.[24]

Upon his release, Worthington declared himself a reformed Christian and raised funds from his remaining followers to take himself, Evelyn and the children back to the United States. On the way they survived a shipwreck, which he no doubt embroidered into a sign of divine providence. The family settled near Poughkeepsie in New York state, and Worthington became ordained as a Presbyterian minister. After he was expelled from the congregation several years later for getting up to his old tricks,[25] he once more hit the road to swindle and deceive in various states. He was arrested in January 1917 and died in police custody in December of that year from a heart attack induced when confronted by an irate recent female victim.[26]

Back in Christchurch, the Temple of Truth became the Choral Hall some time around 1914. By the 1960s it was known as Latimer Hall, and was used as an entertainment venue and dance hall until it was eventually demolished in 1966 to make way for a hostel for young women that never eventuated. For many years it remained a carpark, and is now the site of townhouses knocked up in a tipsy daze of glass-eyed late capitalism.

Chapter 7.

Bumps in the night

Well, sir, I hope
you've done it now!
Oh Lord! I little
thought, sir, yesterday,
When your departed mother
spoke those words
Of peace through me, and
moved you, sir, so much,
You gave me —
(very kind it was of you)
These shirt-studs — (better
take them back again,
Please, sir) — yes,
little did I think so soon
A trifle of trick,
all through a glass too much
Of his own champagne, would
change my best of friends
Into an angry gentleman!

— ROBERT BROWNING,
'MR. SLUDGE, "THE MEDIUM"', 1864

The desire to talk to the dead, whether to seek knowledge or to have proof of an afterlife, is as old as civilisation itself. In the sixth book of Homer's *Odyssey*, Odysseus travels to the edge of the known world and raises the shades of the dead for information on getting home to Ithaca. In the Bible (1 Samuel 28:3–25), King Saul goes to a woman in Endor to seek the advice of the deceased prophet Samuel. British Museum Assyriologist Irving Finkel has traced the concept of the ghost to prehistory, hinted at in the oldest Mesopotamian archaeological remains.[1]

Yet for all that history, it was not until the early nineteenth century that the craze for séances and Ouija boards, the fervent believers in ectoplasm, and accompanying rationalist sceptics and debunkers, kicked off in the United States. This phenomenon is sometimes referred to as the 'Second Great Awakening' or evangelical revival. This was a period in which multiple novel, essentially Protestant, Christian sects came into being in close proximity. The region, in western and central New York state, came to be known as the Burnt-over District for the fiery foment of religious and utopian reform ideas that emerged there — Mormons, Millerites, Adventists (including their spinoff, the Seventh-day Adventists), Jehovah's Witnesses, the Shakers, the Oneida Society and many others.[2]

The story of Spiritualism begins there, too, in March 1848, in a small wooden cabin in Hydesville just outside of Rochester. This cabin, which had a reputation for being haunted, was home to the unexceptionally Methodist Fox family and their two young daughters, Margaret (aged 14) and Kate (11). What set these two sisters apart, though, were the strange phenomena that surrounded them, particularly the mysterious raps produced by no visible means but which could be made to answer questions in a simple alphabetic code.

This became quite the local sensation. The Fox girls called the knocking spirit 'Mr Splitfoot', as if it were the Devil, but through interrogation and neighbourhood gossip a story emerged about a travelling peddler who had been murdered by the earlier occupants of the house; unconfirmed sources even claimed that bones had been found in the cellar.

Interest quickly spread, attracting the curious, along with journalists and clergy. The girls were tested by the *New-York Tribune* founding editor

Horace Greeley and New York Supreme Court Justice John Edmonds, who did not detect any foul play. Others would try — among them doctors, scientists, preachers and journalists. No dishonest contrivance could be found.[3]

America was transfixed. And there is something quintessentially American about the phenomenon: it's so *democratic*. If two very ordinary young girls could contact the other side, then so could anyone. It also struck a chord peculiar to the nineteenth century, a time when rising affluence and standards of living meant that middle-class families tended to be smaller and children more precious, and yet the infant mortality rate was still staggeringly high. It was an age obsessed with the spectre of death but unable to do much to keep it at bay. Is it any wonder, then, that the hope of contacting departed loved ones brought widows, widowers and grieving parents flocking to the séance table?

Tireless debunkers, such as Harry Houdini and others, showed many to be frauds of the same stripe as Robert Browning's fictional Mr Sludge. But Spiritualism became its own culture, with periodicals, churches and summer camps. Mediumship became a realistic career, especially empowering women who were otherwise restricted to the domestic sphere.[4] Spiritualism also filled an important niche in evening group entertainment as nineteenth-century technology created more leisure time for the middle classes.[5] It never really faded away.

By the 1960s, Ouija boards were a mass-market item, competing successfully with the boardgame *Monopoly* in the United States, beating it for top place in 1967.[6] But it was in the late nineteenth and early twentieth centuries that Spiritualism rode a worldwide wave, and New Zealand was not immune.

‡

Spiritualism had already gone through its first rise and decline in Britain and the United States by the time it arrived in Aotearoa in the late 1860s. In his 2000 doctoral thesis on New Zealand Spiritualism, Shaun Broadley sees it as being taken up as a tool within a broader utopian agenda of creating a 'Better Britain' in the South Pacific. He draws parallels with the experimental reformist and progressive understanding of colonisation exemplified by Edward Gibbon Wakefield's systematic approach to settlement and Julius Vogel's public works and liberal reforms of the 1890s.[7]

In reality, Spiritualism was a motley patchwork of ideas, sentiments, processes, beliefs and practices that drew on a wide range of sources and philosophies to create a semi-coherent thesis: that identity and consciousness persisted beyond death in some kind of community, that the dead wished to communicate with the living, and that these spirits wanted to guide the living on the path to some kind of spiritual or social progress. As such, it appealed in colonial New Zealand, where higher learning wasn't often accessible, and where people had to teach themselves, make do and innovate to survive.

From the 1870s onward, the flood of immigration from Britain, and to a lesser extent the United States and Australia, brought settlers with first-hand knowledge of Spiritualism. John Marshman (1823–1913) was Canterbury's provincial treasurer, an immigration agent and the province's first Commissioner for Crown Lands. While an immigration officer and agent general for the New Zealand Company and Canterbury Association in London, Marshman held séances at his house with such prominent figures as the author Samuel Butler (1835–1902), the naturalist Alfred R. Wallace (1823–1913) and the zoologist W. B. Carpenter (1813–1885) in attendance.[8] Butler later painted Marshman's portrait, now in the collection of Christchurch Art Gallery Te Puna o Waiwhetū.

‡

Ground Zero for all this — as often seems to be the case for spiritual movements at the time — was Otago. Although this might seem counter-intuitive today, Dunedin's well-heeled and educated population was receptive to such novelties.

Robert Ellwood links the rise of Spiritualism and Theosophy to the period's rapid phase of immigration, the establishment of the University of Otago (one of the first in the world to allow female enrolment, much as Spiritualism was one of the few religious movements to allow female leadership) and gold-rich Otagoans feeling increasingly dissatisfied with

Sir Robert Stout KCMG, thirteenth premier of New Zealand, Chief Justice of New Zealand, women's suffrage supporter and free-thinker.

their colonial status among newer independent nations and so increasingly pivoting to the United States.[9]

The fashionable of Dunedin were also heavily influenced by trends in Melbourne, the centre of Spiritualist activity in Australia. The forty-fifth parallel north is supposed to have all sorts of paranormal associations, passing through the Auvergne and close to occult centres like Lyon, Venice, Turin, Milan and Belgrade. Perhaps the forty-fifth parallel south, passing through the middle of Otago, exerts a similar effect. It is certainly very close to one of our most famous ghosts, at the Vulcan Hotel in the tiny village of St Bathans; Lake Waihola, to the south of Dunedin, also has a reputation for ghosts and peculiar happenings.[10]

Spiritualism as a social phenomenon became the subject of vigorous debate in the pages of the *Otago Daily Times* in 1869, with the earliest mention being a letter to the editor written a year earlier under the pen name 'Fideles' (Latin for 'faithful'), which urged closet Spiritualists to 'arise, and put foolish fear behind them, knowing that hardly any new science, however true or holy or good it may have been, has at first been favourably received'.[11] Things kicked up a notch in 1870 with the establishment of a Spiritualist Investigation Society and the publication of an anonymous pamphlet directed at the Presbyterian Church, defending the movement and wagering one thousand guineas on Spiritualism's authenticity.[12]

The Dunedin *Echo*, published by future attorney general Robert Stout (1844–1930) — a noted free-thinker who also supported women's suffrage — presented articles for and against Spiritualism, and a notice in the issue for 15 June 1870 suggests around half a dozen spirit circles were operating in Dunedin at the time and claiming positive results. On 25 June, an article by transatlantic celebrity Spiritualist Emma Hardinge Britten (1823–1899) offered 'Rules to be Observed When Forming Spiritual Circles'. Hardinge Britten visited New Zealand in person in 1879.[13]

The Spiritualist craze spread from Dunedin throughout the south of the South Island in ripples. In 1870 the *Cromwell Argus* reported of Otago that 'Spiritualism still maintains its supremacy over the minds of many in this Province' and 'Strange stories pass from tongue to tongue concerning remarkable manifestations and mysterious revelations.'[14] As far north as the South Canterbury port town of Tīmaru, the *Timaru Herald* reported manifestations there.[15] Spiritualist activity sparked with abandon from the alluvial gravels of the goldfields as prospectors sought an edge in finding the elusive metal. In the North Island, one Thames miner wrote to the *Pleasant Creek News*:

> I saved a claim here at the Thames through a spirit communication. It had been neglected, and was liable to be jumped, when I was told by spirit writing that six men were coming at nine o'clock the next morning on the claim to jump the ground, with other particulars of their programme. It was there with the men that I got, just in the nick of time to save the claim. The jumpers came exactly at the time I was told they would do, and they saw at once that they were completely checkmated, and looked sheepishly disappointed and as white as ghosts when they saw we were too much and too strong to be bounced by them. You see by this that I am a Spiritist [*sic*].[16]

We may presume similar sentiments were to be found further south. J. L. Gillies, former secretary of the Otago Harbour Board and editor of the *Bruce Herald* in South Otago, gave a great deal of coverage to Spiritualism in the first part of the 1870s, contributing some himself under the pen name 'Stockwhip'.[17] A small circle is reported as active in Queenstown prior to August 1870, another in Tokomairiro near Milton, and there were reports of séances on the Taieri Plain and in Ōamaru.[18] The Tokomairiro group reportedly consulted the spirits in relation to a robbery in Clyde in August 1870, in which over £12,000 in gold and money were stolen. No doubt they were motivated by the £500 reward. The same group also investigated the possibility of spirit communication as a replacement for the telegraph.[19]

Early in 1873, an *Otago Daily Times* editorial declared that 'Amongst the social movements of the age, the spread of Spiritualism is certainly the most conspicuous, if not the most important.'[20] Even Otago's Provincial Superintendent James Macandrew (1819–1887) was implicated, a *New Zealand Herald* journalist going so far as to claim that he 'consoles himself with the reflection, gleaned from the "Spirit World", by Mr Smith, of Melbourne [Anglo-Australian Spiritualist James Smith (1820–1910), who visited Dunedin in 1872], that our mineral resources are inexhaustible, and that no matter how much waste there may be, our financial position will remain sound'.[21]

‡

Shaun Broadley observes that this Spiritualist outbreak was fuelled by the investigations initiated in Britain in 1869 by the London Dialectical Society — which were not an attempt to debunk the presence of spirits but rather to prove them — and a sympathetic 1871 article in the *Quarterly Journal of Science* by celebrated English scientist William Crookes, pioneer of the vacuum tube, detailing his experiments with the medium D. D. Home.[22]

But the thing that kept the whole movement alive in this distant part of the world was the steady stream of visiting speakers, who would hit the quiescent meat of the New Zealand circuit like a caffeinated jolt of Frankenstein's stolen lightning. Lecture tours of the colony could be quite lucrative. The aforementioned James Smith — who would later fall out of favour for predicting the imminent end of the world and for his attempts to 'magnetically' imprint the knowledge of dead intellects upon the brains of his children — was rewarded by the people of Dunedin for his visit in 1872 with 50 sovereigns.[23]

The following year, two noted American Spiritualists, James Martin Peebles (1822–1922) and his personal medium and secretary 'Dr' Elisha Dunn (1840–1914), arrived in the city and made an impression.[24] Peebles is a perplexing figure — various sources claim that he was a member of the Indian Peace Commission of 1868, United States Consul to Trebizond, and representative of the American Arbitration League at the Paris Peace Conference of 1919.[25] In 1876 he also went on to acquire a fraudulent medical degree from the notorious diploma mill the Philadelphia University of Medicine and Surgery, and was peddling a snake oil cure for epilepsy around the turn of the century.[26] He can't have been a complete quack, though, as he did live to the age of 99, which presumably can be attributed, as outlined in his book *How to Live a Century and Grow Old Gracefully* (1884), to an ovo-lacto diet and abstinence from alcohol, coffee, meat, tea and tobacco.[27]

James Martin Peebles, Unitarian minister, abolitionist, Theosophist, Spiritualist and medium.

A HISTORY OF CALIFORNIA AND AN EXTENDED HISTORY OF LOS ANGELES AND ENVIRONS, HISTORIC RECORD CO., LOS ANGELES, 1915

Before becoming a Spiritualist in the 1850s, Peebles had been a Unitarian minister. Following the American Civil War he converted to the Episcopalian Church and dabbled in Theosophy. He advocated for temperance, the abolition of slavery, the Oddfellows, dress reform and women's rights, and against vaccination, which was a typical mindset for Spiritualists in the English-speaking world of the day.[28] Peebles' hotline to the beyond included Mozart, Jesus' favourite disciple John, the expected native Americans, and a sister of Louis XIV.

Peebles encountered the hulking, impressively moustachioed Dunn in a travelling hypnotist's show in Battle Creek, Michigan, in 1858, and, impressed by his talents, determined to polish the rough and dissipated young man into a protégé. Dunn was the clairvoyant and Peebles the interpreter and teacher.[29] Dunn appears to have been as much a fraud as Peebles — upon his death it was discovered that the impressive collection of curios he had acquired on their travels consisted largely of fakes; the supposed nooses from famous executions were, on inspection, all cut from the same length of rope.[30]

Although the two gentlemen were married — Peebles to a Boston art teacher, and Dunn to a woman by the name of Carrie Etts, back in Rockford, Illinois — the wives were not in the picture, and there was much whispering about the true nature of the men's relationship, to the point that the *Otago Daily Times* felt the need to reassure its readers that 'their relations were those of acquaintances, friends and travelling companions — nothing more'.[31]

The two Americans were highly popular in Dunedin. At the 1873 farewell event hosted for the pair, 200 people attended the Athenaeum and Mechanics' Institute in the Octagon, the hall decoratively festooned in evergreens and flowers. Peebles spoke of Dunn's ability to levitate — a feat never demonstrated during their sojourn — and both men were presented with £100 and two gold-mounted pounamu pendants.[32]

Not all were so fortunate in their wake, however. John Logan, a deacon at Dunedin's Knox Presbyterian Church and Robert Stout's father-in-law, was dragged before the Church session in an ecclesiastical trial for heresy because he had shared a platform with the Spiritualists at one of their events. Logan was excommunicated, and he and his wife would later become active

Elisha Dunn, American hypnotist, clairvoyant and medium.

COURTESY ROCKFORD PUBLIC LIBRARY, ROCKFORD, ILLINOIS, USA

in Spiritualist circles, Mrs Logan finding a hitherto unsuspected vocation as a medium.[33] Their daughter Anna married Robert Stout in 1876, and she would go on to be a prominent suffragist and to help found the Society for the Protection of Women and Children, and the Plunket Society.[34]

‡

As mentioned, the formidable Emma Hardinge Britten arrived in the Antipodes on tour in 1878–1879. Alfred Deakin (1856–1919), destined to be the second prime minister of Australia and an ardent Spiritualist in his youth, described her as a theatrical woman 'of large proportions, excellent appetite and unshakeable self-confidence', who, although she had 'a large share of egotism, was a sincere believer in spiritualist principles'.[35] Hardinge Britten was one of the few people to address the unjust treatment of the Logans, writing of their plight in her 1884 book *Nineteenth Century Miracles*.[36]

Hardinge Britten stands out among the many Spiritualist visitors to these shores in that she showed a specific interest in Māori and their spiritual beliefs, holding them in high regard. During her short visit, she seems to have assimilated a lot of information on the subject, primarily from the Reverend Richard Taylor's book about Māori lore and legend, *Te Ika A Maui* (1855). She even dedicated the first few pages of the New Zealand chapter of *Nineteenth Century Miracles* to the subject, observing that, 'midst the mythological personages of New Zealand, "the Spirits of the dead" ever play a very prominent part, and our chief interest in noticing the Maoris at all, lies in the fact, that belief in, and open communion with these Spirits, still exists'.[37]

This communion, she states, gave Māori the edge over colonial forces, thus giving them prior warning, 'information of the parties sent out to attack them; the very colour of the boats, and the hour when they would arrive; the number of the enemy, and all particulars essential to their safety . . .'[38] These she compared to the oracles of the Old Testament Hebrews.

She also wrote about Te Whiti o Rongomai III and the shameful events at Parihaka, and recounted an example of what might be described, in Spiritualist terms, as Māori mediumship. It is worth recounting in full:

Mr. Marsden had long been prospecting unsuccessfully in the gold regions [of the King Country]. He had a friend in partnership with him, to whom he was much attached, but who had been accidentally killed by a fall from a cliff.

The Spirit of this man came unsolicited, on an occasion when Mr. Marsden was consulting a native seeress, for the purpose of endeavouring to trace out what had become of a valuable watch which he had lost.

The voice of the Spirit was first heard in the air, apparently above the roof of the hut in which they sat, calling Mr. Marsden by his familiar name of 'Mars.' Greatly startled by these sounds, several times repeated, at the Medium's command, he remained perfectly still until the voice of his friend, speaking in his well-remembered Scotch accent sounded close to his ear, whilst a column of grey misty substance reared itself up by his side. This apparition was plainly visible in the subdued light of the hut, to which there was only one open entrance, but no window. Though he was much startled by what he saw and heard, Mr. Marsden had presence of mind enough to gently put his hand through the misty column which remained intact, as if its substance offered no resistance to the touch. Being admonished by an earnest whisper from the Maori woman, who had fallen on her knees before the apparition, to keep still, he obeyed, when a voice — seemingly from an immense distance off — yet speaking unmistakably in his friend's Scotch accents, advised him to let the watch alone — for it was irreparably gone — but to go to the stream on the banks of which they had last had a meal together; trace it up for six miles and a half, and then, by following its course amidst the forest, he would come to a pile, which would make him rich, if he chose to remain so.

Whilst he was waiting and listening breathlessly to hear more, Mr. Marsden was startled by a slight detonation at his side. Turning his head he observed that the column of mist was gone, and in its place, a quick flash, like the reflection of a candle, was all that he beheld. Here the séance ended, and the astonished miner left the hut, convinced he had heard the Spirit of his friend talking with him.

He added, that he followed the directions given implicitly, and came to a mass of gold lying on the stones at the bottom of the brook in the depth of the forest. This he gathered up, and though he prospected for several days in and about that spot, he never found another particle of the precious metal. That which he secured, he added, with a deep sigh, was indeed enough to make him independent for life, had it not soon been squandered in fruitless speculations.[39]

Communion with spirits and the dead frequently formed an important part of Māori responses to the catastrophic upheaval caused by the arrival of Christian missionaries and European culture, providing an impetus to many protest and prophetic movements, starting with the Ngāpuhi tohunga Papahurihia, also known as Te Atua Wera (d.1875) in Northland. The movement that arose around him in 1833 displayed a number of recognisable indigenous parallels to Pākehā Spiritualism, in the employment of trances, mediumship via tohunga (priests) and waka atua (vessels of a spirit), and rituals comparable in the Western mind to the séance.[40]

Some of these Māori groups went so far as to adopt various practices of Pākehā Spiritualism, such as in the Upper Waihou in the Hokianga in the 1890s, set off by the enforcement of the Dog Tax, manifesting in séances and spirit-rapping. Author and playwright Bronwyn Elsmore describes this as 'a further symptom and manifestation of the dissatisfaction felt by the local people because of social and political issues'.[41]

That said, however, the situation is likely analogous to the apparent embracing of Christianity by Māori in the 1830s. As historian of religion Allan Davidson says: 'While it is possible to describe the context in which this took place and point to various factors which made it possible, it is important to recognise that people became Christians for their own reasons.'[42] The same can be said of Spiritualism for both Māori *and* Pākehā in Aotearoa.

In general, the Spiritualism of the 1870s and 1880s was positively disposed and sympathetic to Māori, given that indigenous peoples were often seen as more sensitive or spiritually in tune with the other side, and because Spiritualism held the universalism of humankind as a core tenet.

Traditional Māori spirituality also believed in the enduring immortality of the soul/wairua and that these were everywhere coexisting with the material world. Some Spiritualists and investigators, such as interpreter, writer and land purchase agent Charles Oliver Bond Davis (1817–1888), noted the commonalities despite their different cultural contexts.[43]

‡

One of the most peculiar accounts in the annals of New Zealand spiritualism and spectral activity comes to us from the first half of the 1880s, recorded in the Wellington-based *New Zealand Mail* by its avid Spiritualist editor John Chantry Harris (1830–1895). Although the account is attributed to a rural editor under the name Henry Anderson, it is, as Robert Ellwood points out, undoubtedly the work of William Charles Nation (1840–1930), owner-editor of the *Wairarapa Standard*.[44]

Nation was born in Sydney and moved with his family to Nelson in 1857. His father, a printer, established the newspaper the *Colonist* on arrival, and the young Nation worked there as a printer. Already committed to the temperance movement, Nation organised a Band of Hope — a kind of anti-alcohol support group — for the youth of the community and joined the Nelson Volunteers.

With the onset of the Otago goldrush, for a time Nation moved south to work in the offices of other printers in both Dunedin and Lyttelton, but eventually returned to Nelson. Shortly after marrying Sarah Ann Webley in 1864, Nation took up a printing position with the *Press* in Christchurch for 12 years. He and Sarah produced six daughters and two sons. After a stint at the *Wellington Independent* and its successor publication, the *New Zealand Times*, Nation bought the *Wairarapa Standard* in Greytown from Richard Wakelin in 1881.[45]

While living in Greytown, Nation's interest in Spiritualism was sparked when, in March 1883, one of his daughters, Bertha, 10 years old at the time, appeared to have developed the power of causing small items of furniture to move across the room while she was only touching them lightly. From there, events closely parallel those in the case of the original Fox sisters in the United States:

In a little while they discovered that there was an intelligent force at work. If Mr Nation said, 'Move the table towards the door,' the table straightway made the required movement. 'I then,' says Mr Nation, 'arranged that when the answer should be "yes," the table should tilt slightly three times, according to the number of letters in the word, and tilt twice for "no".'[46]

The association with one of the children is interesting. Was this merely the case of a precociously clever child deceiving a gullible parent, or something more akin to the Poltergeist phenomenon? Nation certainly believed that Bertha was the channel for whatever it was doing these things, and soon she was in considerable public demand as a medium. At the child's command, the table answered all manner of questions by rocking back and forth or sliding around the house to indicate the locations of concealed family members. Bertha's talents also expanded to include automatic writing on a slate provided for the purpose.

A spirit circle quickly formed and met regularly at Nation's house, likely modelled on the format advocated by Hardinge Britten. The group was led by a recently widowed woman known only as Mrs C., who had discovered her talent for mediumship in the circle, as did Bertha's older sister Bella. One of the most fascinating aspects of the case is the response from Māori participants, Ngāti Kahungunu chief Hāmuera Tamahau Mahupuku (c.1840–1904) and tribal leader, farmer and land assessor Te Mānihera Te Rangi-taka-i-waho (1800–1885) of Pāpāwai. Both seemed convinced of the veracity of the experience, comparing it to the traditional communion with the spirit world they had known of in their youth before it was forbidden by the missionaries.

Te Mānihera, in particular, believed contact had been made with the spirit of his dead daughter, which surely would have required a knowledge of the region and te reo simply not available to little Bertha Nation.[47] His health was failing, and he blamed himself greatly for the death of 19 of his 22 children by two marriages, believing they had been caused by his transgression of a tapu, and this may have made him more receptive to the suggestion.[48] The *Mail* article describes a typical evening for the circle:

A circle was formed of five persons, who laid their hands lightly on the top of a heavy dining table, the hands of any one person not touching those of another. In a couple of minutes the table began to oscillate, and then to move round slowly. The movement soon became quicker, until the table spun round as fast as those forming the circle could move with it. The table was a heavy one, with a large solid centre support, and it was impossible to suppose that it could have been moved by the exertion of muscular force on the part of those whose hands rested lightly on its top.[49]

On 15 August 1884, it was claimed that the circle had been visited by no fewer than 20 entities, who made themselves known over a span of nearly three hours, including one who attempted to speak through the medium in 'Swiss', unintelligible to those gathered. At this point the *Mail*'s credulity found its limit, and reporting on the event pointed out that no such language existed, the Swiss speaking German, French and Italian.[50]

Combining his career and creed, in June 1887 Nation launched the Spiritualist newspaper *More Light*, named for Goethe's deathbed words, with the motto, taken from 1 John 1:3: 'That which we have seen and heard declare we unto you.' Nation wrote all the articles and did all the typesetting himself.[51] Aside from Spiritualism, Nation's two other main interests were child welfare and nature. The central role of Nation's children in his spirit circle had convinced him that children had a unique connection with the other side, and he supported a lyceum system for training children as mediums. His fondness for children may also have motivated his campaigning for tree-planting and the introduction of the first Arbor Day in New Zealand, in Greytown in July 1890.

It was not only living children with whom Nation was concerned — the spirit circle often received communications from mysterious child spirit guides. One such instance occurred on Good Friday evening 1883, when two families of children gathered in the circle. There, communications were received. The first described children as terrestrial angels linking this world with the world to come, but it was also ominously conveyed that moral lessons needed to be learned in this life or they would be learned in 'spirit land'. A second message, from a child spirit calling herself Annie

Hansen, told of the wonders that awaited in the spirit land. The third message came from a child spirit called Amy, and warned:

> Bertha must give up entirely for a while. The power is withdrawn from her for a wise purpose because it withdrew a certain amount of force. On any special occasion let her help me. She must be obedient to her parents and go to bed at an earlier hour. She is an excitable little body, and can't be still — she is all hop, skip, & jump. An excitable temperament throws off more force. I shall withdraw the power for a time, though we shall always be about her.[52]

Seeking better prospects, and perhaps wishing to be rid of the hostility of the local clergy, Nation sold the *Standard* in 1893 and moved to Shannon in the Manawatū, going into business with his son Charles Cecil Nation and publishing the *Manawatu Farmer and Horowhenua County Chronicle*. At Shannon, Nation was appointed registrar of births, deaths and marriages. Although he had ceased to publish *More Light*, he maintained his commitment to Spiritualism, and also arranged an Arbor Day for Shannon in 1894. In 1896 Nation moved to Levin to go into competition with a new newspaper that had set up there, successfully enacting a takeover. He sold the paper in 1909, continued as births, deaths and marriages registrar for Shannon, served as coroner for Levin for 17 years, and became a justice of the peace in 1899.

Levin only deepened Nation's Spiritualism. In 1903 he launched another Spiritualist newspaper, the monthly *Message of Life*. Many of the articles in this successful publication found their way into his book *Remarkable Experiences in the Phenomena of Spiritualism in New Zealand* (1907), which ran to three editions in Aotearoa and one in Canada. For 13 years Nation was president of the National Council of the Spiritualist Church and travelled the country supporting isolated circles. Later he joined the Spiritualist Church of New Zealand, and after his death was remembered as the 'Grandpa' of New Zealand Spiritualism and the earliest advocate for the Arbor Day movement in this country.[53] Of his efforts to promote Spiritualism, Nation would write in the 1880s:

Did I suffer in business? Someone may ask. Yes, I did. Being the proprietor of a newspaper, Simon Pure and Co., who belonged to the Church, got at me by withdrawing advertisements, giving up the paper, and getting their jobbing work done in other towns; and my family was almost cut off by these Christian professors, and I realised that when the Church persecutes it has no mercy . . . However, I weathered the storm, and did my best for the advancement of the town, I devoted myself to the welfare of the young people, and the trees that were planted on the road-sides were the outcome of Arbor Day efforts, carried through by my energy. For this I was publicly thanked by the Mayor and Borough Council, and to-day I look back and find pleasure in the thought that I did my duty and held on to the truth of spirit return.[54]

‡

That is not the only strange tale out of the storied Wairarapa. Consider the magnificently named Charles Joseph Bonaventure Golder (1842–1923), who was born in Lower Hutt and who made his living as a watchmaker and jeweller in Masterton. His true calling, however, was as a self-professed prophet of the Old Testament mould. Among other eschatological fancies, Golder believed he was destined to father a new race of human-angel hybrids.[55] Unfortunately, union with his wife Margret Ferguson only produced three perfectly normal human children.

Perhaps this is why in 1881, now living in Waipawa in Hawke's Bay, he began writing gushingly effusive love letters to a young woman. When her father found out, like something out of Chaucer's 'The Miller's Tale', he began replying to Golder in her stead, luring the would-be Lothario to a nocturnal rendezvous. Instead of the young lady, Golder found her father waiting and ended up on the receiving end of the quaint colonial New Zealand tradition of 'tar-tarring' — the equivalent of tarring and feathering, but with toi-toi plumes instead of feathers.[56]

Nor were the spirits to leave the Wairarapa. Over a century later, in 1992, the town of Carterton was the site of a bizarre and brutal ritual murder, when Wallace Iopata and Huia Tawhai killed Tawhai's elderly husband, Lou, before burning down the weatherboard house and standing naked outside on the lawn, chanting in meditation as they waited for a UFO to take them to Australia. Tawhai and the younger Iopata had, in what they described as an exorcism, tortured the old man: they scalded him with boiling water, castrated him and, when he died, dismembered him and attempted to burn his head in a woodburner. Originally three were arrested for the murder — Iopata, Huia Tawhai and her lover and occasional boarder, Jay Sankaran. In the end, Sankaran avoided prosecution by turning witness for the prosecution, revealing a disturbing story of sex acts, violence and evil spirits. Huia Tawhai and Iopata both denied murdering Lou, and during the trail Tawhai declared she had been following Iopata's orders and that it was he who had dismembered the body. Tawhai was found guilty of manslaughter and sentenced to seven years in prison. Iopata was given a psychological assessment, diagnosed as schizophrenic and with severe intellectual impairment, declared unfit for trial and placed in a secure unit in Porirua Hospital.[57]

‡

Spiritualism flourished in both islands throughout the winter of 1884, as diligently recorded in the *Mail* by its sympathetic Spiritualist editor, John Chantry Harris. The Wellington Spiritualist Investigating Association, which Robert Ellwood suggests was likely the same organisation as the Wellington Association of Spiritualists,[58] had been active a mere two months and was already having to turn people away from its meetings. A typical evening went like this:

> [A]fter singing two hymns and reading a portion of scripture, the medium was entranced, and then delivered a very impressive invocation. After the delivery of the invocation, an address on the subject of 'Death' was given by the controlling spirit, who fully described the change called death, and related the experiences of several spirits and their entrance to the spirit world. The address, which lasted about forty minutes, was delivered in a most impressive manner.[59]

This report appeared in the *Mail* alongside a report on the infamous British trial of political activist and atheist Charles Bradlaugh and Theosophist Annie Besant for publishing birth control literature; an extract from *The Harbinger of Light*, a Melbourne-based Theosophical Society magazine, and as such likely the first mention of Theosophy in mainstream New Zealand media; and an article about a man in New York who had killed his fiancée by hypnotising her to obey him. This last item recounted how he had attempted to bring about the hypnotic induction — the dissociative shock that puts the subject into a suggestive state — by pulling a pistol on her, wrongly assuming it to be unloaded, and pulling the trigger.[60]

Closer to home, on 10 June 1886, Mount Tarawera erupted, covering Te Ariki village and the famous Pink and White Terraces in ash and thick volcanic mud. The following day newspapers reported the sighting of a foreboding ghostly waka taua, the so-called 'phantom canoe', on the waters of Lake Tarawera a few days before. Other newspapers around the colony quickly picked up on the story, no doubt fuelled by the popularity of Spiritualism and the predilection of the Victorians for gothic fancy, declaring it an omen of the catastrophic event.[61] As folklorist James Cowan put it in a popular telling, writing in 1925:

> The people were not without warnings of their fate. The waters of the lake rose and subsided in an unaccountable manner; and some days before the catastrophe the phantom canoe was seen on Tarawera's waters by the matakite [someone able to see the spirit world or omens of the future], those of the wise and understanding eye — the ghostly war canoe which was wont to appear before some tribal disaster, gliding across the waters towards the funeral mountain, with its double row of occupants, one row paddling, the other standing wrapped in their flax robes, their heads bowed, their hair plumed as for death with the feathers of the huia and the white heron — these were the souls being ferried to the mountain of the dead.[62]

‡

The Wellington Association of Spiritualists held its meetings at Ingestre Street, Brooklyn, every Sunday at seven in the evening. Men were charged two shillings, and ladies, one. On one occasion the gathering was visited by a spirit calling itself John Mackey, who proceeded to deliver a lecture on prison reform, which perfectly highlights the relationship between Spiritualism and progressive social liberalism:

> The medium, while seated at the table, gave one or two little spasmodic shudders similar to those which are premonitory symptoms in the cases of persons suffering from epileptic fits, and with closed eyelids remained in this position until the hymn was concluded. His corporeal frame was then presumed to have been taken possession of by the controlling spirit, which in this instance was stated to be that of the late departed John Mackey, and in his trance the medium rose and delivered a short prayer, after which he gave a short address relative to the treatment of criminals in the various prisons. The controlling spirit depreciated the present system of treating criminals, who were looked upon more like beasts than human creatures. It should, he said, be recollected that these men were but invalided spirits, who were capable of being taught and elevated to something better.[63]

This furious activity, however, seemed to decline with the decade. In 1888, the *Mail* reprinted a review from the London *World* of the memoirs of the widow of the once internationally celebrated Scottish medium Daniel Dunglas Home (1833–1886), gently consigning him — the original of Browning's Mr Sludge — and Spiritualism to the dustbin of history.[64] While Spiritualism in New Zealand was far from dead, it was ailing.

The Wellington Association of Spiritualists lost a significant number of its officers when resolutions were passed to eliminate the 'quasi-religious' element from the meetings and concentrate exclusively on psychic research. By 1891 the Association was defunct.[65] It is perhaps not entirely coincidental that the fateful year of 1888 was also when Theosophy established itself in Wellington.

The split in the Association reflected a global trend in Spiritualism. By the 1890s a distinct parting of the ways had occurred between the groups that were to evolve into the nonconformist Spiritualist churches and the scholarly psychical or parapsychological research groups who sought a more academic approach. The parapsychologists set about investigating or — more often than not — debunking mediums. The *Mail* devoted considerable attention to the 1894 court case of Wellington brother and sister James and Priscilla Hackett, who were charged with 'exercising enchantment' with much muslin and phosphorescent paint, materialising the dead, including, supposedly, some Māori.

The jury acquitted Priscilla, laying the blame on James, but the judge threw the case out, dismissing it as merely deception, and advised the pair to either leave the colony or to abstain from the practice.[66] Ellwood notes that throughout the month of June, alongside this case, the *Mail* also reported on similar trials involving palmists and other fortune-tellers. The Hacketts were also active in New South Wales, and were exposed by T. Shekleton Henry in his book *Spookland* (1894).[67]

‡

One significant part of colonial society in Aotearoa, however, remained a resistant bulwark against Spiritualism in the 1880s — the various technical, mechanics' and amateur scientific institutes around the country — and they, too, formed an influential national movement. This resistance is encapsulated in a lecture given at the Auckland Institute (which eventually became the Auckland War Memorial Museum), initiated by William D. Campbell in 1883. Campbell was a geological surveyor, engineer, an amateur scholar of Aboriginal Australian culture, and a Spiritualist, as well as being a member of the Auckland Institute from 1881 to 1885 and elected its vice president in 1883.

In September that year he delivered the lecture 'Psychological Investigations' on the subject of Spiritualist phenomena, declaring it real and rightly of the magisterium of science rather than superstition. Naturally this brought a response from the more sceptically minded members, and at the next meeting Edward Augustus Mackechnie, a physician and solicitor, delivered the brutal rebuttal 'The Spell of the Supernatural'.

In his paper, Mackechnie dismissed Spiritualism as hallucinations and delusion, to the enthusiastic approval of his fellow members. It suffices to say Campbell was not re-elected the following year.[68] Nonetheless, Mackechnie was himself fascinated with spirituality, psychic powers and the afterlife, writing extensively on the subject, and it seems his antipathy to Spiritualism may have had as much to do with his conservative politics as anything else.[69]

Mechanics' institutes had begun in Britain in the 1820s as adult education establishments for skilled working men, part of a broader movement of self-improvement and concern for the working classes. Institutes were established in Auckland, Nelson and Wellington by 1842, expanding to over a hundred throughout the country by the mid-nineteenth century. New Zealand's institutes were not much given to theorising, seeing themselves more as collectors and cataloguers, and this closed-mindedness stands in stark contrast to the previous decade and unusual figures such as the watchmaker, mathematician and astronomer Arthur Beverly (1822–1907), a member of the Otago Institute and its vice president between 1879 and 1880. Beverly was highly regarded in the colony, and frequently consulted by the government for his mathematical expertise. An impeccable scientist, he cautioned his friend, the eccentric Canterbury College professor of science and free-love enthusiast Alexander Bickerton, about the latter's speculative theoretical excesses.[70]

At the same time Beverly was agnostically conducting experiments in Spiritualism and the mystico-mathematical theories of Professor C. Piazzi Smyth's *Life and Work at the Great Pyramid* (1867).[71] Pyramidology, the belief that the dimensions of the Great Pyramid at Giza contain some millennial occult secret or that the shape itself had mystical powers, was widely ridiculed in Victorian New Zealand, yet nevertheless attracted some prominent figures with its promises, including Governor Sir George Grey (1812–1898); F. W. Irvine (1821–1883), physician and son of the eighteenth Laird of Drum in Scotland; Archdeacon Arthur Henry Stock (1823–1901) of St Peter's Anglican Church in Wellington; and popular Dunedin evangelist Alfred Brunton (1828–1900).[72] Beverly was regarded as something of an expert on the subject, and the aforementioned American Spiritualist James Peebles declared that Beverly knew 'more about the geometrical and astronomical purposes of the great pyramid *Ghizeh* [*sic*] than any other living man'.[73]

In 1872 Beverly became secretary for the Dunedin Society for Investigating Spiritualism. He was also a friend of the politician, and later New Zealand premier, Robert Stout (1844–1930).[74] His most unique legacy by far is the Beverly Clock, a mechanical clock in a grand wooden case on the third floor of the University of Otago's Physics Department building. Powered by minuscule changes in the ambient air pressure, it has not needed winding since Beverly set it in motion in 1864.[75]

Increasingly, too, both the clergy and the rationalists attacked Spiritualism as being a kind of mental health issue, the product of degenerate mentality and an encourager of sexual vice, with men and women holding hands by dim gaslight or flickering candle flame. Séances were put on a par with the self-pollution of masturbation. This rebuke of Spiritualism coincided with the popularisation of eugenics and an increased concern with improving public health, with many critics observing the preponderance of frailties among mediums, although arguably this was simply because it offered employment and entertainment for the already invalided.

In his book *The Devil's Sword Blunted* (1879), the Reverend Matthew Wood Green (1840–1914), Member of Parliament for Dunedin East between 1881 and 1884, declared Spiritualism to be 'the Enemy of Marriage' and quoted the American preacher, social reformer and ex-Spiritualist Dr Thomas de Witt Talmage (1832–1902):

> I indict spiritualism . . . because it is a social and marital curse. The worst deeds of licentiousness, and the worst orgies of obscenity, have been enacted under its patronage . . . Families innumerable have been broken up by it. It has pushed off hundreds of young women into a life of profligacy. It talks about 'elective affinities,' and 'affinital relations,' and 'spiritual matches,' and adopts the vocabulary of free-lovism.[76]

The patriarchy also noted with disdain the leadership roles to which women often rose in Spiritualism, diagnosing hysteria, female troubles and the supposed inherent weakness of the sex. The Catholic Church invoked

A cartoon published in the *Auckland Observer* in October 1908 warning of the dangers of Spiritualism.

NO SPIRITUALISM.

"*The advance of Spiritualistic ideas amongst our flock is alarming. It's time we got to work and shut the spooks down, and turn their thoughts to more solid spirits.*"

the spectre of demonic possession, the Very Reverend Father Theophilus Le Menant Des Chesnais (1836–1910), vicar general and administrator of the Diocese of Christchurch, warning:

> Even to our first mother Eve, the devil appeared as medium to enlighten her about good and evil, pretending to be very much interested about her spiritual and temporal welfare, whilst making a desperate effort to deceive and ruin her, and, through her, her husband also and all the human race, as he did, alas, with too much success. It is still principally by female mediums this arch-deceiver lies to lead us astray. Let us beware![77]

‡

In the midst of this rather pessimistic outlook for New Zealand Spiritualism, a new champion would arise in the form of Jane Elizabeth Harris (née Francis, 1852/3–1942). Harris was born in St John's Wood in London and emigrated to New Zealand on the *Ida Zeigler* with her mother and stepfather in 1866. They settled in Pārāwai, Thames, and in 1873 Jane married market gardener and Christian Spiritualist Thomas Harris, bearing him seven children. We should observe that, like Dunedin, Thames was a goldrush town that attracted many from Victoria, Australia, and the Spiritualists there were closely aligned with those in Melbourne.

It is also worth noting that in the 1870s there was an attempt to set up in Thames a utopian settlement based on the Harmonial philosophies of American Spiritualist Andrew Jackson Davis (1826–1910), and a company was formed under the name Aurelia Co-operative Land and Labour Association (ACLLA) in 1872. It attempted to canvas for investors in Dunedin and Melbourne, and although a prospectus with pretty plans was published, ultimately it failed in its ambitions and Aurelia never materialised. The project was wound up in 1874.[78]

The couple were passionate autodidacts and read voraciously to improve themselves, which in Jane manifested in an outpouring of creative self-expression in the Thames *Evening Star* under the nom-de-plume 'Jenny Wren', the occasional public lecture, and a burning desire for recognition.

In those days, of course, such recognition was hampered by her gender, which may have been what attracted her to Spiritualism in the first place, there being no such restrictions on leadership in that community.

She initiated a fitful correspondence in 1882 with Governor Sir George Grey, about her ambition to write about land nationalisation, finding herself in agreement with him.[79] This likely was the foundation for a lecture Harris gave to the Thames Mutual Improvement Association in 1884, entitled 'Woman's Work and Destiny', in which she spoke of the struggles of those who worked on the land, and the hope that one day they might 'shake themselves free of the bondage of Wealth and Power', while citing John Stuart Mill on the equality of the sexes and condemning the economic oppression of women and the evils of child labour.[80]

Harris was by no means the only person to be drawn to Spiritualism through literary inclinations. Lady Mary Anne Barker (1831–1911), known for her book *Station Life in New Zealand* (1870), spent three years living on a Canterbury sheep station with her second husband, Frederick Broome, from 1866–68. Following the death of her first husband, George Barker, in 1861 she had expressed a strong belief in his continued presence near her.[81] After she and Frederick returned to London, it was reported in the *Otago Daily Times* that she was allegedly a Spiritualist medium and that her husband had written anonymous articles on the subject in *The Times* of London.[82]

Susan Nugent Wood, wife of the Otago goldfields warden and later resident magistrate of Southland John Nugent Wood, was a prominent Otago writer of verse and prose. She also believed steadfastly that spirits visited the mortal world, and she collected stories of ghosts and hauntings.[83] Her poetry was full of allusions to spirits and the afterlife, as in her poem 'A Matin Song' about a mother whose child has died:

> Blessed be He who lifts our darlings up,
> Yet lets us hear their tiny voices call;
> Bidding us follow them and find the land
> Of ceaseless morning, never-ending spring,
> Where nothing e'er grows old![84]

The Dunedin poet Thomas Bracken (1843–1898), lyricist of the national anthem 'God Defend New Zealand', published an entire collection of Spiritualism-inflected verse, *Behind the Tomb and Other Poems* (1871), and his poem 'The Other Side' is positively overt in its Spiritualism:

> Treasured forms start up before us,
> Softly through the room they glide,
> And we hear, in loving chorus,
> Voices from the other side.[85]

Thomas Harris had joined a spirit circle led by the local Presbyterian minister, the Reverend J. S. Neill. Neill also became a member of the Theosophical Society, which the Auckland Presbytery asked him to resign from in 1893. Jane was not an immediate convert, being disquieted by the séance experience, but was brought around by the death of a son in infancy in 1876 and by reading an article in *The Harbinger of Light* about the purposefulness of the afterlife. From there she became a medium and started writing for the *Harbinger*. In her belief system, Christ was the heavenly medium channelling the will of God and a 'divinely inspired Socialist',[86] and contact with the dead was a natural part of the spiritual advancement of the living.

Things took a turn for the worse, however, when Thomas Harris died in 1887 and Jane was left with six young children, attempting to run the market garden during the day and writing at night. Tragedy struck again the following year when her youngest child, aged just one year, died suddenly. This was a situation all too common among nineteenth-century widows of limited means, and the Spiritualist movement gave Harris the strength to carry on, as it did so many overburdened and bereaved women of the period.

The *Harbinger*'s editor, W. H. Terry, came to Harris's aid and offered her a lecturing engagement in Melbourne. Harris and her family stayed on in Australia until 1896, and she appears to have been well received, producing a book of poetry in 1890, although the mainstream publications were put off by her controversial and outspoken Spiritualist beliefs. She also suffered another loss in 1890 when her 16-year-old son William was fatally injured in a factory accident and joined the ranks of 'the risen ones'.[87]

For all the tragedy in her life, Harris clearly found the Melbourne milieu amenable, given the length of her stay. As Robert Ellwood observes, the Australian Spiritualist Churches were among the first fully-fledged in the world and very different to the informal spirit circles and research societies Harris would have been familiar with in New Zealand.[88] Harris would no doubt have felt supported and at home there.

Back in Aotearoa in early 1896, inspired by the energy and zeal of the Australian churches, Harris delivered well-attended talks at the Auckland Opera House on Wellesley Street (later Fuller's Opera House and host to the first film screening in the country) — the initial lecture being on the subject of 'After death — what then?'. Her earnestness and fervour (Ellwood describes it as 'virtually apostolic') won audiences over. Of her return, she wrote:

> A pleasant surprise awaited me, for I had heard that Spiritualism was dead, or forgotten now. However the large audience that filled the Opera House on our first night showed at least an active interest in our mission and we were able to meet all expenses. Three months there [Auckland], then we were asked to form and start a society, which we easily did, from the audience, willing friends came forward...[89]

Following the instructions of her spirit guides, in 1896 she established the Society for Spiritual Progress in Auckland, followed by groups in Wellington, New Plymouth, Gisborne, Whanganui, Nelson, Christchurch and Dunedin, and a collection of her Wellington lectures was published in 1897. Through these routes Harris promoted political reform and the special role of women as society's moral guardians.

In Christchurch in 1900 she remarried, to Charles Nathaniel Roberts. By 1905, having moved to Auckland, she had adopted the hyphenated surname Harris-Roberts. Roberts died in 1920. Harris-Roberts, sharing the longevity common to many occultists, lived to the age of 90, dying in Paeroa, and while she herself used the title 'Reverend', to her followers and co-religionists she was known as 'The Mater'.[90]

☦

Prior to Harris's return, Spiritualism in New Zealand was practised by entirely informal, or liberal quasi-religious amateur societies with facilities for lectures and séances, but there was no ecclesiastical structure. As Harris travelled around establishing Spiritualist churches after the Australian model, by the squeaky hinge of the century things had changed completely. The first church meetings were held in Wellington in 1900, the year of the first mention of a Spiritualist Church in Auckland. Harris lectured in Christchurch in 1901, and in 1903 the first Spiritualist Church was established in that city in the Hobbs Building in Cathedral Square, later moving to Druid Hall in Worcester Street.

Lectures and demonstrations were reported in the press, listing speakers such as Susannah Harris, an American 'trumpet medium' (that is, a medium who specialises in manifesting spirit voices from a speaking trumpet), along with various well-known Australian Spiritualists, such as the novelist Rosa Campbell Praed, the 'apport' medium Charles Bailey (apportation being Spiritualist jargon for materialising objects and small animals in the séance chamber), and the celebrity medium Vivian (later Vyvyan) Deacon, who visited around 1920.[91] Ellwood reports that among New Zealand occult circles, it was believed that Deacon, using Spiritualism as a sort of soft front, introduced the Ordo Templi Orientis (OTO) to New Zealand, which we will look at in Chapter 12.[92]

Rather momentously, in 1907 the National Association of Spiritualists of New Zealand (NAS) was formed, with former Liberal Party Member of Parliament for Wellington William McLean (1845–1914 — more on him later) as its first president, and Nation as vice president. By 1914 this group had followed the trend of general ecclesiasticisation of such groups to become the National Association of Spiritualist Churches in New Zealand (NASC), excluding individual members where previously they had been accepted.

The outbreak of the First World War brought many to the pews of these churches, both those seeking solace in a life beyond this one and those wishing to contact loved ones killed in battle. But the silver cord between Britain and Aotearoa was strong, and Spiritualists were also active in the war effort, raising money for food parcels, medicine and tobacco. The British Spiritualist publication *Two Worlds* sponsored a Spiritualist Motor Ambulance Fund, supported by the journal *Light* and *The International Psychic Gazette*. The sum of £931 was raised, and with it six ambulances were purchased from the Ford Motor Company and presented to the War Office.

Each vehicle bore the legend 'Jointly subscribed for by the Spiritualists of the Dominion of New Zealand and Great Britain'.[93] Arthur Conan Doyle's very short 1918 essay (a note really), 'The Military Value of Spiritualism', claimed Spirtualists were ideal soldiers because they didn't fear death.[94] This militarism was not universally shared among Spiritualists, however, with one British correspondent attacking *Two Worlds*' patriotic support for the war and accusing its editor of being bloodthirsty and condoning murder.[95]

If Greek national identity was born on the quasi-mythical killing fields of Bronze Age Troy, New Zealand national identity was forged in blood further up the Dardanelles in Gallipoli in the First World War. That battle of war had its own yearning for supernatural protection and peculiar happenings, which were as likely a case of nerves and suggestion as anything paranormal. In 1915 Welsh Private Tom Arnold wrote to his parents from the trenches: 'I have a strange presentiment that something is going to happen, and if I lose my life in tomorrow's battle I want you to banish all sorrow and grief for me.' He was found dead in a gully the next day.[96]

In January 1916, members of the 14th Sikh Battalion claimed to have seen a vision of the warrior guru Gobind Singh mounted on a white horse with a white egret perched on his turban.[97] The ghost of a great general leading living troops into battle is hardly unusual in the mythology of war. This is likely a similar phenomenon to the Angel of Mons, a popular legend about the appearance in the sky to protect British troops at the Battle of Mons on 22 and 23 August 1914. In fact, this was a case of morale-boosting fiction — in this instance the short story 'The Bowmen' by the Welsh fantasy writer Arthur Machen, published in the British *Evening News* on 29 September 1914, retroactively transformed into an urban legend.

As one might imagine, attempts to improve one's luck were also popular in the trenches. An Australian correspondent wrote in 1918, after the fact, of a soldier from Queensland, of Scottish extraction, who wore a silver coin around his neck as a talisman, more in jest than anything else. His battalion at the Gallipoli landing was all but destroyed, yet he survived with only minor injuries.[98] Belief in such lucky mascots seems to have been potent at the battle. During the abdication crisis of 1936, a former member of the British Grenadier Guards sent a letter of support to Edward VIII and enclosed two four-leaf clovers to which he attributed his survival in the 1915 Gallipoli campaign.[99]

During the war a particular cult developed around the idea of pocket Bibles or prayer books having the power to deflect bullets. There is a documented New Zealand example of this phenomenon, and the associated artefact is displayed as part of the long-running *Gallipoli: The Scale of Our War* exhibition at Te Papa in Wellington. Hone Tahitahi (Te Aupōuri) served during the First World War in the First Contingent, and was one of a handful of Māori serving in the Wellington Infantry Battalion. During the attempt on Chunuk Bair in the Gallipoli campaign, an Ottoman bullet struck him in the chest just above the heart. Miraculously the bullet was stopped by the te reo Māori prayer book in his breast pocket, the point lodging by this verse from Matthew 14:27: 'Kia manawanui. Ko ahau tenei. Ahau e wehi.' (Be of good cheer. It is I. Be not afraid.)[100]

A similar tale from an Australian at Gallipoli has the bullet stopping at Jeremiah 38:2–3:

> Thus says the Lord: 'He who remains in this city shall die by the sword, by famine, and by pestilence; but he who goes over to the Chaldeans shall live; his life shall be as a prize to him, and he shall live.' Thus says the Lord: 'This city shall surely be given into the hand of the king of Babylon's army, which shall take it.'[101]

‡

The NASC changed its name again in 1923 to become the Spiritualist Church of New Zealand (SCNZ) and sought incorporation from Parliament in the manner of other nonconformist churches of the time. This was duly granted in the passing of the Spiritualist Church of New Zealand Incorporation Act 1924, recognising them as being no different to any other nonconformist church so incorporated.[102]

Most Spiritualist groups, however, preferred to remain independent of the SCNZ, although some of these were affiliated with the UK-based National Spiritualist Union or Greater World Spiritualist League. With greater official recognition, New Zealand's Spiritualists lobbied for the amendment of the Police Offences Act 1884 — under which mediums were occasionally brought to trial, although the cases were invariably thrown out — it being a direct copy of the British Witchcraft Act of 1735 and other codes.

One such case occurred in 1892, when a fortune-teller working under the splendid name of Madame Zenobia was summoned to court in Auckland charged with 'fraudulent representation . . . with a view to obtain money'. The presiding judge, Dr Joseph Giles, dismissed the case because it didn't fall under the 1884 Act, given that the references to fortune-tellers and necromancers in English law had been sensibly left out of the New Zealand version.[103] Despite the repeal of the Witchcraft Act in Britain in 1951, nothing similar happened in New Zealand law until 1981, when the fortune-telling section was amended to 'acting as a medium with the intent to deceive' in the new Summary Offences Act.[104]

The First World War, with its tremendous loss of life (New Zealand lost around 1 per cent of its population at Gallipoli and fighting on the battlefields of Europe), also did much to foster the desire for families to contact their loved ones on the other side, and so it is hardly surprising that the decades following the Great War would spark a massive revival of Spiritualism's fortunes.

‡

In Dunedin, Thomas Harris worked with William Rough (1850–1924) to establish a Spiritualist Church there. We have already briefly encountered Rough in Chapter 1, dismissing Theosophy as having no more to teach him. Rough was a carpenter, and married Mary Jane Erridge (1854–

1823), a suffragette, in Dunedin in 1874. They lived in Rothesay, part of Ravensbourne, and went on to have nine children.[105] Rough was a member of the Dunedin Psychological Society, at whose meetings he regularly gave 'trance addresses' and carried hot coals in his hands without coming to harm. This group is likely identical to the Dunedin Circle or Metaphysical Club, which the Spiritualist Katherine Bates, who visited Australia and New Zealand in 1887, records in her book *Seen and Unseen* (1907).[106]

According to his book *Forty Years' Experiences of Occult Research* (published around 1920), Rough became interested in Spiritualism in 1882. At this time he received as a spirit guide a being known as The Sage, who supposedly had lived in Atlantis 16,000 years previously; the cynical may observe that Ignatius Donnelly's popular and fanciful pseudo-archaeological *Atlantis: The Antediluvian World* also came out in 1882. Around 1886, Rough formed a Dunedin association of around 60 Spiritualists, gave up meat and liquor, and was contacted by 'an Oriental Band called The Sun Angel Order of Light', which purportedly influenced mortals in their sleep from the Fifth Heaven and prophesied to him of the coming Great War of 1914.[107]

There appears to have been some scandal in 1900, though, with Rough being implicated in the death of a young woman to whom he had provided some herbal medicine. Although he was eventually absolved and the death attributed to natural causes, moves were made to prevent Spiritualists giving out prescriptions, and two months later the family left Dunedin for Wellington. Mary Rough died in 1923; William followed the next year.[108]

Among Rough's associates we can find an example of a Spiritualist who quite blatantly combined contacting the dead with political radicalism. William Mouat Bolt (1838–1907) was a sailor from Lerwick in Scotland who settled in Dunedin in 1863. There, he worked as a storeman for importers Bing, Harris & Co, a role he held for 30 years. Bolt was closely involved in establishing the Dunedin Mutual Improvement Association and the Dunedin Freethought Association.

Aside from his Spiritualist enthusiasms, Bolt belonged to a number of left-wing political organisations in Dunedin, serving as vice president of the Otago Trades and Labour Council, and as secretary of the National Liberal

Association in 1891. Philosophically, Bolt was influenced by socialism and Fabianism as well as his Spiritualism and other Freethought movements, and supported a progressive single-tax system, women's rights, land nationalisation and co-operative settlement.[109]

Indeed, the political left has a peculiar relationship with the occult. As the philosopher Karl Popper (1902–1994) — exiled in Christchurch during the Second World War, having fled the Nazi Holocaust — pointedly observed, Marx's historical dialecticism had more in common with faith than science.[110] In his attempts to debunk astrology with a tongue-in-cheek astrological analysis of the birth of Marxism and the revolutions of 1848, by linking them to the discovery of Uranus, planet of revolution in modern astrology, and also declaring Mendeleev's periodical table superior to alchemical nonsense, Trotsky inadvertently revealed a considerable knowledge of the subject.[111]

Bolt was one of several Spiritualist radicals who formed an important political nexus in Dunedin. Another was Robert Rutherford (1827–1904), an accountant with McLandress, Hepburn & Co, the first mayor of Caversham in 1877, chairman of the Caversham Road Board, chairman of the Caversham School Committee, town councillor, and president of the Ocean Beach Domain Board, Caversham Mutual Improvement Society and Caversham Public Library.[112]

The Dunedin bookseller and publisher Joseph Braithwaite (1848–1917) was, until 1884, a Spiritualist, free-thinker and Freemason, later returning to the Anglican Church. Prior to his prodigal return to the Church of England, Braithwaite was active in the Liberal Association and the Land Nationalisation Association. Influenced by his Spiritualist beliefs, he believed that poverty could be eliminated with the abolition of private land ownership and the imposition of a state-tenure system:[113]

> Spiritualism will re-establish on what professes to be a ground of positive evidence the fading belief in a future life — not such a future as is dear to the reigning theology, but a future developed from the present, a continuation under improved conditions of the scheme of things around us.[114]

The most politically prominent of these Dunedin Spiritualist radicals was undoubtedly William McLean, whom we have already briefly encountered as the leader of the National Association of Spiritualists. Born in Inverness-shire, Scotland, McLean emigrated to Dunedin in 1863 and spent some time on the Otago goldfields. From there he went to the West Coast, where he worked as a schoolteacher and invested in the mines. In Reefton he became the area's first mining and commission agent in 1871. In 1884 he moved to Wellington, where he worked as an auctioneer and sharebroker. He was also secretary of the Wellington Opera House Company, a member of the Excelsior Lodge of Druids, and in 1898 he became the first person to import and drive a motor car in New Zealand.[115]

Although McLean harboured political ambitions, running for Parliament at least five times, he was only successful once, after the Wellington by-election in 1892. He was an unwavering supporter of New Zealand's Liberal Party, and presented himself as a champion of the working man, land nationalisation and single land tax. In 1890 he became president of the US-born international fraternal labour group Knights of Labor order in Wellington, and, consistently supported by Wellington's trade unions, lobbied for reform of the electoral system for itinerant workers and changes to Parliament's Upper House. For the purpose of promoting liberal politics, he and a number of trade unionists established the *New Zealand Times* Company.[116]

McLean regarded himself as the sort of Christian Socialist not untypical among reformist Victorian progressives, but his Christianity was deeply rooted in his Spiritualism.[117] In a well-attended public lecture at the Wellington Opera House in 1887, he articulated this position, declaring that Spiritualism had 'no quarrel' with what he condescendingly described as those who practised their Christianity 'in its simple forms as taught by Christ', and that Spiritualists only wished to 'cleanse it from the dogmas that have crept into the system'. The Spiritualist vision of spiritual immortality and progress found expression in McLean's political views as a humanist universalism on earth and the eradication of poverty and want.[118]

‡

William McLean, goldminer, teacher, Liberal MP and Spiritualist.

> 'Oh, where have you been, my long, long love,
>   this seven years and more?'
> 'Oh, I've come to seek my former vows
>   Ye granted me before.'
> — 'The Demon Lover', anonymous folk ballad (1685)

In 1919 a fantastic case brought Spiritualism once more into the spotlight. A woman named Pearl Burke appeared before the Auckland Police Court, charged with having aided and abetted the suicide of another woman, Jessie West. West, aged 36, had drowned herself in Whangārei Harbour under peculiar circumstances, walking down the steps of the town wharf in her nightgown, accompanied to the water's edge by Burke. Both women worked at the Whangārei Hotel. J. M. Killen, the coroner, gave the first deposition, followed by an older man, William Robert West, a farmer from Cambridge and the husband of the deceased. Jessie West had told her husband she was going to Auckland on holiday, and thence to Whangārei, from where she wrote him her last letter.

Apparently, she had decided to make the arrangement permanent and started working at the hotel. There had been no falling out or abuse in the marriage. According to another witness, Ellen Murphy, who shared a room with her at the hotel, West had been romantically entangled with a man named Fred Potts. Potts was a contractor and builder, also from Cambridge, and a widower with several children, who had fallen into financial trouble. In order to help him, Jessie had married the rich and elderly William. When the young woman failed to extract any money from her new husband, Potts, unable to support himself and his children, committed suicide.

Murphy told the inquest that Mrs West was a believer in Spiritualism and had attended a meeting in Auckland not long after Potts died at which, she said, Potts, a Spiritualist himself, had contacted her. Other witnesses stated that before that meeting West had wanted to drown herself, but after the meeting she had improved in mood, supposedly discovering her ability to communicate with her Freddy on her own. Later, she had told them, Potts conversed with her through table raps and wanted her to join him.

On one occasion, West proposed to Burke and some others that they hold a séance in the bedroom. At 7.30 p.m., West placed a chair bottom on a three-legged flower stand and put the light out. They began to sing the hymn 'There Is a Happy Land, Far, Far Away'. Witnesses heard knocks from the floor, which appeared to be coming from one of the stand's legs. West and Burke continued to hold séances, and the ghost of Potts purportedly expressed its unhappiness that West had not yet joined him.

West once more developed suicidal thoughts and told her friends that she would go to Waikato to drown herself, but her friends threatened to tell the authorities. After this, West became more reserved and transferred her attention to Burke, becoming exceptionally friendly with her a week prior to the suicide, which followed a further séance the two had conducted. A contemporary report in the *New Zealand Times* gives an account of Burke's testimony:

> 'About 7.45 p.m. on June 2nd, the late Jessie West and myself held a spiritualistic meeting in her room. The lights were turned out as usual, and we placed our hands on the table. Deceased said "Jessie loves Freddy," and the table knocked three times, which deceased said meant "Yes." Then she said: "Does Freddy want Jessie?" and the table again knocked three times. Then she said: "Is Freddy happy without Jessie?" and the table knocked once, which deceased said meant "No." This séance lasted until 8.10 p.m., and then the deceased lighted a candle, and said she was going to meet Freddy, and that she would be ever so much happier, and he would be happier, too. She at this time had her costume on. She told me to go and put my coat on. This I did, and I joined her again in her room. She said, "We'll go now," and then we left the hotel by the back entrance. Deceased said, "We'll go down on to the wharf," and accordingly we did so. Deceased on the way to the wharf kept talking about her Freddy calling her at the wharf. Deceased took off her clothing with the exception of her nightdress and a pair of white stockings, and after handing them to me went down the wharf steps and went quietly into the water. After she went into the water I watched her for three or four minutes before I left the wharf to return to the hotel.' The statement added that accused did not tell the truth to the police at first, because West had told her not to say anything.[119]

Pearl Burke went before the Supreme Court in Auckland on charges of having aided and abetted West's suicide, but the Grand Jury returned 'no bill', a term that indicates the jury finds the criminal charges alleged against a suspect are insufficiently supported by the evidence to warrant criminal prosecution. The judge agreed, saying that it seemed to him that West, being the elder and more forceful personality, was the leading mind, and Burke was entirely passive in the affair. Burke was discharged.[120]

‡

It often seems the case that haunted houses have a 'Blue Room', a room that seems to attract ghostly activity. The many examples include, for the United States, the Blue Room at the White House in Washington DC; in the United Kingdom, the Blue Room at Preston Manor in Brighton, and the Blue Room at the infamous Borely Rectory in Essex. Canada offers up the famously haunted The Blue Room Spa in Milton, Ontario. In New Zealand Spiritualism of the early twentieth century, the Blue Room of Dunedin can be added to that list.

> I will take my readers with me to the outlying district of Tahuna in a suburb of St. Kilda, Dunedin, and to a small house lying under the shadow of a beetling cliff out of which stone is quarried for metalling the streets. Indeed, the street in which the house is situated is called Quarry Street, and it is one of those partly-formed thoroughfares upon which the pathways are more or less swallowed up in long grass, and where properly channelled gutters are not to be found.[121]

Thus did the visitor approach what was, perhaps, the most famous Spiritualist salon in the Aotearoa of the Roaring Twenties. Soon after Jane Harris's mission to Dunedin, that city became home to the famous Blue Room, where the young clairvoyant Pearl Judd (1908–1967) demonstrated her extraordinary abilities under the guidance of her uncle, Clive Chapman (1883–1967). There were numerous newspaper accounts of events at the Blue Room, and Chapman, collaborating with an anonymous journalist writing under the initials 'G.A.W.', also recorded

Frontispiece of *The Blue Room*, by Clive Chapman, Dunedin house-painter turned Spiritualist investigator and self-taught 'scientist'.

his version of events in a book titled *The Blue Room* (1927).

Chapman was a strange fellow, a Dunedin house painter turned Spiritualist investigator and self-taught 'scientist'. In the 1920s and 1930s, he supervised a series of séances with Judd as the medium. In the book he variously describes Blakean childhood visions of angels in Kaitangata, and his studies of light, vibration and psychical phenomena as an adult, and how, when his marriage irrevocably broke down, he went to stay with his mother at whose house, by mysterious means, he ascertained the psychic sensitivity of each of his female relatives, concluding that his niece, Pearl Judd, had extraordinary potential.

The two of them embarked on a run of Spiritualist experiments supposedly producing levitations, disembodied voices and materialisations, and the typical cast of spectral advisers: an Arab wise man named Sahanei — and also, coincidentally, the city in Sudan where Kitchener defeated the Mahdists in 1898; the Hollywood actress Martha Mansfield, who starred with John Barrymore in *Dr Jekyll and Mr Hyde* (1920) and died tragically in a studio fire three years later; and a comedic little girl called wee Betty.

Others included Captain Trevor; Ronald; George Thurston; Charlie, a lyric tenor and frequently the spokesperson of the spirits; Dorothy, a soprano; Grace; Oliver; Jack; Vilma; and Granny, Chapman's maternal grandmother. Many of the male spirits, perhaps unsurprisingly, had died while serving in the Great War. These manifestations took place in a room with pale blue wallpaper, blue curtains and blue shades on the electric lights, hence the soubriquet the Blue Room, blue being a spiritual colour.[122]

At the time it was one of the most famous Spiritualist venues in the country, attracting the notable and the curious. Indeed, Arthur Conan Doyle attended during his 1920–21 New Zealand visit. Independent accounts tell of the marvels of the Blue Room. In an incident cited by the psychical researcher Harry Price, in around 1930 William Percy Gowland (1879–1965), professor of anatomy at the University of Otago's medical school, witnessed heavy tables levitate and a locked piano play itself.[123] Three years earlier, an invited journalist from the *Otago Daily Times* also witnessed the self-playing piano, and heard 'The voice of a girl claiming to be that of a well-known singer at the New Zealand and South Seas

Sir Arthur Conan Doyle, author, creator of Sherlock Holmes and promoter of Spiritualism.

Exhibition . . . in one of her favourite numbers . . . If it was trickery it was damnable trickery, for there were many in that Blue Room who believed, heart and soul.'[124]

☦

In the first two decades of the twentieth century there can be no more famous figure in the so-called silver age of Spiritualism than Arthur Conan Doyle (1859–1930), physician, author and creator of the great fictional detective Sherlock Holmes and scientist Professor Challenger. It is unfortunate, perhaps, that the author lacked his celebrated creations' perspicacity and deductive skills.

Early on, an interest in mystery was apparent — one of his first short stories, 'J. Habakuk Jephson's Statement' (1884), helped popularise the story of the ship the *Marie Celeste*, the unexplained vacation of which took place over a decade earlier, in 1872. He was particular fascinated by the mystical and paranormal, and in 1887, in the Portsmouth town of Southsea, Doyle began investigating psychic and supernatural phenomena under the influence of Major General Alfred Wilks Drayson, a member of the Portsmouth Literary and Philosophical Society. This investigation took the form of telepathy experiments and attending séances, and that year he would declare himself a Spiritualist in the pages of the Spiritualist journal *Light*.[125]

In 1889 Doyle became a founding member of the Hampshire Society for Psychical Research, and joined the London Society for Psychical Research in 1893. The following year found him chasing around Devon for poltergeists with researchers Sir Sidney Scott and Frank Podmore.[126] At the height of the First World War, Doyle became irrevocably persuaded of the reality of psychical phenomena, and convinced of the mental powers of Lily Loder Symonds, his children's nanny.[127]

The horrors of war and the deaths of those close to him — his son Kingsley, wounded at the Somme in 1918, and his brother Innes Doyle in 1919 — and the deaths of his two brothers-in-law and his two nephews after the war, had a profound impact on his belief in communication with the dead, leading to his second book on Spiritualism, *The Vital Message* (1919). Doyle appears to have been of the Christian Spiritualist persuasion, and was a member of the famous Ghost Club of British paranormal researchers.[128]

The Ghost Club, which still exists today, is the oldest continuously operating group associated with psychical research anywhere in the world. Founded in 1862, its true origins go back to spooky conversations between the fellows of ivy-clad Trinity College, Cambridge, in 1855. Past members include novelist Charles Dickens, poet Siegfried Sassoon, paranormal investigator Harry Price, speed record breaker Donald Campbell, actor Peter Cushing, author and broadcaster Peter Underwood, paranormal investigator Maurice Grosse, baronet and diplomat Sir Shane Leslie and folklorist Eric Maple.

Doyle's visit to Australia and New Zealand on Spiritualist missionary work is extensively documented in his book *The Wanderings of a Spiritualist* (1921).[129] His celebrity earned him sold-out halls and much attention in the New Zealand press, even if it didn't gain huge numbers of converts. He gave two lectures each in Auckland, Wellington, Christchurch and Dunedin on the theory of Spiritualism and accounts of his own experiences. No doubt many in the audience could identify with the theme of wartime loss. The second lecture of the two introduced to Aotearoa the phenomenon of spirit photography, explained by means of a magic lantern show.

That December, the *Otago Daily Times* was gearing itself up for the media frenzy of Doyle's tour, and public interest in all things spiritual, with a florid article about the faith healing of the prophet Tahupōtiki Wiremu Rātana (c.1873–1939), who was only just emerging into public consciousness. The journalist made showy allusions to Franz Mesmer, Robert Fludd, Paracelsus, Spiritualism and Christian Science before reporting on Doyle's Wellington lectures three days later. This report asserted that Doyle was 'stated to have altered the point of view of many hundreds of people who have attended the lectures he has already given throughout Australia, and in Auckland and Wellington', and that a certain Mr R. S. Smythe — probably the Australian journalist Robert Sparrow Smythe (1833–1917) — had asked Doyle to tour to the Dominions 20 years earlier, but Doyle had been too busy at the time.[130]

At the same time the paper was also publishing anti-Spiritualist sermons from the clergy and letters of endorsement of Spiritualism. The edition for 18 December reported positively on Doyle's Christchurch lectures, stating: 'He has none of the hysteria of the youthful convert, none of the fanaticism of the man anxious to convert all to his point of view', and that he 'states only facts he can prove from his own experience'.[131]

In Christchurch, Doyle even met a pet dog that supposedly had the intelligence of a human being, an encounter he later wrote about to the editor of *The Times* of London :

> Sir, — Without entering into the polemics of spiritualism — a subject upon which no conclusions can be reached save by personal experiment — I would wish to say a word about Darkey, the Christchurch Terrier, which barks out the answer to questions. Hundreds of people have tested this dog's powers and a considerable sum was raised for war charities by their exhibition. A committee of three, Mr. Poynton a well-known magistrate being one, investigated and reported, declaring that they could find no evidence of a trick and that 90 per cent of the questions were correctly answered. I was unable to get equally good results myself, though what I did get was remarkable so far as it went. As to alleged clairvoyant powers I preferred to think, as stated in my book, that thought transference was a more normal explanation. Your critic quotes this as an example of my 'strange credulity.' I should say it was 'strange incredulity,' which in this, as in other cases, refused to face well-attested facts.[132]

‡

When Doyle spoke in Dunedin on 20 December, it was to a packed auditorium despite the rain, and a number of clergymen were in attendance. The *Otago Daily Times* called for 'more psychic research' in response to his lecture on spirit photography,[133] but by and large the photographs were met with cynical incredulity. Spirit photography was early photography's response to Spiritualism, or vice versa, pioneered by an amateur American photographer, William Mumler (1832–1884), who had reused a glass photographic plate without cleaning it properly. Spirit photography took off in the wake of the slaughter of the American Civil War. Pictures taken in dimly lit séance chambers showed mediums extruding ectoplasm (looking suspiciously like muslin or cheesecloth) from mouths, noses or places inexplicable, and floating faces (more often than not resembling papier-mâché, wax or superimposed photographic cut-outs).

The colony of New Zealand was around the same age as the science of photography, and accomplished professional photographers were ubiquitous very early in its history. They knew all about camera trickery and retouching. It did not help that Doyle refused to allow a group of Auckland photographers to examine the prints, claiming that only an expert on spirit photography had the appropriate skill and knowledge to do so and that there were none in New Zealand.[134]

In fact, Aotearoa had its own Spiritualist photographers well before then. In 1870, the photography studio of the Burton brothers in Dunedin, better known for postcards of the Pink and White Terraces, was displaying examples of spirit photography in its front window. Australian Spiritualist the Reverend John Alexander Dowie had displayed 'chromo-lithographs' of spirits and mysterious lights during a lecture in Wellington in 1887.[135] Edward Wyllie, an Anglo-Indian Masterton cartoonist and photographer, would later become something of a celebrity for his spirit photography when he emigrated to the goldfields of California in 1886.[136]

This would not be the last time that photography would show up Doyle's perplexing naïveté: in 1922 he published *The Coming of the Fairies*, a book about his belief in and theories about the 'fair folk'.[137] The book contained the five so-called Cottingley Fairy photographs, purportedly taken by a pair of young girls, Elsie Wright (1901–1988) and Frances Griffiths (1907–1986). Doyle staunchly defended the authenticity of these photographs, even though it was quite apparent to the eye that the fairy figures had been cut from paper and posed. In a 1985 interview on ITV's *Arthur C. Clarke's World of Strange Powers* — a programme with a fond following in New Zealand — a very much older Elsie and Frances admitted the deception: 'Two village kids and a brilliant man like Conan Doyle,' said Elsie, 'well, we could only keep quiet.'

'I never even thought of it as being a fraud,' said Frances in the same interview. 'It was just Elsie and I having a bit of fun and I can't understand to this day why they were taken in — they wanted to be taken in.'[138] This

Emma Hardinge Britten, transatlantic celebrity Spiritualist, author and subject of Spiritualist photographs.

isn't the only evidence of Doyle's obdurate gullibility. For a while Doyle was friends with Harry Houdini, and reportedly no matter how often Houdini tried to explain to his friend that his own feats were trickery and illusion, Doyle refused to believe it.[139]

Over time, Doyle has become almost as famous for his gullibility as for his literary creations. In any case he clearly liked New Zealand, declaring it 'the most wonderful place in the world' and writing in *The Wandering of a Spiritualist* that New Zealanders were far kinder to him than Australians, whose leading papers had been scathing of him.[140]

In 1921 the Christchurch *Press* reported Doyle's general view of the world from Australia:

> Sir Arthur took a gloomy view of things, and felt that if we did not learn something of goodness and temperance of thought, now after the world bad been 'pretty well bled,' then the human race was lost for ever. 'We have,' he said, 'gone through the most frightful tragedy since Atlantis disappeared in the waves, and if we are not going to learn the lessons of the war, then the best I think we can do is to disappear in the waves also. And I shall not be surprised if we do. I believe intensely in the interposition of Providence in these matters. The war has been a warning, and if the world does not take it, it will! If we start on violence and eroticism there is no future for the world.' The remedy was in Spiritualism, and Sir Arthur saw none stirring but the Spiritualists. He asserted that the Roman Catholics, Anglicans, Baptists, and Congregationalists had failed. For 1900 years their doctrines had been tried, and the result was a frightful catastrophe. There was something amiss with other religions when there were 10,000,000 men lying dead on the ground. Yet the adherents of those religions did not apologise.[141]

‡

On 13 March 1929, a most peculiar headline appeared in the Auckland *Sun*: 'Into Mountain Wilds — Spiritualists' Strange Pilgrimage — Search for Lost Airmen'. The text that followed did not disappoint:

Told by the spirits from the Beyond that the airmen, Hood and Moncrieff, had crashed in the Puketoi Ranges, Mr. and Mrs. J. Lawson, of Eden Terrace, Auckland, took a crystal-gazing seeress with them and plunged into the bush country to find the plane and the bodies.

The amazing story of their 71-day trek into the wilderness is now told for the first time. How they gave up their business; how they suffered untold hardships through cold and hunger; and how they returned penniless from their strange pilgrimage into the mountain wilds, makes a fantastic story. They still maintain the airplane is lying in the heart of the Puketois.[142]

The plane in question was a Ryan monoplane named *Aotearoa*, in which two New Zealanders, Captain George Hood and Lieutenant J. R. Moncrieff, had attempted the first trans-Tasman flight, taking off from Sydney on 10 January 1927. Radio contact was lost seven hours in, approximately halfway en route, and they were never heard from again. No wreckage from the plane was found. John and Stella Lawson were Auckland-based Spiritualists; Mrs Lawson claimed medium abilities and Mr Lawson was a converted cynic. Mrs Lawson said that when the plane had gone missing, she had been a given a vision that it had not, in fact, crashed in the logical place of the Tasman Sea, but rather somewhere near Pongaroa in the Tararua district.

On 8 February 1928, the Lawsons were visited by a scryer (one who sees things in a crystal or some other polished surface) by the name of Elizabeth Watson, who told the couple that she had experienced a similar vision and had been guided to them by mystic means. The troika managed to convince a group of young men to go on a fruitless search before setting out themselves from 14 February to 12 March. They likewise found nothing, and returned home on instructions from the beyond that warned of a coming storm, which did indeed occur.

Mr Lawson sold his business to fund a second trip on 19 April, in which the three tramped 300 miles of brush and scrub in cold and rain over 54 days. Eventually they had to return home again, but they remained convinced that the wreckage of the plane and the remains of Hood and

Moncrieff still lay somewhere in the Puketoi ranges. John Lawson recorded the adventure in a diary, now in the collection of the Alexander Turnbull Library, and religious historian Robert Ellwood quotes an example from it:

> Circle held at Maori House on Wednesday night at 8 o'clock. Conditions splendid. Maori spirits all around hundreds of them.
> Medium *Stella*
> Persons present
> John Lawson
> Keepa Tainguru
> E. Pehikore
>
> The Spirit says that we are with the right people. Lovely power lovely people will get great results. Little Star (meaning girl) went to heaven. Kanaaha pleased he say I bring them all here. All coming tonight. All coming through. You have great results. God guide you safely. Kanaaha lead you to his tribe. Bless all people. You soon will be satisfied. No danger go straight ahead. I go and let someone else through... Success too. Hurry up and sing...
> Thurs. Morning. The Spirits are all still with us. & helping us wonderfully. Spirits say we walked 22 miles. Too far.
> Friday— ... two Maories and the dog are quite well & in good spirits & they are both Ratanas so they are the same as us Spiritualists. I think we know more than the people give us credit for.[143]

Kanaaha, supposedly a pre-colonial Māori although with a distinctly un-Māori name, was one of the spirits channelled by Stella Lawson. Others included the more stereotypical Native American spirit guides, Red Eagle, Little Bear and Little Star, a young girl called Marie, and the pseudo-Chinese sounding Yem Sing, who gave health advice. The most interesting thing to take away from this sample is the positive reference to Rātana, then still a very new faith and vigorously opposed by the press, the clergy and — threatened by this unconventional Christian statement of Māori self-determination — the authorities.

It seems entirely odd that John Lawson would attempt to compare members of the Rātana faith to Spiritualists: faith healing and the ngā Anahera Pono (the faithful angels) aside, it wasn't really part of their belief system, particularly as they also rejected the tohunga and their traditional communion with the other world.

Eventually the group had to give up. Lawson's diary records that the party was 'played out' and that the weather was making continuing the search impossible. He was self-aware enough to note that they would likely be thought 'cranks and mad people and [all] sorts of other things but we don't mind as we are going to show them that we are perfectly sane & know what we are talking about'.[144] The plane has never been found, although a possible sighting in the 1960s formed the basis of a major search of the Awaroa part of the Abel Tasman National Park in 2013.[145]

‡

One of the earliest mentions of another New Zealand medium, Violet May Cottrell (1887–1971), comes from Doyle himself, who referred to her in 1925 in passing as having channelled the afterlife rantings of the late English peer and owner of the *Daily Mail* and the *Daily Mirror*, Lord Norcliffe. 'Can anyone imagine,' Doyle wrote in *The Edge of the Unknown* (1930), 'that these forceful words, which can be matched in unpublished communications from the same source in England, could really have come from the mind of the lady in far New Zealand?'[146] A scant five years later, following Doyle's death, similar questions were being asked again as the good lady began channelling the author himself from beyond.

Cottrell was the youngest of eight children of Eliza Jane Fleetham and George William Grainger, a civil engineer employed as clerk of works on the construction of the breakwater for the Napier Harbour Board. In around 1892 the family upped sticks to clear 80 hectares of bush in Kiritaki in the Maharahara East block in southern Hawke's Bay. But George's engineering days were not totally behind him, and he shared his engineering expertise to help out the locals. Until 1909, he was also the postmaster, and the Graingers rose to prominence in the district. As was usual for the time, May's formal education at the local school finished at the age of 13, whereupon the next 10 years of her life were spent contributing

Violet May Cottrell, writer, birdwatcher and medium.

to the family farm. She clearly disliked this life of isolation and toil, and in her later writing of its effects on her mother's poor health we can see the social conscience typical of many Spiritualists.[147]

In around 1910 May made her escape, and five years later we find her in Napier, marrying Horace Spence Cottrell, who worked as a salesman in his father's china and fancy goods store. Her own work life then turned to the domestic front, with housework and, when two children arrived, mothercraft. But it appears that focusing on these alone was not completely fulfilling and May quickly discovered they could offer a springboard to deeper thought and from there an outlet for her literary ability. The subjects she chose were wide-ranging and largely reformist — health, marriage, religion, psychology, philosophy, economics, war (unsurprisingly, given the period) and the taboo topic of sex education.

The latter was deeply important to May, and she and Horace wrote a number of letters to English birth control advocate Marie Stopes, suggesting, rather bizarrely, that the unconscious mind had the potential to sterilise semen before it reached the womb. Again, we see the familiar pattern of the Spiritualist woman as self-taught intellectual.[148]

In the interwar period it was not uncommon for women to suffer from what were then euphemistically described as 'nervous disorders', and which we would recognise today as depression. This was hardly surprising given the huge burden of grief the country bore over the menfolk they had lost in the Great War, followed by the carnage wrought by the 1918 Spanish flu epidemic, which in turn gave way to increasing economic hardship, culminating in the Great Depression. And May was no exception, throughout the 1920s and 1930s suffering from poor mental health.

Around this time she began receiving psychic messages from Norcliffe, her spirit guide Zonia of the Stars (supposedly a philosopher from Arabia in the age of the Pharaohs), Doyle and others. Apparently influenced by the American New Thought movement, she became convinced of the power of the subconscious over the human body, eternal life beyond death, and the destined triumph of good over evil. Many of these channellings were published in *The Harbinger of Light*, which is where Doyle seems to have originally become aware of her.[149]

Among the many articles and obituaries circulating worldwide immediately following Doyle's departure from the mortal realm was a piece in the *Daily Express* claiming that the author and his wife had established a secret code by which means whomever of them died first would attempt to signal the other. This was to be the definitive proof of existence beyond the grave and their way of filtering out fraudulent communications by mediums. No such code, however, played a part in the communications received by May Cottrell, as animatedly reported by Napier's *Daily Telegraph* on 10 July 1930: 'Sir Conan Doyle Speaks to Napier Medium. Mrs H. S. Cottrell [her husband's name, in the formal manner of the time] Receives Message'.

When she was interviewed, May described the medium as a 'human wireless set', and reported that through her Doyle had described his sadness at leaving his friends and family, saying that he was trying to adjust to his new existence, and that he was glad to see his son again.[150] Three days later the same paper reported grumbles and misgivings from Dunedin's Spiritualist community, which called for close investigation of May and her spiritual communications, evidently miffed that the dead author had not chosen to call upon them first.[151]

The announcement of the Doyle message set off a flurry of interest in Spiritualism in Napier, or at least in the Napier *Daily Telegraph* — one wonders what the resident magicians of nearby Havelock North made of it. The newspaper ran a series of interviews with May Cottrell from 11 July. In the 12 July edition of the paper, she said she had discovered her power as a medium when she was experimenting with her sister-in-law, suspending a ring on a thread in the top part of a half-filled glass of water. They would ask the ring a question, and interpret the way it tapped the side of the glass by simple alphabetic code.

They started with simple, general questions, which eventually gave way to communications with acquaintances who had died in the Spanish influenza epidemic a few years before. Among these were May's parents, and the manner of their passing is rather telling about the context for her path to Spritualism in the context of her depression and mental health:

> My father, knowing this — for our loved ones on the other side do know what is happening to us here — most earnestly desired

to help me back to health and happiness. Both he and my mother have written through me many times since then and have succeeded in removing much of the old bitterness from my heart. Their love and understanding have helped me over many difficult places, and the teaching I have received from my spirit guides has completely changed my attitude towards life.[152]

Aside from these unconventional activities, May and her husband were passionate members of the New Zealand Native Bird Protection Society — a forebear of the modern Forest & Bird — and made a thorough study of the gannet population of Cape Kidnappers Te Kauwae-a-Māui. This they developed into a lecture, complete with hand-coloured magic-lantern slides by Horace, which toured the country at the invitation of the American Chautauqua Association — an adult education and social movement of the time — in 1923.

Horace encouraged May to write, and marketed her articles and stories to publications. She was a prolific poet; her verses on topics pertinent to the homemaker with a feminist viewpoint readily found a place in women's magazines. One, 'Pania of the Reef: A Maori Legend', which appeared in a 1930 issue of the British shipping and sea travel magazine *Blue Peter*, was a retelling of the legend of Pania of the sea people, and her ill-fated romance with a mortal. The influence of Longfellow's 'Hiawatha' is palpable:

> Pania, beautiful sea maiden,
> Coming from dark depths mysterious,
> From the ocean's strange, weird caverns,
> Dwelt alone upon the shore.
>
> Well she loved the golden sunlight,
> Glinting, flashing on the waters;
> Gloried in the noontide splendour
> And the rosy glow of sunsets . . .[153]

At the time the story wasn't widely known outside of the Ngāti Kahungunu iwi, but May's poem took root and popularised the legend locally to such an extent that eventually, in 1954, a bronze statue, *Pania of the Reef*, was unveiled on the waterfront and quickly became an iconic symbol for Napier.[154]

Shortly after publication of the poem, the Cottrells lost the china store in the devastating earthquake that struck Hawke's Bay in 1931. Horace took a writing job with Napier's *Daily Telegraph*, and then work as an agent of the Land and Income Tax Department in Wellington. Later, May would herself enter the paid workforce, finding employment with the Rehabilitation Board during the war years. This meant she had to step back from writing, although she did join the New Zealand Women Writers' and Artists' Society in 1939.

That was not the only toll the war took, though. In 1942 tragedy struck when the Cottrells' son, Spence, was killed while on active service as a bomber pilot with the Royal New Zealand Air Force. After the war, all reference to Spiritualism in May's writings stops.

After the Cottrells returned to Napier in 1947, the poems, radio plays and articles on Aotearoa's scenic attractions, birdlife and Māori once more flowed from May's pen. She was particularly inspired by Napier's phoenix-like resurrection from the rubble as a futuristic town of Art Deco buildings. Horace died at Napier in 1960, and May followed him to the spirit lands just over a decade later.[155]

‡

Compared to Dunedin, Christchurch was relatively conservative and far less diverse in philosophical outlook in the nineteenth and early twentieth centuries, although it is a place rich in ghosts on the maddeningly flat plains, and where dark energies can be stirred up by the nor'wester and the dynamo of the River Avon.

We know quite a lot about Spiritualist goings-on in the circumbellum Christchurch of the 1930s and 1940s thanks to a scrapbook in the collection of the Macmillan Brown Library at Canterbury University, put together by the Psychic Research Society of Christchurch, which was established by Edgar Lovell-Smith (1875–1950) in 1940 to investigate Spiritualist and psychic phenomena.

Born to a prominent Christchurch family, Edgar was the son of lithographer and printer William Sydney Lovell-Smith, and brother/brother-in-law of the well-known artist spouses Colin and Rita Lovell-Smith and entrepreneur and community organiser Kitty Lovell-Smith. The family of feminists, Fabians and philanthropists lived in Upper Riccarton; Edgar attended Riccarton School and later the Canterbury School of Art, supporting himself as a lithographer at his father's firm, Smith and Anthony.

In 1920 Lovell-Smith retired in order to concentrate on his passion for early coaching. This led to him purchasing, restoring and using a Cobb & Co coach, which was presented in around 1930 to Canterbury Museum, where it forms part of the Colonial Street display.[156] In the mid-1930s he left the Anglican Church for the Christian Spiritualist Church.

The Christchurch Society for Psychical Research was set up as a counterpart to the one in Wellington, and both groups shared members. Outside of Lovell-Smith we know little of the other members save from the appearance of their names in the minutes recorded in the scrapbook: Violet Barker of Sumner, who was a regular participant in the séances held at the Society's 27 Chancery Lane premises; the medium Lily Hope; Stanley Edlin and his wife, who operated a photography studio and experimented with spirit photography; a Mr O'Brien, who organised a visit to Tīmaru to spread the Spiritualist message; and husband and wife Cecil and Jessie Eyles. Cecil was a member of the Canterbury Society of Arts, and there may well have been an overlap between the group and Christchurch's vibrant bohemian art community of the time.[157]

It seems unlikely, for example, that such a group would be as gauche as Mr S. Oldfield, president of the Quest Club of Auckland's Psychic Institute, who in 1935 wrote a letter of complaint to the editor of the *Auckland Star* about the depiction of Spiritualism in a production of Noel Coward's *Weatherwise* by the boys of Mount Albert Grammar School.[158]

The Christchurch scrapbook itself consists of names and addresses where séances were held or sites of paranormal activity (the suburb of Linwood, for some reason, seems to have been particularly rich in such manifestations), and newspaper clippings and transcribed articles from around New Zealand going back as far as 1876. The scrapbook begins with The Archer Insurance Policy Case, in which the Society tracked down a Linwood family whose deceased son had reportedly communicated about

The scrapbook of the Christchurch Psychical Research Society Inc.

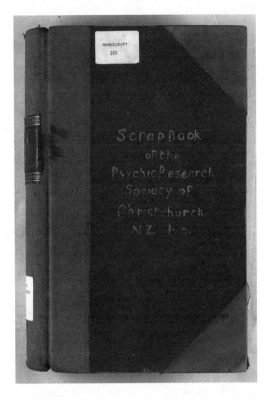

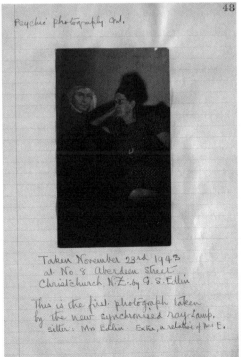

his unclaimed life insurance policy which had been hidden for safekeeping in their garden shed. Letters were sent to insurance companies in New Zealand, Australia and the United Kingdom to no avail, and Lovell-Smith included a sketch of the shed in the scrapbook.[159]

Another page in the scrapbook records a report that Prime Minister Richard Seddon was communicating from the other side, 'he being dead, yet speaketh'.[160] Other pages attest to the understandable influence of the aftermath of the Second World War, with a clipping about British spirit photographer Ada Deane, whose photographs of the Armistice Day service at the Whitehall Cenotaph, London, on Armistice Day, 11 November 1923, supposedly captured the faces of dead soldiers floating in an ectoplasmic cloud merged with the crowds. (In reality, they look more like faces shoddily cut from photographs and superimposed in the dark room.)[161] Dean's spirit photographs are housed in the British Library.[162]

Like that of the vast majority of Spiritualists of the period, the society's work was framed in a Christian worldview. An anonymous note in the scrapbook warns that those who wish to contact the dead 'should start with a prayer through Christ for protection and guidance . . . if it is His will'.[163] The Chancery Lane séances presumably began in this way, and one of these evenings in 1937 was recorded for the *Psychic News* by one of the society's members, Norah Foster, a clipping of which is preserved in the scrapbook.[164]

During the event, the medium, Lily Hope, materialised the spirits of an educated nun by the name of Sister Monica and a Native American girl, Sunrise. The chamber was in darkness except for a single dim red light, and Hope was sewn into a chair with lengths of sateen ribbon (a measure against fraud) in her 'cabinet', which consisted of curtains held up by safety pins in a corner of the room. The walls and ceiling were covered in black cloth. The attendees sat in a circle, and, after singing some verses of 'Abide with Me' and reciting the Lord's Prayer, two voices were heard in the darkness.

The voices requested that the safety pins be undone, and that the singing continue. A Mrs Eddles, who was assisting, undid the pins and noted that, while Hope was warm, her hands were cold. This might suggest that artificial decoy hands had been substituted in the restraints, leaving the medium's hands free — an old trick of the game. Once the curtains were re-pinned, the group began singing a hymn, and two entities made themselves known.

Sunrise merely spoke, while Sister Monica materialised fully and submitted to a request to show her feet. This was considered significant, as Hope had had part of a toe amputated whereas the phantom nun's feet were both seen to be entire and intact. Foster, who had seen Sister Monica materialised in Wellington, described her as having 'a beautiful, cultured voice, sweet facial expression'.

At another point in the séance two carnations fell from the ceiling, apparently a speciality of Sunrise. At the end of the session Hope was freed from her confines, and her feet were found to be strapped in a crossed position whereas they had originally been strapped straight. This would suggest either that a spirit had moved Hope's feet without breaking the ribbons, or — to the more sceptically inclined — that the medium had been at large during the performance.[165]

☦

Spiritualism continued to play an important, though less visible, role in shaping the culture. Mary Manson Dreaver (1887–1961) — journalist, Labour Party activist, Auckland City Councillor (1938–44), MP for Waitematā (1941–43), and member of the now-defunct upper-house Legislative Council of the government, the only woman to hold that position (1946–50) — was a minister at a Spiritualist church in Alma Street, Newmarket, in Auckland, and president of the Spiritualist Church of New Zealand.[166] Another prominent post-war Spiritualist and medium was Beatrice Swaby (1905–?), who was attached to the Petone Spiritualist church,[167] which was a potent force in New Zealand Spiritualism well into the 1980s, when it was presided over by Mary and Warwick Fry.

Warwick officiated and Mary was the clairvoyant, with Mary rising to public attention with her twice-monthly call-back show on Wellington's 2ZB, which ran from 1983 to 1985 until multiple wowsers called the station's integrity into question and the show was discontinued.[168]

Throughout the 1980s, census data shows a continuous growth in people identifying Spiritualist churches as their religion.[169] Today there are Spiritualist churches in Christchurch, Hastings, Paraparaumu, Nelson, Petone, Auckland, Napier and Wellington, with individual practitioners and healers around the country. The national church is known as Spiritualism New Zealand, as earnest, sober and respectable an organisation as one could hope for, complete with a board, a constitution and a code of ethics.

As a volunteer-run organisation it has no central headquarters, but like other nonconformist churches its ministers are recognised as marriage celebrants, and as such are able to officiate at weddings and funerals, although technically anyone can officiate at a funeral.[170]

Spiritualism New Zealand, with its focus on healing, personal responsibility, karma and universal brotherhood, is an earnest force for good in the world. The nadir of the Spiritualism phenomenon in Aotearoa, however, is very likely the Australian–New Zealand television co-production *Sensing Murder*, which screened on TVNZ's TV2 from 2006 to 2018. Hosted by Levin-born, Australian-based actor Rebecca Gibney until 2017, and thereafter by New Zealand actor Amanda Billing, the format consisted of sending three professed psychics to a New Zealand location associated with an unsolved murder armed only with a photograph of the victim, and incorporated dramatic re-enactments of the events surrounding the crimes.

The programme's producers made the claim that they tested around 70 psychics and mediums in Australasia with a solved case prior to each season, the most accurate being shortlisted for the show's roster. This claim was reiterated with each episode. The three most often chosen were the Australian Deb Webber and New Zealanders Sue Nicholson and Kelvin Cruickshank.

In its run, *Sensing Murder* accumulated significant criticism for playing on the hopes of vulnerable people, with the New Zealand Police clarifying that 'spiritual communications were not considered a creditable foundation for investigation'.[171] In a 2007 episode of the media and current events satire show *Eating Media Lunch*, the programme was ruthlessly mocked in a section called 'Sensing Bullshit' that centred on Australian TV Channel 7 video footage of Webber talking about a sceptical journalist's completely fictitious sister.[172] TVNZ was heavily criticised for cross-promoting *Sensing Murder* on its *Breakfast* programme with ambiguous claims about missing toddler Aisling Symes.[173]

In 2012 the New Zealand Police found the body of Jane Furlong at a beach in Port Waikato. In 2007, *Sensing Murder* had claimed that her body was either in the Auckland Domain or at a demolition site.[174] Despite all this, somehow in 2006 the programme managed to win Qantas Media Awards for Best Director, Non-Drama, and Best Reality Format, and in 2008 Best Format-Reality Series, which is probably the only otherworldly mystery in the whole proceedings. No crime has ever been solved with *Sensing Murder*'s assistance.

Chapter 8.

The women of the Beast

The name written on her forehead was a mystery: BABYLON THE GREAT, THE MOTHER OF PROSTITUTES AND OF THE ABOMINATIONS OF THE EARTH.

— REVELATION 17:5

Aleister Crowley (1875–1947) is the most infamous name in British occultism, a pioneering ceremonial magician, a poet, painter, novelist of questionable quality, mountaineer, and prolific author of magickal writings — he added the 'k' to 'magick' to distinguish it from illusionists and stage magicians. Crowley had a connection to Aotearoa of sorts: his great-great-grandfather, Abraham Crowley (1795–1864), had been one of the first and most enthusiastic emigration agents for the New Zealand Company, responsible for promoting the British settlement of much of the country.[1]

Born into the wealthy bosom of an upper-middle-class family of pious Plymouth Brethren in Royal Leamington Spa in Warwickshire, the younger Crowley liked to joke that, appalled by his mischievous tendentiousness, his mother declared him 'the Great Beast' of the Book of Revelations. Crowley was educated at Trinity, Cambridge, where it is claimed by some that he was recruited by British intelligence. In 1898 he joined the Golden Dawn and was trained by Samuel Liddell MacGregor Mathers. Thereafter he lived a peripatetic life, basing himself variously at Boleskine House on the shores of Loch Ness, the mountains of Mexico, and India to study the religions of the East. He had an independent income from an inheritance and a remarkable knack for getting people to give him money.

In March 1899, while on honeymoon in Cairo, his wife Rose, following an invocation of Thoth, Egyptian god of wisdom, went into a trance during which a momentous message was delivered. Rose — one of the many 'Scarlet Women' who would embody goddess sexuality in Crowley's life — told her husband that 'They were waiting' for him, and that he should write down everything that happened over the following three days.[2]

So when a being named Aiwass, a messenger of Horus, began to speak to him, dictated through Rose as medium, Crowley duly transcribed the utterances. The result was *Liber AL vel Legis*, or *The Book of the Law*, which he self-published in 1909.[3] Aiwass told Crowley to redirect his efforts from ceremonial magick to sexual magick, and the sacred marriage between the feminine principle (animus, love, the Egyptian goddess Nuit as a kind of oversoul, and her emissary, the Scarlet Woman) with the masculine (anima, life, the Egyptian god Hadit, and his emissary, the Beast).[4]

From this beginning, Crowley founded the occult philosophy of

Aleister Crowley, magician, writer, artist, mountaineer and co-founder of Argenteum Astrum, in Golden Dawn regalia.

Thelema (Koine Greek for 'will') to guide twentieth-century humankind into the 'Æon of Horus', often summed up by its core injunction: 'Do as thou wilt be the whole of the law. Love is the Law, love under will. There is no law beyond Do what thou wilt.'[5]

Three years later he and British chemist and occultist George Cecil Jones (1873–1960) co-founded an esoteric order of the Argenteum Astrum (A∴A∴, though in Crowley's system this stands for multiple things in various languages), through which they developed and spread the teachings of Thelema. Following a stint in Algeria, in 1912 Crowley was initiated into the German-based Ordo Templi Orientis (OTO, see also Chapter 12), eventually to become the leader of the British branch. Bringing this part of the OTO into line with Thelema, he established his own branches around the Anglosphere.

Rose, spiralling into alcoholic dementia, divorced Crowley around 1910. Crowley committed her to a mental asylum in 1911, and then rode out the First World War in the United States, campaigning for Germany, although it later transpired that he had infiltrated the pro-German faction in the United States on behalf of British intelligence. In 1920 he and his followers established the Abbey of Thelema, a commune of his inner circle of followers, in Cefalù, Sicily. It was named after the indulgently debauched establishment that features in François Rabelais' picaresque sixteenth-century novel *The Life of Gargantua and of Pantagruel*, Rabelais himself being a monk, free-thinker and libertine.

The residents of Thelema included Raoul Loveday, a 23-year-old Oxford undergraduate who died suddenly while there; Loveday's wife and elder by six years, the singer, dancer and model Betty May Loveday; the Swiss-American Leah Hirsig, for a time Crowley's Scarlet Woman; acolyte Jane Wolfe; and assorted others at various times.

Reports of polygamy, arcane rituals and general squalor scandalised readers of the British newspapers, their chief source being a distraught Betty May, who had been sending letters to the newspapers even before Loveday's death; in fact, since their arrival at the abbey in the autumn of 1922. Mussolini's regime stepped in and put an end to the abbey when it evicted the household in April 1923, somewhat ironic given Il Duce's tolerance for the capers of playwright, poet, womaniser, decadent and political agitator Gabriele D'Annunzio, who held sway over an equally (albeit unmagickally) debauched fiefdom, the so-called 'free state' of Fiume (1920–24) in what is now Croatia. Speaking of the recently dead D'Annunzio in 1938, Mussolini is alleged to have said, 'When you have a rotten tooth you have two possibilities open to you: either you pull the tooth, or you fill it with gold. With D'Annunzio it was always easier to fill him with gold.'[6] Apparently, with Crowley it was less effort to pull him out.

For the rest of his life Crowley moved between Germany, France and England, promoting the Thelema faith and guiding humanity into the Æon of Horus. He died, penniless, of chronic bronchitis aggravated by pleurisy, in a boarding house his friends had found for him in Hastings, Sussex, in 1947.[7]

Much of Crowley's notoriety came from his reputation for bisexuality, insatiable libidinousness and propensity for narcotics. While indubitably a colossal egoist of the first water, he was far from the pantomime villain the popular media has tried to tar him as being. Crowley never visited Aotearoa, aside from the local presence of OTO (addressed in Chapter 12), but he does have several connections to this archipelago through four women who are in one way or another associated with him.

☥

To begin with, we should dispel one insidious myth. Leila Ida Nerissa Bathurst Waddell (1880–1932) — renamed the more propitious 'Laylah' (by means of gematria, the Kabbalic art of assigning letters numerological equivalents) by Crowley — was a talented violinist, author and occultist, and Crowley's muse and mistress in the 1910s. For Crowley she was the 'Divine Whore', 'Mother of Heaven', 'Sister Cybele', 'Scarlet Woman' and 'Whore of Babalon' (Crowley's gematrical spelling) — the embodiment of the anima and female sexuality.

Waddell was born in Bathurst, New South Wales, and began her musical career as a violin teacher at schools in the area until ambition took her to Britain. In 1906 she attracted the attention of the composer and impresario Henry Hayward (1865–1945), who recruited her for The Brescians, an Anglo-Italian cinema orchestra that worked for T. J. West and his West

Leila Waddell, violinist, 'Divine Whore', 'Mother of Heaven' and 'Scarlet Woman'.

Pictures in New Zealand. With The Brescians she performed Charles Flavell Hayward's 'Grand Concert Duet (Olde Englande) on English Airs, for Two Violins' and Francesco Paolo Tosti's 'Beauty's Eyes'.[8]

She remained with The Brescians until 1908, after which she departed for England to study with the internationally renowned violin teacher Émile Sauret (1852–1920). She performed in a gypsy band at Daly's London Theatre, and it was in London that she met Crowley. He immediately fell in love with her, and Waddell took the ritual role of Crowley's Scarlet Woman, and lover, for seven years. Her violin playing was an important part of Crowley's publicly attended series of 'Rites of Eleusis' — entrance fee, the exorbitant sum of £5 5s a head in old money — in late 1910.[9] Details of the first performance of these astrologically based A∴A∴ events even found their way to Aotearoa, appearing in the *Hawera and Normanby Star* alongside a recipe for scones on 15 December 1910:

> STRANGE RITES PERFORMED IN SEMI-DARKNESS. Harmless eccentricity is the chief quality to be found in 'The Rites of Eleusis,' the first of which was performed at the Caxton Hall in London some six weeks ago. One is told that Mr Aleister Crowley, who presides over these rites, has invented a new religion, and that his idea is to plant Eastern transcendentalism in English soil under the guise of ceremonial magic. And if one may judge by the first act of the Rite of Saturn, Mr Crowley's sole claim to originality is the belief that what would merely be yawned at in the light becomes impressive in darkness or semi-darkness. And perhaps even that error has been made before. An atmosphere heavily charged with incense, some cheap stage effects, an infinity of poor reciting of good poetry, and some violin playing and dancing are the ingredients of the rite. There is nothing to give offence to the most sensitive. The Mother of Heaven [Waddell], who plays the fiddle with considerable technical skill but no inspiration, is probably not intended to represent any figure in other religions. Some of the poetry, such as passages from Swinburne, is mildly erotic, but, rendered in a sing-song voice, with little expression, was void of passion. Positively the only relief in a dreary performance was afforded by a neophyte falling off his

stool: which caused mild hilarity among a bored and uncomfortable audience, most of whom were perched on small wooden stools a foot from the floor. Mr Crowley says that the end and aim of his rites is ecstasy. Somebody ought to tell him that ecstasy of any kind is impossible when your foot has gone to sleep.[10]

In 1913, Waddell became Grand Secretary General of the M∴M∴M∴ (Mysteria Mystica Maxima), the British section for first-degree initiates of the OTO, and shortly thereafter decamped with Crowley to New York to wait out the Great War. While touring US cities, she played lunchtime concerts in factories, organised by the YMCA. The venues were barns, sheds and gardens, and the audiences were mostly male migrant workers. The men sang along with the arias and would give her posies of wildflowers. She loved this experience and considered it the greatest work of her career.

Already a seasoned writer, Waddell came to wider notice with 'Two Anzacs Meet in London', her memoir of her acquaintance with the author Katherine Mansfield, published in New York's *Shadowland* magazine in 1923 shortly after Mansfield's death.[11] Details are murky, but it seems this led to contracts for a novel and a book of short stories with a London publisher. Crowley, meanwhile, had set up his abbey in Sicily with his new consecrated Scarlet Woman Leah Hirsig, whom Crowley called his 'Ape of Thoth'.

It was time to move on. In the year the Mansfield piece was published, Waddell returned to Sydney to take care of her ailing elderly father, supporting herself by performing with various orchestras and teaching. At the time of her death in 1932 she was teaching violin at the Convent School of the Sacred Heart in Sydney's Elizabeth Bay.[12]

In his 2008 book *Notorious Australians: The Mad, the Bad and the Dangerous*, Toby Creswell picks up on a popular story that Waddell was part-Māori,[13] something also mentioned by Richard Kaczynski in his 2010 biography of Crowley, *Perdurabo: The Life of Aleister Crowley*.[14] The origin of the claim seems traceable to Francis King's 1977 *The Magical World of Aleister Crowley*.[15] Looking at photographs of her, her particular dark beauty might indeed pass for wahine Māori, but there is no evidence for this, and the record of the New South Wales Office of Births, Deaths and Marriages shows that her paternal grandparents came from Coventry and Fort William, Inverness, and that her paternal grandparents both came from Monaghan in Ireland. That isn't to say it's impossible — Māori were great travellers in the nineteenth century — it's just astronomically unlikely.

‡

Marguerite Frieda Harris, Lady Harris (née Bloxam, 1877–1962) — who went, at her own preference, by the technically incorrect but assertive Lady Frieda Harris — was the daughter of John Astley Bloxam, FRCS, a no-nonsense consulting surgeon at Charing Cross Hospital in London and a former British Army surgeon. In 1901 she married Englishman Percy Harris (1876–1952), who came from a wealthy Jewish business family, but one with roots in Aotearoa, as we shall see. This provides her chief connection to Aotearoa.

Frieda's schooling had been rather unorthodox for a young Victorian lady. She had been sent to what was presented as a traditional girls' boarding school in Bourne End in Buckinghamshire, presided over by an American, Alice Marie Davis. Davis was the mother of Rosamond Lehmann, whose novels with their gay and lesbian themes scandalised England in the 1920s, 1930s and 1940s. Lehmann was still writing in the 1970s and 1980s, but by then the English were far less shockable. Davis's husband, Rudy Lehmann, was a Liberal MP, a barrister, the editor of *Punch*, a rowing enthusiast and a Spiritualist.[16] It is presumably here that Frieda first became acquainted with occult matters.

Although lacking a formal higher education after school, Frieda was a voracious autodidact, devouring books on a wide gamut of subjects, including art, mysticism and various esoteric spiritualities and alternative philosophies. Frieda was deeply interested in Anthroposophy and was also a Co-Mason (a special role open to women), designing a set of tracing boards for the Craft degrees of Entered Apprentice (1°), Fellowcraft (2°) and Master Mason (3°).[17] Through her mother's 'sentimental reading' of *The Light of Asia* — Sir Edwin Arnold's verse translation of the *Lalitavistara Sūtra*, which details the Buddha's journey to enlightenment

— Frieda had an early introduction to Buddhism.[18] She also dabbled in Christian Science,[19] and was friends with fellow mystic creatives: surrealist painter-poet Ithell Colquhoun (1906–1988); artist, illustrator and writer Maxwell Armfield (1881–1972); and poet George Russell (1867–1935, better known by his nom-de-plume 'Æ', short for 'Æon').[20]

In this highly artistic circle Frieda taught herself to draw and paint. Her intellect appealed to her future husband, Percy: 'We exchanged books . . .' In 1947, Percy wrote of their relationship: 'We also discussed every kind of subject from political economy to the newest form of poetry or play.'[21] They had two children together, Jack (1906–2009) and Thomas (1908–?).

Percy Harris's father, Wolf or Woolf Harris (1833–1926), the son of a rabbi, had emigrated in the 1850s from Poland to Dunedin, where he established a trading company with another Jewish immigrant, Adolf Bing, importing mining supplies during the heady goldrush years. That trading company went on to become the clothing import–export company Harris, Bing & Co, a major player in the local and national economy. Frieda and Percy's elder son, Jack, migrated to New Zealand in 1926 to take charge of the business. Peppered among the largely pastoral pre-goldrush Scots Presbyterians of Dunedin, there were only five Jewish families: Harris, Casper, Nathan, Fogel and Bing.

As the economy boomed, many more families came to join them, and a synagogue was built on Moray Place in 1868 to house the southernmost Jewish congregation in the world. These Jewish immigrants became prominent in Dunedin business and society, and included well-known names such as Maurice Joel (1829–1907), Abraham Solomon (1835–1900), Bendix Hallenstein (1835–1905), the Theomin family, and the noted politician and future premier Sir Julius Vogel (1835–1899).

Woolf Harris married Elizabeth Nathan, the daughter of a prominent Christchurch businessman, Hyam Nathan (b.1862). Through his business connections in Britain, Woolf became friendly with the Porter family, whose daughter Jessie would marry John Bloxam — Frieda's parents. The families socialised at gatherings in London when the Harrises were there on business and visiting their son, and Percy and Frieda ultimately began courting.[22] Frieda and Percy had likely met through the Lehmanns already.[23]

There was little impediment to a union. Frieda's father was an atheist and didn't have the usual prejudices about Percy's Jewish heritage, and Percy was every inch an assimilated English gentleman. In his 2007 memoir, their son Jack wrote that his father 'always felt he was English not Jewish'.[24] The pair married on 2 April 1901.

☦

The Harrises spent their first two years of married life in New Zealand, where Percy worked in the family business. On their return to Britain, Percy entered politics, as a candidate for the Liberal Party.[25] It was not at all uncommon at the time for New Zealanders to enter British politics, as they were themselves British citizens. He was first elected to Parliament in May 1918 in the seat of Harborough in Leicestershire, and when he was made a baronet in 1932, Frieda adopted the honorific.

Frieda's family always believed her to have psychic gifts. For example, when, in 1926, her son Jack (later Sir Jack Harris) returned to Aotearoa to take up his grandfather's business, just as he was boarding ship his mother gestured to a young woman in the group ahead of him, and said, 'That girl is your future wife.' And so it came to pass.[26]

Frieda Harris is mainly known to posterity as the artist who illustrated Crowley's Thelemic tarot deck, *The Book of Thoth*. Crowley had only intended to devote six months to bringing the imagery and symbolism of the tarot into line with his magickal system, but he procrastinated and there were financial and production issues, along with personality clashes, so that even with Harris managing the project, coaxing and prodding Crowley along, it ended up taking five years, from 1938 to 1943. Both had died before the OTO published the first deck in 1969. The overhaul — drawing heavily on the traditional Marseilles tarot in a conscious rejection of the Rider–Waite–Smith version — was extensive: the trumps were renamed, the symbolism revised, and the sequence reordered.[27]

Harris largely got the job by chance. In 1937 Crowley had asked his friend, the playwright Clifford Bax (1886–1962), to find him an artist who could illustrate the new deck. The first two artists Bax invited failed to attend the appointment at the Royal Automobile Club. So when Bax sent along Harris, then a woman of 60, and Crowley asked her to take on the project, it would be fair to say the invitation was made partly out of frustration. But he was also impressed by her occult knowledge and psychically sensitive presence. She brought her own interest in Anthroposophy to the project — the latter evident in her designs, which owe much to the projective synthetic geometry favoured by Rudolf Steiner[28] — and she also contributed many of her own insights, which are recorded in letters she and Crowley wrote to each other.[29]

Harris went on to provide the artwork for several of Crowley's books, including *Little Essays Toward Truth* (1938), *Thumbs Up!* (1941), *Olla: An Anthology of Sixty Years of Song* (1946), *The Last Ritual* (1948) and *Liber Aleph: The Book of Wisdom or Folly* (1962); this last, although it had gone to press at the time of Crowley's death in 1947, was not published for another 15 years.[30] Harris preferred to remain anonymous, not wishing to receive special treatment because of her status, and worked under the pseudonym 'Jesus Chutney'.[31]

Harris and Crowley often worked together at the home of a mutual friend, the London socialite Greta Valentine, and Crowley eventually initiated Harris into the A∴A∴, where she took the magickal motto Tzaba, Hebrew for both 'painter' and 'hosts' or 'armies'. In Crowley's gematria this adds up to 93, representing the Thelemic value of its core philosophical values: 'Do as thou wilt be the whole of the Law' and 'Love is the law, love under will.'[32] Crowley also initiated Harris into the OTO directly at rank of IV°, recognising her Co-Masonry degrees.[33]

Prone to prodigality, Crowley was living well above his means, and Harris provided him a stipend while also using her society connections to attract backers. On 29 May 1942, Crowley wrote to a Mr Pearson, the photoengraver of the Thoth deck: 'I should like to emphasise that I am absolutely devoted to Lady Harris, and have the evidence of countless acts of kindness on her part, indicating that her feelings toward me are similar.'[34] He paid tribute to her in the introduction to *The Book of Thoth* with the obligatory phallic allusion:

> She devoted her genius to the Work. With incredible rapidity she picked up the rhythm, and with inexhaustible patience submitted

to the correction of the fanatical slave-driver that she had invoked, often painting the same card as many as eight times until it measured up to his Vanadium Steel yardstick![35]

For her part Harris relished working with Crowley, but that's not to say that she didn't, from time to time, stand up to the 'fanatical slave-driver' when she felt the need. When Crowley suggested in a letter that she should imitate the artist Aubrey Beardsley in her design, she wrote back: 'Know what you *won't* do shall be the whole of my Law! . . . I can bear many things, chilblains included, but I will *not* draw a lady like Aubrey Beardsley.'[36] The two remained close until the Great Beast drew his last breath. There is a surviving portrait of Crowley on his deathbed, sketched in pencil by Harris's hand.

When Percy Harris died in 1952, Frieda Harris moved to India to study Hinduism and Buddhism at the invitation of the Indian dancer Ram Gopal, whom she had met when he brought his ballet company to England in 1951. She remained in India for the rest of her life, dying on her houseboat in Srinagar on 11 May 1962.

☦

In his 2017 book *Hard Frost: Structures of Feeling in New Zealand Literature, 1908–1945*, John Newton opines that Aotearoa's emerging blokey, patriarchal modernism of the 1930s and 1940s was unnerved by the symbolist and psychological element in the work of Katherine Mansfield (1888–1923). Battened on Auden and pragmatic Protestant materialism, literary gatekeepers like Frank Sargeson couldn't see a place for Mansfield in the New Zealand canon. Newton writes: 'In contriving to forget Mansfield, the nationalist generation deny themselves access to another new world, the "twilit jungle" of modernist interiority with all that it offers in terms of complexity and psychological intelligence.'[37]

I would define it more in terms of Mansfield's mystical imagination, not that she would have seen herself in a New Zealand context anyway, despite being born and raised in Thorndon, Wellington. Her father, Harold Beauchamp, was the chairman of the Bank of New Zealand

and was knighted in 1923. Her maternal uncle Joseph Frank Dyer was married to Phoebe, the daughter of Premier Richard Seddon. Creativity was in Katherine's genealogy — her extended family included the author Countess Elizabeth von Arnim, and her great-great-uncle was Victorian genre painter Charles Robert Leslie.[38] In England Mansfield fell into the orbit of the Bloomsbury set and wrote marvellous short stories that took a scalpel to society. What interests us here, however, is Mansfield's pursuit of higher truths.

The Bloomsbury set and Crowley's circle brushed up against each other in London and Paris and shared ideas transmitted through the medium of then-burgeoning modernism. Virginia Woolf's 'vibrations' have mystical underpinnings; E. M. Forster had something of the mystic about him. Both Forster's and Lytton Strachey's fathers had been close friends of Edward Bulwer-Lytton, after whom Strachey was named. Crowley was bisexual, as were several of the Bloomsbury members, and both groups existed outside of polite society, shocking the mainstream and struggling with the residue of Victorian mores.

From 1911 to 1913, Mansfield's husband, John Middleton Murray (1889–1957), published the literary journal *Rhythm* with the mystico-spiritually inclined Michael T. H. Sadler — Sadler translated Kandinsky's *Concerning the Spiritual in Art* in 1914. Mansfield joined the journal with the fifth issue as assistant editor and was a major contributor.[39] Murray had first met Crowley through his Oxford friend Frederick Goodyear (1887–1917) around 1910. Goodyear's lead article for the first issue of *Rhythm* was titled 'The New Thelema', and articulated a utopian, free-thinking, anything-goes vision for humanity unencumbered by religion or conventional social morality. Although Goodyear's inspiration was Rabelais, some sort of connection with Crowley's Thelema seems likely, too.

For a 1912 issue of the journal, Mansfield reviewed *The Triumph of Pan* (1910) by Crowley's co-occultist and occasional lover, Victor Neuburg (1883–1940), admiring aspects of its poetic prose by eviscerating its 'perverted sensuality' and mysticism.[40] Another issue later that year contained a review by Wilfred William Gibson of Crowley's play *Mortadello, or The Angel of Venice: A Comedy*. Gibson was not impressed, describing it as 'an amazingly juvenile performance', and 'at its giddiest . . .

a dull, stupid affair'.[41] Already Mansfield and Crowley's social circles were brushing at their fringes.

They met that year at a Chelsea party hosted by their mutual friend Gwen Otter. Ida Baker, Mansfield's devoted confidante, recorded in her diary that Katherine was 'caught up briefly in an odd group of people . . . with an interest in the occult', naming Crowley, and noting that Mansfield was invited to an 'Evening' at which hashish was indulged in.[42] The poet Kathleen Jones imagines it thus in her book *Katherine Mansfield: The Story-Teller*: 'She smokes cannabis for the first time hoping for some kind of psychic revelation. Instead she gains insight into her own character. While others are in lotus-land she sits on the floor arranging matches into mathematical patterns.'[43]

This rose-tinted description is presumably based on Baker's second-hand account of the event, which described Mansfield as 'pink and paradisical' and 'arranging and rearranging with the greatest exactitude the matches from a box which she had in her hand, making patterns on the floor'.[44]

James Laver (1899–1975), author, critic and Keeper of Prints, Drawings and Paintings at the Victoria and Albert Museum, was at the event and recalled it this way:

> 'The stuff is beginning to work,' [Crowley] said. 'She's not going to be interesting; she's only going to sleep.'
> Katherine lay on the sofa and lit a cigarette. She threw the match on the floor and lay crookedly on the carpet. This caused her such acute distress that Gwen put it straight. 'That's much better,' said K.M. 'Pity that stuff had no effect.'[45]

Another account, of unclear origin and reliability, tells that, as she came down off her high, Mansfield hallucinated 'hundreds of parcels on shelves identically marked *Jesus Wept*'.[46] Her relationship with Crowley soured swiftly after that, and she would later describe him as 'a pretentious and very dirty fellow'.[47]

‡

Mansfield would eventually find her guru. The magnificently moustachioed George Gurdjieff (1866/1872/1877?–1949) was a Russian spiritual teacher of Caucasus Greek and Armenian descent, who, after a period travelling in the East, synthesised his philosophy of the 'Fourth Way'. He believed that most people existed in a state of disunified consciousness, flitting between fragmented versions of the self, moment to moment, in a kind of hypnotic waking sleep. His method for wakening the mind to a higher, unified consciousness and potential, 'the Work' (which perhaps inspired the Havelock Work), was derived from studying the spiritual practices of Eastern Orthodox monks, and Indian fakirs and yogis. The Fourth Way was later widely popularised through the writings of the Russian esoteric and author P. D. Ouspensky (1878–1947).[48]

Mansfield was introduced to Gurdjieff by the influential editor of the British magazine *The New Age*, A. R. Orage (1873–1934), who had published a number of Mansfield's stories.[49] It was Orage who had encouraged her to go to Gurdjieff's Institute in 1922, when the desperate Mansfield was seeking increasingly unorthodox treatment for her tuberculosis.[50] At the institute Mansfield was placed under the care of Olgivanna Lazovitch Hinzenburg (1898–1985), a Montenegrin disciple of Gurdjieff who later married the architect Frank Lloyd Wright, and spent most of her time with Orage, who was frequently in attendance on his master. Mansfield's final letters to Murray detail her adoption of some of Gurdjieff's teachings.[51]

Because she was a guest of the institute rather than a pupil, Mansfield was not required to undergo the rigorous ascetic routines of the students,[52] but the damp and draughty conditions at the institute's prieuré greatly aggravated her condition, and on 9 January 1923 she died of a pulmonary haemorrhage after running up a flight of stairs.[53] John Middleton Murray held Orage partly responsible for Mansfield's early death.

‡

Some might argue that including Rosaleen 'Roie' Norton (1917–1979), the 'Witch of King's Cross', is, perhaps, stretching the ambit, as she did not personally know Crowley and moved to Australia when she was a young child. Even so, her veneration of the god Pan and devotion to sex magick was heavily indebted to Crowley's writings, and her connection to Aotearoa is worth celebrating.

Norton was born in Dunedin to unexceptional English-immigrant Anglican parents — her father a captain in the merchant navy and a cousin of the composer Vaughan Williams, her mother a 'conventional, highly emotional woman, far too absorbed in her family'[54] — but she was a far from unexceptional child. She was born during a thunderstorm, and later in life she would claim that being born with pointed ears, blueish marks on her left knee and a hymenal tag marked her out as a witch from the beginning.[55] From age three she was drawing what she called 'nothing beasts' — animal-headed ghosts with tentacular arms.[56] As a five-year-old she once had a vision of a shining dragon beside her bed. This and other unusual events convinced her from an early age that another, spiritual word existed.[57]

The family moved to Sydney in 1925, settling in Lindfield, a rapidly developing bush-clad middle-class suburb of double-brick California bungalow and federation-style houses. Norton had a strained relationship with her parents in her teens — she lived in a tent in the garden for three years, and collected assorted animals as pets.[58] Increasingly alienated by the mainstream, around the age of 14 she was expelled from her Anglican girls' school because her drawings of witches, devils and vampires were thought disruptive.[59]

She then enrolled at East Sydney Technical College, where her artistic talents were encouraged by sculptor Rayner Hoff (1894–1937),[60] and where she began reading the writings of Éliphas Lévi, Dion Fortune, the Kabbalah, and especially Aleister Crowley.[61]

After leaving college, Norton supported herself with various menial jobs, marrying Beresford Lionel Conroy in 1940. They divorced in 1951 and Norton moved into an eccentric boarding house in Merangaroo.[62] To support herself she took on illustration work with the magazine *Pertinent*, which started in 1940 and was edited by the Welsh-born poet Leon Batt. Batt admired Norton's work greatly.[63] Buoyed by such encouragement, in 1943 Norton had a major exhibition with fellow artist Selina Muller.

In an article about the show in *Pix* pictorial magazine, Norton talked about her experiments with self-hypnosis and how she drew on her

Rosaleen Norton, artist and putative witch.

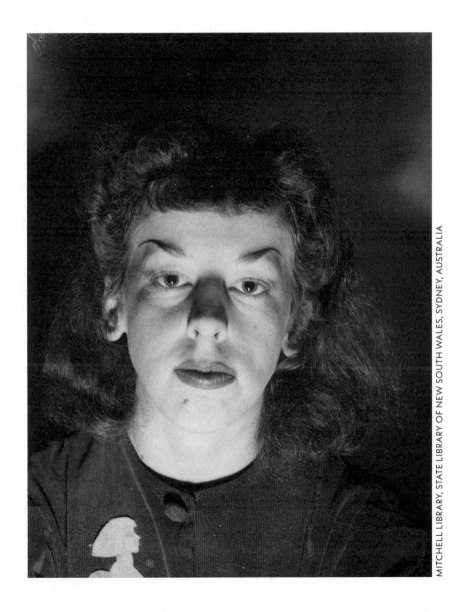

unconscious for material.[64] In style and content Norton's art strongly resembles English artist and magician Austin Osman Spare (1886–1956), who had briefly associated with Crowley before going on to found his own sigil-based system of Chaos magic.

While working at *Pertinent*, Norton met the younger poet Gavin Greenlees (1930–1983), and by mid-1949 they were looking for a venue in Melbourne for Norton to have another exhibition. Norton showed 46 paintings at the Rowden White Library at the University of Melbourne, but within two days of it opening the police came and removed three works, deemed obscene, and Norton was charged under the Police Offences Act 1928. Norton successfully won the case on the grounds that the paintings had already been published in a recent book that the Australian censors deemed acceptable.[65]

By now Norton and Greenlees were lovers, and they soon moved to louche King's Cross, notable for its bohemianism and red-light district.[66] Their eccentricities drew the attention of the Sydney police, and in September 1951 they were arrested on vagrancy charges — a technicality the authorities could level at anyone without steady employment whom they didn't like, irrespective of whether they had a fixed abode.

The publisher Walter Glover arrived as their white knight, employing the two full-time as assistants and releasing in 1952 a limited-edition book of *The Art of Rosaleen Norton*, in which Greenlees's poems were put to Norton's pictures.[67] The black-and-white drawings of provocatively nude goddesses and copulating demons proved too spicy for some, and the book was banned in the United States. A court order ruled that certain plates had to be blacked out if it was to be legally sold in New South Wales, gaining Norton's work much publicity, although bankrupting Glover.[68]

‡

In 1955, another New Zealander, whom we will discuss in greater detail in the following section, enters the picture: Anna Karina Hoffman. At the time Hoffman was an adolescent, struggling with mental health. She was arrested in Sydney for swearing at a police officer and charged, claiming at the trial that her problems were the result of attending a Satanic Black

Mass officiated by Norton. Norton, of course, rejected any idea that she was anything other than a pagan, and Hoffman later admitting to making the whole thing up. Nonetheless, the tabloids latched onto the fiction, gleefully labelling Norton a devil worshipper and 'the witch of King's Cross'.

Reacting to the public outcry, the police began a campaign of harassment against Norton. First, they took the proprietor of a Kashmir restaurant in King's Cross to court for displaying her paintings, and then they raided the flat she and Greenlees shared on the suspicion of their performing an 'unnatural sex act', the evidence for which was a photograph of Greenlees in costume posed thrashing Norton's naked buttocks. The photograph had been taken at Norton's birthday party, and subsequently stolen by Francis Honer and Raymond Ager, two members of Norton's circle, who intended to sell it to the Sydney *Sun* newspaper.[69] All of this, however, was nothing compared to the scandal to follow.

In 1947 the British classical composer and conductor Eugene Goossens (1893–1962) had arrived in Australia to take up the role of conductor for the Sydney Symphony Orchestra and the directorship of the New South Wales State Conservatorium of Music. He had an interest in the occult, particularly Crowley. Having seen a copy of *The Art of Rosaleen Norton*, the married composer wrote to the artist, and they met in the early 1950s, becoming lovers in a sort of informal *ménage à trois* with Greenlees.

Norton's relationship with Goossens was an intense one, and was recorded in a collection of erotically charged letters in which he variously called her 'Roie' and 'Roiewitch', and which he had urged her to destroy but which she had kept, hiding them behind a sofa. One of Goossens' letters reads:

> Contemplating your hermaphroditic organs in the picture nearly made me desert my evening's work and fly to you by first aerial coven. But, as promised, you came to me early this morning (about 1.45) and when a suddenly flapping window blind announced your arrival, I realised by a delicious orificial tingling that you were about to make your presence felt . . . I need your physical presence very much, for many reasons. We have many rituals and indulgences to undertake. And I want to take more photos.[70]

Rosaleen Norton, *Three Witches*, c.1951.

These letters were stolen from Norton's home in 1955 by Sydney *Sun* reporter Joe Morris, who had infiltrated her circle undercover. In March 1956, after returning from a trip to London, Goossens was detained by police at Sydney Airport, and was found to have tried to bring around 800 pornographic photographs, an explicit film and rubber masks into the country. Goossens was interviewed by the police a few days later and confronted with the evidence of his long-time affair with Norton. Rather than face an even greater humiliation, Goossens pled guilty to pornography charges under section 233 of the Customs Act. He was fined £100. His reputation utterly in tatters, he was forced to resign from his positions and returned, disgraced, to Britain.[71]

By this time Norton's relationship with Greenlees had fallen apart. Greenlees, not especially stable at the best of times, was admitted to the sandstone confines of Sydney's Callan Park Hospital with a mental breakdown in 1955, and diagnosed with schizophrenia two years later. Norton continued to visit him in hospital, taking him in during his temporary release to the community in 1964. Alas, this proved premature, and Gleenlees was soon readmitted to Callan Park following a psychotic knife attack on Norton. He was permanently discharged from institutional care in 1983, four years after Norton died.

Meanwhile the tabloid attention around Norton intensified and began to attract tourists to her home. In later years Norton became more reclusive, and in 1979 she entered the Sacred Heart Hospice for the Dying with colon cancer, saying, shortly before her death, 'I came into the world bravely; I'll go out bravely.'[72]

‡

Shortly after the 1955 incident and a stint in Sydney's infamous Long Bay prison, Anna Hoffman (1938–2014) was deported back to Aotearoa. Born Lorna Ann Jenks in Taumarunui, the 16-year-old had travelled to Sydney earlier that year as a stowaway on a ship. A stopover in Sydney was part of her grand plan for getting to Paris to study the violin, even though she didn't have a passport. According to the first volume of Hoffman's autobiography, *Tales of Anna Hoffman, Volume One* (2009)

— and almost everything in it needs to be taken with a generous pinch of sodium chloride — her impetus for fleeing Auckland had been witnessing Frederick Foster shoot his ex-girlfriend Sharon Skiffington in the face in Somervell's Milk Bar on Queen Street earlier that year.[73]

Hoffman's friend Vera Shrubsall, a member of the Auckland Operatic Society, furnished an introduction to her cousin, Eugene Goossens, which is how she ended up in Norton's circle. While studying at the Sydney Conservatory, supporting herself with café work and as an artist's model, she discovered Buddhism, Marxism (which didn't take), hashish, opium and witchcraft (which did).[74]

What Hoffman's circumstances actually entailed, at any point in her life, is not entirely clear from the biography. All three volumes of *Tales of Anna Hoffman* frustratingly metronome between the sensational and the demure. She says Norton sexually initiated her herself — not, Hoffman hastens to clarify, that she participated out of any lesbian inclination.[75] 'The seduction emanating from [Norton] was too powerful to resist,' she writes. 'I felt the shackles of convention slip away before this unfathomable woman... as she laid me on the fur cover before taking her appointed place. I plunged into the great void... As the red and black robed magician stepped forward... I caught a whiff of the unmistakable odour of goat.' And thus, like something out of a Hammer Horror, 'I became a Priestess in my own right.'[76]

There is little evidence that any of this, in fact, happened outside of Hoffman's febrile imagination. It's unclear whether she really even met Norton, and if she did, it seems unlikely they would have known each other very well. Hoffman had a propensity for embellishment and notoriety-seeking, retroactively positioning herself Zelig-like at every nefarious event, a practice that endured her entire life. In the 1960s and 1970s she was a somewhat eccentric habitué of Auckland's nocturnal demimonde, friends with everyone from Shanghai Lil pianist Billy Farnell to gossip columnist David Hartnell.

She claimed to have witnessed the 1963 Bassett Road machine-gun murders despite being in Australia at the time, and in 2012 she declared herself in possession of the skull of Australian bushranger legend Ned Kelly, supposedly given to her by a mysterious man in uniform at a dinner in Melbourne in 1980.[77]

For all that she always feyly signed herself off 'Best Witches', in terms of genuine occultism Hoffman was a manqué witch more than anything else.[78] It was yet another affectation to bolster her infamy in the goldfish bowl of Auckland, a performance, and to seed reports of her supposed magical activities in the pages of excitable tabloids. Hoffman and Farnell, for example, she claimed, kept goats which they milked at midnight in Grafton Gully, attracting the attention of the police.

At this time, prior to the creation of the motorway, the gully was still full of cottages and dense bush. The police and the police reporter from *Truth* arrived one night and Hoffman drew them along, telling them that they were just in time to witness an animal sacrifice. She convinced the reporter to drink a mug of goat's milk, telling him it was the animal's blood, proclaiming it an aphrodisiac, and then ordering him to strip off in order to ride one of the goats in moonlight. The reporter got as far as his hat and shoes before the police intervened, and all was dutifully reported in *Truth* the next day under the headline, 'Gruesome Goings-On in Grafton Gully'.[79]

If it seems extraordinary that someone would believe any of this, this is about the same period, according to poet and performing artist Alan Brunton, that the short-lived psychedelic band Ministry of Fog — in which former Mount Roskill Grammar pupil and future star actor Roy Billing played bass — practised in the liminal setting of the gully by candlelight, and supposedly rustled a sheep on Mount Eden and then slaughtered it in the bath.[80] The gully is a weird place, now an island of wilderness in the midst of the metropolis, overlooked by the melancholy concrete rainbow of Grafton Bridge, once synonymous with suicides, below which is the Symonds Street cemetery, where so many embittered scions of the Empire lie in alien earth very far from home.

Hoffman once said that her witch persona was merely 'mad, mad fun' that people wanted to believe and so she obliged them. In an interview conducted in 2012, shortly before she was diagnosed with the cancer that would take her life a couple of years later, she stated that she took it more seriously by then.[81] But who is to say?

Chapter 9.

In science's robe

Then she got into the lift, for the good reason that the door stood open; and was shot smoothly upwards. The very fabric of life now, she thought as she rose, is magic. In the eighteenth century, we knew how everything was done; but here I rise through the air; I listen to voices in America; I see men flying — but how it's done I can't even begin to wonder. So my belief in magic returns.

— VIRGINIA WOOLF, *ORLANDO: A BIOGRAPHY*, 1928

As science emerged from the rest of philosophy as an intellectual process in ancient Greece, for a long time it remained intrinsically entangled with natural magic — the inherent magical virtue of things in nature independent of spirits or demons. Astronomy was still part of astrology, and chemistry had yet to separate itself from alchemy. Because it derived from nature, the Church had no problem with it. Bishop of Cologne and Catholic saint Albertus Magnus (c.1200–1280) could write about the magical properties of stones and herbs, confident that these were gifts from God, and that this was as much science as his work on geometry on the authority of Roman writers like Pliny the Elder.

When the Renaissance philosopher Marsilio Ficino (1433–1499) wrote about the power of astral spirits in *De vita libri tres* (1489), he compared them to hellebore — a dangerous drug, but a natural one, its effects hidden (occult) and a puzzle, but an aspect of its natural physical properties nonetheless.[1]

The Age of Reason can be said to have begun with Isaac Newton (1642–1727), but his alchemical studies, interest in Rosicrucianism and attempts at biblical eschatological prophecy caused twentieth-century economist John Maynard Keynes (1883–1946) to say of him: '[he] was not the first of the age of reason, he was the last of the magicians'.[2] Newton's contemporary, mathematician, philosopher and intellectual nemesis Gottfried Leibniz (1646–1716), dismissed gravitation as 'a scholastick occult quality' that threatened to drag the Enlightenment 'back again into the Kingdom of Darkness'.[3] To Leibniz, laws of agency that apparently worked by continuous miracles without a theory of concrete material mechanism smacked of the magical. His magic is today's scientific fact.

The boundaries between science and the occult in the late nineteenth and early twentieth centuries were more porous than at any other time since the Renaissance. Some of the period's leading scientists — William Crookes, Oliver Lodge, Camille Flammarion, Alfred Russel Wallace, Thomas Edison, Nikola Tesla and Jack Parsons — were all variously involved in forms of Spiritualism or occultism. When he discovered isotopes (different forms of the same element that contain equal numbers of protons but different numbers of neutrons in their nuclei), Francis

Aston (1877–1945), who received the Nobel for chemistry in 1922 for this breakthrough, was actually looking for a mystical element predicted by Theosophists Annie Besant and Charles Leadbeater in their 1908 book *Occult Chemistry*.[4] Theosophy's founder Helena Blavatsky was only too happy to chip in on subjects scientific, or to appropriate scientific discoveries as supporting 'evidence' for her cosmological worldview.

While this sort of mental flexibility is a lot rarer in the sciences these days, in a letter to Max Born in 1947 Albert Einstein felt moved to describe quantum entanglement as 'spooky action at a distance'. James George Frazer and Max Weber were both influences on Keith Thomas's keystone study *Religion and the Decline of Magic* (1971).[5] Having surveyed historical sources from the medieval up to the onset of modernity circa 1700, in the final pages of his book Thomas states, with uncharacteristic hesitation, that if belief in magic had not died out completely in the West, it had 'greatly decayed in prestige'.[6]

‡

But had magic declined — or had it merely gone underground? As science became the dominant way of understanding the world, the impulse to the occult and esoteric increasingly adopted a kind of drag of scientific trappings in order to retain plausible currency and acceptability. Much enthusiastic pseudoscience might just as easily be classified as occult or esoteric.

Some early, difficult to categorise, New Zealand examples include the theories of Benjamin Betts (1832–?). Betts, who was English, had trained as an architect — where is not clear — and travelled in India to study Eastern philosophy before settling in Auckland, where he worked as a trigonometrical computer for the provincial government. He became obsessed with the notion of representing human emotional states from the zero or animal base state to full consciousness as geometrical, splitting the psychological spectrum as Newton did that of white light.

The exquisite diagrams he produced were based on the growth patterns of plants and crystals, and he was convinced that the secret to understanding the human condition was love. To that end he attempted to engage the

Benjamin Betts, plate from
Geometrical Psychology, 1887.

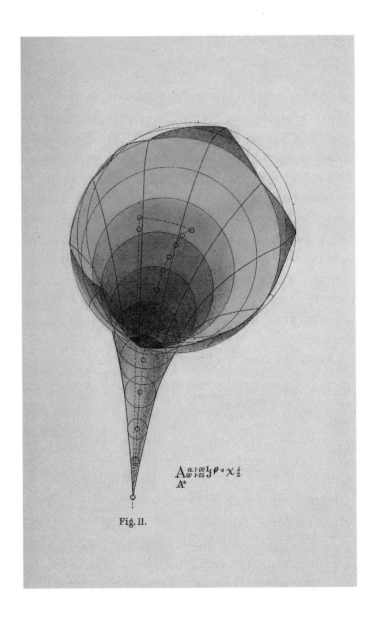

critic John Ruskin (1819–1900), who rebuffed him. He then approached his sister's friend Mary Everest Boole (1832–1916) — the self-taught mathematician and educator, and widow of the English mathematician George Boole (1815–1864) — and she was sufficiently interested to share Betts's diagrams with various scientists and artists. Eventually a book of his theories and diagrams was published, *Geometrical Psychology, or, The science of representation: An abstract of the theories and diagrams of B. W. Betts* (1887), edited by Louisa S. Cook.[7]

‡

A later example of this quasi-scientific presentation of the mystical is that of Edgar Roy 'Chook' Brewster (1905–1978) of New Plymouth, although as a church-going Anglican he would certainly refute any association with the occult. Brewster was a beekeeper turned philosopher who, from studying his apian charges, came to the conclusion that utopia could be achieved if only humanity could reconstruct civilisation around the hexagon like the cells of a beehive. He believed that right angles were antithetical to harmonious living, and strove to eliminate them from his life as part of his Norian (NO Right ANgles) philosophy. The world was round, the God-consciousness — symbolised by the halo — was round. Right angles did not occur in nature, and evil was manifest in the 20 right angles of the Nazi swastika.

As the culmination of his theories he built a house in Sanders Avenue, New Plymouth, with hexagonal windows, hexagonal units of construction and hexagonal furniture. Rather disappointingly the elevation of the walls consisted of typical right angles like any normal house, though grouped around a hexagonal centre. Brewster even went so far as to cut the corners off a print of the *Mona Lisa* to make it hexagonal, correcting Leonardo da Vinci's failings. International magazines *Pix* and *Popular Mechanics* published articles about the house and it became something of a tourist attraction: 250,000 people visited between 1953 and 1974.[8]

Brewster and his wife Nettie were enthusiastic musicians and composers (together they wrote 'Beekeeper's Song' and 'Lovely Egmont') and when Her Majesty Queen Elizabeth II visited New Plymouth in January 1954 —

Edgar and Nettie Brewster's Beehive House, New Plymouth, in the mid-1950s.

not long after the potent magical ritual of her coronation — the Brewster's song 'Welcome Queen Elizabeth II' (Roy on lyrics, Nettie composing the music) was, according to the surviving sheet music, performed by a choir of 160 schoolchildren at Pukekura Park.[9] It was later recorded under the TANZA label. History does not preserve what the Queen thought of the experience.

Brewster expressed his philosophy in verse in a book-length epic titled *Norian Thoughts* (c.1973):

> Roundways and by the use of them
> The Holy City — New Jerusalem,
> The Bride of Christ — it must arise
> Pure and perfect before our eyes.
> And then it will be heard by some
> The Spirit and the Bride Say Come.[10]

Brewster believed that God had commanded him to create a hexagonal ideal Norian city — a New Jerusalem — at the base of Taranaki's near-perfect cone, and there await the second coming of Christ. Acting on the divine instruction, in 1976 Brewster dismantled his house and planned his holy city, but he died two years later having never got past designing the triangular and hexagonal subdivisions.[11]

Aotearoa is primarily known for its sheep and dairy exports, but it has proven surprisingly adept at exporting alternative faiths as well. One such instance is the interesting case of Charles A. Simpson (1882–1958), who started out in life as an electrical engineer, a thoroughly scientific and rational career, and ended up as a spiritual healer in the United Kingdom. Simpson was born and raised in Britain but emigrated to New Zealand in 1907. Here, he married his first wife, Grace, who, it seems, like many New Zealand women at the time, was interested in Spiritualism and attempted to involve her husband. The early signs were not auspicious, though, and Simpson was evidently inclined to nod off at Spiritualist gatherings.

When Grace became terminally ill with breast cancer, stress drove Simpson to prayer. During an intense state of prayer, he was contacted by a spirit guide, Dr Lascelles, who is said to have relieved Grace of her pain for the remaining three months and four days that the incorporeal physician had (accurately) predicted was her remaining allotted time in this world. Two years later, Simpson married his second wife, Florence, and in 1921 they returned to England.[12]

Under the direction of Dr Lascelles, in 1926 Simpson gave up his career as an electrical engineer and established the Guild of Spiritual Healing in London, which later became the Seekers Centre. Cures of conditions regarded as incurable were reported, and Simpson's influence proliferated throughout Britain through associated Harmony Prayer Circles that provided spiritual healing in absentia. In 1933 the organisation relocated to grander premises in the 'The Lilacs', Addington Park, West Malling in Kent, and at its height boasted over 5000 members connected by the prayer circles.[13] This organisation still exists at the same location as the Seekers Trust.

Another free-thinking philosophy that enjoyed considerable popularity in Aotearoa in the twentieth century was the School of Radiant Living, established by Dr Herbert Sutcliffe (1886–1971). Sutcliffe — not to be confused with the 1940s New Zealand test cricketer of the same name — was born in Lincolnshire, England, and at an early age joined the Lincoln Cathedral choir, leading to a passion for singing that remained with him throughout his life. Among his qualifications, Sutcliffe was an active Freemason, a Doctor of Divinity and a Fellow of the Faculty of Scientists in London. At one point he worked as a telegraph engineer, but his primary interest was in nutrition.

In the early 1900s he emigrated to Australia to work on the then new telegraph cables, and married Hilda Gertrude Wilson in Brunswick, Melbourne, in 1915. In Australia Sutcliffe became interested in the work of Freud, Adler and Jung, and joined the Australian Psychological Society, of which he was president from 1925 to 1930.

With a doctorate in psychology under his belt in 1931, throughout the rest of the decade Sutcliffe developed his new philosophy for balanced living, gaining a vigorous following in the United States, the United

Kingdom, Hong Kong, China, and Canada. By 1936 he was styling himself a 'metaphysician' and was establishing Radiant Living centres in Australia and New Zealand. He settled in Havelock North in 1942, initially staying at Whare Rā with Harriot and Ethel Felkin. 'On yonder hill you will pitch your tent,' Ethel prophesied, and pointed towards Te Mata Peak.[14]

For his base he purchased 'Swarthmoor', the former home of the Quakers John and Maggie Holdsworth, on Te Mata Road at the base of the hill. He renamed it 'Peloha' — a portmanteau of peace, love and harmony.[15] Peloha became the centre of all Radiant Living activity worldwide, which at its height consisted of 36 summer schools, 12 of which were in Aotearoa. Peloha was also the meeting place for Sutcliffe's followers, particularly at Christmas and Easter, a training facility for accredited teachers of Radiant Living, and a clinic where Sutcliffe gave advice on diet and exercise and provided therapy to paying guests. As well, of course, it was Sutcliffe's home, where he lived with his second wife, Phyllis, his first wife Hilda having died in Australia in 1944.[16]

A typical routine for a Radiant Living summer school went like this:

> 7:00 Dressing bell
> 7:45 Lemon drinks
> 8:00 Physical Culture exercises
> Breakfast with school songs [from the official song books published by Sutcliffe]
> Followed by tidying rooms
> 10:00 Silence [meditation led by Sutcliffe 'with two senior teachers']
> 10:45 Tea and sandwiches
> Eye tests and Eye Class Lecture by Founder
> Lunch Rest
> 3:00 Eye-exercise classes [pseudoscientific exercises to strengthen sight though exercises, many of which, such as staring into the sun, would now be considered highly dangerous]
> 3:30 Tea Class for teachers
> 6:00 Dinner
> 8:15 Sutcliffe lecture[17]

At first glance this doesn't seem overly esoteric or occult, and indeed I hesitated to include Sutcliffe in this book, as he more or less fits comfortably within a broader context of mid-twentieth-century self-improvement, eugenics and assorted health fads. But then we arrive at the religious component of Radiant Living, embedded in a version of Christianity of a distinctly Theosophical flavour. Correspondence from Sutcliffe and many of his followers would be signed off 'T.U.F.' for 'Thank you, Father'.

In his self-published and undated book *Healing Rays and Consciousness*, Sutcliffe writes that: 'this physical body is held together by an etheric substance called the Etheric Double, which never leaves the human form, even in sleep. The Etheric Double is the outer covering or garment of the Etheric body, and is connected to it by what may be termed a silken or silver cord', and that 'The Etheric Body itself is, in turn, the clothing or outer shell of the Astral Body.' He also claimed to receive communications from entities he called the Hierarchy, or 'Rays of Spiritual Existence beyond the Astral plane', which guided him in life and in directing the business of the movement.[18]

☦

For all that, the focus of Radiant Living was practical and directed at the body as the vehicle of the soul. This was a two-pronged approach, which Sutcliffe described as '*Health* — through Diet, Physical Exercises, Breathing. *Understanding* — through Psychology and Mental Analysis. *Spiritual Growth* — through co-operation with Divine Laws.'[19]

The process began with a strict elimination diet that — through a complex, largely vegetarian menu of the sort familiar from most fad diets — sought to correct previous poor eating. This was supported through breathing exercises, physical exertion — hula-hoop competitions were a fixture, and Sutcliffe even in advanced age was known to come on stage via a gymnastic tumble to deliver lectures — positive affirmations and a call to joy to create the appropriate vibrations for maximum human potential. 'Thought,' stated Sutcliffe, 'is as truly a natural force as electricity or light . . .' He explained:

> Thought radiates from the mind of the thinker, travels over space and produces effects upon other minds at a greater or less distance from its thought. Each kind of thought has its own rate and character of vibration . . . Thoughts of a positive, constructive, uplifting nature blend and harmonise whilst those of a negative, destructive, deteriorating nature produce discord.[20]

The vibrations of health and joy had the power to disperse diseased cells. Reminiscent of Steiner and Whare Rā, colour therapy also played a role — red was a stimulant, green calmed, blue purified, and adherents of Radiant Living were warned emphatically never to wear black.[21]

Although Sutcliffe never adopted an overt political position or attempted to influence political direction in Aotearoa, public officials were regularly present at the openings of Radiant Living schools and celebrations. As public health grew in importance in government policy and popular thinking, Sutcliffe was praised in speeches, though this is not an unusual thing for officials to do when interacting with a local group with any significant following. Sutcliffe and Radiant Living were, however, involved with two more mainstream groups intent on bringing about a better New Zealand.

Sutcliffe's words, without attribution, were also to be found in the broadsheets of another organisation, the Crusade for Social Justice.[22] Of this group little is known beyond it being an organised Christian movement operating in Auckland in the 1930s and 1940s that actively campaigned for progressive social causes and against the war, and promoted the policies of Prime Minister Michael Joseph Savage.

In another instance, the 1942 Dominion Reconstruction Conference, held in Auckland by the Moral, Spiritual and Social Advancement Movement of New Zealand, was widely supported and attended by politicians, doctors, educators, businesspeople and religious leaders, and brought together many health and wellbeing-focused groups to discuss improvements to the country.[23]

At the time the country was at the height of its obsession with public health as a moral imperative and with eugenics, which would rapidly lose favour when confronted with its most extreme manifestation in Nazi

Germany. Sutcliffe attended the conference representing Radiant Living and was quoted in 'The People's Plan' report produced by the conference; the youth activities of Radiant Living were introduced by a certain Edmund Hillary (1919–2008), the future conqueror of Everest.

The Hillary family was imbued with a profound conviction of moral purpose for which traditional Christian worship proved insufficient. In the late 1930s, with Europe fast approaching the Gethsemane of the Second World War, the entire Hillary family enthusiastically joined the Radiant Living movement. Hillary's father, Percy, was briefly vice president, his mother Gertrude was the first Auckland secretary, his brother Rex became a teacher, and his sister June led the communal singing. The young Hillary, deeply conflicted between his pacifism and his desire to serve his country, was the most involved of all.[24] As Sutcliffe would later write:

> For five years, from 1938 to 1943, the Hillary family was closely associated with the Auckland School of Radiant Living. I am glad to have on record the many times they testified to the fact that Radiant Living came into their lives bringing harmony and understanding to each member of the family and the family as a whole just when it was needed.
>
> Father Percy Hillary was so appreciative that he requested me to take Edmund with me on lecture campaigns because he could not think of anything better for Edmund's future.[25]

Something of the flavour of the teachings can be found in a notebook kept by Gertrude Hillary:

> The radiance you express will be in accordance with the ideal you tenaciously hold.
>
> Prayer: To ask earnestly and reverently as in worship; to make known one's desires to God. And what is prayer but the expansion of oneself into the living ether.
>
> Love is divine emotion. I surround my child with infinite love and wisdom.[26]

Hillary became an associated teacher of the organisation — it is not clear whether this means he was accredited or not — and Sutcliffe's secretary, and was deeply appreciative of the confidence Radiant Living instilled in him, stating in his autobiography:

> A Dr Herbert Sutcliffe was in town and he was talking about a new philosophy — Radiant Living. My family and I went along to his first lecture and were very impressed. It was a combination of Christianity, psychology and health and fitness and it just seemed to fit our needs at the time. We became members and when Dr Sutcliffe introduced training classes I qualified first in the course and became a Teacher of Radiant Living. I gained quite a lot from Radiant Living — I learned to speak confidently from the platform and even started thinking more freely on important topics. But finally my enthusiasm faded, as it always seemed to do. I developed the conviction that I was trying to escape from ordinary life, so I reluctantly withdrew from the organisation.[27]

Hillary remained open to thinking outside of orthodoxy throughout his life. In 1953 both he and sherpa Tenzing Norgay claimed to have seen a yeti on Everest. Although they later changed their minds about this, in 1960 Hillary nonetheless led an expedition to search for this cryptozoological creature.[28] No doubt out of kindness, he also contributed an ill-advised foreword to Martin Doutré's fallacious *Ancient Celtic New Zealand* (1999), a work which for the most part has been politely ignored by media and scholarship.

Doutré's premise, for which there is no credible evidence were we to even entertain such an absurd assertion, is that Aotearoa was occupied by a migration of Celtic peoples who were invaded and supplanted by Māori a millennium ago.[29] Hillary's contribution freely admits to being insufficiently informed to pass judgment on Doutré's assertions, and has a diplomatically encouraging tone, leading one to wonder whether he was fully aware of the purposes to which his words would be put.

Hillary's yearning for higher truths led to his interest in Buddhism and Hinduism, and no doubt contributed to his seeking out of high and

Edmund Hillary with Radiant Living founder Herbert Sutcliffe in 1940.

desolate places. The mountains of New Zealand, ancestors of Māori, have a peculiarly powerful place in the Pākehā imagination. The writer, poet and penal reformer Blanche Baughan (1870–1958) writes as much in her 1910 book *Snow Kings of the Southern Alps*:

> As one stands here upon this rocky-vantage point and sees this mountain-world, Man does not count; one does not think of him. There is no sign of visible habitation; it is the actual presence of these mighty forms that engrosses one's whole attention, not the remembrance of their scanty mortal associations; while, as for the citizen surnames imposed (often with what manifest incongruity!) upon their august majesties, far from them humanizing the landscape, the landscape has de-humanized them; warm meanings of flesh and blood they now connote no more, but stand only for splendid entities, motionless, pure, of silent rock and ice. This ocean of the snows, in brief, is so immense, the barque of human enterprise upon it so small, that the effect upon the mind at gaze is that of a quite shipless sea, a solitude still inviolate.[30]

For Māori, the connection is a far more intimate one, that of whakapapa. Baughan asserted that the tangata whenua kept away from the snowline of the Southern Alps, regarding the vertebrae of Te Waipounamu 'always with veneration and awe, and, fearing to profane, avoided them'.[31] This is, of course, nonsense, and Māori had extensively explored what was accessible, recording the territory accurately in story and tradition rather than European maps.

That Radiant Living had a loyal following in Aotearoa in the 1940s through to the 1970s is reflected in the number of schools the movement bought or self-built over that time. As the movement established each of these various schools, founding-day banquets became a popular celebration, to which local body politicians, MPs and other dignitaries were often invited. And there is a sense that the movement's work was appreciated, with, for example, Prime Minister Peter Fraser reportedly claiming that if more people embraced the principles of Radiant Living, he would be closing hospitals instead of opening them.[32]

Phyllis Sutcliffe continued to run the organisation from Havelock North after Herbert died in 1971. When she in turn died, in 1981, the house was sold to Weleda, the multinational manufacturer of herbal beauty products and naturopathic medicines.

In 1989, proceeds from the sale were invested in a large endowment for Victoria University to establish scholarships in Sutcliffe's name for disadvantaged students.[33] Radiant Living continued to exist as a movement in New Zealand until the 1980s, and an echo of it exists in the name by multiple alternative naturopathic and nutrition-based health companies and groups around the world. Perhaps its most significant legacy is the idea, outside the practitioners of yoga of course, that being able to touch your toes is an exercise.

‡

It would be appropriate to provide a thorough treatment of Bruce Cathie (1930–2013) in a later volume on UFOs and their attendant subculture in Aotearoa, but the fundamentals of his worldview originate from a substrate of occult concepts. Cathie was an airline pilot who lived in Takapuna on Auckland's North Shore. Upon seeing a UFO over Manukau Harbour in 1952 and learning from other pilots that such sightings were not uncommon, Cathie took to theorising why these sightings seemed to be more common in some places than in others, and then began writing books about his ideas. It's probably not that outlandish to suggest that, at the height of his popularity, his profile in the United Kingdom and the United States was higher than that of more significant Takapuna authors such as Frank Sargeson.

Cathie believed that he could mathematically describe a grid of electrodynamic fields that encompassed the Earth. These powered UFOs and dictated where and when nuclear bombs could be detonated, by means of tapping into particular harmonic frequencies. He claimed to have predicted the French nuclear tests at Mururoa atoll, based on harmonic calculations derived from trigonometry, latitude and longitude. He outlined these theories over six books, starting with *Harmonic 33* in 1968, and finishing with *The Harmonic Conquest of Space* in 1994.[34] His early books were published by A. H. & A. W. Reed, but later editions appeared in the United Kingdom and the United States. Sphere Books in the United Kingdom, for example, published an edition of *Harmonic 33* in 1980.

American television drew attention to his theories twice, and he was interviewed in the season-four episode 'UFO Australia', of the Leonard Nimoy-hosted series *In Search Of...* in 1979.[35] His ideas were discussed on the 'Ancient Architects' episode of season 12 of *Ancient Aliens* in 2017.[36] A documentary, *The Harmonic Code — The Harmonics of Reality* (the title punning on Dan Brown's 2006 novel *The Da Vinci Code*) was released in 2007.

Comparisons are easily drawn between Cathie's ideas of harmonics and R. Buckminster Fuller's (1895–1983) nigh-on-incomprehensible theory of 'synergetics', which combines geometry and the study of all systems, from biology and physics to sociology, mathematics and engineering, reducing everything to energy vectors;[37] similarly with Nikola Tesla's (1856–1943) theories about constructing a free energy grid for the entire world based on induction.[38] It is, however, possible to trace the notions of such a network of energy lines to the pseudo-archaeological belief in ley lines, which was first formally postulated by Herefordshire miller Alfred Watkins in his book *The Old Straight Track: Its Mounds, Beacons, Moats, Sites and Mark Stones*, first published in 1925 and reprinted many times since after it was picked up by the counterculture in the 1960s.[39]

Ley lines, as Watkins postulated, were straight alignments that could be drawn between various ancient structures and natural landmarks, but over time they accumulated associations with energy flows detectable to dowsers — dowsing, the finding of lost things by studying the motion of handheld pendulums, sticks or metal rods having been practised in New Zealand since the colonial period — and even as UFO flight paths. The chief argument against the existence of ley lines can also be directed at Cathie's energy grid: if you play fast and loose enough with geography and numbers, you can make them fit just about anything.

Cathie died at the North Shore Hospice in Takapuna in 2013, survived by his wife, two sons and a hardcore following of fervent believers in his theories.[40]

✣

> ULYSSES: . . . but when the planets
> In evil mixture to disorder wander,
> What plagues and what portents! what mutiny!
> What raging of the sea! shaking of earth!
> Commotion in the winds! frights, changes, horrors,
> Divert and crack, rend and deracinate
> The unity and married calm of states
> Quite from their fixure!
> — Shakespeare, *Troilus and Cressida*, Act I, Scene iii (1609)

In 2010 and 2011 Christchurch and other Canterbury communities were devastated by terrible earthquakes from which they have still to entirely recover. Titarangi local Ken Ring claimed to have predicted them in a tweet on Valentine's Day earlier in 2010, based on his theory of how the moon influences the Earth.[41] He also predicted in a tweet another massive quake in Marlborough and North Canterbury in March 2011, which mercifully failed to materialise but did cause panic and a small exodus from Christchurch.[42] This led to considerable attention for Ring and widespread condemnation from the scientific community.

Ring is a prolific author, particularly of books about weather and climate, and a compiler of popular almanacs. His first book, *Pawmistry* (1999) was a spoof on palm-reading for cats. His subsequent books take themselves in deadly earnestness. He has also, according to various biographical notes, worked as a maths teacher, speech therapist, musician, actor, clown, part-time teacher's college lecturer and 'maths magician'.[43] He has a considerable following, writing columns for farming and fishing publications, for a time delivering weather reports for Australia's Channel 7 television programme *Today Tonight*, and apparently consulting for Olympian-rower-turned-event-organiser Ian Ferguson, the All Blacks (allegedly) and, until 2020, the Gisborne City Council.[44]

The basis of Ring's theory is the demonstrable and incontrovertible fact that the moon controls the tides. Although a connection between the moon and tides had been known since antiquity, mentioned by Pytheas of

Massalia in 325 BCE and Pliny the Elder in his *Natural History* in 77 CE, it wasn't until the 1700s that mathematics and gravitation had advanced to the point of a modern scientific understanding of tidal mechanics.[45] Ring's supporters like to compare him to a persecuted Galileo, which is ironic as Galileo actively lampooned the idea that the moon had anything to do with the tides in his 1616 essay *'Discorso Sul Flusso E Il Reflusso Del Mare'* ('Discourse on the Tides').

In 1999 Ring self-published his theories in the book *Predicting the Weather by the Moon*, which seems heavily influenced by a book published 10 years earlier by Waikato umbrella-maker Harry Alcock, *Lunar Effect: Moon's Influence on Our Weather*, which Ring praises on his website.[46] Where Ring diverges from general scientific consensus is where he asserts that the known cyclical interactions of the natural variations in the lunar orbit, in conjunction with the 11-year solar cycle, can, in a very localised way, predictably impact weather patterns and even disturb the Earth's crust to cause earthquakes.[47] What this overlooks is the fact that even the combined gravitational pull of the sun and moon aligned, with the moon at its closest to Earth, is too weak and distributed to have specific effects in a very localised area. A small fridge magnet is more powerful that the gravitational pull of the Earth because you can use it to pick up pieces of iron. The kind of energy required to disturb a continental plate is vastly more than all the nuclear weapons in the world going off simultaneously could shift.

Conveniently, Ring concedes this is not an 'exact science' (i.e. not a science at all). Which is just as well, as various professional and amateur scientists have demonstrated that the data produced is highly unreliable, and that Ring's so-called successes can be attributed to luck and retrospective confirmation bias.[48] It's pseudoscience, and makes claims for the cycles of the heavens that even astrologers wouldn't put forth.

This is nothing new in Aotearoa. Before Ring came English immigrant Joseph Taylor (1858–1942), who was born in Audley, Staffordshire. Following an education at Buckley's Academy, Winsford, Cheshire, and later at the Theological Institute, Owen's College, Victoria University, in Manchester, Taylor arrived in Nelson in 1894. Here, he lived for the next 40 years working as a mining engineer, discovering and developing the

Pūponga coalfield, and investigating the Parapara iron deposits.[49] Taylor was a prolific writer about sunspots, solar physics and seismology, and published storm and earthquake predictions in the *Nelson Evening Mail* based on the motions, gravitation and electromagnetism of the planetary bodies. Taylor gave lectures about his theories around the South Island, calling his 'science' Psycho-Radio-Cosmics, writing in one of his newspaper columns in 1909:

> It was by proceeding on these principles, and by coupling them with certain psychic perceptions, that I was enabled to arrive at my recent scientific, confident, and successful prediction of what I termed in general 'the coming cosmic strain' . . . I could foretell with certainty, yea, even with mathematical precision all important disturbances both in the atmosphere of the Earth and in the atmosphere of the Sun.[50]

In the same column he noted that his methods gave him information on droughts, storms, pestilences and epidemics, comparing himself to the omnipresent Clement Wragge.

‡

The following year Taylor was touring the West Coast of the South Island, lecturing to large audiences on the subject of Halley's Comet, which was looming impressively in the skies that year. It is a testament to the strength of certain superstitions that there was a popular belief in the Empire that the comet caused the death of Edward VII, and the spectroscopic discovery of cyanogenic compounds in the comet's tail led to panic that humanity would be gassed.[51] It is unknown whether Taylor addressed these subjects, but he does appear to have mooted the notion of building a spa at the hot springs of the Upper Buller, as well as the mining possibilities of the West Coast which he promoted to Parliament's then Upper House.[52]

Surprisingly, it was his career in mining that caused him trouble, not his predictions. Having established his coal-mining operation, he had been charged in 1902 with defrauding the company over a wharf that never materialised, resulting in a sentence of two years' hard labour.[53] This

Joseph Taylor, mining engineer, 'Psycho-Radio-Cosmics' proponent and founder of the philosophy of Absolutism.

NZ TRUTH, 12 SEPTEMBER 1929

does not seem to have held Taylor back unduly. Later in life he became an advocate for a government sanatorium and astronomical observatory at Maruia in the Lewis Pass, and for the establishment of a state iron foundry.[54] He also continued giving lectures from his 'Universal Institute' about his theories, including a philosophy he'd developed and named Absolutism,[55] which he defined thus:

> Absolutism teaches that whether we realise it or not, we are always obliged to assume the fact of Absolute Truth as the fundamental premise of all our thinking, that the fact of the Absolute is recognised natively as a primary intuition, being, when once truly recognised, above proof and beyond doubt, and that this light arises directly in virtue of our own participation in the Absolute Divine Essence.[56]

After this we lose track of him, but at some point he appears to have moved to Wellington, where he died in a hospital after an illness of two months.[57] He was survived by his wife, four sons, two daughters and 'many grand-children and great grand-children'.[58] Absolutism, as a movement, left no such legacy.

Chapter 10.

The Age of Aquarius

So it is with my generation, which straddled the years of the sixties and seventies. To look at the international context, these were the years of hope and optimism, personified by John Kennedy's reign in a mythic American Camelot. It was the Age of Aquarius. It was the age of our own Kennedy, the late Norman Kirk. Of Vietnam protests. Of 'No Maoris, No Tour'. It was the time when we were looking, Maori and pakeha, for a way out of a cul-de-sac. Of trying to mould a new future.

— WITI IHIMAERA, 'MAORI LIFE AND LITERATURE: A SENSORY PERCEPTION', 1982

Up until the 1960s the occult was just that, occult — hidden, obscured, concealed — but as a younger generation discovered their in-scapes through music, psychedelics, free love and alternative spiritualities, the occult became a minority enthusiasm. By the 1970s, it was a craze. Had Crowley been born a generation or two later he would have been a major celebrity. Even in death he did quite well for himself: in 1970 Jimmy Page of Led Zeppelin bought Boleskine House, where Crowley had attempted the Rite of Abramelin[1] on the shores of Loch Ness in around 1900. The Rolling Stones were devotees briefly, and The Beatles included him (appropriately enough) between guru Sri Yukteswar and Mae West in the back row, far left, on the cover of *Sergeant Pepper's Lonely Hearts Club Band* in 1967[2] — the same year that the musical *Hair* announced the dawning of the Age of Aquarius.

According to Western astrology, astrological ages last 2160 years, which is approximately how long the northern vernal equinox (our spring equinox) — when the plane of the Earth's equator intersects with the geometric centre of the sun and day and night are of equal length — takes to move through any particular Zodiacal constellation. The Age of Aquarius, much as the 1967 song of the same name states, is supposed to usher in a new era of peace, understanding and cosmic enlightenment, if only we knew whether it has actually started. Unfortunately, astrologers have, for the last two millennia or so, ignored the important discovery made by an ancient Greek astronomer named Hipparchus (190–120 BCE), that the Earth's axial rotation actually changes over time like a spinning top.

The upshot of that is that the actual Age of Aquarius, as determined by the International Astronomical Union, will not begin until the year 2600.[3] Astrologers, on the other hand, can't seem to agree, with their calculations ranging from present-day Australian astrologer Terry MacKinnell, who says it started in 1477, to British astrologer John Addey (1920–1982), who said it wouldn't start until 3597.[4] For the sake of sanity it's probably best if we just refer to 'the New Age'. American occult author Mitch Horowitz provides a useful general definition of what characterises this New Age:

1. Belief in the therapeutic value of spiritual or religious ideas
2. Belief in a mind–body connection in health

3. Belief that human consciousness is evolving to higher stages
4. Belief that thoughts, in some greater or lesser measure, determine reality
5. Belief that spiritual understanding is available without allegiance to a specific religion or doctrine.[5]

In the United States, the radical left embraced Marxism and its attendant explicit atheism, and the Youth International Party, or 'Yippies', staged a mock exorcism and levitation of the Pentagon in October 1967.[6] But while the 'Summer of Love' might have blossomed in San Francisco's Haight-Ashbury district that year, as with most things there was a time-lag until it reached Aotearoa, which it finally did properly in the 1970s.

By the late 1960s, a mod version of the psychedelic aesthetic had already appeared on New Zealand television screens via the youth music show *C'mon* (1967–69), hosted by Peter Sinclair. The music was fairly vanilla and tame, but the sets — conceived by designer Roy Good and inspired by the Op Art of Bridget Riley and Eastern religious imagery — popped in black and white. Popular occult and New Age paperbacks, although often diluted and misinformed, abounded. *The Morning of the Magicians* (1963, an English translation of the 1960 *Le matin des magiciens*) by French journalists Louis Pauwels and Jacques Bergier was very on-trend with its spurious explanations of secret societies. Swiss author Erich von Däniken's *Chariots of the Gods?* (1968) convinced many that the Egyptian pyramids must have been made with the help of ancient aliens, despite all archaeological evidence and common sense to the contrary.

Then the pace started to accelerate. The Woodstock festival took place on Max Yasgur's dairy farm in Bethel, New York, in August 1969, the same month that cult leader Charles Manson sent his followers on their murderous rampage in the Hollywood Hills. Woodstock arrived at one remove in New Zealand in the form of Atlantic Records' expensive three-LP boxed set *Woodstock: Music from the Original Soundtrack and More* and the Oscar-winning documentary in 1970.

That same year, back in Aotearoa, impresario Phil Warren was promoting his Redwood 70 festival in West Auckland. Rather tame by comparison with Woodstock, it headlined on-sabbatical Bee Gee Robin Gibb backed by a string quartet. This was followed in quick succession in 1971 by the Englefield Rock Festival at Belfast, Christchurch, and at Waikanae over the Easter weekend, and the University Arts Council's Jam Factory in July. But it wasn't until 1973 that Aotearoa experienced anything approaching Woodstock: the Great Ngāruawāhia Music Festival in January, headlined by Black Sabbath and Sandy Denny, and, further down the bill, Blerta, Mammal, Billy T.K. and Powerhouse.[7]

New Zealand and Australia had been dragged into the United States' war in Vietnam (1960–75), and more than 3000 New Zealand military and civilian personnel eventually served in South East Asia.[8] There were protests throughout the period, concentrated on Anzac Days and the visits of South Vietnam's Premier Air Vice-Marshal Nguyen Cao Ky in 1967 and US Vice President Spiro Agnew in 1970.[9] American protest songs formed an important part of those actions.

The counterculture also brought with it an interest in Eastern spirituality, the *I Ching*, the *Kama Sutra* and *The Tibetan Book of the Dead*, although this manifested in a heavily orientalist misrepresentation of Eastern permissiveness. It also brought a flourishing drug culture, primarily cannabis and hashish, but heroin as well, leading to police vice squads being set up nationally in 1965 to tackle the problem. By the mid-1970s, any idea of innocent homegrown hippie hedonism had clearly been hijacked by gangs and much darker, highly organised, big-business drug syndicates with an international reach, which were importing Buddha sticks, and eventually heroin, from South East Asia. The most notorious of these was the Mr Asia drug ring, which came to a bloody end at the close of the decade.[10]

LSD was present but not nearly as popular, despite the northern hemisphere hyperbole, although hallucinogenic trips could also be had by less synthetic, more shamanic means in the form of magic mushrooms (*Psilocybin*) harvested in the southern autumn, or by playing Russian roulette with datura (*Datura stramonium*) and angel's trumpet (*Brugmansia candida*), both of which were to be found in many New Zealand suburban gardens.

‡

The 1960s and 1970s were the decades of tuning in, turning on and dropping out, to paraphrase Timothy Leary, guru of the acid trip. Disenchanted with the conventions and constraints of the post-war nuclear family, young New Zealanders headed for the hills, setting up communes like Wilderland (1964) and Karuna Falls (1976) on the Coromandel Peninsula and the Tui community in 1984 at Golden Bay, all of which survived on necessary tedium into the twenty-first century.[11] (Life in the 1970s in the isolated Manaroa commune, deep in Marlborough's Pelorus Sound, and to a lesser extent the Riverside commune in Nelson, is memorably recounted in Miro Bilbrough's memoir *In the Time of the Manaroans* [2020]).[12]

The poet and sometime mystic James K. Baxter (1926–1972) attempted to establish a commune at remote Jerusalem on the Whanganui River in 1969. Although the basis of his communal vision was a mix of Catholicism and Māoritanga, extolling voluntary ascetic poverty 'without money or books',[13] Baxter's notoriety as a political countercultural firebrand and 'corrupting' influence on youth attracted press attention. The commune quickly attracted a chaotic and overcrowded following, which upset the locals and caused the Whanganui authorities to intervene out of health and sanitation concerns. This iteration of Baxter's Jerusalem only lasted until 1971, but a smaller, more dedicated and cohesive group returned the following year, outliving the poet by three years.[14]

Aotearoa's most perdurable urban commune, Chippenham, was established in 1971 in an old Victorian mansion in the Christchurch suburb of Merivale. A centre for Greenpeace, HART (Halt All Racist Tours), homosexual law reform and women's refuge activism, it survived into the early twenty-first century as part of the Heartwood Community. Marion Hobbs, later a Labour member of Parliament from 1996 to 2008, was a one-time resident.

Other notable individuals who lived on communes at various times include perennial Waitākere, then Invercargill, mayor Tim Shadbolt, who lived at the Huia commune west of Auckland in the 1970s, and Green Party co-leader Rod Donald (1957–2005), who, along with activist Elsie Locke (1912–2001), lived in a loose community in the loop of the Avon River in Christchurch. When not roaming the highways and byways in their jaw-dropping hand-decorated bus, the wild theatre and music troupe Blerta ('Bruno Lawrence's Electric Revelation and Travelling Apparition') had a commune at Waimārama in Hawke's Bay.[15] The times were ripe for seeking out new, less materialistic ways of living.

In a somewhat counterintuitive (and potentially uncool) way, the Establishment was to step in and offer a helping hand to those trying to rebel and escape it. In October 1973, perhaps in a move akin to a parent calling the bluff of their rebellious teen, Labour Prime Minister Norman Kirk lent his government's support to the back-to-the-land movement. By approving kibbutzim-style communities on Crown land leased at 4.5 per cent of the land's market value, they were effectively finding the runaway a flat and contributing to the rent. Called 'ohu', te reo Māori for voluntarily working together as a group, it was hoped that these settlements would give rebellious, alienated youth a stake in the country, working the land, and a sense of community.

Unfortunately, the land on offer was often poor and inaccessible, and bureaucratic delays meant that only eight ohu were ever established. Following Kirk's sudden death in 1974, and National's return to government the next year, the scheme eventually collapsed, with only three ohu surviving in 1983. The last — Ahu Ahu ohu in the Whanganui hinterland — disbanded with the new millennium.[16] Although not occult, there was a mainstream openness to these New Age anti-materialist lifestyles.

☦

It is a mistake, however, to assume that this revolution started in the 1960s. Or that the escape to the land necessarily involved the land of your birth. If anything, it streamed from the same Victorian-Edwardian teat as had the Golden Dawn, and Aotearoa was already exporting it early along with the newly refrigerated lamb carcasses. One of these early up-takers was Noel Street, who, although his birth and death dates are not altogether certain, like a disconcerting number of Spiritualists seems to have lived a good, long life. Born and raised in Aotearoa, at some point, probably the early 1900s, he moved to the United States and was ordained

Members of the theatre and music troupe Blerta ('Bruno Lawrence's Electric Revelation and Travelling Apparition') with their families in 1971. Lawrence is standing at far right.

in the largest Spiritualist church in the country, the Universal Church of the Master (founded in 1908). Thenceforth he travelled America with his wife, Coleen, lecturing and performing psychic readings and healings.

In 1917 the Streets set up the Lotus Ashram, a Spiritualist fellowship, in Miami, Florida. This later relocated to a larger site in Port Lucie, Florida. Noel led as a medium, combining Eastern religion and philosophy with what were claimed to be traditional Māori teachings. Coleen, apparently lacking the psychic gift, taught yoga and vegetarian cooking. Noel was still active well into the 1970s, publishing pamphlets on topics ranging from mediumship and reincarnation[17] to Eastern and Māori spirituality, and opened another spiritual centre in Chillicothe, Ohio, which moved to Texas in 1977.

‡

Esoteric and occult concepts frequently find ready homes in the experimental arts. The Red Mole company was founded in Wellington in 1974 by poet Alan Brunton (1946–2002), his partner and later wife, performer Sally Rodwell (1950–2006) and jack-of-all-trades Peter Fantl (1952–2001). It had sparked late in the previous year from a chance meeting of a group of New Zealand creatives in an opium den behind the Shell service station in downtown Luang Prabang in Laos.[18] The company grew to include performers and creators who would go on to individual cultural prominence — names including Deborah Hunt, Ian Prior, Jan Preston, Jean McAllister and Martin Edmond. The core of the group was the *ménage à trois* of Brunton, Rodwell and Hunt.

Brunton had always been interested in the ritual and magical in theatre. His 1968 bachelor's degree thesis at Victoria University had been on the subject of ritual and dream in Shakespeare's *The Tempest*.[19] He was quick to recognise the magical power of language to liberate the psyche from the constraints of a conventional world. It was a realisation that informed every Red Mole production. The company was an intriguing collision of the rough-and-ready and highly polished, a heady mélange of New Zealand sentimentality and crudity with European avant-garde of the early twentieth century, devised by Brunton and Rodwell or collectively.[20]

Alan Brunton, poet, theatrical producer and founder of Red Mole.

Red Mole quickly became Aotearoa's best-known alternative theatre company when it toured the towns and community halls of the country in 1978. By then, Red Mole had generated its own private unwritten gospel. As Martin Edmond writes:

> There was a poetic and prophetic tone to *Ghost Rite* not present in Red Mole's work up to this time. In the programme of *Ghost Rite* Red Mole used a quotation from the Dadaist Hugo Ball which focuses attention on New Zealand as an image of paradise (under threat): 'Somewhere, perhaps, there is a little island in the South Pacific that is still untouched, that has not yet been invaded by our anxiety. How long could that last before that too could be a thing of the past?' Like 'some day all theatre will be like this,' the Ball quotation became a leitmotif attached to a lot of Red Mole publicity, especially in America.[21]

The Red Mole mythos — that paradise cannot exist without apocalypse, and vice versa — was particularly evident in its shows from the late 1970s and early 1980s. 'Apocalypse,' writes Edmond, 'is poised simultaneously at the point of collapse into total ruin and the revolutionary rebirth into a new (and better — perfect?) world. Apocalypse is the ideal phantasmagoria, the bright moment of simultaneously disappearing and re-forming, a magical act, a "ghost rite".'[22]

This vision is distinctly occult in orientation, and stems from the revolutionary air of the 1960s, which Brunton saw as magical. He writes in the introduction to the poetry anthology *Big Smoke* (2000) that the young generation abandoned the churches in favour of a utopian pagan idea of a battle betwixt good and evil on an occult level. That evil dwelt in the Pentagon. 'The great magical event of the Sixties was the attempt to levitate the Pentagon during the 1967 march,' he wrote. 'Christianity tried to bring the young back to the faith — cardinals at the Vatican II Council (October 1962) attempted to shock the Roman Catholic church out of its feudal condition by abandoning Latin and the altar rail.'

The only tangible upshot of this, according to Brunton, was liberation theology in South America and Protestant apocalyptic fundamentalism in the United States; 'but it was too late, young people were gazing at the exotic, and, out there, the apocalypse was real'.[23] Asked what it meant to him to be a poet in the modern period, he replied: 'I wanted to write stuff, once, that was so dangerous it would have to be destroyed. This was my fantasy. I thought I was making magic . . .'[24] He once stated that the future of poetry will be 'magical':

> It will be about charms, it will useful against our enemies and head lice, speaking it will cure mangy skin, the blind will SEE; charms must be spoken; there has to be a performance; in the performance there is pleasure; it is the pleasure the adept takes in the performance that makes the charm powerful; performance makes 'texts an event'.[25]

It is possible to get the flavour of the experience from the 1979 Sam Neill-written and -directed documentary *Red Mole on the Road*. Brunton, raised alone by his grandmother in a fundamentalist Christian household in Hamilton, was an enigmatic, charismatic figure who even today retains an aura of awe and mystery in some circles. Hunt might manifest Prime Minister Robert Muldoon as a spot-on impression of a pig-man hybrid caricature; Edmond would often appear as an undertaker, a combination of Baron Samedi (the Vodou avatar of death) and circus ringleader. Between 1978 and 1988, the troupe would impress more sophisticated audiences in the United States and Europe with a unique blend of psychodrama, allegorical masque and cutting topical satire, enhanced by disturbing and extraordinary props, costumes, masks and puppets.

The Western theatre has its origins in ritual, going all the way back to the late sixth century BCE in Athens as part of the Dionysia festival in honour of the Greek god of wine, fertility, madness and religious ecstasy, Dionysos.[26] Even in the Christian era, performance retained a religious role in the mystery plays — hybrids of Biblical narrative and folktale — and the carefully staged re-enactments of Christ's Passion. Even modern theatre is a ritual of sorts that distracts the audience from self-awareness and changes and intensifies its perception of reality.

Red Mole certainly played into that idea, and was Dionysian in its pursuit of catharsis and frenzied ecstasy, deriving its imagery from a variety of esoteric sources — alchemical allegory, cabaret, Dada, Egyptian mythology, surrealism, circus, street performance, Jungian archetypes, and distinctly New Age ideas about short-circuiting the programming of the conscious mind and perceptually shifting the complacent, mainstream perception of reality.

Red Mole created a manifesto with five stated principles: 'to preserve romance, to escape programmed behaviour by remaining erratic, to preserve the unclear and inexplicit idioms of everyday speech, to abhor the domination of any person over any other, and to expend energy'.[27] 'But none of us knew we had a manifesto,' Martin Edmond said in a 2020 interview with David Herkt to promote his book on Red Mole, *Bus Stops on the Moon: Red Mole Days 1974–1980*.[28] 'We had this manifesto but no-one had been told about it.'[29]

The last Red Mole production was *The Book of Life* in 1992. With the deaths of Brunton in 2002 and Rodwell in 2006, this vibrant, feverishly creative experiment in guerrilla theatre and evangelical catharsis finally came to an end.

‡

It must be strongly iterated to the reader that Waitaha were and are an actual people of the South Island, not to be confused with the Bay of Plenty iwi of the same name. Traditionally Waitaha was said to have arrived in Aotearoa on the waka *Uruaokapuarangi*, led by Rākaihautū, his wife Waiariki-o-āio and son Te Rakihouia, the tohunga kōkōrangi (astronomer) Matiti, various members of Te Kāhui Tipua, Te Kāhui Roko, Te Kāhui Waitaha and others. Rākaihautū (although Sir Apirana Ngata disputed this) then headed south to Te Waipounamu (The Greenstone Waters, the South Island) and settled peacefully with Te Kāhui Tipua, Te Kāhui Roko, Te Rapuwai, Ngāti Hawea and Ngāti Wairangi, living collectively as Waitaha until the sixteenth century, when Ngāti Māmoe migrated from the north and assimilated them. Then Ngāi Tahu migrated south and assimilated Ngāti Māmoe.[30]

The descendants of Waitaha are still to be found, predominantly in Canterbury and North Otago, and in recent years have begun to reassert their identity. Waitaha are not remotely mythical, but their limited visibility has led to an appropriation and embroidering of their identity as quasi-magical people or non-Polynesian pre-Māori by certain streams of New Age belief. Occasionally this industry has been aided by some entrepreneurial Māori, not about to let scruples get in the way of monetising Pākehā credulity, or to pursue an internal iwi agenda.

The main primogenitor of this Waitaha neo-myth is the curious character Barry Brailsford, author of the 1989 book *Song of Waitaha: The Histories of a Nation* and subsequent titles.[31] Brailsford was born in Cobden, Greymouth, on the West Coast, in 1939, and is quite the paradox. Despite being what some would describe as a purveyor of pseudo-history and 'mythistory', he gained an MA in history from the University of Canterbury, was a principal lecturer at the Christchurch College of Education, is a former member of the New Zealand Archaeology Association Council, and in 1990 was awarded an MBE for services to education.[32]

Those qualifications tend to lend far more weight to Brailsford's theories than is warranted, although his first book, *The Tattooed Land* (1981) was a thoroughly unremarkable, mainstream account of South Island historical sites. This and another relatively uncontroversial text, *Greenstone Trails: The Maori and Pounamu* (1984) were later reissued by StonePrint Press in the 1990s, significantly revised into alignment with his later pseudo-historical views.[33] According to Brailsford's narrative, he was approached by 'Te Pani Manawatū at Tuahiwi . . . Chief of Tūāhuriri Ngāi Tahu', who, impressed with Brailsford's expert testimonial during Ngāi Tahu's Waitangi Tribunal settlement hearings, asked Brailsford to assist a group — nominally included within Ngāi Tahu but identifying as Waitaha with their own claim — and gave him access to Waitaha's secret lore. Te Pani (1911–1991), a member of the 28th New Zealand Battalion and a sergeant in the Second World War, contributes an introduction to *Song of the Waitaha*, and a posthumous one to Brailsford's 1995 book *Song of the Stone* (reissued in 2008). The latter reads:

> You [Brailsford] have been chosen to write the record of our ancestors and tell the story of Waitaha because of your skill and the

awhi [cherishing, support] you gave the people of Ngāi Tahu during the Tribunal hearings. This is not the easiest of tasks because of the things that have been hidden away from the majority of the people. People will ridicule all the things you say and do in the name of Waitaha.[34]

As social anthropologist Michael Goldsmith notes, disagreements within Waitangi claimant coalitions over who should get what are not uncommon, and Te Pani represented a contingent identifying as Waitaha who wanted their own nation recognised as distinct from Ngāi Tahu. Goldsmith also suggests that Te Pani was one of those criticised, but discreetly unnamed, by Ngāi Tahu chief negotiator Sir Tipene O'Regan for politicising history.[35] It is doubtful that Te Pani realised quite how far Brailsford would embroider and embellish legitimate Waitaha lore:

> Waitaha was a nation, an ancient gathering of many peoples from Europe, Africa, Asia and the Americas. That nation, founded in the ways of peace, was swept aside by invading warrior tribes several hundred years ago. Yet when it was destroyed, the sacred knowledge it had cradled for fifteen hundred years did not die. The women who survived carried it into the new tribes.[36]

As a message it hits all the right New Age buttons — inclusiveness, diversity, life-affirming, pacificism — and can even draw in the latest scientific discoveries about Pacific migration from Asia, trade with South America, and mitochondrial Eve (the most recent matrilineal common ancestor of all humans traceable through mitochondrial DNA). Of course, there is not a skerrick of archaeological, genetic, linguistic, paleo-botanical, or any other evidence for this grand coalition of peoples, and it effectively erases Waitaha's whakapapa as tangata whenua.

‡

There is often a tendency in such appropriation of elements of indigenous cultures to New Age ends to rely on the face value of dubious historical reports, such as the brief mention in 1898 that at Christchurch the police were searching the Dallington sand dunes, 'where some bones were unearthed the other day. Dr. Symes [Dr William Henry Symes, Medical Officer of Health for the colony, police surgeon and president of the Philosophical Institute] has examined the jawbone, and believes it to be that of some old Maori warrior. It must have belonged to a man of giant stature of comparative youth.'[37]

Other instances include Clement Wragge's 1910 claims of stone-age monolithic sites in the Bay of Islands.[38] The New Zealand-born American artist K. M. Ballantyne (1885–1961), writing in 1930, was convinced, on his Art Deco-derived stylistic interpretation, that Māori visual culture was directly related to Egyptian, Babylonian, Hittite, Assyrian, Indian, Chinese, and North and South American Art,[39] which would certainly cover a lot of purely imaginary bases.

In its most benign form this New Age revisionism results in such absurdities as Judith Hoch, a white anthropologist from the United States with a background studying the Yoruba of Nigeria, the Cree of Québec and Vodou in New Orleans, who is now based in Nelson and who claims an eco-spiritual psychic connection with the ancient Waitaha and their knowledge.[40] At its most malign, in the 1970s these notions played directly into the pseudo-ethnographical agendas of people such as Barry Fell and R. A. Lochore,[41] and more recently Kerry Bolton (whom we will meet again in Chapter 11 as New Zealand's one-time most prominent Satanist),[42] and Martin Doutré,[43] whose pseudo-histories of pre-Māori settlement have Pākehā nationalist implications and help to undermine Māori assertion of customary rights and special status as Aotearoa's first people, and have been enthusiastically taken up by the Hobson's Pledge movement.[44]

Brailsford has more or less reinvented himself wholeheartedly as what some might see as a kind of Pākehā tohunga and is regarded with varying degrees of acceptance and scorn from Māori, including Waitaha, and Pākehā. Makere Stewart-Harawira (Waitaha), a professor of indigenous, environmental and global studies at the University of Alberta, Canada, writes:

The author's ascribing to himself of a Waitaha whakapapa and the highly imaginative re-interpretations of the events surrounding the writing of *Song of the Waitaha* in the subsequently published *Song of the Stone*, have all become useful weapons in the hands of others wishing to discredit the whanau and hapu of Waitaha. In the context of a government-orchestrated lolly-scramble contestation for rapidly diminishing resources, the misappropriation of Waitaha histories and identity has been wielded as a tool to construct the continuance of the people of Waitaha into the present day as pure fabrication. In the hands of authors such as Brailsford and his colleagues, the indigenous tribes of Aotearoa are now being displaced through fanciful reconstructions that place immigrant groups from Europe and elsewhere beyond the Pacific as the earliest arrivals in Aotearoa. Numerous articles such as those by Gary Cook in *Rainbow Network* magazine promote an interpretation of ancient mounds and stone walls which attempts to support their claim of an earlier migration of non-Polynesian antecedents.[45]

Brailsford's Pākehā critics variously depict him as a self-promoting New Age showman,[46] and he is regarded by other spiritual nonconformists as a slightly buffoonish character rather too willing to adopt Māoritanga and spiritual abilities.[47]

In 2022, partly inspired by so-called 'freedom villages' that had sprung up around the country protesting Covid-19 mandates, a group claiming tino rangatiratanga and Native Title in the name of Waitaha and Ngāti Māmoe began camping in the Burwood section of Christchurch's River Avon corridor of the Red Zone, a large area of currently wilding land left in the wake of the Christchurch earthquakes. This occupation was vigorously repudiated by the local hapū, Ngāi Tūāhuriri, who also claim whakapapa to Waitaha and Ngāti Māmoe.

Te Maire Tau, the upoko (head) of Te Ngāi Tūāhuriri Rūnanga, stated that the protest group had been misinformed by *The Song of the Waitaha*. He recalled the tensions that had been caused by the book within the hapū, saying: 'None of our elders' whakapapa or traditions support this publication. All families in Tuahiwi were offended. Our upoko at the time was quite clear that we were to have no engagement with them.' The protest group allegedly had connections to Kyle Chapman, formerly the leader of New Zealand white supremacist group the National Front.[48]

‡

Another fascinating New Zealand export is Jani King, born some time in the 1940s near Putāruru in the southern Waikato. After leaving school and a string of jobs that took her to Australia, she had an encounter with a glowing extra-terrestrial in 1961, and allegedly developed the power to mentally communicate with whales and dolphins. In 1989 she had an audience with the psychic channeller Azena Ramanda and spoke with an entity named St Germain. This St Germain — perchance the legendary immortal eighteenth-century alchemist Count St Germain? — explained that King had been abducted by a UFO in 1947 and medically examined, and that the being she had met in 1961 was from the Pleiades and named P'taah (which sounds a lot like the name of the Egyptian creator god Ptah).

It's probably worth noting that around this time King was also reading Whitley Strieber's 1987 book *Communion*, the self-proclaimed 'classic account of alien encounter'.[49] In 1989 King made her first public appearances channelling P'taah, and by 1991 a semi-permanent group was gathering around her in North Queensland. These channelling sessions set out the teachings of P'taah, resulting in a book, *An Act of Faith* (1991), and subsequent volumes. According to P'taah, star people have been coming to Earth for centuries, and differ from humans in that they remember their divine nature and reincarnations. P'taah also describes coming changes in the world coinciding with the blossoming of Goddess energy on Earth. In the 1990s King, who lives in Queensland, emerged as a major figure in the Australian New Age movement.[50]

‡

In 1986, Roy Wallis argued in the *Journal for the Scientific Study of Religion* that British settler societies, New Zealand especially, were, among developed societies, particularly open to new religious movements despite the relatively low attendance of traditional churches.[51] Throughout the 1970s and 1980s, a veritable tsunami of new religious groups and spiritualities poured into Aotearoa from Asia, Australia, Europe and the United States. We don't really need to go into any of them in too great detail, as most lack an overt occult component or would be better discussed in the context of new faiths, cults or UFO-centred movements. These include communities like Centrepoint in Auckland, and new religious movements including the Hare Krishnas (ISKON) in their saffron robes, Ananda Marga, the multiplanetary Aetherius Society, Soka Gakkai, the Art of Living Foundation, Transcendental Meditation (TM) levitating away, Brahma Kumaris, Landmark Education Corporation, Eckankar, Maitreya, Neuro-linguistic Programming (NLP) — British comedian Jimmy Carr is a fan — the UFO-communing Raëlians, Subud, and the Unification Church more colloquially known as the 'Moonies'.[52]

Transcendental Meditation (TM) attempted to get a foothold in New Zealand politics in 1996 when Tim Irwin (a graduated TM practitioner since 1983, the first Māori to do so), originally from Bluff, ran for Parliament as the candidate for the Natural Law Party.[53]

Others have had more traction. Zenith Applied Philosophy — or, to use its catchier acronym, ZAP — stands unique among these movements in that it is almost entirely an original product of Aotearoa, specifically Christchurch. It seems almost purpose-built for the aspirational drive and motifs of its time, with a name that suggests both being struck by a mystical Damascene gnosis with science-fictional, comic-book onomatopoeia, while indirectly suggesting the country's favourite flavoured-milk drink of the day. The origins of ZAP can be traced back to 1974. Its founder John Dalhoff (1944–2001) was born to Danish parents and grew up in Golden Bay near Nelson — a place rich in alternative lifestyles and alternative worldviews. His own exploration of alternative spirituality began when he fell into the gravitational pull of Scientology as a student at Massey University in the early 1960s. He went on to become a full-time Scientology worker in Aotearoa after travelling to the Saint Hill Manor Scientology Centre in the United Kingdom in 1965 to study.

Accused of failing to comply with the group's 'ethical codes', in 1972 he was expelled from Scientology. Clearly undeterred from his spiritual journey, two years later he claimed to have reached the 'ultimate' state — presumably something like Operating Thetan Level VIII in Scientology — and thenceforth went by the name 'John Ultimate'. His new philosophy was a curious, heady and rather toxic cocktail of tenets lifted from L. Ron Hubbard's 200 axioms, Eastern religion, and the usual far-right flummery from the ultra-conservative US John Birch Society, anti-unionism, anti-Communism, alleged anti-Semitism and New World Order conspiracy theories — a proto-QAnon if you will.

For a while ZAP also had an ambiguous relationship with another Christchurch-based libertarian-minarchist group, the Tax Reduction Integrity Movement (TRIM). (If ZAP is obscure, TRIM is virtually invisible.) The Church of Scientology, no more tolerant of heresy or competition than any other religious group, declared Ultimate 'suppressive' — which is about the worst thing you can be as a Scientologist — and forbade Scientologists to have anything to do with ZAP not long after.[54]

Very occasionally ZAP members can still be seen in Christchurch's CBD, approaching young, white, male passers-by and asking them if they have an interest in world affairs or offering personality tests, and proffering flyers selling ZAP applied philosophy courses. This approach is obviously another aspect of the movement lifted straight from Scientology. In 1980, the Christchurch *Press* somewhat hysterically declared there to be between 4000 and 5000 ZAP students, an estimate that seems more to reflect the penchant for cult panics characteristic of the period than serious statistical enquiry. By 2008 the same newspaper had revised its estimate to a more realistic few hundred at ZAP's 'feisty peak', wasting away to a mere 20 or 30 adherents by 1990.

☦

That said, at its height in the late 1970s and early 1980s, ZAP held considerable influence in Christchurch. For example, it ran several fast-food restaurants, notably Sandwich Factories — whose ZAP connection only came to light in 1981 when what is now the Service and Food Workers Union brought a successful action against them. The food outlets Luigi's Pizzas, The Dog House, Farmer John's Chicken House, American Burger

Bar and Roasters Restaurant were also implicated. ZAP also ran the company Natrodale Organics Plus, and likely still does.

At this time it was regularly claimed that many prominent Christchurch business, political and civic leaders were members of ZAP. In 1995 ZAP briefly even boasted a radio station, Radio Liberty, which folded after a few months.[55]

The relative success of ZAP in the 1980s clearly had a lot to do with the way its aggressive pro-business, pro-wealth, pro-success philosophy chimed with eagerly aspiring individualism of the decade. Some might regard it as, essentially, a cult for yuppies, but, despite its high profile, its actual doctrines remained maddeningly vague or borrowed — its source material being generic free-enterprise material such as Frédéric Bastiat's *The Law* (1850) and Gary Allen (at the time a spokesperson for the John Birch Society) and fellow John Birch Society member and businessman Larry Abraham's *None Dare Call it Conspiracy* (1971), a book that was itself bursting with conspiracy theories.

Its anti-mixed economy, anti-union, anti-communist stance held a certain appeal at the time. Members were known to randomly bang on the roofs of Lada cars, berating their owners for driving a communist vehicle.[56] At the time, Lada cars were sold by the New Zealand Dairy Board, which took them in lieu of hard currency from a bankrupt Soviet Union for mutton and butter, an arrangement that ended in 1990.[57]

The name aside, John Ultimate was clearly in a messianic mould, at one point claiming to have personally absorbed an earthquake that would have destroyed Wellington, and declaring his Burnside home the 'centre of the universe'. 'Jesus talked about being the son of God,' Ultimate is reported to have written in late 1978, 'but no-one has talked about attaining the ultimate state. This has been obtained here at the centre of the universe . . . I am the ultimate now I have talked to many people recently in other places though different means (e.g. in their dreams, on their telephones). 'Many people from other places are now on the way to the centre of the universe . . .'[58] Many aspects of the group, including the reported cleansing rituals, the tight controls on members' finances, the strict forbidding of drugs, and members isolating from their families, are distinctly cult-like.[59]

Concern about ZAP's nature and influence ran sufficiently high that in

1985 Philip Burdon, the National Party MP for Fendalton, from where the group operated, asked for a Parliamentary inquiry. It never eventuated. Ultimate apparently made himself very comfortable from tithes and ZAP course sales, investing in the US stock market and giving generously to various right-wing causes. He existed at a Hubbard-like distance from the gatherings at his large Clyde Street house, communicating only by intercom, or telephoning his followers, having grown morbidly obese and averse to face-to-face interaction. Many followers had not seen him in 10 years by the time of his death in 2001, despite being in regular contact.[60] 'I am above nothing or below nothing,' Ultimate once wrote. 'I am not god, and I have no wish to go down to that level.'[61]

To what degree Ultimate and his higher-ranking followers believed his shtick is difficult to determine. Geoffrey Russell, an 'advanced' member responsible for TRIM, is quoted as saying in 1982: 'Perhaps Zap does look weird, but it depends on what you think is weird. There are some pretty extraordinary things supported by the establishment.' Regarding Ultimate's propensity for L. Ron Hubbard-esque mystery, Russell said: 'He has a sense of humour.'[62] One wonders if the Covid anti-mandate activity of the early 2020s has sparked off a little revival among the remaining members.

‡

With its pseudoscience, science-fictional moniker, Quantum Dynamics or QD (sometimes known as 'People Dynamics' or 'Quest for Freedom') emerged to prominence at the end of the 1990s, surfing the back of a decade of abuse panic and self-improvement. Led by homeopath Janee Child, also known as Jane Thompson, Jane Ball and then, by deed poll in 1998, the more self-consciously exotic Yasmine Child, like ZAP it used some distinctly Scientology-esque techniques to control its adherents. Child, ex-wife of potter Barry Ball (the brother of *Footrot Flats* creator Murray Ball), allegedly presented herself as a victim of ritual abuse who had created QD as a way of healing herself.

Those drawn to QD were often already vulnerable victims of past sexual abuse, or were essentially conditioned into believing they had suppressed memories of being ritually abused. Those who resisted this indoctrination were told they weren't ready for QD, accused of being lazy and not working hard enough for it, and cast out. Those who stayed often distanced themselves from their families, split from partners, and some even became suicidal. QD trainees were required to analyse the key relationships in their lives and re-enact past traumas, frequently graphically sexual, in front of as many as 30 strangers. In other words, a textbook cult of the classic model.

Participants plotted out their deepest thoughts onto triangle diagrams, their path to enlightenment, over which Child would wave her hands and diagnose their life 'blocks'. Those who kept to the 'Divine Plan' were promised eventual reincarnation on a higher plane, while on this plane they were financially milked through expensive courses as they moved up the ranks to QD teacher. It was clearly lucrative in neurotic Auckland: the year she became Yasmine, Child moved her operation from Hillsborough to a country retreat near Albany.[63] Child's last known whereabouts was Western Australia.

Chapter 11.
Witchcraft and neopaganism

The real defect of rationalism or exclusive intellectualism lies in its attempt to prove Faith, or, I should rather say, in its belief that it has succeeded in demonstrating what cannot be demonstrated. Rationalism tries to find a place for God in its picture of the world. But God, 'whose centre is everywhere and His circumference nowhere,' cannot be fitted into a diagram. He is rather the canvas on which the picture is painted, or the frame in which it is set.

— WILLIAM INGE, *FAITH AND ITS PSYCHOLOGY*, 1910

New Zealand's nineteenth-century European settlers came primarily from the British Isles, and were often people from rural areas seeking a better life for themselves and their families. In many outlying parts of the Great Britain and Ireland, ancient folk beliefs — particularly relating to fairy lore and witchcraft — persisted well into the twentieth century to be recorded by folklorists and oral historians.[1] For the Irish, particularly those associated with the Celtic revival, folk beliefs were not merely quaint superstition but rather a matter of nationalism, cultural patrimony and heritage. The Irish Famine of 1845–49 brought immigration into Britain and the Empire, and the Irish brought their rich supernatural lore with them.[2]

And belief in witches and pagan figures were not solely the demesne of illiterate countryfolk. Fairy fever had been sparked among the antiquarians of the Romantic era and burned fiercely throughout the reign of Queen Victoria, among scientists, historians, theologians, folklorists, anthropologists and authors. More than a few reputable Victorians and Edwardians genuinely believed in fairies, albeit rationalised as the remnants of non-Indo-European cultures or Platonised as personified natural forces.

In a letter cited in the acknowledgements of his friend Jonathan Cott's 1973 fairytale anthology *Beyond the Looking Glass* author and founding *Rolling Stone* editor David Dalton observed, 'how elemental the Victorians were, how intact that cord was that tied them to the savage Celtic tradition, almost like an underground railway transporting treasures from the incredible depths of the past to the very door of the crystal palace'. That cord really was more of a Gordian web of pixie dust and ectoplasm.

Even so, popular nineteen-century writers on the subject of the supernatural — Sir Walter Scott, for example, and his rather banal *Letters on Demonology and Witchcraft* (1830) — were expected to maintain a critically hostile stance to superstition. Anglicans and Methodists stoutly denied that such supernatural forces existed.[3] Not so Catholics, who had a reputation for awe and miracles to maintain. The tone was repeated in New Zealand, and we find *The Wellington Independent* in 1863 reprinting a piece from *The Times* of London ascribing nineteenth-century reports witchcraft to the influence of unconscious suggestion.[4]

‡

Yet this scepticism difficult to square with the contemporaneous and ubiquitous popularity of literary ghost stories, and the occult pursuits of prominent historical figures of the nineteenth century — Napoleon, Byron, Lord Castlereagh and Tsar Alexander I of Russia, to name just a few — as reported in the press.[5] Between 1860 and 1899, British newspapers published over 462 reports about outbreaks of witchcraft, with the highest number being 162 in the 1860s and declining thereafter.[6] This decline gained momentum around 1900 and rapidly accelerated in Britain after 1930.

In part this is likely due to increased affluence and access to healthcare which gave individuals far greater personal control over their worlds and made them feel less the plaything of other forces In Britain this can be associatedwith such social advances s as the granting of universal suffrage for men in 1918, votes for women in England in the same year and in Wales and Scotland in 1928, the National Insurance Act 1911 and the National Health Service Act 1946.[7] New Zealand had a head start on Britain, passing the Public Health Act in 1872, granting women the vote in 1893, and passing the Unemployment Act in 1930, and the Social Security Act in 1938. It's also likely people stopped talking about the witchcraft, fairies and other folk beliefs unguardedly, lest they be mocked, or attract scrutiny of the authorities.

But inevitably, such beliefs were carried to the young colony, most of them being relatively benign, such as apotropaic items of clothing or dead cats secreted in wall cavities, as well as the more usual lucky horseshoes and the throwing of spilled salt over the shoulder.[8] There was an easy coexistence of old and new: Victorian reprints of Nicholas Culpeper's *Complete Herbal* (1653), with its advice on dispelling hexes, and William Lilly's *Christian Astrology* (1647), could be found on bookshelves next to farmers' almanacs and family Bibles. Thomas Arnold the Younger (1823–1900), second son of the celebrated headmaster of Rugby School, brother of the poet and classicist Matthew Arnold (1822–1888), emigrated to New Zealand in the mid-nineteenth century to try his hand at farming. He made the following observations about Pākehā settler superstition in the Nelson area in 1848:

Albrecht Dürer, *The Witch*, c.1500. Fantastical depictions like this have for centuries tended to colour the witch in the popular imagination.

> Living so long with these people, I have learnt many things that I had little idea of before. Their superstitions and belief in ghosts astonished me. In an age of materialism and steam, here are people who firmly believe that a fiery serpent as big round as a man's leg, once appeared in an iron furnace at Tunbridge a few years ago . . . More than one of the ghost stories which they have told me in the most simple natural way, have something quite poetical and beautiful about them. For my part, I confess that it is a relief for me to find, that this faith in Providence and its visitations and warnings from the unseen world, still holds its ground firmly. Real life wears such a harsh and forbidding aspect for the English poor, that one must rejoice if some belief or other, though it be but a superstitious one, remains to poetize and ennoble their daily life.[9]

And what is one to make of this 1871 court report in the *Auckland Star*:

> (Before R.C. Barstow, Esq. RM)
> SHADOWS ON THE PAVEMENT.
> Bridget Lestrange, an elderly woman with an evil eye and weird countenance, was charged with drunkenness.
> The old woman scowled upon the constable, darted a severe look at the Clerk of the Court, and roared out, 'Guilty, and what of it?'
> Fined 10s and costs.[10]

Interesting things happen when these folkways encountered Māori magical traditions in which whakapapa was the GPS that orientated the individual in a complex landscape of human and non-human ancestors, but what specifically resonated was the belief in mākutu or malign occult powers. European colonists brought a host of diseases to which Māori had no previous experience or immunity — influenza, whooping cough, tuberculosis, cholera, typhoid, measles, and others. Understandably Māori, at least initially, interpreted this as mākutu, and British missionaries were often accused of being 'he iwi mākutu', of the tribe of evil sorcerers.[11]

In 1835 the Reverend Henry Williams was participating in a large iwi gathering when andhis cloak was torn by an angry rangatira who accused him of 'makutuing people'.[12] During the land wars between 1845 and 1872, it was not uncommon for Māori accused of mākutu to be put to death by their own people, with the colonial government not involving itself except, on one occasion, to dismiss a rangatira responsible for one such execution from his salaried position as a land assessor.[13] The missionaries made the eradication of mākutu a priority, as the Reverend Thomas Buddle (1812–1883) wrote at the beginning of the 1850s:

> The belief in Witchcraft was deeply rooted in the mind of the New Zealander. Like most other nations they have had their '*hai makutu*,' i.e., sorcerers, wizards, and witches. Throughout the Pacific, sorcery has been one of Satan's most powerful agencies. It has exerted a fearful influence—stultified the intellect, called into existence a thousand fears, destroyed mutual confidence, perpetuated their mental and spiritual bondage, and as much if not more than any other superstition, impeded the progress of the Gospel. When we remember how very extensively a belief in the existence of witches, and in their power over the fates of men has prevailed, even in the civilized nations of Europe, and especially in England, we cannot feel surprised to find it among the New Zealanders, whose mythology brings them into such close and constant communication with infernal spirits, and whose ignorance and superstition make them the easy dupes of designing men.[14]

This relationship changed dramatically at the century's turn. The imposition of British education and the spread of Christianity put an end to indigenous witch-killings,[15] and in 1893 the colonial government, emulating similar laws in Britain against magical con artists, prescribed hard labour for anyone claiming to 'exercise or use any kind of witchcraft, sorcery, enchantment, or conjuration'.[16]

Naturally this also applied to the Pākehā community, but not so (with some very rare exceptions) the Tohunga Suppression Act of 1907, which was brought in by the new Dominion of New Zealand with the endorsement of some Western-educated Māori. That Act specifically targeted the younger, new style of self-proclaimed tohunga emerging at the time with a mishmash of traditional practices, a hit-and-miss understanding of native herbalism, Christianity and snake oil.[17] It also gave the authorities a convenient weapon against resistant Māori prophetic movements, such as that of Rua Kēnana (1869–1937) of Tūhoe, who was arrested for sedition in 1916.

The state-funded te reo Māori press ridiculed belief in mākutu, and attempted to popularise the idea of 'mate Māori' — a sort of psychosomatic malaise of no obvious cause attributed to transgressions of tapu.[18] Fascinatingly there are two examples of Pākehā women being arrested under the Tohunga Act accused of peddling quackery to Māori: Mary 'Saint' Elizabeth Curry, in 1917, an elderly woman who may have been some kind of herbalist;[19] and another elderly woman, Mary Ann Hill, in 1914, a certified midwife who sold a concoction that 'looked like tomato sauce and smelled like furniture polish' and professed clairvoyance.[20]

In both cases the women had amassed large followings among Māori who were understandably mistrustful of Western medicine in the wake of multiple epidemics of newly imported diseases: 1898–1899, influenza; 1900–1901, bubonic plague; 1902–1903, scarlet fever and measles; 1907, pertussis; 1911, typhoid; 1913, smallpox, and 1916, polio. Possibly the women represent the survival of imported European 'cunning' or healer traditions.

It is important to understand this history because the upshot of attempting to stamp out belief in mākutu among Māori was to, by means of the so-called Streisand Effect by which attempts to hide or censor in fact increases attention make Pākehā aware of it to the point of assimilating fear of it into their own beliefs. At the extreme end we find Kimble Bent (1837–1916), one of the so-called Pākehā-Māori who naturalised into Māori life and identity among Ngāti Ruanui, deserting his army regiment during the land wars and becoming a follower of Tītokowaru, a healer and caster of mākutu in South Taranaki.[21] It might be more accurate to say Pākehā-Māori were tolerated by their hosts as mascots and go-betweens to the Europeans.

‡

One of New Zealand's most internationally popular authors, even today, was Frederick Maning (1812–1883) — Arthur Conan Doyle was a huge fan — a Pākehā-Māori of Anglo-Irish extraction who wrote a number of books describing his first-hand experience (likely embroidered for effect) of mākutu and other magical practices. On one occasion he narrates an attempt by an old, one-eyed tohunga to cast mākutu on him, writing: 'I remember I felt a curious sensation at the time, like what I fancied a man must feel who had just sold himself, body and bones, to the devil. For a moment I asked myself the question of whether I was not actually being then and there handed over to the powers of darkness.'[22]

The appeal of tikanga and Māoritanga could be profoundly seductive to the handful of Europeans primed for an interest in spiritual matters. The best-known example of this is undoubtedly that of the missionary the Reverend Thomas Kendall (1788–1832) who, in the parlance of an earlier era, famously 'went native'. He would write in 1822, 'All [Māori] notions are metaphysical and I have been poisoned with the apparent sublimity of their ideas that I have been almost completely turned from a Christian to a heathen.'[23] When Kendall took the daughter of a rangatira for his de facto wife the following year, the Reverend Samuel Marsden, his superior in the Church Missionary Society, put it rather differently:

> His mind has been greatly polluted by studying the abominations of the heathens, and his ideas are very heathenish. No change will ever be produced in his sentiments and feelings while he remains here. He will never recover from his fall, as he is now a man without strength and in the most awful state as it respects his soul. 'Strangers have devoured his strength, and he knoweth it not.' (Hosea 7:9)[24]

Curiously, though, belief in mākutu also infected more conventional colonists. Tohunga stood on the boundary line and cursed the land stolen by Pākehā in the Waikato.[25] Pākehā farmers might blame such curses when the land failed to prosper, and newspapers report crop failures as 'a mākutu seems to be upon the land'.[26] In 1924 North Island farmers informed a government minister that the land was under the influence of mākutu.[27]

Consider the construction of the Rangiriri highway, opening the following year and now part of the Waikato Expressway. Beset with disasters and obstacles and requiring the moving of an urupā (Māori burial site), it took three years to construct just 27 kilometres, a journalist reporting: 'The men on the job speak mysteriously of "mākutu". Sometimes it is with bated breath, sometimes a twinkle may be detected in the eye, but the purport is the same — the Rangiriri job has been under a potent spell.'[28] In 1929 the bursting of the Mount Eden reservoir was blamed on the curse of an old kuia,[29] and by the breaking out of the Second World War, mākutu was regarded as thoroughly assimilated into New Zealand English.[30]

A faint echo of this belief was discernible when, in 2002, work on another stretch of the Waikato Expressway, this time near Meremere, was halted due to the belief of Ngāti Naho (a subtribe of Tainui) that a taniwha (a spirit creature associated with water) inhabited the local swamp. Work on a 12-kilometre stretch across the swamps had halted earlier after sinking earthworks blew the $56 million construction budget, and local Māori attributed a high number of car crashes on State Highway 1 to the entity. Transit New Zealand responded to the issue under the same protocols as for found human remains.[31]

Similar beliefs are still active in Scotland, where in 2020 plans for an organic salmon farm on the Isle of Skye were scuppered by a group called Friends of the Eilean Fhlodaigearraidh Faeries, who warned that a variety of mermaid called an *ashrai* might feel threatened and retaliate by luring workers into the sea.[32] Increasingly, though, New Zealand is in the forefront of recognising other knowledges and worldviews in the area of 'biocultural conservation'.[33]

‡

The Waikato is rife with high strangeness. Perhaps it's because for a short period a considerable amount of agency and attention was concentrated there: anger, death, anguish and misery during the land wars, on top of centuries of Māori habitation and belief. In the 1880s, for example, there was the case of the Waikato saurian, a mysterious cryptid that plagued the area around Paeroa and Waihoa, variously attributed to a hoax, Māori having returned from Australia with crocodile eggs and leaving them near the river, a taniwha,[34] a sea lion,[35] or a tuna tūoro — a quasi-legendary giant black eel considered an ill omen by Māori.[36] Not incidentally, reptiles were associated by Māori with Whiro-te-tipua, the atua of misfortune.

The mining township of Waihi was beset by psychic disturbances during the 1920s, ranging from multiple nocturnal sightings in the streets of a white, spectral figure carrying a candle[37] to the remarkable case of Mr and Mrs Collins, who became convinced their Walmsley Street house was oppressed by a malign poltergeist that would only allow the use of one chair in the home. The couple was later found wandering in a daze at the Auckland Railway Station and taken to Avondale mental hospital by the police for observation. Was it mere *folie à deux* brought on by a recent lecture on the supernatural by travelling ex-Primitive Methodist minister-cum-knife-grinder Samuel Barrett, as thought by many in Waihi?[38]

Certainly ghost scares were not unusual in the Waikato in those days, with similar outbreaks occurring in Paeroa and Thames, which the cynical might attribute to boredom and the fearsome amount of alcohol consumed in those communities. Was it even, perhaps, repressed anxiety and shame, for the inhabitants of Waihi in the 1920s were the strike-breakers who replaced the 'Red Fed' (New Zealand Federation of Labour) miners in 1912?

In the late 1930s, a respectable Cambridge farming woman saw, in broad daylight, for all of 10 seconds, the ghost of an elderly, tattooed Māori warrior leaning on his taiaha, gazing wistfully towards confiscated Maungakawa. Perhaps news of the tensions in the Pacific agitated a psychic turbulence in the area and stirred up this old martial spirit? This was reported in a newspaper story in 1941, which also told of an 'old-time farmer acquaintance' of the writer, 'many years ago', droving his stock from Waikato to Auckland, overnighting in an abandoned hut by the wayside, only to be troubled the whole night by heavy footsteps and clanking chains (haunting tropes that date all the way back to the Stoic philosopher Athenodorus and the Rome of 44 BCE)[39] with no visible human cause.[40]

At the lesser end of the scale, in 1982 workers laying a railway culvert in Waimiha, south of Te Kuiti, found not one, but *two* separate instances of live frogs entombed in rock in the same day, describing them as lethargic and 'black-as-black'.[41] This appears to have been one of the last such examples of this puzzling Fortean phenomenon[42] recorded in the OECD.[43]

State Highway 1 in the Waikato is something of a strange attractor of anomalies and high weirdness, particularly UFO sightings. There is a certain spirit of wonder and ritual in driving along a highway that becomes almost a meditation, especially with the Luxor-silhouette of the Huntly Power Station over the river or the small white pyramid at Pōkeno with its gothic finial of rifles. Many religious texts are merely attempts at a *Highway Code* to life.

‡

Despite, as historian Nile Green notes, the tendency of an 'occult' to emerge from the interaction of distinct geographies, cultures and languages — as in the case of the peculiar mutation of Buddhism that arose from the meeting of the United States and Meiji Japan, or the Anglo-Indian nature of Theosophy — this simply didn't take lasting coherent form in Aotearoa.[44] Perhaps the old believers sensed that in a land of vast realms of forest and ocean, their little household spirits were out of their league in a standoff between Māori gods like Tāne and Tangaroa, and the imperial old-world Jehovah.

A sense of this made an impression on author James Cowan (1870–1943), writing of Mokoia Island in Lake Rotorua for the *Otago Daily Times* in 1913:

> There are some places in New Zealand where the 'genius loci' of the ancients seems a very real thing. New though the land is from the standpoint of civilised man, it has secluded spots which hold for those who have that too rare quality, poetic imagination, a soul of immemorial antiquity, a familiar spirit, a perdurable element of mysticism and enchantment, built up of the lives and loves and traditions of generations of mankind. In these places it is the dead who are of more importance than the living, in a sense, for the minds of people of the brown race [Māori] are prone to contemplate the past — perhaps rather more than is good for them.[45]

This was a perennial theme in Cowan's writing. Even as late as 1931, couched in romantic sentiment and tongue-in-cheek though it may be, we can find him writing: 'I can never enter such a bush without something of the Maori veneration for the ancients of the Wao-nui-a-Tane' and 'The tree-worship of the olden woodsmen seems the most natural thing in the world in such a forest as Waipoua . . . It seems sacrilege to lay crosscut saw to the remaining groves of so chieftanlike a tree.'[46]

These instances, scattered to begin with, had largely faded from the collective Pākehā consciousness by the middle of the twentieth century, especially as ethnography became an emphatically scientific discipline under the influence of anthropology. One exceptional vestige was to be found in the visual arts of the 1930s and 1940s in the motif of the dead tree in the work of Christopher Perkins, Eric Lee-Johnson, Gordon Walters, Rita Angus, Russell Clark, John Holmwood and Mervyn Taylor. On a superficial level these are prosaic *memento mori* evoking the pastoral conquest of the land, but the anthropomorphic tendencies in their depiction have more than a little of the dryad slain by progress in them.[47]

The old folkways and superstitions of Europe were mostly forgotten or ridiculed as a pitfall for the credulous. Nevertheless, it does seem a little strange that the Table of Duties for New Zealand's 1899 Customs Tariff would include '82. Proprietary medicines, or medicaments . . . n.o.e. [not otherwise enumerated], prepared by any occult secret or art, 40 per cent. *ad valorem* [according to value]',[48] although in all likelihood 'occult' in this context just means 'undisclosed'.

In the late 1920s a number of New Zealand newspapers covered the UK trial of 'Cornish gypsies' for tricking Britons out of cash with threats of the evil eye,[49] and while readers of Gisborne's *Poverty Bay Herald* were regaled with thrilling details of the trial in Karlsruhe of Berta Vögtle, the 'Witch of Groetzingen', for embezzlement in 1935,[50] they could rest easy in the knowledge that it wasn't the sort of thing that happened here — or at least, not openly. A Mr F. B. Adams in 1930 delivered an address to the Otago University Club luncheon on the subject of witchcraft, declaring that 'this most lamentable of human superstitions' consisted of a fully developed medieval Christian notion grafted onto the lapsed gods of older mythologies, and spoke at length about the mob violence such beliefs encouraged, including the assault on a priest in France in 1926 for supposedly having cursed someone.[51]

There were exceptions, however. An opinion piece in the *Otago Daily Times* in 1909 suggests a revival of witchcraft might be a much-needed antidote to the disenchanting atmosphere of Nietzsche, Ibsen and Tolstoy,[52] and cites Oliver Madox Heuffer's *The Book of Witches* (1908). Heuffer (1877–1931) was the grandson of Pre-Raphaelite painter Ford Madox Brown, and younger brother of author Ford Madox Ford. In his book he argues that belief in witchcraft and the occult is so prevalent in history that it is culturally unhealthy to dismiss it as trivial superstition and, indeed, it is important to human psychological happiness to embrace it.[53]

At times, though, relicts of paganism would manifest in unexpected places. Consider the large canvases produced by renowned artist Rita Angus (1908–1970) in the mid-to-late 1940s and early 1950s, notably two oils, *A Goddess of Mercy* (1945–47, Christchurch Art Gallery Te Puna o Waiwhetū) and *Rutu* (1951, Museum of New Zealand Te Papa Tongarewa, Wellington), and a watercolour, *Sun Goddess* (1949, private collection).[54] These goddess paintings were Angus's woman-centred, peace- and life-affirming response to the aftermath of the Second World War and what she saw as a male world of death and destruction. In a rare public statement in 1947 she wrote: 'My paintings express a desire ... to create a living freedom from the afflicting theme of death.'[55]

Each painting is a syncretic, hieratic hybrid of European, Asian and Pacific spiritual motifs, *Rutu* being a self-portrait, or rather, a self-apotheosis icon as haloed bodhisattva. Curator and art writer Ron Brownson has suggested that they trace the seasons winter, spring and summer.[56] The result is as much an expression of esoteric spirituality as anything produced by European Symbolists as the nineteenth century closed. Wildly presumptive colonial appropriation by our standards, yes, but a brighter, more utopian mysticism than that cloaking the slaughter which provoked it.

‡

The average Pākehā rarely engaged with tikanga or Māoritanga except as a curiosity or a kitsch ornament to nascent nationalism, as in the case of the Savage Clubs. The Savage Club, conceived of in London by journalists and artists, was a social club first transplanted to Invercargill in 1885 and spread around New Zealand. The club emphasised stage performance, with evenings featuring singing, musical items and recitations. In New Zealand it adopted the trappings of pseudo-Māori ritual, leaders being called 'rangatira' and 'ariki', and members dressed up in piupiu (flax skirts) and carried faux mere (clubs).[57]

Such organisations were neither occult nor esoteric, but some secularised aspects of Anglo-Celtic paganism certainly proved remarkably tenacious. The ancient English fertility ritual of Morris dancing is recorded as far back as the fifteenth century,[58] and dancers first migrated to New Zealand in the 1870s, although aside from the existence of bush bands there are no records of Morris dancing until the 1920s. Morris dancing began to take off in New Zealand in the 1920s and 1930s, largely in response to the folk revival in Britain, and British groups like Mary Neal's Espérance Club.[59]

The Bloomsbury-esque arts and literature community in Christchurch took to Morris dancing under the auspices of the sculptor Francis Shurrock (1877–1977), who in 1924 had emigrated from Warrington in Lancashire to teach art.[60] The Morris revival was kicked off in Britain by the rural revivalist Rolf Gardiner (1902–1971), who also popularised organic farming and naturism and is somewhat controversial for his public approval of the German youth movement and its *Völkisch* tendencies, though his flirtations with Nazism are likely exaggerated.[61] Gardiner conceived of Morris dancing very much in magical terms, insisting it be an exclusively masculine activity, and, far from merely being a 'communal dynamic for all men':

> [T]he Morris and Sword dance are not popular dances; they are essentially selective magic dances which only a peculiarly fitted and trained elite is capable of executing. It is ridiculous to suppose that *any* man is fit to dance the Morris; the old 'traditional' folk knew this well enough in making membership of their 'sides' something of a privilege, and their training of dancers an initiation.[62]

By and large, though, the faint echoes of paganism reside in secular contexts. It could also be argued that Anzac Day every 25 April, coincidentally close to southern hemisphere Samhain (30 April–1 May), constitutes a non-Christian holy day when thousands converge on cult sites around the country at dawn to honour the powerful dead, a fact its critics do not seem to appreciate. Samhain is the Gaelic festival of the transition from harvest into the season of the dead. In the northern hemisphere Samhain is coeval with Halloween and All Soul's Day in most Christian calendars.

The imagery surrounding Anzac Day is articulated in a pagan vernacular of triumphal arches and obelisks, poppies and eternal flames, contradictions that were understood at the time the holiday was initiated.[63] Indeed, in Dunedin in 1923 there was considerable public agitation that the city's proposed cenotaph would take the form of an obelisk, one correspondent to the *Otago Daily Times* describing it as a 'hotch potch of pagan and Christian presentiment'.[64]

On the other hand, you also have purely secular organisations consciously playing at pagan, as in the case of the United Ancient Order of Druids. This group originated in Britain in 1781 as the Ancient Order of Druids, an alternative to Freemasonry to which it bears a superficial resemblance, and is based on a romantic antiquarian understanding of the iconography of ancient Celtic Druidry.[65] As the organisation grew and lodges proliferated around Britain (barring a difficult period during the French Revolution when the British government cracked down on secret societies), some in the organisation wished to adopt a more democratic model similar to the Odd Fellows and other friendly societies. This resulted in a schism, and several lodges, nearly half the organisation, left to form the United Ancient Order of Druids (UAOD) in 1833.[66] It was uncontroversial and tame enough that Winston Churchill was inducted in 1908. The UAOD arrived in New Zealand in 1876 with the founding of the Pioneer Lodge by Past Arch Druid Brother Solomons of Melbourne, who was at that time residing in Dunedin, followed by the Hope and Mistletoe lodges in Christchurch.[67]

The UAOD grew to 50 lodges around the country within a decade. As late as the 1970s, Druids could be recognised in processions, parades and other public events by their long grey beards, white hoods and gowns.[68] By

The United Ancient Order of Druids in their Grey Lynn, Auckland, headquarters in 1909.

then they were probably best known for acting as insurance agents, and — although aspects of their ceremonies and costumes were heavily influential on the earnest revival of a spiritual Neo-Druidry in the nineteenth century — they are emphatically a secular, friendly and benevolent fraternal society, even going so far as to prohibit religion as a topic of conversation.[69]

While the New Zealand order was officially wound up in 1995, nonetheless the presence of the UAOD helped prepare the ground in Aotearoa for Druidic neopagan groups. One such is the Grove of Summer Stars, who have established a Druid grove, substituting native trees for the usual European varieties, in the hills of Pukerua Bay in one of the last surviving stands of kohekohe on the Kāpiti Coast.[70]

This group is a member of the international mystery school the Order of Bards, Ovates & Druids (OBOD), which was founded in England in 1964 by historian-poet Ross Nichols, and the writer and founder of the Tolkien Society Vera Chapman, who were both members of the Ancient Order of Druids.[71] It also draws somewhat on the Welsh Gorsedd of Bards cultural revival movement. With a Tolkien-linked pedigree and an emphasis on forest conservation, there is a certain aesthetic satisfaction that an OBOD grove would eventually establish itself on these shores.

☦

Returning to witchcraft, the practice of a more formal sort enjoyed a Western renaissance in the twentieth century, kicked off by the dubious anthropological musings of Anglo-Indian Egyptologist, archaeologist, anthropologist, historian and folklorist Margaret Murray (1863–1963) and her now thoroughly debunked 1921 book, *The Witch-Cult in Western Europe: A Study in Anthropology*. In this text Murray argued for the existence of an enduring ancient fertility religion centred on goddess worship and ritual witchcraft, whose practitioners were persecuted during the Counter-Reformation witch trials in England and Scotland, which reached their peak between 1580 and 1630.[72]

These theories became part of the mix of folklore, indigenous and Western ceremonial magical practices, Freemasonry, and mythological archetypes upon which former colonial civil servant and amateur anthropologist Gerald Gardner (1884–1964) based a new neopagan religion which became known as Wicca. Characteristically, Wicca has no central authority and is eclectic, with individual covens adopting their own idiosyncratic rituals and identities, which is further complicated by self-initiated individual adherents, yet it does nonetheless have some consistent beliefs. Wicca is often heterosexually dualistic, usually women-affirming,[73] and eco-spiritual, based in the cycles of nature and centred on the worship of a fertility mother goddess and her subservient male consort.[74]

Gardner's books, especially *Witchcraft Today* (1954), spread the Wiccan movement to other English-speaking countries — the United States, Canada, Australia and New Zealand.[75] According to Eleanor 'Ray' Bone (1911–2001), a prominent member and force in Gardnerian Wicca from its early stages, before joining Gardner she had been initiated by a hereditary coven in Cumbria in 1941.[76] According to Wicca scholar Julia Phillips, a later coven which Bone led in Cumbria eventually relocated to New Zealand, though it has never been traced.[77] The Oak Grove coven in Auckland perhaps has a lineage from the Bone line and the *Covenentus Quercus* (Covenant of the Oak) coven that operated in Sussex in the 1960s, but has only been active for the past 20 years.[78]

Worshipping the Goddess as a manifestation of feminist spirituality — and so-called 'Dianic' Wicca (after the Roman virgin goddess of the hunt and moon Diana)[79] shorn of the movement's patriarchal roots without the emphasis on gender polarity — began to appear in New Zealand in the 1970s. Unlike other Western countries, where feminist witchcraft was a minor offshoot of a broader Wiccan and neopagan scene, in New Zealand until relatively recently woman-centric feminist practice was dominant over other varieties.[80] This was partly transplanted via feminist support material from the United States, but also through influential publications such as Carol Christ and Judith Plaskow's *Womanspirit Rising* (1979), Starhawk's *The Spiral Dance* (1979) and Zsuzsanna Budapest's *The Holy Book of Women's Mysteries* (1980).

It appealed to women, often urban with a tertiary qualification and predominantly Pākehā, who felt the feminist movement needed a more spiritual side, or who were attracted to a woman-affirming spirituality that embraced nature. This came with a certain amount of pushback from radical feminist activists, who were concerned that a turn to the spiritual was a distraction from political activism and might lead to complacency.[81] Unlike the United States, where such groups have appropriated elements of Native American ritual such as talking sticks, smudging, sweat lodges and shamanic dream journeys, seeing them as more in touch with an authentic spirituality, in Aotearoa this has not been the case. While outdoor gatherings will acknowledge the tangata whenua, Māori 'cultural property' tends to be respected.[82]

This can be seen as an emergent form of 'bio-regionalism' in magical practice — an ethics associated with place, the *terroir* of a magical or animistic system.[83] Also the idea of an immigrant or descendent of colonists attempting to connect with a still very culturally engaged spiritual world they do not whakapapa to is both absurd and, from the magical point of view, foolhardy. Juliet Batten recommends taking a courteous cue from Māoritanga — respect for the land, observing the cues of the seasons in indigenous nature, finding parallels in the Celtic traditions, without imposing a European worldview upon it.[84] Below is an example of an invocation from around 2004 originating in this practice, incorporating the names of Māori deities:

> Hine-tītama, goddess of the east and the air, dawn maiden, you are the mother of all and you greet us in death . . . Mahuika, goddess of the north, the one who gave the world fire, you warm us with your energy . . . Taranga, goddess of the west, who gave birth to Māui in the ocean, you keep us alive with the water of life . . . Papa-tūānuku, goddess of the south, who came forth from Te Pō, the darkness, you are our mother earth . . . Hine-ahu-one, the essence of all living things, breathe with us now and energize us with your power.[85]

But traditional or hereditary witchcraft was not entirely out of the picture. A reminder came in the form of the Pickingill Papers, named for George Pickingill, a well-known 'cunning man' (a solo practitioner, usually operating out of a rural community and skilled in cures, dowsing and other problem-solving) born in Canewdon, Essex, in 1816. Supposedly, for many years he led a traditional coven in England until his death in 1903.

The papers were published in the 1970s in the British periodicals *The Wiccan* and *The Cauldron*, purportedly written by an E. W. 'Bill' Liddell (sometimes using the pseudonym 'Lugh', the Irish Celtic god of arts, crafts and the law), who had been living in New Zealand since the 1960s, later emigrating to Australia.

The texts, with their traditionalist emphasis on a Man in Black and a Magister (master), were seen by modern Goddess-centric Wiccans as a direct attack. Liddell claimed that he had been instructed by both Gardnerian and hereditary elders to publish the papers to disseminate their views on organisation and ceremony, although he also claimed not to agree with all of them.[86] While the Pickingill Papers have not received any academic support and may even be a hoax, the possibility of a continuation of a non-Wiccan witchcraft tradition in New Zealand is an intriguing one. Perhaps Liddell was a member of Bone's lost coven.

‡

In more recent years, the other flavour of neopaganism to establish itself in Aotearoa is derived from Nordic and Scandinavian traditions. In the broadest sense, as a loose movement this is sometimes referred to as 'heathenry', although this encompasses a diverse range of groups, including *Ásatrú*, *Vanatrú*, or *Forn Sed* in Scandinavia, *Fyrnsidu* or Theodism in Anglo-Saxon affiliated groups, Irminism for those with an emphasis on the German pantheon, while the old-guard white-supremacist groups often go by Odinism, Wotanism, Wodenism or Odalism.

A schism exists between groups with an emphasis on *Völkisch* ethno-nationalism that excludes non-whites, and benign universalist groups that see their practices and beliefs as being open to all. Another schism exists between those Nordic and Scandinavian groups that see themselves in a traditional continuity with the old faith, and newer reconstructionist groups with a mystical or occultist obsession with a pan-Indo-European identity. Heathenry's origins lie in the Romantic cultural revivals in nineteenth-century Europe, Wagner's operas being a popular expression, although actual veneration of Germanic and Nordic deities first manifested in Germany and Austria in the early 1900s. For many years, because of the association of such groups with Nazism, this version of neopaganism remained underground. It has become visible only relatively recently. Although many of these varieties can be found in Aotearoa, only a very few have made much impact on popular awareness.[87]

Surprisingly, it can be argued that veneration of Odin first arrived in New Zealand in 1934 with a German Jewish refugee fleeing the Nazis — the poet, writer and journalist Karl Wolfskehl (1869–1948), blind as Milton, an Ovid cut off in an antipodean Tomis. Around 1900, Wolfskehl was a member of the Munich Cosmic Circle, whose other members were the esotericist Alfred Schuler (1865–1923), philosopher Ludwig Klages (1872–1956), writer Ludwig Derleth (1870–1948) and journalist Fanny zu Reventlow of Schwabing (1871–1918) — the so-called Bohemian Countess — among others.

Drawing on research into imagined matriarchal prehistory by the Swiss scholar Johann Jakob Bachofen (1815–1887), the group concocted a doctrine based on the idea that Western civilisation was rapidly declining due to the disenchanting effects of Christianity. This could only be reversed, they reasoned, by embracing a cosmic worldview rooted in the pagan past.[88] Wolfskehl was also the bridge between Cosmic Circle and the elite cultural figures and aesthetes surrounding the German symbolist poet Stefan George (1868–1933). George's circle was also of a mystical, though more classically homophile, bent, in which George, and to a lesser extent Wolfskehl, were vessels for divine inspiration for imitation by other members.[89]

Both groups represented a kind of anti-modernist radical conservativism in German politics, initially opposed to Nazism. As Nazism took hold in Germany, Wolfskehl, who had by then turned to Zionism, was forced out of both groups by the emboldened anti-Semitic sentiments of other members.

The private cultus of George's circle concerned a particular kind of nationalism that revered the idealised *Geheimes Deutschland* or 'Secret Germany' — the cultural soul of the German people, a mystical sibling of Deep England and *France profonde*. This Secret Germany was personified in Wotan, the Germanic equivalent of Odin, an image that was very important to Wolfskehl although in his personal mythos it also accommodated Jewish and classical German identities. Wolfskehl believed he had twice experienced visions of Wotan, about which he was very private, but which nonetheless informed many of his poems, particularly *An die Deutschen* (*To the Germans*).

This poem, his most personal, was revised in 1944 in his New Zealand exile. The refrain 'Wo ich bin ist Deutscher Geist' ('Wherever I am is the German soul') suggested that he was the avatar of Secret Germany, and that the spirit of the 'true' Germany, in contrast with its Nazi parody, had travelled with him to Aotearoa, which he sometimes referred to as a Thule of the south. (Thule is a mythical utopian land in the far north, and was often presented as the origin of the German peoples.)[90]

In a 1936 essay, the psychologist Carl Jung determined that Wotan represented a view of the Germanic peoples as poets and philosophers, and that modernity's disenchantment had interrupted that archetype and resulted in the national schizophrenia of Nazism.[91] He argued that the Cosmic Circle had mistaken Wotan for a cosmogonic Eros — that is to say, in the manner of the ancient Greek poet Hesiod's Eros, an all-infusing, liberating force of creation.

Jung pointedly excluded Wolfskhel from even this flawed communion with the German spirit, in the same way the Cosmic Circle rejected Wolfskehl's Zionism as existing in competition with their Wotanic vision, describing the poet and his fellow Zionist Jews as Molochites after the Old Testament's brutal Semitic deity Moloch.[92] This perhaps hints that Jung was not quite as antipathetic to the Nazis as he later affected, and as is officially endorsed today.

In 1981 the Wellington newspaper the *Star Weekender* reported on the formation of the Church of Odin, noting that 24-year-old Kerry Bolton was both a member of the church and national secretary of the Petone-based far-right white-nationalist group New Force. The Christchurch-based southern leader of New Force, David Crawford, was likewise said to be a follower of the Church of Odin. According to the *Star Weekender* article, the church described itself as the 'true religion of the European race', predating the 'alien and destructive creed of Judaic Christianity'.[93] Nazi Germany notably also struggled with Christianity's Jewish origins, leading to both the casuistries of Nazi 'Positive Christianity', which erased

Jesus' Jewishness and the significance of the Old Testament, and *Völkisch* neopagan manifestations of varying degrees of fundamentalism.[94]

This Church of Odin was ultimately a scion of the First Anglecyn Church of Odin, founded in Melbourne in 1936 by the Australian barrister, author and fascist sympathiser Alexander Rud Mills (1885–1964),[95] though the New Zealand Church regarded its parent organisation as the Mills-inspired Odinist Fellowship, founded in 1969 by Danish neopagan and far-right activist Else Christensen (1913–2005) and run out of her mobile home in Crystal River, Florida, in the United States.[96]

‡

The Church of Odin is related to another prominent group of Heathens to be found in Aotearoa: Asatru. As a religious faith, Asatru first appeared in Iceland as *Ásatrúarfélagið* or fellowship of the Æsir faith,[97] recognised by the Icelandic government in 1973 as Iceland's largest non-Christian denomination and founded by farmer and poet Sveinbjörn Beinteinsson (1924–1993), prominent businessman and former hippie Jörmundur Ingi Hansen (b.1940), Theosophist journalist Dagur Þorleifsson, and Thorsteinn Gudjónsson, a leader of a group dedicated to the theories of geologist, philosopher and spiritualist Helgi Pjeturss (1872–1949).[98] This group, in as far as can be ascertained within Iceland's rather introverted and monocultural political landscape, is largely apolitical or even secular-progressive, and should not be confused with the right-wing and racialist American variant, heavily influenced by Mills, founded by Stephen McNallen (b.1948) around 1994, from which the group found in New Zealand springs.

McNallen, a Texan, first became fascinated with Scandinavian traditions during his college years, and around 1969–70 founded the Viking Brotherhood and its newsletter *The Runestone* to promote his version of Asatrú, which bears little resemblance to Icelandic *Ásatrú* beyond the name, pantheon and some of the rites. After a four-year stint in the United States Army, McNallen transformed the Viking Brotherhood into the Asatru Free Assembly (AFA). The AFA was predicated on McNallen's concept of metagenetics, which argued that certain religions were only suitable for people of certain ethnic ancestries, and unsurprisingly began attracting a neo-Nazi element which conflicted strongly with the hippie neopagan faction. McNallen expelled the neo-Nazis and racialists, and disbanded the AFA in 1987. After moving to California and working as a journalist for *Soldier of Fortune* magazine for a time, he returned to Heathenry circles.[99]

In 1993 Else Christensen — who would eventually be arrested and imprisoned in 1999 for trafficking cannabis and heroin — handed McNallen the membership list, which formed the nucleus of a new organisation, the Asatrú Folk Assembly, the following year.[100] For all that the AFA attracts a strongly alt-right element, partly to avoid the conflicts that came to a head in 1987, the various kindred movements are autonomous and there is no overarching political ideology, making it quite difficult to attribute a particular ideology to the AFA.

While it is fairly safe to assume that a disorganised form of Asatru has probably existed in New Zealand since the late 1990s through the connectivity of the internet, an official group, the Fensalir Kindred, was only founded by IT consultant Cameron Mottus in Christchurch in 2018.[101] In photographs accompanying a 2019 article on the group by Andrea Vance in *Stuff*, Mottus with his square, hipster glasses and professional white dress shirt seems an unlikely leader of a small group of white men with Viking beards and the occasional head polished like a coffin handle. They idealise the warrior and practice *glíma*, the ancient martial art of the frozen north, not the gentle poet-seer *seidr*. That article drew a connection between the movement and the 2019 Christchurch mosque attacks, and was partly ruled against by the New Zealand Media Council in June that year.[102]

Mottus is closely connected to McNallen, and the group seems to conform to Asatrú's emphasis on warrior patriarchy and ethnic exclusivity, although ironically this doesn't particularly reflect the realities of Nordic mythology and culture as revealed by archaeology and scholarship. Indeed, medieval Scandinavians, exposed to Asia, Persia and China by way of trade or service in Byzantium, clearly found Islam intriguing enough to import their textiles and imitate their designs on textiles. This includes at least one case of imitating the name Allah in Arabic Kufic script on grave clothes, and remains in excavated graves in Sweden have genetically tested positive for Persian origins.[103]

Chapter 12.

The Rosy Cross and the OTO

Before that threshold in the morn's first light,
In wonder lost, in ecstasy of joy,
I stood: Thou spirit to the end attain'd,
Thou crown'd adept, thy long probation done,
Was that the Temple of the Rose and Cross?

— W. E. WAITE, 'THE ROSY CROSS', c.1916

We have already briefly canvased the origins of Rosicrucianism and noted the extensive and tenacious influence of its various iterations on Western esotericism, often in tandem with Freemasonry. That first obscure notice, the *Fama Fraternitatis RC* of 1614, that a secret Rosicrucian fraternity had been born to radically reform religion in Europe, instigated a range of reactions. Certainly, many European intellectuals recognised the fingerprints of Marsilio Ficino's Christianised Kabbalah, the alchemical tradition, and the millennial undertones.[1] Rosicrucianism was, and often still is, highly secretive. What texts that were available were encrypted with hidden codes and signed with pseudonyms or initials, and their true origins remained mysterious.

Nonetheless, the promise of Rosicrucianism was exciting: a utopian New Jerusalem of reformed religion and society, underpinned by a rejuvenation of the arts and natural sciences. The *Fama* told the story of Christian Rosenkreutz, a German knight who had voyaged to the East and returned with mystical wisdom. It also claimed that his concealed tomb had been found in 1604 — 120 years after it was sealed and hidden — and that its walls were a veritable encyclopaedia of arcane knowledge.

Modern scholarship generally attributes authorship of the *Fama* and two other Rosicrucian documents to a theology student, Johann Valentin Andreae (1586–1654). Andreae lived in Tübingen, the same Lutheran university city in Swabia as the lawyer and Paracelsian physician Tobias Hess (1586–1614), whose apocalypticism was clearly an influence, and the law professor Christopher Besoldus (1577–1638), whose library of esoteric books provided an invaluable resource.[2]

In the centuries since then, disparate organisations have identified as the heirs of Herr Rosenkreutz, making it very difficult to define Rosicrucianism. Academic and esoteric sources agree that Rosicrucianism draws on ancient Gnostic and Hermetic sources for its version of gnosis or knowledge of spiritual mysteries promising the salvation of the spirit from the sullen bonds of matter. This view owes much to Jung's recycling of Lutheran Protestantism's attempt to link Rosicrucianism to a supposedly more authentic primitive, pre-Catholic Christianity in the seventeenth century. And yet little of that ascetic, salvational Gnosticism was particularly evident prior to the twentieth century and the emergence of the neo-Gnostic *Lectorium Rosicrucianum* in the 1930s, which drew on a motley gamut of sources, including the German theologian Jakob Böhme (1575–1624), the Swiss physician and alchemist Paracelsus (c.1493–1541), heavily coloured by twentieth-century Jungian interpretation.[3] In truth, Rosicrucianism in the late nineteenth and twentieth centuries took many forms and influenced many occult and esoteric societies, including groups like the Ordo Templi Orientis, where those Rosicrucian roots are not to the fore, and heavily entangled with Gnosticism, Illuminatism, and then submerged in a robust topping of Crowleyan Thelema.

☦

The first of the two Rosicrucian organisations to set up shop in Aotearoa was the Ordo Tabulae Rotundae, or Order of the Table Round (OTR), not to be confused with the Theosophical Society's Order of the Round Table, and the Masonic Societas Rosicruciana in Anglia (SRIA). We have already met the OTR in connection with Whare Rā as something Robert Felkin brought from England and established in parallel with the Stella Matutina. If it, as rumoured, still exists today, it is now difficult to separate from the SRIA.

This latter is an esoteric Christian organisation started in the United Kingdom some time between 1865 and 1867 by clerk and Freemason Robert Wentworth Little (1840–1878), who based the rituals and degrees on documents he found in the storeroom of the Freemason's Hall in London. Arthur Waite of the Golden Dawn believed these elements to have originated with the German Orden des Gold- und Rosenkreutz of the 1750s, by way of another organisation, the Societas Rosicruciana in Scotia (the Scottish branch), active in the 1830s.[4]

In 1910 Felkin, a member of the SRIA, met Rudolf Steiner and was deeply impressed with the latter's links to the German Rosicrucian orders. Later that year, unable to personally study with Steiner, he sent to Berlin as emissary the impressively monikered Neville Gauntlett Tudor Meakin (c.1876–1912), a fellow Bahá'í and Adeptus Minor fellow member of Stella Matutina.[5] Judging from a lecture he gave at the General Assembly of the Metropolitan College of the SRIA in London in 1916, in which he cites many of the familiar tropes of root races and Steiner's Cultural Epochs, and namedrops Blavatsky,[6] by the time of Felkin's membership, the SRIA, or at least his interpretation of it, had been thoroughly contaminated with ideas taken whole and undigested from Theosophy and Anthroposophy.

Meakin is something of an enigma. Supposedly when he turned 21, his stepfather, the Reverend Henry Meyers Meakin, told young Neville that his real surname was Tudor and presented him with family papers allegedly revealing him to be the rightful Grand Master of the OTR.[7] According to Meakin, this magical esoteric Gnostic order, dedicated to Arthurian chivalry and Grail Christianity, had existed since the time of Camelot, handed down through the generations of the Tudor family with a three-century break until revived by Meakin's grandfather. It suffices to say that this is almost certainly errant tosh, as all official records suggest that the Reverend Meakin was indeed his father and no such person by the name Tudor had ever existed.

Meakin had a talent for fantasy, as evidenced by his 1902 novel set during the Crusades, and two others co-authored with the angler Hugh Tempest Sheringham (1876–1930), which were published by Heineman in 1904.[8] He presumably initiated Felkin into the OTR in around 1909.

Meakin suffered from tuberculosis, and fearing that he would die without an heir to take over as Grand Master of the OTR, in 1910 he appointed Wellesley Tudor Pole (1884–1968). Pole, also a Bahá'í and a Spiritualist, claimed descent from Owen Tudor, founder of the Tudor royal dynasty, and was directly involved in the recovery of the artifact known as the blue bowl of Glastonbury, which, rather than a sacred Celtic relic seen in a vision, turned out to be no older than the nineteenth century.[9] Meakin incorporated many of Pole's Arthurian ideas into the OTR and initiated Pole in 1910.

Meakin died in 1912, having (according to Felkin) changed his mind, leaving the office of Grand Master to Felkin instead. Pole initially contested this on the grounds that Felkin was not a member of the 'family', but then seems to have let it go. Felkin consulted Arthur Waite about the matter, and with his approval accepted the role, taking the signs, symbols and rituals of the Order with him when he settled in New Zealand.[10]

In 1917 Felkin had also been appointed Chief Adept of the SRIA for

New Zealand, a role he held until just before his death, and Felkin College No. 68, the New Zealand SRIA province, is named after him.[11] Induction into SRIA can only be obtained by Master Masons, and Felkin adopted the same principle in inducting members of Whare Rā into the OTR.

☨

The story of the Ordo Templi Orientis (Order of the Temple of the East, OTO) begins in Bavaria with Theodor Reuss (1855–1923), an extraordinary personage. Reuss was the son of an Augsburg innkeeper and at various times a singer — performing in the 1882 premier of Wagner's *Parsifal* and later supporting himself in English music-hall — a journalist, a tantric occultist, a neo-Gnostic bishop, a Freemason and, allegedly, an anti-Socialist spy for the Preußische Geheimpolizei, the Prussian secret police.

In 1880, while living in Munich, Reuss attempted a revival of the old Bavarian Illuminati. The Illuminati, the 'illuminated', has over the years been applied with varying degrees of accuracy to many groups, real and imaginary. Historically, though, the name usually refers to the Bavarian Illuminati, one of several secret Enlightenment societies (the Rosicrucians and the Freemasons being others) founded in Bavaria by philosopher Adam Weishaupt (1748–1830) in 1776 and dedicated to opposing superstition, the political influence of religion over public life, and the authoritarian abuse of state power. In 1784, with the support of the Catholic Church, all secret societies were banned by Charles Theodore, Elector of Bavaria. Political conservatives and clergy vilified the group over the years, blaming them for social and political uprisings throughout Europe, the French Revolution especially. Hungarian astronomer and diplomat Franz Xaver von Zach was the second-in-command. Professed members include Duke Ferdinand of Brunswick, Duke Ernest Frederick of Saxe-Coburg-Saalfeld, writer Johann Wolfgang von Goethe (author of *Faust*), and philosopher and poet Johann Gottfried Herder.

In Britain Reuss became friendly with William Wynn Westcott, whom we previously encountered as one of the founders of the Golden Dawn, and who as Supreme Magus of the Societas Rosicruciana in Anglia authorised

Reuss to start a German branch in 1902. The previous year, Gérard Encausse, better known as the occultist 'Papus', had chartered Reuss as a Special Inspector of the Martinist Order of esoteric Christianity.[12] But it was years earlier, in 1895, when Reuss had met the Viennese inventor-industrialist and mystic Carl Kellner (1851–1905), that the OTO was born.

Like Reuss, Kellner was a Freemason, a student of Rosicrucianism, and fascinated by Eastern religions. He had made his fortune as co-developer of various chemical improvements in industrial paper manufacture. This capital funded extensive world travel, during which Kellner claimed to have met with a Sufi and two Hindu tantric adepts — variants on the invisible ascendant masters type — who were members of the quasi-mythical Rosicrucian group the Hermetic Brotherhood of Light. They initiated him into a special understanding of Freemasonry's complicated vocabulary of symbols and the use of sex magic. In fact, Kellner's understanding of sex magic would seem to have more to do with the writings of American occultist Paschal Beverly Randolph (1825–1875) than Rosicrucian mysteries. Regardless, sex magic likely became a small part of the impetus for founding the women-welcoming OTO, as most versions of Freemasonry did not admit women.

Much like the Golden Dawn, the original OTO was modelled after a Masonic structure, its inner circle based on the highest degrees of the Memphis-Misraim Rite and the wisdom of the Hermetic Brotherhood of Light.[13] The new organisation was slow to take off, as Reuss was still distracted by his attempts to resuscitate the Illuminati — something Kellner didn't approve of — but in 1903 they managed to cobble together a manifesto, which was published the following year.[14] Kellner did live to see the OTO blossom, but died from a heart attack shortly after, in mid-1905.

Reuss met Aleister Crowley in 1910, while he was living in London, and made him a seventh-degree initiate of OTO, based on Crowley's irregular 33 degree of the Masonic Scottish Rite, which he acquired in Mexico City. (The Scottish Rite is, in fact, French in origin, and is an elaborately esoteric appendant body of Freemasonry not recognised by the English lodge.) In 1912 Reuss conferred upon Crowley the ninth degree and appointed him National Grand Master of the OTO over the United Kingdom and Ireland.

With this authority, Crowley quickly set to work establishing the lower, Masonic degrees of OTO, the Mysteria Mystica Maxima (M∴M∴M∴), created the important OTO Gnostic Mass while in Moscow — referring to it as the Order's 'central ceremony of its public and private celebration'[15] — and rose to the rank of Grand Master of the Rite of Memphis-Misraïm in 1913.[16] We will pause here because it's important to acknowledge the centrality of the Gnostic Mass (technically *Liber XV* of the Crowley corpus) to the philosophy and praxis of OTO.

The Gnostic Mass, its structure loosely based on the Roman Catholic and Eastern Orthodox Masses, was intended by Crowley as a performative, direct way of experiencing the principles of Thelema and unity with the individual's inner divinity, while also satisfying the human religious instinct. Crowley writes of it in his *Confessions*:

> Human nature demands (in the case of most people) the satisfaction of the religious instinct, and, to very many, this may best be done by ceremonial means. I wished therefore to construct a ritual through which people might enter into ecstasy as they have always done under the influence of appropriate ritual... I resolved that my Ritual should celebrate the sublimity of the operation of universal forces without introducing disputable metaphysical theories. I would neither make nor imply any statement about nature which would not be endorsed by the most materialistic man of science. On the surface this may sound difficult; but in practice I found it perfectly simple to combine the most rigidly rational conceptions of phenomena with the most exalted and enthusiastic celebration of their sublimity.[17]

The ceremony requires five officers: a priest, a priestess, a deacon and two acolytes referred to as 'children'. The congregants enter the ritual space where the deacon waits at a small altar, which represents the sphere of Tiphareth (beauty, spirituality) of the Sephirotic Tree of Life. Placing the Thelemic Book of the Law on the altar in the East, behind the Veil, which is not closed at this point (dividing sacred and profane, this world and the other), the deacon proclaims the Law of Thelema in the name of IAO (the divine name or formula containing the names of the Egyptian gods Isis, Apophis and Osiris, or birth, death and resurrection).[18] The Law of Thelema is proclaimed, and the Gnostic Creed — modelled after the Nicean Apostolic creed of mainstream Christianity — recited (notes in square brackets are mine):

> I believe in one secret and ineffable LORD; and in one Star in the company of Stars of whose fire we are created, and to which we shall return; and in one Father of Life, Mystery of Mystery, in His name CHAOS, the sole viceregent of the Sun upon Earth; and in one Air the nourisher of all that breathes.
>
> And I believe in one Earth, the Mother of us all, and in one Womb wherein all men are begotten, and wherein they shall rest, Mystery of Mystery, in Her name BABALON. [Babylon, the Scarlet Woman, the sexual and maternal anima cognate with the biblical Whore of Babylon in the Book of Revelations.]
>
> And I believe in the Serpent and the Lion, Mystery of Mystery, in His name BAPHOMET. [The deity the Templars were accused of worshipping,[19] which by way of Éliphas Lévi's Goat of Mendes making and unmaking, becomes Crowley's βάπτισμα (baptism) and Μῆτις (wisdom), Pan, Mithras, Lust.]
>
> And I believe in one Gnostic and Catholic Church of Light, Life, Love and Liberty, the Word of whose Law is THELEMA. [The Will, a concept that may have been influenced by Crowley's reading of Nietzsche and Schopenhauer.]
>
> And I believe in the communion of Saints.
>
> And, forasmuch as meat and drink are transmuted in us daily into spiritual substance, I believe in the Miracle of the Mass.
>
> And I confess one Baptism of Wisdom whereby we accomplish the Miracle of Incarnation.
>
> And I confess my life one, individual, and eternal that was, and is, and is to come.
>
> AUMGN, AUMGN, AUMGN. [Combining the Hindu cosmic syllable AUM with the Christian Amen and various sacred syllables, conferring power over the manifest phenomenological universe.][20]

The entire ceremony is a complex and aesthetic process full of allegory as the soul symbolically passes through the various stages of initiation into the mystery, concluding at its climax with a eucharistic sacrament, which is simply a distillation of the same archetypes that inform the Christian rite.

☦

A divergence of sorts between the old OTO and a Thelemic form under the other's umbrella gradually formalised in 1918 when Reuss, by then biding his time in Switzerland, issued his German translation of Crowley's Gnostic Mass. Greatly impressed by Crowley's Thelema, Reuss took to referring to himself both as Sovereign Patriarch and Primate of the Thelemically inclined Gnostic Catholic Church, and as Gnostic Legate to Switzerland of the Église Gnostique Universelle of the original OTO.[21]

A year earlier, in 1917, Reuss had released a synopsis of OTO degrees and instruction, all heavily modelled on Freemasonry. The peripatetic Crowley, having gone to the United States to avoid the war, attempted to establish this Masonic OTO in Detroit, Michigan, but was rebuffed by the local Masonic Council of the Scottish Rite on the grounds that its Masonic elements were far too orthodox for them, leading a chastened Crowley to completely rewrite them.[22]

In the spring of 1920, Reuss suffered a stroke. Crowley, ever the opportunist, raised the question of Reuss's competence to continue to lead the OTO, resulting in a rapid deterioration in their relationship. Crowley proclaimed himself Outer Head of the Order, and when Reuss died in 1923 — with the leadership intestate and Crowley putting it about that Reuss had anointed him successor — Crowley was officially elected to the position after a heated and chaotic Conference of Grandmasters in 1925.[23]

During the Second World War the European OTO was virtually extinguished, and only a scattering of individual initiates in various countries — including Australia, and the Agapé Lodge in Hollywood, California, led by the rocket engineer Jack Parsons — remained. After being released from a Nazi prison camp, Karl Germer ('Frater Saturnus', 1885–1962), Crowley's German representative, emigrated to the United States. In 1942 he was officially appointed as Crowley's successor as Outer

Head of the Order, and he took office when Crowley died in 1947.[24]

Germer attempted to keep the OTO running with an ailing Gerald Gardner (founder of Wicca)[25] as the Order's main representative in Europe. In 1951 Gardner was replaced by Frederick Mellinger (1890–1970). Germer also granted a charter to Crowley's former secretary Kenneth Grant (1924–2011) to run an OTO Camp in the United Kingdom. Grant was expelled a mere four years later, and set up his own Thelemic organisation, the Typhonian Order. The Typhonian Order loosely follows OTO ideas but is altogether more Luciferinan in orientation. Over the years it has become less hierarchical and today has an unorganised presence in Australia and New Zealand, often through UFO enthusiasts and Chaos Magick practitioners. After Grant's hasty exit, the OTO in the United Kingdom was led by Noel Fitzgerald (1908–1958) until his death.[26]

Germer died in 1962 without having named a successor, leaving the OTO leaderless until 1969, when Grady McMurty (1918–1985) invoked Crowley's emergency authorisation post-mortem to become OTO Frater Superior. McMurty eschewed the title of Outer Head of the Order, stipulating that this was an international office, and the moribund organisation was at that point in time incapable of fulfilling that aspect of its constitution. He began performing initiations in 1970.[27]

☩

Although the group extant in Aotearoa today dates to the early 1980s, the first attempt to establish a branch of the order can be dated back to 1920 and the English Spiritualist Vivian (later Vyvyan) Deacon (1895–1938). Deacon was the son of an itinerant herbalist and healer father, Cornelius, and his mother, Elizabeth, was a cousin of the poet Robert Browning. Browning was himself well-versed in the classics and Western esoteric traditions by his half-uncle, Elizabeth's father, Reuben Browning.[28] The Browning family connection brought the young Vivian into the sphere of many eminent Victorians, including Oscar Wilde, who lived next door, and Arthur Conan Doyle. W. B. Yeats was another friend, and it was he who introduced Elizabeth to various members of the Golden Dawn.[29]

In 1895 Elizabeth Deacon met James Ingall Wedgwood (1883–1951), a regular correspondent with Robert, who would become Vivian's tutor. Wedgwood was also the founding bishop of the Theosophy-adjunct Liberal Catholic Church, and eventually went to Australia. When aged only 17, at the invitation of the Australian Theosophical Society, Deacon also struck out for the Antipodes, where he came under the sway of Charles Leadbeater. He also became friendly with the Australian decadent painter Norman Lindsay and his circle.[30]

Not long after arriving in Melbourne, Deacon became besotted with the 15-year-old Eunice Mary Lew Tong, and having secured the permission of her widowed mother, they married and moved to Sydney, a move prompted by Deacon's friend Veni Cooper-Mathieson ('Sister Veni', 1867–1943), a charismatic American proponent of the New Thought movement. In Sydney, Deacon established himself as a psychic medium and herbalist with the help of two Theosophists, Frank Bennett and Wedgwood. Bennett was recognised (or self-proclaimed, depending on the source) as Crowley's appointed OTO, and Vivian, or by then Vyvyan (after Oscar Wilde's son), became absorbed in OTO's teachings, along with those of Theosophy, before founding his own group, the Christian Mystics of the Rosy Cross (CMRC) in 1917.

Despite their mutual contacts, Deacon did not meet Crowley in person until 1931, after he had returned permanently to the United Kingdom. Crowley's interest seems mainly in Deacon's successes with defamation lawsuits directed at newspapers that doubted his authenticity.[31] Keith Richmond's 2004 biography of Bennett, *Progradior and the Beast*, says, however, that Bennett first met Deacon in the early days of the Great War and failed to persuade him to join the OTO. Richmond asserts that later in life Deacon embroidered his negligible association with the OTO to promote his CMRC, and that this misled some authors into assuming his leadership of the OTO in Australia when, in fact, he was never a member.[32]

In 1920 Deacon was approached by a group of New Zealand Spiritualists to visit and prepare the way for Arthur Conan Doyle's tour later that year, and so he set off for Christchurch that May. His sojourn in Aotearoa was to last two years. The flavour of his teaching was a blend of Theosophy, Fabianism, New Thought, Marx, Freud, Darwin and the New Testament. Human consciousness was a 'triune':

> The conscious mind corresponds to the economic world, the object world, and is the mind one always used in the present. Man's subconscious mind corresponds to the subject world and from the depth of the subconsciousness come the demands for those things that are termed 'the rights of the people' ... Man's super-conscious mind corresponds to the ideal world and holds within it all the desires and possibilities of the future. Intuitions from the super-conscious mind might be said to emanate from the spirit of man — the highest part of him.[33]

It is entirely possible that the OTO influence has been overstated, or that this was his attempt to reform Crowley's OTO into something more in keeping with its Rosicrucian roots. Crowley himself did not think much of Deacon, writing to Bennett in 1923: 'I am glad you are quite through with Deacon. If he is using our name to acquire wealth, I think you should complain to the authorities. It is obtaining money under false pretences.'[34] However, according to Australian occult researcher Gregory Tillett, Deacon arrived in Australia in 1908 bearing the original pre-Crowley order as Frater Memnon, the first Grand Head of the Order in that country, having been authorised by Reuss.[35] Richmond disputes this.

Shortly after relocating to Wellington, Deacon fell ill and was joined by his mother, Elizabeth, who had already followed him to Australia, and then Eunice. They all returned to Australia in Easter 1922 to coincide with Annie Besant's visit. And, in the end, any OTO or Rosicrucian seeds that might have been sown by Deacon in Aotearoa do not appear to have taken root in any meaningful way.[36]

☩

We pick up the story again six decades later, in December 1981, with the appearance on the scene of the personage of 'Soror (Sister) Egeria', who had been working as an assistant for Grady McMurtry, Hymenaeus Alpha of the Order, and was chartered by him to establish the Order in Aotearoa. She herself had been initiated into OTO in California in the late 1970s, and now, after basing herself in Bygrave Place, in the Christchurch suburb of Bishopdale (Margaret Mahy fans will recognise this as the Gardendale of her 1984 book *The Changeover*), she began initiating people into OTO.[37]

In Dunedin she was billeted to a house in Challis Point (in blogging her memories, Egeria rather charmingly calls it 'Chalice Point') on the Otago Peninsula. Her hosts were two women who turned out to be the priestesses of Sisters of the Silver Star (SSS), a Typhonian triad[38] led by a man who had initiated various Dunedin women into the group with sexual rites of his own devising. The women complained of being coerced into having sex, which repulsed Soror Egeria and further emphasised the need for an official OTO presence.

In Dunedin the SSS held their rituals in a room above a nightclub called Pharaoh's (probably Pharaoh's Tomb on Stafford Street). One OTO member initiated by Soror Egeria, identified in her online memoir as 'GA', would go on to found the first 'tribes' (now known as 'camps') — the smallest local unit of OTO — and 'oases' — the smallest local body of OTO able to perform initiations to the third degree and required to perform the Gnostic Mass six times a year. These were Penguin Tribe in Dunedin (which later became Dogfish Tribe), the Sea Stars in Christchurch, AVA in Wellington, and Kantharos in Auckland.

Soror Egeria remained in New Zealand for six months, based in Christchurch but travelling around the country, in Wellington connecting with and initiating Pat and Chris Zalewski (see Chapter 4), who went on to establish AVA, and even initiating a member of an Ānanda Mārga group in Auckland.[39] After a few months in Sydney, Soror Egeria returned to New Zealand in 1983 and moved into a house on Tole Street in Ponsonby, where other OTO members lived. This became the site of the Kephra Abbey, the first home of the Oceania Lodge.[40]

Today, OTO in Aotearoa is a thriving organisation with bodies in Auckland (Kantharos), Hamilton (Prana), Christchurch (Te Ahi Ka) and Wellington (Eschaton). Unlike many similar groups, it is open and public about its existence and purpose, maintaining a regularly updated website.

‡

Soror Egeria, responsible for rejuvenating the presence of the OTO in Aotearoa from the 1980s.

COURTESY BILL HEIDRICK, TREASURER OF OTO DURING THE CALIPH YEARS

Also known as the Ancient and Mystical Order Rosæ Crucis, Antiquus Mysticusque Ordo Rosæ Crucis (AMORC) is the largest Rosicrucian-identified organisation in the world and a truly international presence. In keeping with other primarily Rosicrucian organisations, it identifies itself with what it regards as an ancient primordial philosophy. Its objective history is difficult to unpick from its internal narrative, which at times borders on the outright fanciful.

In 1909 the American occultist and mystic Harvey Spencer Lewis (1883–1939) had gone to France — not Germany, for some reason, as was usually the case — in search of the relict Rosicrucian Brotherhood. Apparently, he was successful, and, according to the official account, was initiated in Toulouse and instructed to establish a chapter in the United States. A manifesto was issued in the United States in 1915. Lewis's AMORC co-founder, a Mrs May Banks Stacey (1846–1918), claimed to have been the descendent of a group of Rosicrucian colonists who settled in New England in the late seventeenth century, and to have been an initiate of the Eastern Rosicrucians.[41]

The business of America is, of course, business, and even ancient mystic wisdom is apparently not immune to the influence of rampant capitalism. Lewis, as first Imperator of the Order, saw free enterprise as an essential part of the AMORC project, and in 1929 published a book on the application of AMORC principles to business.[42] Railway magnate Arthur Stilwell (1859–1928) — also known for getting business guidance from mysterious, as he described them, 'brownie' voices[43] — was a member of the Order, as were, allegedly, at least for a time, Walt Disney (the 2010 AMORC convention was held at Disneyland in California) and *Star Trek* creator Gene Roddenberry.[44] The Mexican artist Diego Riviera was a known member.[45]

AMORC has a fairly high public profile in North America and Europe, with newsletters, books, social media and a YouTube channel. Its teachings are the standard fare of such organisations — 'sacred sciences' from classical philosophy; science; New Age spirituality; traditional healing; meditation; alchemical, Rosicrucian and Masonic symbolism; and a loosely Masonic structure of degrees grouped together under the titles Postulant, Neophyte and Initiate. The end goal is to achieve some level of unity with the divine with a distinctly flamboyant Egyptian aesthetic — putting the 'luxe' into Luxor.

AMORC headquarters moved from New York to San Francisco to Tampa, Florida, before settling in San Jose in California, where its elaborately Egyptian-themed complex can be found today. AMORC's New Zealand presence, like its diffuse one in Asia, is administered from its rather more modest Grand Lodge in Strathalbyn, South Australia, brought together in 1996 with the Australian Grand Lodge (founded in Sydney in 1930) and English-speaking AMORC-affiliated groups in Singapore, Hong Kong, China, and the Philippines.

In Aotearoa, AMORC is headquartered at a lodge in Coleridge Street in Auckland's Grey Lynn, and was listed as incorporating as a private company on 4 November 1959. Prior to amalgamation, the Auckland Lodge published a bulletin from 1976 to 1981, and a Wellington chapter published a newsletter from 1970 to 1972.[46] An advertisement placed in the *Evening Post* reveals that the US organisation was attempting to recruit, or at least sell books, in New Zealand as early as 1940:

> A New Life Open to You. Rosicrucians Reveal A New World of Possibilities. Strange Book Loaned To Those Seeking New Start. At last, a new method of mastering our lives and putting all the obstacles to success and happiness in their proper place, has been outlined by the Supreme Council of the Rosicrucians. And, by a special concession, copies of this new plan and an explanation of what it will do, will be loaned to those who wish to make a new start in life and change the course of their career. The Rosicrucians have ever been known for their rational, simple, and thorough knowledge of the arcane facts of life. Through all the ages they have held the Light of Knowledge as a sacred trust, and thousands of eminent writers and historians have conceded the highest tribute to them. The new book, called 'The Secret Heritage,' will be mailed to sincere inquirers without obligation and postage prepaid. Write a letter (not a postcard) addressed to: SCRIBE C.H.O. The Rosicrucians — AMORC— SAN JOSE, CALIFORNIA. 'The Rosicrucians are NOT a religious organization.'[47]

☦

The Lectorium Rosicrucianum or Spiritual School of the Golden Rosycross is another neo-Gnostic Christian organisation, attributing its theology to Rosicrucian sources, the purported beliefs of the medieval Cathars as interpreted by French mystic Antonin Gadal (1877–1962), Hermeticism and Alchemy. It was founded in Haarlem in the Netherlands in 1935 by three Dutch occultists, Jan van Rijckenborgh (1896–1968), his younger brother Zwier Willem Leene (1900–1988), and the mystic Catharose de Petri (1902–1990). The three had met as members of the Rosicrucian Fellowship established by the Danish-American astrologer and Christian occultist Max Heindel (1865–1919) in 1909.[48]

The Lectorium's cosmology divides the universe into two natural orders: the material, dialectical order of birth, death and matter; and an imperishable, static spiritual or divine order of God. This is relatively true to historical Rosicrucian doctrine and Gnosticism. A 'divine spark' of the latter, sometimes known as the 'Rose of the Heart', is latent in every human being.[49] The distinction and terminology of 'dialectic' and 'static' suggests at the very least a passing awareness of Marx and an attempt to offer an attractive alternative to his theory of dialectical materialism.

The divine spark manifests in most people as a sense of undefined yearning, which the Lectorium aims to educate about, providing the initiate a path of 'transfiguration' from the material back to the spiritual order through an esoteric interpretation of Scripture. This entails the 'rebirth from the spirit' of John 3:8, or, as Paul puts it in 1 Corinthians 15:31, 'daily dying' — the daily rebirth in the spirit from a daily dying of the material. This relies on conflating the message of Luke 17:21 that 'the kingdom of God is within you', with the Rosicrucian concept of macrocosm and microcosm, the body contains the divine plan of the spiritual order: as above, so below.[50]

Having survived Nazi persecution in Europe, following the Second World War the Lectorium continued to evolve throughout the 1950s and 1960s, until the death of van Rijckenborgh in 1968. This event provoked a schism within the organisation between de Petri, now leader, and van Rijckenborgh's son Henk Leene (1924–2014). Henk departed with a number of students to form a splinter group, the Sivas Esoteric Community, named after the Domaine de Sivas region in the French Alps, which Leene associated with the Indian god Shiva.[51] Since de Petri's death in 1990, the Lectorium has been under the direction of the International Spiritual Directorate (ISD), a college of senior students at the school.[52] The Lectorium spread internationally, establishing in Australia in Adelaide in 1974, and then setting up in Sydney and Melbourne in 1999.

In Aotearoa, the Lectorium is based out of the Golden Rosycross centre, a large weatherboard farmhouse with a terracotta tile roof in Karāpiro in the Waikato, although when Robert Ellwood was writing his survey of alternative spiritualities in New Zealand in the early 1990s it was still located in Auckland. Ellwood describes it as appearing to be primarily a study group for esoteric Christianity, and regarded its teachings as 'a more thoroughgoing reconstruction of the profound cosmic dualism of the Manichaeans, radical Gnostics, or medieval Cathars . . . than any other modern group of which I am aware'.[53]

Chapter 13.

The Devil rides out

Better to reign in Hell than serve in Heaven.

— JOHN MILTON, *PARADISE LOST*, I, CCLXIII, 1667

Satan. Lucifer. Set. Iblis. Ahriman. The Adversary. The Bible actually has very little to say about the personification of Evil, and it is only a broader Christian tradition that pulls together the serpent in Eden, God's gambling partner in the Book of Job, the fallen star of the morning in Ezekiel, and the tempter of Christ in the New Testament into some sort of coherent narrative: the fallen angel who sets himself — rather futilely, it must be said — against Jehovah. There is no unambiguous reference to this entity in the Torah. Interestingly it is Islam's Qur'an, of all the faiths of the book, which offers direct injunction that he, Shaitan, should not be worshipped.[1]

Over the centuries various groups have been accused by ecclesiastical authorities of conscious Satan worship — the Templars, the Cathars, and other heretical groups in the Middle Ages for example — who one suspects would have admitted to anything, no matter how outlandish, under torture. In the early modern period there are, of course, the infamous witch trials of Europe and North America. The Catholics accused the Protestants, the Protestants accused the Catholics, and in the 1890s Léo Taxil (1854–1907) accused the Freemasons in a scandalous hoax.[2] Taxil's fictions — over the top even by 'Penny Dreadful' standards — were eagerly reported in Aotearoa by the Catholic magazine the *New Zealand Tablet*.[3]

Certainly, there were Black Masses — the diabolical inversion and abomination of the Catholic Mass. The oldest surviving mention of this, dubious though it is, comes from Epiphanius of Salamis (c.310/320–403) in his *Panarion*, and Theodoret of Cyrrhus (c.393–c.458/466) in his *Haereticarum Fabularum Compendium*, both of whom allege this of a group of libertine Gnostics known as the Borborites.[4] In the medieval period up to the Council of Trent (1545–63), particularly in France, the Black Mass ultimately took on a more structured form as a spinoff of the Low Mass or Votive Mass (Masses said to influence God towards a desired outcome) by way of the Mass of Vain Observance.

The latter was often a by-product of the great surplus of clerical students in ratio to parishes, what the medievalist and historian of religion Richard Kieckhefer calls the 'clerical underground'. These students, often embittered and cynical, drifted around France as *clerici vagantes* (wandering clerics), evolving increasingly edgy parodies of the Mass and

Félicien Rops, *Le Calvaire*, 1880–82. In fin de siècle nineteenth-century Europe, the Decadent movement in art and literature developed an obsession with satanism and black masses as a lurid counterpoint to bourgeois propriety.

quite prepared to perform the sacrament for anyone willing to pay and for whatever purpose the client desired.⁵

From the sixteenth to the nineteenth centuries in France, the Black Mass became a quasi-literary trope linked to gossip, fashionable celebrity and scandal, often with little evidence to back up its concrete existence. Jean Bodin (c.1530–1596), for example, has one performed for Catherine de Medici in his *De la démonomanie des sorciers* (1580). Ironically the most lurid notions of what went on were largely based on libels directed against early Christianity by Judaism and the Romans.

Here we must also include the fantastical allegations that emerged from the inquisitions of the fifteenth century, and the witch trials of the sixteenth and seventeenth centuries, which perhaps find their ultimate origins in the persecution of Jews and heretical Christian sects. We must also consider historically well-documented individuals who are identified as devil-worshippers in justification of horrific serial murder sprees, such as the French nobleman Gilles de Rais (c.1405–1440), companion to Joan d'Arc and model for Bluebeard; the German bandit Peter Niers (c.1540–1581); and German farmer, cannibal and self-professed werewolf Peter Stumpp (c.1535–1589).

Louis XIV's mistress Madame de Montespan (1640–1707) supposedly had a Black Mass performed for her in secret, in which she lay naked on the altar, in the hope of maintaining the Royal affections. In the subsequent investigation as part of the infamous *l'affaire des poisons*, de Montespan's accomplices were arrested, and the trial records would influence the further refinement of the ceremony.⁶ By the eighteenth century the Black Mass was little more than a masque for blasphemous revelry, an aesthetic psychodrama at best, associated with the likes of the Marquis de Sade (1740–1814) and the Hellfire Clubs of England, enjoying a revival among the Decadents of the *fin de siècle*, with the publication of Joris-Karl Huysmans' novel *Là-Bas* (1891), though the seeds were planted by Charles Baudelaire's *Les Fleurs du Mal* (1857).

In Western occult terms, Satanic worship falls under the category of the 'left-hand path', a modern term deriving from the Sanskrit Vāmācāra (left-handed attainment), which is a heterodox, tantric path to dharmic enlightenment at odds with the orthodoxy of the texts of Hinduism,

Buddhism, Sikhism and Jainism, but in practice tends to be a matter of local culture and personal preference. More generally, practices of the left-hand path are characterised by a rejection of convention and status quo, the breaking of taboos, the questioning — if not outright rejection — of religious and moral dogma, the prioritising of the individual will, and sometimes sexual or blasphemous imagery.[7]

What the Satanists and fellow travellers of today usually get wrong is that you're not supposed to enjoy these violations: they are supposed to be a form of abasement — not penance or expiation per se, but more like an ascetic mortification to remove oneself from the mundane quotidian world.

‡

Modern Satanism proper begins with the American Anton LaVey (1930–1997) and his Church of Satan in 1966. This organisation was primarily sceptical, libertarian atheism in orientation, dressed up in theatrical drag and drawing heavily on the Miltonic Satan as a Romantic-Enlightenment ideal of pride and individuality rather than thinking of Satan as an actual entity.

LaVey's rationalistic, materialistic Satanism shows the influence of Nietzsche's nihilism and Ayn Rand's objectivism. There is also an unexpected New Zealand connection: the 1896 Social Darwinist tract *Might Is Right; or The Survival of the Fittest* by Ragnar Redbeard, known variously as Arthur Uing, Richard Thurland, Desmond Dilg, Gavin Gowrie and, to his mother, Arthur Desmond (c.1859–c.1929). Redbeard/Desmond was either born in England or New Zealand, and was a drover in Hawke's Bay until entering politics in 1884 as a parliamentary candidate. A radical political agitator, he is notable for his public defence of Te Kooti, and edited the Auckland *Tribune*.

Desmond moved to Sydney in 1892, becoming involved in the Australian labour movement alongside Billy Hughes, Henry Lawson and Jack Lang. However, the flavour of his politics is far more in the fascist vein, or at the very least Nietzschean, in idealising the alpha male man of action — an unpleasant variant of the New Zealand modernist 'man alone'

— and rejecting the notion of inalienable universal human rights. At some point he moved to the United States, and various locations are given for his death, ranging from Mexico to Palestine. Even the identification of Redbeard with Desmond is considered speculative and is contested in some circles. Curiously it is largely the neo-fascist presses of Odinism and Satanism that keep him in print today.[8]

As a rhizomatic wave of movements, twentieth-century Satanism falls loosely into two groups: the atheistic or philosophical, and the theistic or religious. The atheistic Satanists are primarily rooted in the precepts of the Church of Satan, where Satan represents an intellectual and countercultural protest against conformity and religious worldviews. Theistic Satanists, in contrast, regard Satan, or an equivalent entity like the Egyptian god Set, as an actual individual spiritual power or entity.[9] An example of this is the group known as the Order of Nine Angles (ONA or O9A; note 'angles', not 'angels'). Supposedly established in the United Kingdom in the 1960s, it only really came to public attention in the 1980s and 1990s because of its neo-fascist associations, and it has links to groups in Australia and New Zealand.[10]

ONA regards itself as 'traditional Satanism', centring on the 'dark forces' of Satan and his consort, a Kali-esque Baphomet, and seven other angles, with which members attempt to unite in order to evolve into higher states of being. The nine angles would seem to represent the nine realms of the Qliphoth — the evil inversion of the Sephiroth described in Lurianic Kabbalah and Hermetic Qabalah — although ONA would probably reject this as implying some influence of Jewish thought.

> These realms intersect at nine angles; three of space, one of 'causal' (or linear) time, two symbolically seen as 'positive' and 'negative' (though in essence these are one) and one of acausal time. Life is an expression of the intersection of the causal and the acausal and consciousness is the primary place in which the acausal can be apprehended, understood and especially through 'the Star Game', a carefully prepared board game, to enable individuals to increasingly develop their consciousness.[11]

Although ONA claims this knowledge descends across 8000 years from a culture they call the Lemurian civilisation, structurally and functionally it seems very similar to the Golden Dawn family of magical groups, with the Star Game being somewhat analogous to the Golden Dawn's Enochian Chess. ONA has strongly white-supremacist foundations, rejects what it regards as Nazarene Christianity because of its Semitic origins, and advocates human sacrifice or culls of those they deem inferior, either magically or, so it is claimed, by physical murder. Organisationally ONA is structured around secretive cells called 'nexions', but it is entirely unclear how active or widespread they are. Other Satanist groups like the Temple of Set and the Church of Satan are strongly opposed to their interpretation of Satanist ideas.[12]

There are other types of Satanism as well, as defined by the Canadian organisation Ontario Consultants for Religious Tolerance, including Stereotypical or Gothic Satanism — the stuff of Hollywood and Dennis Wheatley novels, which lies behind the various Satanic panics with their lurid tales of ritual child abuse and animal sacrifices, and is responsible for the more excitable elements of ONA. Aotearoa has had its own ritual abuse panics, and, while it is certainly not out of the question that opportunistic ritual abuse has occurred, the notion that it is widespread has been exaggerated in the public imagination by the existence of groups such as Kay Rosaline's Ritual Action Group in Wellington and articles like 'Getting Beyond Ritual Abuse: Thoughts for Counsellors and Clients from a Survivor' in the feminist magazine *Broadsheet* in 1994.[13]

‡

An outbreak of ritual abuse reports in Christchurch in the 1990s was very likely linked with a workshop held there by Ritual Action Network in 1991 and the resulting media reportage.[14] Expert opinion on the actual extent of ritual abuse ranges from total scepticism to borderline apologism,[15] and is largely outside the ambit of this book. Ritual abuse tropes were raised in the Christchurch Civic Crèche case centring on childcare worker Peter Ellis (1958–2019).[16] These themes were picked up by the Dunedin historian Lynley Hood in her book on the subject,

A City Possessed: The Christchurch Civic Crèche Case (2001).[17]

Complaints of alleged abuse of children at the crèche were first made in 1991, no doubt influenced by Ritual Action Group. Around 118 children were interviewed by sexual abuse specialists during the subsequent investigation, and five staff members were arrested in 1992. The investigation raised several questions about the reliability of the interview process, which, contrasting with less outlandish accusations, included claims of satanic rituals, cannibalism, child sacrifice, Masonic lodges, Asian men dressed as cowboys, and one boy apparently stating his belly button had been removed with pliers.[18]

Only Ellis, the sole male member of the crèche staff, stood trial and was convicted, with the more bizarre claims having been dropped by the time of his trial. In an unusual step, in 2019 the New Zealand Supreme Court heard a posthumous appeal for the Ellis case, thereby recognising for the first time in New Zealand law the tikanga that a person's mana exists after death. As was noted at the time of various appeals relating to the case, the high-profile case came off the back of a number of other prominent Christchurch cases with questionable claims and suspect child-interviewing methods, resulting in mass diagnoses — in a redux of the Satanic abuse panic in California in 1982 and elsewhere throughout the 1980s.[19] The Supreme Court's decision, delivered in October 2022, unanimously exonerated Peter Ellis and quashed all of the convictions, finding that a significant miscarriage of justice had occurred.

The other of these Satanist types is Teenage Satanism, familiar as the rebellious adolescent with a penchant for inverted pentacles and niche goth and metal bands.[20] These two categories need not overly concern us. However, researcher John Latham does draw a further distinction between Satanism proper as a formal, philosophically coherent belief system, and devil-worshippers who are still operating within a Christian paradigm — from the losing side as it were — and who get their kicks from sadism, vandalism and blasphemy. At their most extreme, these types of devil-worshippers encompass the excesses of Charles Manson, Nordic Black Metal and the more exotic biker gangs.[21]

Such groups anecdotally met at places like William Larnach's tomb in Dunedin's Northern Cemetery,[22] or in Christchurch at the grave of murder

The Dunedin Northern Cemetery mausoleum of businessman and politician William James Mudie Larnach CMG, long a popular gathering place for would-be teenage Satanists.

victim Margaret Burke in the Barbadoes Street Cemetery (prior to the 1962 removal of the purportedly supernaturally bloodstained headstone)[23] and Witch Hill in the Port Hills,[24] Bolton Street Cemetery in Wellington, the Grafton and Waikumete cemeteries and the Michael Joseph Savage Memorial in Auckland.

Aotearoa is particularly rich in Black Metal bands who make use of Satanic or otherwise left-hand path neopagan and occult imagery in their music and album art. The most prominent — indeed, likely the most prominent Black Metal band in Australasia — is certainly Sinistrous Diabolus, which emerged in Christchurch in 1991.[25] Which is not to say that their choice of aesthetic expression in any way poses a threat to anyone or implies criminality of any kind.

☨

Robert Ellwood, in whose footsteps we respectfully plant ours, has this to say about Satanism in New Zealand:

> Apparently there are Satanists in New Zealand. I have heard rumours of a Satanist church in Eastbourne, and a motorcycle gang, Satan's Slaves, was in the news in 1988. The 1986 census reported 186 self-confessed Satanists (165 males and 21 females), a category unreported in previous censuses. Although some of these responses may have been frivolous, it could well be the case that in 1986, for the first time, there were scores of New Zealanders, mostly male, who seriously thought of themselves as worshippers of he whom the dominant faith considers the antagonist of God and of all that is good. I was able to learn nothing of these people. But they must not be confused with those who are merely followers of what they account the old religion revived.[26]

I concur with researcher John Latham that the mention of the motorcycle gang Satan's Slaves is somewhat ridiculous — their connection with Satan being in name only — although I disagree with his following assertion that Ellwood's final sentence 'can be equally applied to Satanism which also claims to be a "faith of pre-Christian Europe" and that it is an "old religion revived". If we accept this to be true of Witchcraft and other pagan or Neo-pagan religions then we must accept it of Satanism.'[27] Neopagan revivalism is, for the most part, a pastiche founded in a quasi-anthropological approach to extant cultural mythology and folkloric traditions, whereas Satanism's source material is almost entirely based in literary fiction, historical hoaxes and theological calumnies. That is not to say that this doesn't give it power and authenticity, but revival it is not. Norman Cohen concurs. 'There is in fact no serious evidence,' he writes, 'for the existence of Devil-worshippers anywhere in medieval Europe. One can go further: there is serious evidence to the contrary. Very few inquisitors claimed to come across these devil worshippers, and most of those few are known to be fanatical amateurs...'[28]

Satan came to Aotearoa with the missionaries. Māori had no need for an overarching personification of evil in their pantheon — the closest equivalent being Whiro-te-tipua, the atua of misfortune — but for all the progressive and reformist trends of the nineteenth century, as we saw in Chapter 11 many prejudiced missionaries regarded traditional Māori spirituality as a kind of devil worship, or at the very least the product of metaphorical diabolical misguidance and error. For example, upon seeing 17 mokamokai (preserved heads) at a gathering of Ngāpuhi in the Bay of Islands in 1832, the missionary Henry Williams (1792–1864) wrote: 'The countenances of all around seemed to partake of the image of their father the Devil. It is truly satanic, a grin was on every countenance.'[29] The Reverend Ruawai Rakena writes of Methodist missionaries and the theology they imparted on converted Māori: 'Having dismissed most if not all elements in Maori society as of Satan's own creation and design, the disassociation which ensued was only to be expected.'[30]

Some of the clergy clearly regarded the Māori prophetic movements that emerged from 1862 onwards, with their Christian borrowings, as being of a Satanic bent. These movements — going back to that established by Papahurihia (also known as Te Atua Wera) in the 1830s and Tikanga Hou in the 1840s — include that of Te Whiti o Rongomai and Tohu Kākahi at Parihaka, the quasi-military movement of Tītokowaru and Te Kooti, the Tariao and Pao Mīere (not to be confused with the similarly named Pai

Mārire) movements in the Waikato, and Kaingārara in the South Island. Anyone reading an account of the 1865 execution of the missionary Carl Völkner by Kereopa Te Rau under the auspices of the Pai Mārire[31] movement might certainly be forgiven for seeing in its ritual nature a blasphemous parody of the Crucifixion.

These prophetic movements were one of many ways explored by Māori to try to access the benefits of the colonisers' world while bypassing the colonisers themselves. They were also natural reactions to the upheaval, dislocation and social stress resulting from the imposition of the colonial system, and served as focal points of resistance to occupation. In an undated journal sent to the Native Secretary and Land Purchase commissioner Sir Donald McLean (1820–1877), an unknown correspondent reported of the presence of Pai Mārire in South Taranaki:

> Some of the Manuwapo [Manawapou] natives had gone to Patea, others were writing to Mr. Taylor respecting their new doctrine, and imagined that the Revd. gentleman would have coincided with a belief which I am sure he dreads and is trying to suppress as soon as possible. Met Mr. Hough on his way to Waimate, requested me to warn the natives against the foolish tikanga they were adopting. He stayed with me, and with him were a few natives requesting his advice on the subject, which was that he considered the influence they laboured under, a satanic influence, and wrote a strong sarcastic letter to point out how much they were going astray.[32]

As the historian James Belich has observed, even when not specifically Christian, as in the case of prophetic movements that identified with Judaism, these groups were still biblical in foundation.[33] In 1880 the *Tablet* reported a lecture in Ōamaru given by a Mr J. J. Croft on the literal reality of Satan, diabolism and evil sorcery, condemning the pagan gods of old as demons, with copious reference to the Bible and the stories of the saints. Croft concluded his talk with:

> Let Christianity grow weak or die out, let secular education be continued, and the materialistic tendencies of the age be more

developed, and we shall again see the days when the nations took for their guides the demons of Delphi, of Dodona and Prenestse [presumably Praeneste, now modern Palestrina in Italy]. Rationalist pride is soon at an end; humanity feels the want of a superior guidance — take from it the gospel and the Church, and it will to-morrow consult the devils, either divine faith or diabolical superstition.[34]

Anxious strangers in a strange land, the colonists' attitudes did not shift until the near-universal conversion of Māori by 1880 and the suppression of traditional beliefs and practices. Actual Satanism, however — not the mere fever dreams of priests — would not arrive in Aotearoa until the 1970s, and then as a primarily Pākehā phenomenon.

☦

According to John Latham, the Satanic group known as the Order of the Left Hand Path (OLHP) first made its presence officially known in Petone, Lower Hutt, in 1990, although it would change its name two years later to the more gentrified-sounding Latin cognate, Ordo Sinistra Vivendi (OSV).[35] The name-change was an artefact of the group's reinvention to remove so-called 'oriental' influences — presumably Eastern tantra and maybe Indo-Aryanism.[36] Some understanding of this group's beliefs and practices can be drawn from the booklet *Satanism in New Zealand: The Shocking Tale of Sinister Conspiracy* (1998) by K. Thomson, purportedly a Christian investigation into the subject, but — according to Latham — actually an attempt by OLHP's founding Magister, Faustus Scorpius, to stimulate a broader audience for Satanism and neo-fascist ideas in Aotearoa under a pseudonym.[37]

Faustus Scorpius is the occult name of high-profile far-right nationalist Kerry Bolton (b.1956), a prominent figure in New Zealand's neo-fascist and occult circles since the 1970s.[38] He was a co-founder of the Nationalist Workers' Party (it is impossible to know whether the similarity in name to the German National Socialists or Nazi Party is deliberate or not), in 1997 was secretary for the New Zealand Fascist Union for a short period of time, and by 2004 was involved with the New Zealand National Front before, paradoxically, falling out with that organisation's white-supremacist elements.[39] According to some disputed sources, Bolton allegedly formed OLHP after a rupture with the Temple of Set,[40] a largely internet-based and highly successful breakaway rival of the Church of Satan.[41] Rather than being Satanic, it is perhaps more accurate to collect these and the following various groups together as 'Saturnian': the planetary demiurgic spirit of Saturn encompassing all the archetypes venerated, associated with blood, death, sacrifice, nemesis, Nietzschean fatalism, secrecy, opposition to light and egalitarianism, the desire and promise of power, and the restoration of a dark, gloomy, dethroned, solitary force in exile.[42]

OLHP/OSV produced a substantial paper trail of newsletters, stickers, and even a correspondence course, Collegium Satanas. While its literature presents the group as 'non-sectarian' and 'non-dogmatic', and a LaVeyan forum for discussion of occult ideas that 'enhance the individual Will through a Nietzschean-type Self-Overcoming', in practice the tendency to form breakaway groups would suggest otherwise, and the emphasis on ritual puts it more in the magico-religious camp than not, and with distinctly ONA influences.[43] OLHP's most publicly obvious expression was a small magazine called *The Watcher*, which first appeared in 1990, edited and published by Bolton. *The Watcher* became *The Heretic* in 1992.[44]

In 1996 the journalist Gilbert Wong interviewed two members of OSV for the *New Zealand Herald*: Ray Livingstone, a former printer based in Wellington, whom Wong described as the founder of the OSV in 1991; and a female member in Manawatū going by the pseudonym 'Talisman'. The report opens with an OSV invocation: 'Hail Lucifer, Lord of Light, thy chosen are with thee, and holy art the seed of thy loins, knowledge; Sovereign lord and avenger of man, lead us to glory in the hour of our triumph.'[45] Immediately it is possible to hear echoes of the two supernal prayers of Roman Catholicism, the Lord's Prayer or Our Father, and the Hail Mary, although both Livingstone and Talisman were quick to distance themselves from mere theatrical blasphemy. 'If they believe in the Devil and the upside-down cross and perform blood sacrifices,' says Talisman, 'we can be sure they are not Satanists. They could be called Christian Satanists. Most are drug addicts, and their concept of Satanism only exists with the bounds of Christianity.'[46]

Wong's article provided a useful summary of OSV cosmology. Although the group identifies as Satanistic, that is more of a catch-all polytheism for the dark deities of various pantheons in a broad light–dark duality. These deities include Lucifer, Pan, Kali and Hel, among others, and rather than being simply one side of a strict good–evil binary, in fact represent all polarities and complex states. Satan is God and anti-God, humanity and nature, while Christianity is regarded as a blasphemous parody of those earlier religions.[47] This interpretation has strongly Thelemic notes to it.

Livingstone described being led to Satanism by his reading of Nietzsche and takes an abstract, rationalist approach to it, whereas Talisman always felt alienated by the mainstream, psychic, and was more intuitively drawn to it. Wong was careful to stress the normality of their lives aside from their faith, but he also provided a tantalising glimpse of an OSV initiation ritual in which the neophyte, having passed a written test, must bury a quartz crystal inscribed with the Dark Lord's sigil at the site of the ritual:

> On the night of the full moon, just before the ritual is to be performed, disinter the quartz crystal. After inscribing the pentagram, in blood, on the paper intended for burning, pass the crystal widdershins, or moonwise [counterclockwise — the opposite direction of the sun's path through the sky; the use of neopagan/Wiccan terminology is suggestive of OSV's degree of syncretism], through the smoke from the incense.[48]

The fumigation of a crystal may hint at the influence of Solomonic magic, where the invocation of spirits requires the appropriate incense to make the sacral space pleasant and pure for them. The crystal is then fixed about the initiate's neck so that it rests on the solar plexus — the Manipura or City of Jewels chakra, where the energies of the body meet and are in balance — and an order name, the equivalent of the motto in OTO for example, is conceived.[49] The OSV would eventually undergo another transformation into the Order of the Deorc Fyre (ODF) — Anglo-Saxon for 'dark fire' — which wound up in 1997 or 1998, largely concluding this particular Satanic lineage.

‡

The Order of the Sword of Damocles (OSD), led by an individual calling themselves Nemesis, emerged in the Wairarapa around the same time as the Order of the Left Hand Path, and nominally aligned with the latter. It was public enough that it gave interviews to the *Wairarapa Times-Age*, and operated an occult mail-order business named, pragmatically enough, Equipus Spiritae (Spiritual Equipment). According to Thomson, a member of OSD named Lilith, thrown out for her drug habit, founded a splinter group in Masterton, although this seems to have been little more than a front for consuming drugs and alcohol.[50] It seems plausible, in so far that this splinter group may have been what Talisman of the Manawatū OSV was alluding to by 'drug addicts' and 'Christian Satanists'.[51] Neither the OSD nor the splinter group appears to have endured.[52]

The OSD's main claim to prominence was that it served as a basis for the personal fiction of a Palmerston North police detective, Brent Garner, who claimed he had been attacked and his Ashurst house burned down by a group of Satanists. Garner was found a short distance from the burning building, bound, gagged and dowsed in petrol, and claimed he had been attacked by a man called 'The Executioner', who had carved a pentagram into his back. Garner was later convicted of arson and fraud, and received a five-year prison sentence. It is likely that this 1996 event provided the impetus for Wong's article, which was published later that week.

It seems even the Satanist community wasn't entirely sure what was going on either, as Livingstone emphatically distanced OSV from the situation, stating: 'We repudiate those types altogether on the basis that these people aren't mentally balanced. We want balance and exclude people who have an unnatural interest in inflicting pain upon others for the pleasure of it. Man is part of nature and anything out of tune with nature is anti-Satanist.' Both Livingstone and Talisman admitted, however, to encountering people who did fit that definition.[53] In 2003 Garner was found dead by his own hand in his car near Edgecumbe, in the Bay of Plenty. The incident was later made into a 2015 television movie, *Mars and Venus*, named for the two investigations undertaken by the police.[54]

‡

Kerry Bolton departed OSV in 1994 to found another group with, as the name suggests, an even more pronounced far-right ethno-nationalist alignment, the Black Order of Pan-Europa,[55] and established an accompanying newsletter, *The Flaming Sword*, and a related publication, *The Nexus*.[56] Bolton had established the Black Order as a sub-group of the OSV and recruited members through advertisements in *The Heretic*, and appears to have been influenced by Heinrich Himmler's ambitions for the SS as a kind of mystical Aryan knighthood. Rather than using Satanism as a gateway to ethno-nationalism, it seems to present the esoteric aspects of Nazism as a kind of 'blood and soil' socially conservative spiritual renewal for people of Northern European descent, combined with a Satanist nihilism and accelerationist-apocalyptic impetus.[57]

Although the Black Order had a primarily New Zealand-based membership, its mail-order structure encouraged an influx of members from North America, who were less interested in spiritual renewal than they were in race-war conspiracies about a Zionist New World Order, and a sewer of the most rabid white supremacism from the Klu Klux Klan to the Aryan Nation. Bolton once more moved on, and the Black Order rebranded as the White Order of Thule in 1996 under Grandmaster Abaaner Incendium, the former editor of Black Metal publication *Key of Alocer*.[58]

Allegedly this eventually resulted in a mass exodus of the North American contingent when they became aware that Abaaner Incendium was openly homosexual with a penchant for cross-dressing. The White Order struggled on, until finally fizzling out in 2001 with the usual story — accusations of financial impropriety.[59]

Around this time, Bolton, disgruntled by the direction of wider neopaganism, converted — or perhaps defaulted back — to Christianity, the faith he had once decried as slave religion with a Nietzschean fervour. This move was less ironic than pragmatic: American-style Christian conservatism seemed a more secure bastion of European 'white' culture and values.[60] In the revised 2006 preface to his 2001 biography of the prominent American fascist and leader of the US National Renaissance Party James H. Madole, Bolton explicitly repudiates his occult past and proclaims his Christianity.[61]

The observant reader will no doubt have noticed that Satanism in New Zealand tends to list to the extreme right wing, although quite why vastly powerful cosmic entities, who are to us as we are to paramecia, would care about the melanin content of one's skin is anyone's guess. In theory Satanism shouldn't, in fact, be particularly compatible with neo-Nazism, neo-fascism or white supremacism. Neo-fascism's regimented conformity, and white supremacism's elevation of even the most incompetent and inferior white people, are at odds with the basic Satanist precepts of individualism and aspiration.[62]

Then again, as seen in mainstream politics in the anti-communist endorsement by free-market economist Friedrich Hayek of the authoritarian regimes of António de Oliveira Salazar and Augusto Pinochet, the rise of conservative libertarian philosophy typified by conservative libertarian philosopher Frank Meyer and Austrian School economist Hans-Hermann Hoppe, and the embrace of libertarianism and individualism by the alt-right while espousing fascistic values, are all similarly contradictory and paradoxical.[63] Or is it as simple as the observation by George Orwell — someone who understood fascism better than most — that the idea of occultism as a secret thing limited to a small circle of initiates held great appeal for the sort of person who feared the emancipation of women, public education and welfare, and the 'lower orders' getting above themselves?[64]

In the case of the alt-right, Satanism may well have been in the vanguard. Indeed, the quasi-magical trappings of the alt-right — the conflation on 4Chan of the cartoon meme Pepe the Frog with the Egyptian god of primordial darkness Kek — implies some occult influence beyond mere edginess. The alt-right's use of memes to project a worldview also suggest an awareness of the theories of YouTuber, shirtless leather-jacketed BitChute personality and 'agnostic independent Satanist' Tarl Warwick.[65] Warwick's concept of 'Occult Memetics' has a clear provenance in the sigil magic of Austin Osman Spare (1886–1956), by way of the terrible distortions of it introduced by the libertarian bad boys of Chaos Magic since the 1970s.[66]

In essence, memes became the kind of magic charm known as *historiolae*: brief narratives built into incantations providing a mythological or scriptural precedence for a desired magical outcome. These can be found recorded in Ancient Egypt and Mesopotamia, and the Greek magical papyri of the Graeco-Roman period.[67]

This association between certain types of occultism and the far right emerges in the late nineteenth and early twentieth centuries, feeding into a political structure of secret societies variously clinging to traditional hierarchies, anti-liberalism, anti-democracy, the fetishisation of the pagan past in the name of nationalism, anti-modernity conservativism, and distrust of a Christianity with Semitic roots growing, at least in some aspects, ever more liberal. One of the prominent thinkers in this movement was Julius Evola (1898–1974), whose hostility to Christianity, virulent reactionary conservatism and occult beliefs find immense appeal with fascists and Satanists alike.[68]

Evola was a sort of weaponised Schopenhauer, where, in the absence of God, the individual Will must make itself God. He gained quite a lot of traction among pre-war Italian Fascist circles, and it seems likely that he was partially responsible for Mussolini's adoption of the racial politics in which El Duce had previously shown little interest.[69] A substantial element of the alt-right regard Evola as their founding philosopher.[70]

Then, of course, there is Nazism's early flirtations with the occult, which have become fodder for many lurid pop-cultural stereotypes from *Indiana Jones* to *Hellboy*. Historian Nicholas Goodrick-Clarke offers an extensive analysis in his classic 1985 book *The Occult Roots of Nazism*, teasing out the links with the racial ideas of Ariosophy — essentially the white-supremacist remix of Theosophy and Anthroposophy cooked up by Jörg Lanz von Liebenfels (1874–1954) in the early 1900s.[71] Von Liebenfels was, to put it mildly, cracked — an occultist who preached a revival of German paganism, and divided humanity between god-like, blue-eyed, blond-haired Aryans and the 'sodomite-apes' he believed should be sterilised and preferably exterminated.[72]

Hitler was apparently an early fan, as was the Swedish poet August Strindberg (1849–1912), and, allegedly, British Field Marshal Lord Herbert Kitchener (1850–1916). Aside from the usual fads for astrology, alchemy and whatnot in Nazism's early days, we may also include the Thule Society, a group of pseudo-antiquarian ethno-nationalist occultists who emerged in 1918, and whose membership list, according to Hitler biographer Sir Ian

Kershaw, 'reads like a Who's Who of early Nazi sympathisers and leading figures in Munich'.[73] We may also consider the elite, pseudo-chivalrous cult fostered by Heinrich Himmler around the SS at their castle base at Wewelsburg.

Left-wing Satanism does, however, exist. One such example is the Satanic Reds, who, under the banner of social realism, model their beliefs on Satan as described in Giosuè Carducci's 1865 poem 'Hymn to Satan' — the 'People's Satan', if you will.[74] Their philosophy is a combination of the politics of Russian anarchist Mikhail Bakunin,[75] the cosmic nihilism and Cthulhu mythos of American pulp horror writer H. P. Lovecraft,[76] and the belief that early modern witch trial victims were a persecuted peasantry rallying around a mythological and symbolic Devil against Church-backed feudalism.

If there has ever been an 'organised' left-wing Satanism at work in Aotearoa, it has either not flourished or is very secretive. On the other hand, there are New Zealand Satanic groups that are very public about their social concerns and charity work, such as the Dunedin-based Satanic New Zealand, a LaVeyan-style group co-founded by Frankie Vegas. In 2017 the *Otago Daily Times* reported that its charity Soles for Satan was purchasing socks, hats and warm clothing for people in homeless shelters and children living in poverty. Vegas was also responsible for the blood-donation drive Blood for Satan. These initiatives were inspired by similar charitable projects run by the international non-theistic Satanist organisation The Satanic Temple (founded in 2012 and headquartered in Salem, Massachusetts, of witch trial fame) to which Satanic New Zealand affiliates itself.[77]

Epilogue

It's an old country. One day in the back of beyond you come across a small town, run down because many of its young people have headed for the city. In an unpretentious building you discover a local art gallery-cum-museum. A solitary caretaker puffing a pipe turns on the lights and you are startled by the paintings on the walls . . . Here are old images of heaven and hell that now have a surreal air. You'd like to understand this odd iconography but the caretaker has a curiously literal approach — he tells local stories about the paintings as though he were pointing things out to you through a window.

— ROGER HORROCKS, 'THE INVENTION OF NEW ZEALAND', 1983

Not only is Aotearoa as weird as anywhere else, as I hope you will have gleaned from these pages, but it is quite possibly even weirder and quite distinct. Far from being bland and bucolic, New Zealand has a history — one of multiple rich and fascinating unknown histories in this country — that mainstream scholarship is only now beginning to investigate. This thread, however, does not float independently of the rest in the complicated tapestry of our relatively short history as a nation state. It is intimately bound up in a skein with the good and the bad.

In her book *A Demon-Haunted Land: Witches, Wonder Doctors, and the Ghosts of the Past in Post-WWII Germany* (2020), historian Monica Black postulates that post-war Germany's fascination with the occult and the supernatural, its obsession with alternative medicine and healing, was a kind of sublimation of all the Nazi atrocities they couldn't bring themselves to talk about.[1] Likewise, Pākehā New Zealand is built on a legacy of atrocity and theft that even today is too little acknowledged. Perhaps that is why Aotearoa has remained such a peculiarly fertile soil for eccentric and novel spiritualities and an enduring obsession with the occult, the esoteric, the magical and the supernatural. The old traditions never fully transplanted, or, already mutated by the Romantic peculiarities of the mid-Victorian mind, morphed into new things, or had to be grafted onto indigenous rootstock to survive in alien soil.

In contrast, some things like ghosts and evil spirits are universal across cultures. In several instances New Zealand occulture gives us insight into the psychology of the national relationship with Great Britain and the rising power of the United States. Some things did not travel well, like the Celtic fairy faith. North America had its occasional outbreaks of vampire panic into the nineteenth century, and superstitious rustic responses to outbreaks of tuberculosis,[2] but none that I'm aware of in New Zealand.

In Aotearoa, occultism has tended to fall into three loose categories. The first are broadly reformist and popular movements including Theosophy, Anthroposophy and Spiritualism, and to a lesser extent Celtic-based neopaganism and Wicca. The second is the more typically esoteric, elitist and secretive, or at least private, groups associated with the Golden Dawn, Thelema and Rosicrucianism. The final category consists of the groups and movements that are actively involved in ethno-nationalism and far-right politics. It is also interesting to observe that, for the most part, these groups and movements arrived in a fully developed form, although often in an early enough stage to see a paradigm shift into a second generation, often transmitted by publications and charismatic touring speakers.

Spiritualism was already well developed when it arrived here, but it remained in small circles for some time before the first Spiritualist churches appeared. The Theosophy of Blavatsky and Olcott found a home here, but it was the Theosophy of Besant and Leadbeater that made the most impact. The remnants of the Golden Dawn arrived here only after it had spectacularly imploded in Britain, but here it thrived and lasted for most of the twentieth century.

The most eye-opening aspect is the influence these groups have had on governance and social development in these islands. Occult movements such as Spiritualism and the Theosophical Society sometimes gave otherwise marginalised groups — women in particular — opportunities to rise to positions of influence. For example, they acted as early networking vehicles for social progress in the Labour movement, universal suffrage and environmentalism, and often welcomed Māori at a time when many social venues preferred to exclude. I have only cursorily explored that history in these pages, and no doubt there is much to be done by future historians.

As for the future, much depends on the direction of spirituality in Aotearoa as a whole. We are undoubtedly becoming a more secular society as formal religious observance retreats from everyday life and congregations shrink. The established Christian churches are faltering, being circled hungrily by younger, fundamentalist Pentecostal and Evangelical variants. By and large, Pākehā are growing increasingly less religious and more secular. Māori, Pasifika and other immigrant groups are the lifeline of the churches, although the minority interest in the pre-Christian traditions of the Pacific is significant. Of the two other Abrahamic faiths, Judaism remains a small but stable presence and Islam is on the ascendant, as are the two largest Eastern worldviews, Buddhism and Hinduism. It seems likely that religion, or rather, religiosity, will become an increasingly divisive issue within society

The internet will continue to democratise and make accessible a panoply of magical practices and sources, occult and esoteric groups and alternative faiths, although in most cases without the institutional strength of the established churches and faiths. Traditionally, uncertain and insecure times have seen the flourishing of eclectic alternative spiritualities and magical practices, and, given that these times are very uncertain and insecure, I see no reason for twenty-first-century Aotearoa to be any different.

☦

There are many topics that this book has not tackled. For example, I am aware of non-Haitian Vodou practitioners in New Zealand, and, in an era of instantaneous globalism and immigration from South East Asia, Latin America and Africa, it will be interesting to see whether magical and occult practices will travel from those regions as well. Brazilian Pentecostal churches have established themselves in Aotearoa's main centres, so it doesn't seem unreasonable that the Afro-Latin folk religions Candomblé and Kimbanda — which fuse Roman Catholicism with indigenous and quasi-magical beliefs — would also.

There are hints that Philippine 'black magic' Kulam and Gaway, and Tagalog-centric neopagan Dayawism might have made their way here. Thai magical tattoos (Sak Yant) and necromantic traditions are becoming a subject of greater interest, although any Thai practitioners would have been mortified by artists Tessa Laird and Tiffany Singh whimsically installing a South East Asian spirit house, *Wihaan*, as a temporary installation in Auckland's Albert Park in 2010. In Thai custom, at least, it is to court absolute disaster to meddle with spirit houses, or even to look at them in some locations.

Regarding the arts, it would take an entire book in itself to look at the influence of occult and esoteric thought on New Zealand artists. Obvious examples are the photographer Fiona Pardington and the multimedia artist Julia Morison, and there are much less overt examples by many other artists that could be discussed. Another subject that would require a book, possibly several, is a history of Freemasonry in Aotearoa. I barely scratch the surface except to set the stage for the other actors.

⹋

There were subjects that proved just too emotionally overwhelming to attempt to tackle. The Christchurch mosque attacks of 2019 made the public aware of the use of Nordic (particularly Odinist) neopagan imagery by dangerous far-right and ethnonationalist groups. Just as the internet can give the impressionable young person in the provinces the tools to self-initiate into Wicca or Druidism, it can also give access to other groups which are likewise on the rise, although, as I have shown, they have already been with us since the 1970s. That is something to be ever vigilant for, although, just as elements of the far-right have rebranded as the alt-right, the neopagan traditionalists are giving way to the slick and savvy libertarian practitioner subset of Chaos Magic, who don't believe in anything much at all except to do as they please and watch the world burn.

Anecdotally, occult beliefs and magical practices are becoming less fringe and odd, and more acceptably mainstream. To borrow a metaphor from Robert Ellwood, the established religions are the whales of the spiritual ocean, and the various occult and esoteric groups, movements and beliefs we have looked at are but amoebae to those whales, smaller and weaker like the amoebae, but also, like the amoebae, truly immortal.

Notes

Introduction

1. Bernard Reid, *Conjurors, Cardsharps and Conmen: A Comprehensive History of One of the Most Popular Theatrical Entertainments of Nineteenth-century New Zealanders* (Mangawhai: Mary Egan Publishing, 2015).
2. Chris Gosden, *The History of Magic: From Alchemy to Witchcraft, from the Ice Age to the Present* (New York: Farrar, Straus and Giroux, 2020), 406–07.
3. '"I'm no snowflake" — Ethan De Groot entertains with tattoo yarn', *1 News*, TVNZ, 8 July 2021, www.tvnz.co.nz/one-news/sport/rugby/im-no-snowflake-ethan-groot-entertains-tattoo-yarn
4. Christopher Partridge, 'Occulture is Ordinary', in *Contemporary Estoteris*, eds Egil Asprem and Kennet Granholm (London: Routledge, 2013), 124.
5. Christopher Partridge, 'Occulture', in *The Re-Enchantment of the West, Vol. 1: Alternative Spiritualities, Sacralization, Popular Culture, and Occulture* (London: T&T Clark, 2004), 4.
6. See Andrew Paul Wood, 'Magical Thinking: The Photography of Fiona Pardington', in *Black Mirror 2— Elsewhere*, eds Jesse Bransford, Judith Noble and Dominic Shepherd (Somerset: Fulgur Press, 2019), 107–25.
7. Max Weber, *The Sociology of Religion*, trans. Ephraim Fischoff (Boston: Beacon Press, 1993); Richard Jenkins, 'Disenchantment, Enchantment and Reenchantment', *Max Weber Studies* 1, no. 1 (2000): 11–32.
8. John A. Hall, *Ernest Gellner: An Intellectual Biography* (London: Verso, 2010).
9. Jason Josephson-Storm, *Myth of Disenchantment: Magic, Modernity, and the Birth of the Human Sciences* (Chicago: University of Chicago Press, 2017).
10. Wouter J. Hanegraaff, *Esotericism and the Academy: Rejected Knowledge in Western Culture* (Cambridge: Cambridge University Press, 2012), 155; Alex Owen, *The Place of Enchantment: British Occultism and the Culture of the Modern* (Chicago: University of Chicago Press, 2004), 27.
11. Rudolf Otto, *Das Heilige: Über das Irrationale in der Idee des Göttlichen und sein Verhältnis zum Rationalen* (Munich: Beck, 1987), passim.
12. George Grote, 'Grecian Legends and Early History', *Westminster Review* 39 (May 1843): 285–328, summarised in *The Minor Works of George Grote*, ed. A. Bain (London: J. Murray, 1873), 173–74.
13. Gosden, *Magic*, 11–14.
14. The construction of the first gothic revival buildings and publication of gothic romances in eighteenth-century England coincides with the publication of popular grimoires including Ebenezer Sibley's (1751–1799) *New and Complete Illustration of the Celestial Science of Astrology* (1784) and *A Key to Physic, and the Occult Sciences* (1792), and the rather more serious *The Magus* (1801) by the occult grifter Francis Barrett (b.1770–1780 — d. after 1802). These are of the same period as Horace Walpole's house 'Strawberry Hill' (built between 1749 and 1766) and his novel *The Castle of Otranto* (1764).
15. Nick Freeman, 'The Black Magic Bogeyman, 1908–1935', in *The Occult Imagination in Britain, 1875–1947*, eds Christine Ferguson and Andrew Radford (London and New York: Routledge, 2018), 108, n. 11.

16 British occult author, the reliably waspish Francis X. King (1934–1994), once compared the writings of influential and popular French occultist Éliphas Lévi (1810–1875) to the gothic revival wedding cake of London's St Pancras train station. He quipped that by comparison, the 'hippy-occult magazine *Gandalf's Garden* could aptly be described as being Lévi out of Henry Miller'.
17 John Rockey, 'An Australasian Utopist: Robert Pemberton FRSL', *New Zealand Journal of History* 15, no. 2 (October 1981): 157–78. Owenites were the followers of Robert Owen (1771–1858), a wealthy Welsh manufacturer, social reformer, utopian idealist and later Spiritualist. The best-known attempt at an Owenite settlement was New Harmony, Indiana, United States, which lasted from 1825 to 1829. Owenism was also closely associated with the British trade union movement and the Mechanics' Institute movement.
18 Lytton Strachey, *Eminent Victorians* (Garden City: Garden City Publishing, 1918), 20.
19 Jean Lorrain, 'Lanterne magique', in *Histoires de Masques* (Paris: Librairie Paul Ollendorff, 1900).
20 Robert Ziegler, *Satanism, Magic and Mysticism in Fin-de-siècle France* (Basingstoke: Palgrave Macmillan, 2012), 1.
21 M. B. Soljak, 'Superstitions: A sinister revival', *Auckland Star*, 11 February 1933.
22 Ibid.
23 See, for example, the interdisciplinary research network 'Okkulte Moderne' and the resulting De Gruyter book series.
24 Kendall Clements, Garth Cooper, Michael Corballis, Doug Elliffe, Robert Nola, Elizabeth Rata and John Werry, 'In Defence of Science', *New Zealand Listener*, 31 July 2021, 4.
25 Anna Lux, 'On All Channels: Hans Bender, the Supernatural and the Mass Media', in *Revisiting the 'Nazi Occult': Histories, Realities, Legacies*, eds Monica Black and Eric Kurlander (Rochester: Camden House, 2015), 223–41, at 224.
26 Cited in Denis Dutton, 'Theodor Adorno on Astrology', *Philosophy and Literature* 19, no. 2 (1995): 424–30.
27 See Blaise Pascal, *The Art of Persuasion* (Volendam: LM Publishers, 2019).
28 The literature on this subject is legion. See Peter Laslett, *The World We Have Lost* (New York: Routledge, 2004); Stuart H. Hughes, *Consciousness and Society: The Reorientation of Social Thought, 1890–1930* (New York: Vintage, 1961); Mark J. Sedgwick, *Against the Modern World: Traditionalism and the Secret Intellectual History of the Twentieth Century* (New York: Oxford University Press, 2004); Morris Berman, *The Reenchantment of the World* (Ithaca, NY: Cornell University Press, 1981); Keith Thomas, *Religion and the Decline of Magic* (New York: Charles Scribner's Sons, 1971); Robert Darnton, *Mesmerism and the End of the Enlightenment in France* (Cambridge, MA: Harvard University Press, 1968).
29 C. H. Legare and A. Visala, 'Between Religion and Science: Integrating the Psychological and Philosophical Accounts of Explanatory Coexistence', *Human Development* 54, no. 3 (2011): 169–84; C. H. Legare and S. A. Gelman, 'Bewitchment, Biology, or Both: The Coexistence of Natural and Supernatural Explanatory Frameworks Across Development', *Cognitive Science* 32, no. 4 (2008): 607–42.
30 Eric Kurlander, *Hitler's Monsters: A Supernatural History of the Third Reich* (New Haven: Yale University Press, 2018), xvi–xvii.
31 Ibid; Charles Taylor, *Modern Social Imaginaries* (Durham, NC: Duke University Press, 2004), 23–25, 185–87.
32 Ferguson and Radford, *The Occult Imagination in Britain*, 10.
33 Mark S. Morrison, 'The Periodical Culture of the Occult Revival: Esoteric Wisdom,

Modernity, and Counter-Public Spheres', *Journal of Modern Literature* 31, no. 2 (2008): 1–22, at 3.

34 New Zealand Te Urewera Act 2014.

35 New Zealand Te Awa Tupua (Whanganui River Claims Settlement) Act 2017, s 14.

36 Te Anga Pūtakerongo — Record of Understanding, 5.5.2.

37 Robert S. Ellwood, *Islands of the Dawn: The Story of Alternative Spirituality in New Zealand* (Honolulu: University of Hawai'i Press, 1993), 5.

38 To give a sense of how ubiquitous Freemasonry is in New Zealand, in 1939 and again in the 1951 reprint *Aunt Daisy's Book of Handy Hints* suggests with sunny pragmatism that Masonic aprons 'May be beautifully cleaned with Dixon's Carpet Shampoo — follow directions on bottle and do not make apron too wet.' Freemasonry is indeed esoteric, but it is not occult. Public familiarity, and the many books available on the subject, would make discussion of it here redundant. Exposés of Freemasonry are almost as old as Freemasonry itself; one of the earliest, Samuel Prichard's *Masonry Dissected*, was first published in 1730. Although, as John Dickie puts it, 'Freemasonry lubricated the machinery of imperial dominion . . .' and 'turned the [British] Empire into spectacle', for the most part in Australasia it was a benign force that fostered democracy and softened class divisions. There was one significant exception in Australia, although I can find no equivalent case in Aotearoa. One of the many crimes and indignities visited upon Aboriginal Australians with the arrival of European settlers in 1788 was the desecration of indigenous burial sites for skulls and arm and leg bones to use as Masonic 'Emblems of Mortality'. This came to light in 2002 following an amnesty when the lodges of the state of Victoria handed over to Melbourne Museum a large uncatalogued collection of remains, tragically alienated from family, tribal grouping and place. John Dickie, *The Craft: How the Freemasons Made the Modern World* (New York: Public Affairs, 2020), 430–31.

39 We find a lengthy column by John Liddell Kelly (1850–1925) in the *Auckland Star*, 6 October 1923, describing the history and theory of Hermeticism in considerable detail, even specifying his sources as the dubious *The Alpha* (an 1855 guide by Ramus Randolf) and the just-as-dubious *The Kybalion* (1908, likely the creation of 'New Thought' pioneer William Walker Atkinson). Kelly was a Scottish-born journalist and poet who emigrated to New Zealand for his health in 1880, serving as sub-editor for the *Auckland Star*, working for periods at the *Lyttelton Times* and the *New Zealand Times*, and publishing his mystically-themed poems in the Auckland *Observer*: 'Kelly, John Liddell (1850–1925)', in *The Oxford Companion to New Zealand Literature*, eds Roger Robinson and Nelson Wattie (Melbourne: Oxford University Press, 1998); Douglas B. W. Sladen, *Australian Poets, 1788–1888* (New York: Cassell Publishing Company, 1890), 265.

40 As is often the case with transliteration from Hebrew, there are variations in English spelling. I have settled on 'Kabbalah', which I will also use for the Christian version (often spelled as variations on 'Cabbala') and the esoteric version (often spelled as variations on 'Qabalah').

41 This definition is loosely based on that of Antoine Faivre: Antoine Faivre and Karen-Claire Voss, 'Western Esotericism and the Science of Religions', *Numen* 42, no. 1 (1995): 48–77, at 60–64.

42 See Wouter J. Hanegraaff, 'A Dynamic Typological Approach to the Problem of "Post-Gnostic" Gnosticism', *Aries* 16 (1992): 5–43.

43 Daniel Ogden, *Magic, Witchcraft, and Ghosts in the Greek and Roman Worlds: A Sourcebook* (Oxford: Oxford University Press, 2002), 4.

44 Arthur Schopenhauer, *The World as Will and Idea*, trans. R. B. Haldane and J. Kemp (London: Kegan Paul, Trench, Trübner & Co., 1909), passim.
45 See Robert Anton Wilson, *Cosmic Trigger I: The Final Secret of The Illuminati* (Grand Junction: Hilaritas Press, 1977).
46 Steve Rose, 'Moore's Murderer', *The Guardian*, 2 February 2002, www.theguardian.com/film/2002/feb/02/sciencefictionfantasyandhorror.books
47 Hendrik Hertzberg, 'Roboflop' (interview with Dan Quayle), *The New Republic*, 31 October 1988, https://newrepublic.com/article/74620/roboflop

Chapter 1. The not-so-secret doctrine

1 Robert S. Ellwood, *Islands of the Dawn: The Story of Alternative Spirituality in New Zealand* (Honolulu: University of Hawai'i Press, 1993), 96.
2 Robert Twigger, *White Mountain: Real and Imagined Journeys in the Himalayas* (London: Weidenfeld and Nicolson, 2016), 127–31. The chapter, leaving no ambiguity, is titled 'Madame Blavatsky Did Not Go to Shigatse'; Martin Brauen, *Dreamworld Tibet: Western Illusions* (Trumbull, CT: Weatherhill, 2004), 24–37.
3 Loren Graham and Jean-Michel Kantor, *Naming Infinity: A True Story of Religious Mysticism and Mathematical Creativity* (Cambridge, MA: Belknap Press, 2009).
4 See Stephen J. Luecking, 'A Man and His Square: Kasimir Malevich and the Visualization of the Fourth Dimension', *Journal of Mathematics and the Arts* 4, no. 2 (2010): 87–100.
5 For Rasputin, Papus and many other strange religious sects in late nineteenth-century Russia, see Douglas Smith, *Rasputin: The Biography* (London: Macmillan, 2016); Bernice Glatzer Rosenthal (ed.), *The Occult in Russian and Soviet Culture* (Ithaca, NY: Cornell University Press, 1997).
6 Sylvia Cranston, *H.P.B. The Extraordinary Life & Influence of Helena Blavatsky, Founder of the Modern Theosophical Movement* (New York: G. P. Putnam's Sons, 1993), 18–19.
7 Ellwood, *Islands of the Dawn*, 97.
8 Stephen R. Prothero, *The White Buddhist: The Asian Odyssey of Henry Steel Olcott* (Bloomington: Indiana University Press, 1996).
9 Ibid., 23.
10 Here one is inescapably reminded of Plato's parable of the origin of love in the *Symposium* where humans are originally spherical hermaphrodites with two faces, four arms and four legs, who become so powerful that Zeus splits them all in half, creating male and female, and condemning each half to search for their lost soulmate.
11 See Bruce F. Campbell, *Ancient Wisdom Revived: A History of the Theosophical Movement* (Berkeley: University of California Press, 1980); Gary Lachman, *Madame Blavatsky: The Mother of Modern Spirituality* (New York: Jeremy P. Tarcher/Penguin, 2012).
12 Kevin Brehony, ' "A Dedicated Spiritual Movement": Theosophists and Education 1875–1939' (paper presented at the XIX International Standing Committee Conference for the History of Education, National University of Ireland, Maynooth, 1997), 30.
13 David Sweetman, *Paul Gauguin: Complete Life* (London: Hodder and Stoughton, 1995), 440–41.
14 Alfred Percy Sinnett, *The Occult World: Teachings of Occult Philosophy* (London: Trübner & Co, 1881), 6.
15 Sue Middleton, 'New Zealand Theosophists in "New Education" Networks, 1880s–1938', *History of Education Review* 46, no. 1 (2017): 42–57, at 44.
16 'Some Notes of the Convention', *Theosophy in New Zealand* 24, no. 2 (1926): 48–50.

17   Emma Hunt, 'Golden Jubilee of the New Zealand Section of the Theosophical Society 1896–1946', *Theosophy in New Zealand* 7, no. 2 (April–June 1946): 31.
18   Tony Ballantyne, *Webs of Empire: Locating New Zealand's Colonial Past* (Vancouver and Toronto: University of British Columbia Press, 2012), 93.
19   'Deaths', *Auckland Star*, 17 August 1898.
20   Henry Steel Olcott, *Old Diary Leaves: The True History of the Theosophical Society* (Sixth Series) (Adyar: Theosophical Publishing House, 1898), 239.
21   Ellwood, *Islands of the Dawn*, 97.
22   Jack Patterson, 'The History of Theosophy in Auckland', https://hpb.theosophy.org.nz/history; Ellwood, *Islands of the Dawn*, 261, n. 4.
23   Letter from Sturdy to the New Zealand Section of the Theosophy Society, 30 March 1940, published in *Theosophy in New Zealand* 1, no. 5 (August–September 1940): 20; *Theosophy in New Zealand* 7, no. 2 (April–June 1946): 59; Ellwood, *Islands of the Dawn*, 98.
24   Letter from Sturdy to Emma Hunt, 24 October 1939, published in *Theosophy in New Zealand* 1, no. 3 (April–May 1940): 17; Mary K. Neff, *How Theosophy Came to Australia and New Zealand* (Melbourne: Australian Section Theosophical Society, 1943), 43–44; Ellwood, *Islands of the Dawn*, 99.
25   Atkinson was hardly the only New Zealand prime minister to take up with fringe ideas. William Massey (1856–1925) and Governor-General Lord Jellicoe (1859–1935) were both members of the British Israelite movement, who believed that the British descended from one of the lost tribes of Israel.
26   Ellwood, *Islands of the Dawn*, 101.
27   Bishop Charles Leadbeater, *Australia and New Zealand: Home of a New Sub-Race*, facsimile ed. (Tauranga: Ashford Kent, 1912/1973), 1–6.
28   Emma Hunt, 'The Contribution of the Maori', *Theosophy in New Zealand* 2, no. 1 (1940): 11–13, at 11. Conversely, the indefatigable Reverend Samuel Marsden of the Church Missionary Society was convinced that Māori were descended from one of the lost tribes of Israel: Samuel Marsden, concluding remarks, *Journal of Proceedings at New Zealand*, 29 July 1819–19 October 1819, ms. copy made in New South Wales, signed by Samuel Marsden. Ms. 177B, Hocken Collections, University of Otago.
29   Leadbeater, *Australia and New Zealand*, 1; Joy Dixon, *Divine Feminine: Theosophy and Feminism in England* (Baltimore and London: Johns Hopkins University Press, 2001).
30   Edward Tregear, *Hedged with Divinities* (Wellington: Coupland Harding, 1895).
31   Ellwood, *Islands of the Dawn*, 118.
32   Olcott, *Old Diary Leaves*, 240.
33   Ibid., 240; Jack Patterson, 'History of Theosophy in Auckland', https://hpb.theosophy.org.nz/history; obituary, *Auckland Star*, 8 May 1920.
34   In the eighteenth century, the Swedish Lutheran theologian Emanuel Swedenborg (1688–1772), living in England, claimed to have received a revelation from God of a new church to come. The most distinctive part of this new theology was its view of the afterlife, which was taken up by Spiritualism in the nineteenth century. The Swedenborgian New Church consists of mixed congregational and episcopal polities and still exists today.
35   Gertrude M. Hemus, 'Early Days of the Theosophical Society in Auckland', *Theosophy in New Zealand* 7, no. 2 (April–June 1946): 49–52; Lilian Edger, 'Memories of Colonel Olcott', *The Theosophist* (Adyar, India) 61, no. 11 (August 1940): 370; Ellwood, *Islands of the Dawn*, 106–07.
36   Ellwood, *Islands of the Dawn*, 108.
37   Ibid., 106–07; citing Olcott, *Old Diary Leaves*, 249.
38   Patterson, 'History of Theosophy in Auckland'.

39   Email correspondence with Jo Atkinson, senior librarian, Theosophical Society in New Zealand Inc, 14 December 2020.
40   Patterson, 'History of Theosophy in Auckland'.
41   New Zealand Historic Places Trust, 'Theosophical Society Hall (HPB Lodge) (Former)', www.heritage.org.nz/the-list/details/2650
42   Helena Blavatsky, *The Secret Doctrine*, Vol. 1 (London: Theosophical Publishing House, 1893), 83.
43   New Zealand Vegetarian Society, www.vegetarian.org.nz/about/history
44   Geoffrey Hodson, 'The Story of My Life', three-part audio recording, www.theosophy.world/resource/audio/story-my-life-geoffrey-hodson; 'The Geoffrey Hodson Story', www.theosophy.world/resource/articles/geoffrey-hodson-story; John Kirk Robertson, *Aquarian Occultist* (self-published, 1971), passim.
45   *Theosophy in New Zealand* 15, no. 4 (March–July 1955).
46   Alan Senior, 'Mountains: Symbols of Ascent', *Theosophy Society Scotland*, www.yumpu.com/en/document/view/36374463/mountains-as-symbols-of-ascent-theosophical-society-scotland
47   'Mr. Douglas Fawcett', obituary, *The Times*, 18 April 1960.
48   Maurice Isserman and Stewart Weaver, *Fallen Giants: A History of Himalayan Mountaineering from the Age of Empire to the Age of Extremes* (Devon: Duke & Company, 2008), 61–63.
49   'School of Radiant Living — Edmund Hillary', https://nzhistory.govt.nz/culture/radiant-living/edmund-hillary-radiant-liver; 'School of Radiant Living — The Havelock Work', https://nzhistory.govt.nz/culture/radiant-living/the-havelock-work
50   'Theosophical Society Hall (HPB Lodge) (Former)', New Zealand Historic Places Trust, www.heritage.org.nz/the-list/details/2650
51   James Joyce, *Ulysses* (Paris: Sylvia Beach, 1922), 184.
52   Correspondence in the archives of the New Zealand Section of the Theosophical Society, Epsom, Auckland, cited by Ellwood, *Islands of the Dawn*, 126.
53   *Theosophical Women's Association* (pamphlet), Wellington, n.d.; *Newsletter of the Theosophical Women's Association*, May 1947 and March 1948.
54   Untitled item, *London Gazette*, iss. 247209 (May 1879): 3296.
55   'Lecture at Knox Church', *Otago Witness*, 14 August 1869; 'Spiritualism', *Otago Witness*, 9 October 1869; untitled item, *Echo*, 11 June 1870; [Meers], *The Ultimate of Man* (pamphlet), n.d.; untitled item, *The Press*, 22 October 1909; untitled item, *New Zealand Herald*, 12 September 1879; untitled item, *Echo*, 2 March 1872.
56   Olcott, *Old Diary Leaves*, 231–34.
57   Tessa Kristiansen, 'Wilson, John Cracroft', *Dictionary of New Zealand Biography*, first published in 1990, updated May 2002. *Te Ara — the Encyclopedia of New Zealand*, https://teara.govt.nz/en/biographies/1w31/wilson-john-cracroft
58   Robyn Jenkin, *New Zealand Mysteries* (Wellington: A. H. & A. W. Reed, 1970), 91–92.
59   Greg Roughan, 'Repertory Theatre Sure to Rise Again', *The Press*, 10 September 2010.
60   *The Architectural Heritage of Christchurch 8: The Legacy of Thomas Edmonds* (Christchurch: Christchurch City Council Environmental Policy and Planning Unit, 1993), 8–10.
61   Ibid., 8.
62   Edmonds, 'Brand history', https://edmondscooking.co.nz/brand-history
63   Helena Blavatsky, *The Key to Theosophy*, Vol. 1 (London: Theosophical Publishing Society, 1889), 57–58.
64   H. H. Wilson, *Rig Veda*, Vol. 3 (Poona: Ashtekar & Co, 1926), vi.

65 Blavatsky, *The Key to Theosophy*, Vol. 1, 83–84.
66 *The Architectural Heritage of Christchurch 8*, 9–10.
67 The facilities were also used by Theosophy-adjacent groups such as the Liberal Catholic Church of Saint Francis. The upper floor of the building was eventually occupied by the Christchurch Lodge of Universal Co-masonry and the Esoteric Society.
68 *The Press*, 26 July 1926.
69 Penelope Jackson, 'White Camelias Revisited', *Christchurch Art Gallery Bulletin* 196 (29 May 2019); Penelope Jackson, 'Daisy Osborn (1888–1957): An Artist of Note' (MA thesis, University of Auckland, 2001).
70 *CSA Jubilee Catalogue 1881–1930*, 1930, no. 40.
71 Cited in Martin Edmond, *Dark Night: Walking with McCahon* (Auckland: Auckland University Press, 2011), 112.
72 Francis Porter, *Historic Buildings of New Zealand: South Island* (Auckland: Methuen, 1983), 87.
73 The architect of both buildings, Benjamin Mountfort (1825–1898), was a Freemason, and it is tempting to see in the towers of these two buildings a reflection of the twin pillars of Boaz (the earthly Adam) and Joachim (the divine Adam) mentioned in Jeremiah 52:21–22, 1 Kings 7:13–22, 41–42, and in Josephus 8.3, and significant in Masonic symbolism.
74 Blavatsky, *The Key to Theosophy*, Vol. 1, 364 (italics in original).
75 Ibid., Vol. 2, 387.
76 Alison Yvonne Atkinson, 'The Dunedin Theosophical Society, 1892–1900' (BA Hons dissertation, University of Otago, 1978).
77 Ellwood, *Islands of the Dawn*, 108–09.
78 Ibid., 107.
79 C. Watt, 'Theosophy', *Evening Star*, 29 October 1896.
80 Ellwood, *Islands of the Dawn*, 111; Atkinson, 'The Dunedin Theosophical Society', 53–55.
81 Countess Wachtmeister via her secretary H. A. Wilson, 'Theosophy v. the Champions of Christianity', *Wairarapa Daily Times,* 16 March 1896.
82 Charles Kingsley, *Hypatia: or New Foes with an Old Face* (London: John W. Parker & Son, 1853).
83 James Neil, *Spiritualism and Theosophy: Twain Brothers of the Anti-Christ* (Dunedin: Budget Print, c.1901), Hocken Collections, University of Otago.
84 Atkinson, 'The Dunedin Theosophical Society', 55–57.
85 Ibid., 4–7.
86 'Altiora Peto', letter to the editor, *Evening Star,* 28 May 1894.
87 'Agnes Inglis' (unpublished history of the Dunedin Lodge, collection of the Dunedin Lodge of the New Zealand Theosophical Society, undated); Dunedin Theosophical Society, 'Our History', www.theosophy-dunedin.org/our-history.html
88 Jonathan Chilton-Towle, 'Former hotel new home for society', *Otago Daily Times*, 2 February 2015.
89 B. F. Campbell, *Ancient Wisdom Revived: A History of the Theosophical Movement* (Berkeley: University of California Press, 1980), 3.
90 Aleister Crowley to Montgomery Evans II, 22 October 1926, Evans Papers, cited by Richard Kaczynski, *Perdurabo: The Life of Aleister Crowley* (Berekley: North Atlantic Books, 2010), 434.
91 *New Zealand Free Lance*, 4 September 1909, 4.
92 C. F. Scott-Moncrieff, 'The Coming Christ and the Order of the Star in the East: A paper

read to a meeting of clergy and other members of the Church of England, in London, 27 November 1911' (Auckland: Lotus, n.d.); *The International Theosophical Year Book, 1937* (Adyar: Theosophical Publishing, 1936/1937), 235; Ellwood, *Islands of the Dawn*, citing *Crockford's Clerical Directory* (1941), 124, 264, n. 49.

93 D. W. M. Burn, *Pedlar's Pack* (Dunedin: Coulls Somerville Wilke, 1932); obituary, *Evening Star* (Dunedin), 7 July 1951; *Theosophy in New Zealand* 27, no. 3 (May–June 1929); see also his entry in *The Oxford Companion to New Zealand Literature*, eds Roger Robinson and Nelson Wattie (Melbourne and Auckland: Oxford University Press, 1998).

94 Ellwood, *Islands of the Dawn*, 120–21.

95 Ibid., 123–24.

96 'New Zealand artists. Seven and Five Society. Exhibition in London', *New Zealand Herald*, 8 May 1929.

97 'Broadcast ban on Krishnamurti', *The Dominion* and *New Zealand Herald*, 28 March 1934.

98 Ellwood, *Islands of the Dawn*, 124–25.

99 Ibid., 114.

100 *The Sun* (New York), 8 April 1910.

101 Charles W. Leadbeater and Annie Besant, *The Lives of Alcyone* (Adyar: Theosophical Publishing House, 1924); Gregory Tillet, *The Elder Brother: A Biography of Charles Webster Leadbeater* (London: Routledge and Kegan Paul, 1982), 465.

102 Gregory Tillett, 'Charles Webster Leadbeater 1854–1934: A Biographical Study' (PhD thesis, University of Sydney, 1986), 905.

103 Mary Lutyens, *Krishnamurti: The Years of Awakening* (New York: Avon, 1976), 202.

104 Leadbeater, *Australia and New Zealand*; Tillet, *The Elder Brother*, 163–164; Jill Roe, *Beyond Belief: Theosophy in Australia, 1879–1839* (Sydney: New South Wales University Press, 1986), 216–17; Ellwood, *Islands of the Dawn*, 116–17.

105 Tillet, *The Elder Brother*, 197; Ellwood, *Islands of the Dawn*, 117–18.

106 Lutyens, *Krishnamurti*, 155.

107 'Monstrous Mahatmas', *NZ Truth*, 16 January 1909; 'Loathsome Leadbeater', *NZ Truth*, 17 July 1909; 'Leadbeater's lives', *NZ Truth*, 22 August 1914; '"Messiah" billed to appear next year in heavenly glory before the elect at Balmoral Stadium', *NZ Truth*, 31 December 1925; 'Theosophical scandal', *NZ Truth*, 6 June 1926.

108 Ellwood, *Islands of the Dawn*, 118.

109 *Theosophy in New Zealand* (19 December 1904): 181.

110 Ellwood, *Islands of the Dawn*, 114–15, citing *Theosophy in New Zealand*, new series, 1, no. 1 (April 1903): 5. The reviewer then begrudgingly acknowledges how Besant undermines Kiplingesque fustian in her vision of imperialism by grounding it in the Theosophical understanding of the cyclical rise and fall of civilisations, and the observation that the British were almost entirely ignorant of the traditions and beliefs of the people over which they ruled.

111 For example: 'NZ's strangest community', *NZ Truth*, 18 August 1956.

112 Caren Wilton, 'Communes and communities — Early communities', *Te Ara — the Encyclopedia of New Zealand*, www.TeAra.govt.nz/en/communes-and-communities/page-1

113 Ellwood, *Islands of the Dawn*, 150.

114 'Human relationships out of step with social conventions', *Sunday Morning Post*, 19 July 1955; 'NZ's strangest community'.

115 Ray Hansen, 'Beeville', 1971, Ngā Taonga Sound and Vision archives, reference number 292763, https://ngataonga.org.nz/collections/catalogue/catalogue-item?record_id=303170

116   Ellwood, *Islands of the Dawn*, 150–51.
117   Cited by Ellwood, *Islands of the Dawn*, 151–52; Cf. folders 84-204-09 and MS-Group-1584, Manuscripts Collection, Turnbull Library, National Library, Wellington.
118   Ans Westra, Museum of New Zealand Te Papa Tongarewa, Wellington. Reference: O.008998.
119   Ellwood, *Islands of the Dawn*, 152; Cf. folders 84-204-09 and MS-Group-1584, Manuscripts Collection, Turnbull Library, National Library, Wellington.
120   Nancy Swarbrick, 'Animal welfare and rights', *Te Ara — the Encyclopedia of New Zealand*, www.TeAra.govt.nz/en/animal-welfare-and-rights/print
121   See Jane Abbiss, 'The "New Education Fellowship" in New Zealand: Its Activity and Influence in the 1930s and 1940s', *New Zealand Journal of Educational Studies* 33, no. 1 (1998): 81–93.
122   Middleton, 'New Zealand Theosophists', 42–57.
123   Rita Kramer, *Maria Montessori* (Chicago: University of Chicago Press, 1976), 340–41; Paola Trabalzini, 'Maria Montessori Through the Seasons of the Method', *The NAMTA Journal* 2 (Spring 2011): 165.
124   'Montessori in Aotearoa New Zealand', www.montessori.org.nz/montessori/montessori-new-zealand
125   Lee Kenny, 'Rudolf Steiner school's name change dilemma', *The Press*, 21 September 2019.
126   John Paull, 'The Library of Rudolf Steiner: The Books in English', *Journal of Social and Development Sciences* 9, no. 3 (2018): 21–46.
127   Kenny, 'Rudolf Steiner school's name change dilemma'.

Chapter 2. Children of the Golden Dawn
1   Christopher McIntosh, *Eliphas Lévi and the French Occult Revival* (Albany: State University of New York Press, 1972/2011), 12.
2   R. A. Gilbert, *The Golden Dawn Companion: A Guide to the History, Structure and Workings of the Hermetic Order of the Golden Dawn* (Wellingborough: Aquarian, 1986), 1–2.
3   Freud would later clothe his theories in scientism and classical allegory, but few who have read Jung's *Black Books* and *Red Book* would doubt his worldview was thoroughly esoteric and that of an adept magus.
4   See Alison Butler, *Victorian Occultism and the Making of Modern Magic: Invoking Tradition* (Basingstoke: Palgrave Macmillan, 2011), 1ff.
5   Ibid., 248.
6   Donald Michael Kraig, *Modern Magick* (St Paul: Llewellyn, 1988), 9; Ronald Hutton, *The Triumph of the Moon: A History of Modern Pagan Witchcraft* (Oxford: Oxford University Press, 1999), 82.
7   Mary K. Greer, *Women of the Golden Dawn: Rebels and Priestesses* (Rochester: Park Street, 1995), 57.
8   Gilbert, *The Golden Dawn Companion*, 45.
9   A. E. Waite, *Shadows of Life and Thought: A Retrospective Review in the Form of Memoirs* (London: Selwyn and Blount, 1938), 218–19.
10   Ibid., 225.
11   Chic and Sandra Cicero, *The Essential Golden Dawn: An Introduction to High Magic* (St Paul: Llewellyn, 2003), 49.
12   Waite, *Shadows of Life and Thought*, 219.
13   Francis King, *Modern Ritual Magic: The Rise of Western Occultism* (Bridport: Prism Press, 1989), 79–93.

14 Frances Yates, *The Rosicrucian Enlightenment* (Routledge and Kegan Paul: London, 1972); Carl Edwin Lindgren, 'The Way of the Rose Cross: A Historical Perception, 1614–1620', *Journal of Religion and Psychical Research* 18, no. 3 (1995): 141–48; Pierre Martin, *Lodges, Orders and the Rosicross: Rosicrucianism in Lodges, Orders and Initiating Societies Since the Early 16th Century* (London: Edition Oriflamme, 2017).

15 See Florian Ebeling, *The Secret History of Hermes Trismegistus: Hermeticism from Ancient to Modern Times*, trans. David Lorton (Ithaca, NY: Cornell University Press, 2011).

16 J. Gordon Melton (ed.), *Encyclopedia of Occultism and Parapsychology*, Vol. 2 (Farmington Hills: Gale Group, 2001), 1327; Francis X. King, *Modern Ritual Magic: The Rise of Western Occultism* (Paris: Prisma Press, 1989), 66–101; Israel Regardie, *What You Should Know About the Golden Dawn* (6th edition) (Tempe: New Falcon Publications, 1993), 18–19.

17 Peter M. Dunn, 'Robert Felkin MD (1853–1926) and Caesarean Delivery in Central Africa (1879)', *Archives of Disease in Childhood: Fetal and Neonatal* 80 (May 1999): 250–51.

18 Robert S. Ellwood, *Islands of the Dawn: The Story of Alternative Spirituality in New Zealand* (Honolulu: University of Hawai'i Press, 1993), 164–65.

19 John von Dadelszen, 'The Havelock Work 1909–1939', *Te Mata Times*, 9 September 1983. This text was also presented as a paper at the 6th Annual Conference of the Archives and Records Association of New Zealand, Taradale, Hawke's Bay, 26–27 August 1983.

20 'John Herman von Dadelszen, 1913–1988', New Zealand Law Society, www.lawsociety.org.nz/news-and-communications/people-in-the-law/obituaries/obituaries-list/john-herman-von-dadelszen-1913-1988

21 *The Forerunner*, 1 May 1909.

22 Von Dadelszen, 'The Havelock Work 1909–1939', 10.

23 Ellwood, *Islands of the Dawn*, 167.

24 See Michael Hurd, *Rutland Boughton and the Glastonbury Festivals* (Oxford: Clarendon Press, 1993); Michael Hurd, 'The Glastonbury Festivals', *The Musical Times* 125, no. 1698 (August 1984): 435–37.

25 Gareth Knight, *Dion Fortune and the Inner Light* (Loughborough: Thoth Publications, 2000), 115–82.

26 J. B. Priestly, *The Edwardians* (New York: Harper and Row, 1970), 92–93.

27 Cited in Mathew Wright, *Havelock North: The History of a Village* (Hastings: Hastings District Council, 1996), 97.

28 Harriot Felkin, 'A Wayfaring Man', cited in Ellwood, *Islands of the Dawn*, 173–75.

29 Gilbert, *The Golden Dawn Companion*, 42.

30 Robert Felkin, 'Preliminary Adress [sic] 1912', quoted in Timothy Worrad, 'A Cure for Disenchantment: Smaragdum Thalasses Temple, Havelock North, New Zealand', *Preternature: Critical and Historical Studies on the Preternatural* 9, no. 2 (2020): 276.

31 Nick Farrell, *Beyond the Sun: The History, Teachings and Rituals of the Last Golden Dawn Temple* (Cheltenham: Skylight Press, 2017), 57.

32 Ithell Coloquhoun, *Sword of Wisdom: MacGregor Mathers and 'The Golden Dawn'* (New York: Putnam, 1975), 217.

33 S. W. Grant, *In Other Days: A History of the Chambers Family of Te Mata — Havelock North* (Waipukurau: Central Hawke's Bay Printers and Publishers, 1980), 130–31.

34 Wright, *Havelock North*, 98–99.

35 Cited in ibid., 157.

36   Ibid., 94.
37   Harriot Felkin, 'A Wayfaring Man Part II', collected in *The Lantern — A Wayfaring Man Part II*, Vol. 2 (New Zealand: Sub Rosa Press, 2015), 19–160, at 120.
38   Harriot Felkin, 'A Wayfaring Man, Part I', collected in *The Lantern — A Wayfaring Man*, Vol. 1 (New Zealand: Sub Rosa Press, 2012), 76, and cited in Worrad, 'A Cure for Disenchantment', 271.
39   Worrad, 'A Cure for Disenchantment', 270.
40   Farrell, *Beyond the Sun*, 52.
41   'Legend of Te Mata Peak is a tragic love story', *Hawke's Bay Today*, 4 November 2017.
42   S. W. Grant, *Havelock North: From Village and Borough 1860–1952* (Hastings: Hawke's Bay Newspapers, 1978), 83.
43   Ellwood, *Islands of the Dawn*, 180; Farrell, *Beyond the Sun*, 54–55.
44   Farrell, *Beyond the Sun*, 69.
45   David V. Barrett, *The Atlas of Secret Societies: The Truth Behind the Templars, Freemasons and Other Secretive Organizations* (Alresford: Godsfield, 2008), 109; Robert A. Gilbert, 'Hermetic Order of the Golden Dawn', in *Dictionary of Gnosis and Western Esotericism*, eds Wouter J. Hanegraaff, Antoine Faivre, Roelof van den Broek and Jean-Pierre Brach (Leiden: Brill, 2006), 547.
46   D. P., 'The Magic of Havelock North', in *The Lantern — A Wayfaring Man*, Vol. 1 (New Zealand: Sub Rosa Press, 2012), 1–35, at 29; Worrad, 'A Cure for Disenchantment', 279.
47   C. S. Lewis, *The Magician's Nephew* (London: HarperCollins, 1998), 114.
48   Francis X. King, *The Magical World of Aleister Crowley* (New York: Coward, McCann & Geoghegan, 1978), 24.
49   This is not an outlandish suggestion when one considers many New Zealand politicians, and most governors-general, were Grand Master Freemasons, and Freemasonry had been closely associated with the Golden Dawn from the beginning, with Masonic Lodges often stops on official tours. The governor-general at the time of Whare Rā's closure, Lord Porritt (1900–1994), was a member of multiple Masonic Lodges, and during his tenure was Grand Master of the Grand Lodge of New Zealand, as was Lord Bledisloe (1867–1958).
50   Farrell, *Beyond the Sun*, 89–90.
51   Grant, *Havelock North*, 83–84.
52   Patrick and Chris Zalewski, *The Golden Dawn Correspondence Course: A Brief History of Its Origins and Content* (pamphlet) (Wellington: Thoth-Hermes Temple, n.d.); Christina Mary Stoddart, *Light-Bearers of Darkness* (London: Boswell, 1930), passim.
53   Written down in 1992 and cited in D. P., 'The Magic of Havelock North', 29.
54   Pat Zalewski, *The Secret Inner Order Rituals of the Golden Dawn* (Los Angeles: New Falcon Publications, 2016), passim; Gilbert, *The Golden Dawn Companion*, passim. Zalewski asserts that the final three grades have no great astral significance or power and are merely temple civilities. Therefore, he did not include them for his Thoth-Hermes Temple. According to some anecdotal sources, the ultimate revelation of the third order was that the invisible masters were merely symbolic abstractions, and did not in fact exist as persons. If this sounds a little like Scientology, it is to be remembered that L. Ron Hubbard was allegedly at one point a member of the Ancient and Mystical Order Rosæ Crucis (AMORC) in 1940, and heavily involved with rocket engineer Jack Parsons' lodge of Crowley's Ordo Templi Orientis in Pasadena, California: Hugh Urban, 'The Occult Roots of Scientology? L. Ron Hubbard, Aleister Crowley, and the Origins of a Controversial New Religion', *Nova Religio* 15, no. 3 (February 2012): 91–116.
55   Zalewski, *The Secret Inner Order*, 100–01. Addendum in square brackets mine.

56   Ethel Felkin, 'A Wayfaring Man', in *The Lantern,* Vol. 1 (New Zealand: Sub Rosa Press, 2012), 176.
57   Zalewski, *Secret Inner Order*, 9.
58   Ellwood, *Islands of the Dawn*, 177.
59   Ken Edney, *Dr. Robert William Felkin and the S.R.I.A.*, Felkin College of the Societas Rosicruciana in Anglia, Napier, www.mastermason.com/felkincollege/felkin-bio.htm
60   King, *Modern Ritual Magic*, 106–27. One is reminded of Merkabah Jewish mysticism, which centred on visions of ascent (rather a 'descent' in Hebrew) to the various heavens and palaces of God. Of this the Talmud offers the legend of the *pardes*, the garden of esoteric Talmudic knowledge experienced on these episodes: 'Four entered the *pardes* — Ben Azzai, Ben Zoma, Elisha ben Abuyah and Rabbi Akiva. One looked and died; one looked and went mad; Elisha ben Abuyah looked and apostatized; Akiva entered in peace and departed in peace' (Toseftah *Hagigah* 2:2, Babylonian Talmud *Hagigah* 14b, Jerusalem Talmud *Hagigah* 9:1).
61   'Flight Lieutenant Samuel Denys Felkin', Trent Park House, www.trentparkhouse.org.uk/latest-news/flight-lieutenant-samuel-denys-felkin
62   National Portrait Gallery, www.npg.org.uk/collections/search/portrait/mw93804/Alfred-Laurence-Felkin
63   Wright, *Havelock North*, 224–25.
64   'Autumnal Equinox 1960', collected in *The Lantern – A Wayfaring Man Part II*, Vol. 2 (New Zealand: Sub Rosa Press, 2015), 182.
65   Zalewski, *Secret Inner Order*, 41–42.
66   The 72 Goetic spirits would be regarded as demonic in character by most traditions, and quite antithetical to the Enochian angelic spirits of the Golden Dawn practice. They have since made their way into popular culture with the mention of Paimon and Valak in several Hollywood movies, including the former in *Hereditary* (2018) and the latter in *The Conjuring 2* (2016).
67   Whare Rā Pentagram Ritual, papers in the collection of the Golden Dawn Ancient Mystery School, Phoenix, Arizona.
68   Farrell, *Beyond the Sun*, 91.
69   Ellwood, *Islands of the Dawn*, 179.
70   Farrell, *Beyond the Sun*, 76–77.
71   'Letter to Smaragdum Thalasses Members, 24 August 1978', quoted in Farrell, *Beyond the Sun*, 88.
72   Farrell, *Beyond the Sun*, 75.

Chapter 3. The Empire Sentinels
1   *Tuahiwi School Centennial 1863–1963* (commemorative pamphlet), 1963; Margaret Esplin, 'Cossgrove, David and Cossgrove, Selina', *Dictionary of New Zealand Biography, Te Ara — the Encyclopedia of New Zealand*, https://teara.govt.nz/en/biographies/3c34/cossgrove-david
2   Lieut-Coloniel Cossgrove V. D., *The Empire Sentinel's Handbook & Ritual* (Christchurch, n.d.).
3   Ibid., 5.
4   S. M. Adkins, 'Freemasonry, Scouting and the Order of the Arrow', www.phoenixmasonry.org/freemasonry_soucting_and_the_order_of_the_arrow.htm
5   Alistair Hugh MacLean Millar, 'Boy Scouts', in *An Encyclopaedia of New Zealand*, ed. A. H. McLintock, *Te Ara — the Encyclopedia of New Zealand*, www.TeAra.govt.nz/en/1966/youth-organisations

6   George W. Kerr, 'Freemasonry and the Scout Movement', *The Philalethes: The Journal of Masonic Research and Letters* 48, no. 6 (December 1995): 132.
7   Israel Regardie, *The Golden Dawn* (6th edition) (St Paul: Llewellyn, 1990), passim.
8   Annebella Pollen, 'The Kindred of the Kibbo Kift', *Fortean Times* 206 (2016): 34–39.
9   Daniel Carter Beard, *The American Boys' Book of Signs, Signals, and Symbols* (Philadelphia: Lippincott, 1918), 91.

Chapter 4. The Golden Dawn: A coda
1   Peter Clarke, *Paul Foster Case: His Life and Works* (Covina: Fraternity of the Hidden Light, 2013), 8.
2   Mitch Horowitz, *Occult America: The Secret History of How Mysticism Shaped Our Nation* (New York: Random House, 2009), 209.
3   Robert S. Ellwood, *Islands of the Dawn: The Story of Alternative Spirituality in New Zealand* (Honolulu: University of Hawai'i Press, 1993), 153.
4   Ibid., 153.
5   Horowitz, *Occult America*, 211.
6   Ibid., 213.
7   Ellwood, *Islands of the Dawn*, 153–54; David Allen Hulse, *The Western Mysteries: An Encyclopedic Guide to the Sacred Languages and Magickal Systems of the World* (Woodbury: Llewellyn Publications, 2002), 148.
8   Ellwood, *Islands of the Dawn*, 154–55.
9   Nick Farrell, *Beyond the Sun: The History, Teachings and Rituals of the Last Golden Dawn Temple* (Cheltenham: Skylight Press, 2017), 79.
10 Ibid., 77–78.
11 Ibid., 78.
12 Ibid., 78–79.
13 *Builders of the Adytum New Zealand 50th Jubilee — 26–27 October 2013*, pamphlet (BOTA, 2013), 3.
14 Farrell, *Beyond the Sun*, 79.
15 Ibid., 85.
16 Pat Zalewski, *Secret Inner Order Rituals of the Golden Dawn* (Los Angeles: New Falcon Publications, 2016), 16.
17 Farrell, *Beyond the Sun*, 85.
18 *Builders of the Adytum New Zealand 50th Jubilee*, 3.
19 Farrell, *Beyond the Sun*, 79.
20 Zalewski, *Secret Inner Order*, 16–17.
21 *Builders of the Adytum New Zealand 50th Jubilee*, 6.
22 Letter from Margaret Weir on behalf of Ann Davies, to Percy Dowse, 24 March 1969, ARCH 6177, 'Mayoral files of Percy Dowse, Files W', Hutt City Council Archives.
23 Thanks to Laura Jamieson, senior advisor, archives, Hutt City Council, for this information.
24 Untitled items, *Hutt News*, 25 February, 4 March, 11 March 1969.
25 *Builders of the Adytum New Zealand 50th Jubilee*, 4.
26 Farrell, *Beyond the Sun*, 80.
27 John Latham, 'The Darker Side of the Moon: Satanic Traditions in New Zealand as Magick Systems' (MA thesis, Victoria University of Wellington, 2001), 53.
28 Farrell, *Beyond the Sun*, 81.
29 Clarke, *Paul Foster Case*, 43–56; Mitch Horowitz, *Occult America: White House Seances, Ouija Circles, Masons, and the Secret Mystic History of Our Nation* (New York: Bantam, 2010), 211–12.

30   Ellwood, *Islands of the Dawn*, 154–55.
31   Tammerlin Drummond, 'Secretive order peers inward for enlightenment', *Los Angeles Times*, 17 December 1991.
32   'Historic city temple expected to sell for up to $1m', *New Zealand Herald*, 2 December 2014.
33   *The Great Adventure* (BOTA pamphlet), n.p.
34   This has been speculatively pieced together from various anecdotal sources, online groups and chat-rooms, BOTA's internet presence, and general reference texts such as Hulse, *The Western Mysteries*, and the entry on BOTA by David Barrett in Peter Clarke and Peter Bernard (eds), *Encyclopedia of New Religious Movements* (Abingdon-on-Thames: Taylor & Francis, 2004), 86. Parts may be unreliable.
35   'Bitter Suite: The Making of a Musical,' *Topps Official Xena Magazine* 3 (May 1998); Paul Foster Case, *The Book of Tokens: 22 Meditations on the Ageless Wisdom* (Los Angeles: Tarota, 1934).
36   Rob Tapert, email to the author, 27 January 2021.
37   'Pat Zalewski', https://enacademic.com/dic.nsf/enwiki/2446296
38   Ibid.
39   Gerald Suster, *Crowley's Apprentice: The Life and Ideas of Israel Regardie* (York Beach: Samuel Weiser Inc, 1990), 175; 'Pat Zalewski', https://enacademic.com/dic.nsf/enwiki/2446296
40   Suster, *Crowley's Apprentice*, 75.
41   Zalewski, *Secret Inner Order*, 18.
42   Ibid., 59.
43   'Pat Zalewski', https://enacademic.com/dic.nsf/enwiki/2446296; see also Ellwood, *Islands of the Dawn*, 177, 272 nn.34, 38, 41, 273 n.43.

Chapter 5. Rudolf Steiner and Anthroposophy
1   Robert A. McDermott, 'Rudolf Steiner and Anthroposophy', in *Modern Esoteric Spirituality*, eds Antoine Faivre and Jacob Needleman (Freiburg im Breisgau: Herder & Herder, 1992), 288–310, at 299–301.
2   Rudold Steiner, *The Essential Steiner: Basic Writings of Rudolf Steiner*, ed. Robert McDermott (Great Barrington: Lindisfarne Books, 2007), 3–11, 392–95; Carlo Willmann, *Waldorfpädagogik: Theologische und religionspädagogische Befunde* (Cologne: Böhlau, 1998), Chapter 1 passim.
3   See Peter Schneider, *Einführung in die Waldorfpädagogik* (Stuttgart: Klett-Cotta, 1997).
4   Garth J. Talbott, 'Anthroposophy in the Antipodes: A Lived Spirituality in New Zealand, 1902–1960s' (MA thesis, Massey University, 2013), 16; Geoffrey Townsend, *Outline of the History of the Anthroposophical Society/Movement in New Zealand* (Havelock North: Anthroposophical Society in New Zealand, 2001), 3.
5   Philippa Fogarty, 'Wells, Ada', *Dictionary of New Zealand Biography*, first published in 1993, *Te Ara — the Encyclopedia of New Zealand*, https://teara.govt.nz/en/biographies/2w11/wells-ada
6   National Council of Women, Minutes and Reports, Lovell-Smith Papers 1886–1973, MS-Papers-1376-04, Alexander Turnbull Library, Wellington.
7   Talbott, 'Anthroposophy in the Antipodes', 21.
8   Ibid.; Helen Snowden, 'Appendix 2 — Three Personalities', in Townsend, *Outline*, 39.
9   See Ian Church, 'Parris, Robert Reid', *Dictionary of New Zealand Biography*, first published in 1990, *Te Ara — the Encyclopedia of New Zealand*, https://teara.govt.nz/en/biographies/1p8/parris-robert-reid
10 *Nelson Evening Mail*, 11 August 1868.

11 Frances Porter, *Born to New Zealand: A Biography of Jane Maria Atkinson* (Wellington: Allen & Unwin/Port Nicholson Press, 1989), 397, n.93; Gert Christeller, 'The Beginnings: Emma Jane Richmond', in *The Richmond-Atkinson Papers*, Vol. 1, ed. Guy H. Scholefield (Wellington: R. E. Owen, Government Printer, 1960), 838; 'Obituary: Mrs. E. J. Richmond', *Auckland Star*, 11 October 1921.
12 Talbott, 'Anthroposophy in the Antipodes', 26.
13 'News of the Day: Theosophy', *The Press*, 31 March 1897; Christeller, 'The Beginnings', 29.
14 Talbott, 'Anthroposophy in the Antipodes', 26–27.
15 Mathew Wright, *Havelock North: The History of a Village* (Hastings: Hastings District Council, 1996), 168.
16 'Two Sisters' legacy lives on', *Hawke's Bay Today*, 3 April 2017.
17 Townsend, *Outline*, 9.
18 Doris Prentice, 'Christobel Mary Twyneham', *New Zealand News Sheet* 64 (July 1968): 2–3; Snowden, in Townsend, *Outline*, 39–40.
19 Henry Malden, 'A Little History', *The New Zealand News Sheet* 6 (May 1936): 9.
20 *New Zealand News Sheet* 14 (March 1945): 2–5.
21 Ibid., 8.
22 *New Zealand News Sheet* 15 (June 1945): 13.
23 Jean Menteath, 'Ruth Nelson (1894–1977)', *New Zealand News Sheet* 90 (December 1977): 2–3.
24 Mollie Parry, 'A History of the Wellington Group' (unpublished typescript, 1985, collection of Rudolf Steiner House, Auckland), cited in Talbott, 'Anthroposophy in the Antipodes', 56.
25 Talbott, 'Anthroposophy in the Antipodes', 61–63.
26 *New Zealand News Sheet* 43 (June 1960): 3–5; *New Zealand News Sheet* 44 (September 1960): 2.
27 Talbott, 'Anthroposophy in the Antipodes', 66.

Chapter 6. Gomorrah on the Avon
1 Richard S. Hill, 'Worthington, Arthur Bently', *Dictionary of New Zealand Biography*, first published in 1993, *Te Ara — the Encyclopedia of New Zealand*, https://teara.govt.nz/en/biographies/2w32/worthington-arthur-bently
2 Ibid.
3 'Muchly Alias Ward', *Bismarck Weekly Tribune* (North Dakota), 8 February 1889.
4 'Students of Truth', *Christchurch Star*, 6 July 1894.
5 O. T. J. Alpers, *Cheerful Yesterdays* (Auckland: Whitcombe & Tombs, 1930), 89.
6 Hill, 'Worthington, Arthur Bently'.
7 'The Temple of Truth Apostle', *Oamaru Mail*, 1 June 1893; 'The Christchurch Temple of Truth scandals', *Bay of Plenty Times*, 12 June 1893; 'Students of Truth', *Poverty Bay Herald*, 5 June 1893; 'Students of Truth', *Temuka Leader*, 6 June 1893.
8 'The Students of Truth', *South Canterbury Times*, 9 November 1893.
9 Letter to the editor, *Oxford Observer*, 26 November 1892.
10 'The Worthington Lectures II', *Ellesmere Guardian*, 26 September 1891.
11 Ibid.
12 Alpers, *Cheerful Yesterdays*, 130.
13 'What is Pantheism?', *The Press*, 8 June 1891.
14 'A.B. Worthington', *Wanganui Chronicle*, 18 September 1902.
15 John Hosking, *A Christchurch quack unmasked, or, The life and teaching of A. Bently*

	Worthington, alias Samuel Oakley Crawford . . . and Mary H. Plunkett, examined and exposed (Christchurch: H.J. Weeks, 1893).
16	'Debate on Christianity', *The Press*, 8 December 1891; 'Theological debates', *The Press*, 11 December 1891.
17	Hill, 'Worthington, Arthur Bently'; 'Robin Goodfellow', 'Christchurch acid drops', *Oxford Observer*, 10 June 1893; 'The Students of Truth', *South Canterbury Times*, 5 June 1893; 'A tragic occurrence', *The Press*, 8 June 1901.
18	Hill, 'Worthington, Arthur Bently'.
19	'The Students of Truth', *South Canterbury Times*, 28 October 1893.
20	From the *Otago Witness*, reported in 'The Students of Truth', *South Canterbury Times*, 9 November 1893.
21	'The Students of Truth', *Lyttelton Times*, 6 August 1895.
22	Hill, 'Worthington, Arthur Bently'; 'The Students of Truth', *South Canterbury Times*, 5 June 1893; 'Students of Truth', *Christchurch Star*, 5 August 1895; 'Supreme Court', *Christchurch Star*, 28 November 1894.
23	Alpers, *Cheerful Yesterdays*, 91.
24	Hill, 'Worthington, Arthur Bently'; 'The Worthington Trial', *Waimate Daily Advertiser*, 20 October 1902; 'A.B. Worthington', *Wanganui Chronicle*, 18 September 1902; 'Society', *Bulletin*, 13 September 1902.
25	'A holy fraud', *Christchurch Sun*, 29 October 1916.
26	Hill, 'Worthington, Arthur Bently'; 'Worthington dead', *The Press*, 17 December 1917.

Chapter 7. Bumps in the night

1	Irving Finkel, *The First Ghosts* (London: Hodder & Stoughton, 2021).
2	Whitney R. Cross, *The Burned-over District: The Social and Intellectual History of Enthusiastic Religion in Western New York, 1800–1850* (Ithaca, NY: Cornell University Press, 1951); Judith Wellman, *Grassroots Reform in the Burned-over District of Upstate New York: Religion, Abolitionism, and Democracy* (London: Routledge, 2000); Linda K. Pritchard, 'The Burned-over District Reconsidered: A Portent of Evolving Religious Pluralism in the United States', *Social Science History* 8, no. 3 (1984): 243–65.
3	Barbara Weisberg, *Talking to the Dead: Kate and Maggie Fox and the Rise of Spiritualism* (New York and San Francisco: HarperOne, 2004), 12–13.
4	See Ann Braude, *Radical Spirits: Spiritualism and Women's Rights in Nineteenth-Century America* (Bloomington: Indiana University Press, 2001).
5	See Simone Natale, *Supernatural Entertainments: Victorian Spiritualism and the Rise of Modern Media Culture* (University Park: Pennsylvania State University Press, 2016).
6	Mitch Horowitz, *Occult America: The Secret History of How Mysticism Shaped Our Nation* (New York: Random House, 2009), 67.
7	Shaun D. Broadley, 'Spirited Visions: A Study of Spiritualism in New Zealand Settler Society, 1870–1890' (PhD thesis, University of Otago, 2000), 2–3.
8	H. F. Von Haast, *The Life and Times of Sir Julius Von Haast* (Wellington: self-published, 1948), 322, 541–42; Peter Raby, *Samuel Butler: A Biography* (Iowa: Iowa University Press, 1991), 107.
9	Robert S. Ellwood, *Islands of the Dawn: The Story of Alternative Spirituality in New Zealand* (Honolulu: University of Hawai'i Press, 1993), 30.
10	'The Waihola ghost', *Bruce Herald*, 5 August 1889; 'Waihola notes', *Bruce Herald*, 10 January 1899.
11	'Spiritualism', *Otago Daily Times*, 22 August 1868.
12	Spiritualism, to the Reverend of the Synod of the Presbyterian Church of Otago and

Southland, 11 January 1870, Robert Stout Collection, Victoria University of Wellington Library.
13. Ellwood, *Islands of the Dawn*, 30–31.
14. 'Dunedin', *Cromwell Argus*, 9 March 1870.
15. 'Local news of the month', *Timaru Herald*, 30 July 1870.
16. Cited in untitled item, *Southland Times*, 8 February 1870.
17. Untitled items, *Bruce Herald*, 24 July 1872; 31 July 1872; 7 August 1872; 14 August 1872; 21 August 1872; 28 August 1872.
18. 'Spiritualism', *Otago Witness*, 13 August 1870; 'Spiritualism', *Oamaru Times*, 11 June 1872.
19. 'Nemo me impunt lacessit', *Bruce Herald*, 17 August 1870; 'The Clyde robbery', *Otago Witness*, 20 August 1870.
20. Untitled item, *Otago Daily Times*, 30 January 1873.
21. 'Parliamentary notes', *New Zealand Herald*, 15 August 1872.
22. Broadley, 'Spirited Visions', 16–17.
23. Ellwood, *Islands of the Dawn*, 52; *Otago Daily Times*, April–May 1872, passim; James Smith, 'Spiritualism, or the Magnetic Teaching, Its Method and Its Objects, Being Three Lectures, Delivered in Dunedin, April 28, May 5, and May 12, 1872' (pamphlet), Robert Stout Collection, Victoria University of Wellington Library.
24. Untitled item, *Otago Daily Times*, 30 January 1873.
25. James Miller Guinn, *A History of California and an Extended History of Los Angeles and Environs*, Vol. 3 (Los Angeles: Historic Record Company, 1915), 527–33; Joseph Osgood Barrett, *Spiritual Pilgrim: A Biography of James M. Peebles* (Boston: William White and Company, 1871), passim.
26. Larry B. Massie and Peter J. Schmitt, *Battle Creek, the Place Behind the Products: An Illustrated Business History* (Eugene, OR: Windsor Publications, 1984), 62; 'Dr. Peebles Institute of Health: A Fraudulent and Dangerous "Cure" for Epilepsy', *Journal of the American Medical Association* 64, no. 5 (1915): 455–56.
27. J. M. Peebles, *How to Live a Century and Grow Old Gracefully* (New York: M. L. Hollbrook, 1884).
28. Barrett, *Spiritual Pilgrim*, 37; see Logie Barrow, *Independent Spirits: Spiritualism and English Plebians, 1850–1910* (London and New York: Routledge and Kegan Paul, 1986); Ann Braude, *Radical Spirits: Spiritualism and Women's Rights in Nineteenth-Century America* (Boston: Beacon, 1989).
29. Ellwood, *Islands of the Dawn*, 33.
30. Kathi Kresol, 'The enigmatic Dr. Elisha Dunn', Haunted Rockford, www.hauntedrockford.com/the-enigmatic-dr-elisha-dunn
31. Untitled item, *Otago Daily Times*, 30 January 1873.
32. Untitled item, *Otago Daily Times*, 21 March 1873.
33. Untitled item, *Dunedin Echo*, 8 March 1873; Emma Hardinge Britten, *Nineteenth Century Miracles, or, Spirits and their work in every country of the earth: A complete historical compendium of the great movement known as 'modern spiritualism'* (New York: Lovell, 1884), 270; J. M. Peebles, *Around the World: Or, Travels in Polynesia, China, India, Arabia, Egypt, Syria, and Other Heathen Countries* (Boston: Colby and Rich, 1875), 102–03.
34. Ellwood, *Islands of the Dawn*, 37.
35. Alfred Deakin, 'Autobiographical Notes', Collection of the National Library of Australia, series 3: Notebooks and General Manuscripts 1873–1917, subseries 3_22.
36. Britten, *Nineteenth Century Miracles*, 270.
37. Ibid., 264.

38 Ibid.
39 Ibid., 264–65.
40 Judith Binney, 'Papahurihia: Some Thoughts on Interpretation', *Journal of the Polynesian Society* 75, no. 3 (September 1966): 321–31.
41 Bronwyn Elsmore, *Mana From Heaven — A Century of Maori Prophets in New Zealand* (Tauranga: Moana Press, 1989), 342–45.
42 Allan K. Davidson, *Christianity in Aotearoa: A History of Church and Society in New Zealand* (Wellington: Ministry of Education, 1991), 16.
43 *New Zealand Herald*, 'Correspondence', 1 May 1877; 'Spiritism', 4 May 1877; 'Theories on Spiritism', 9 May 1877.
44 'Henry Anderson', *New Zealand Mail*, 30 May 1884; Ellwood, *Islands of the Dawn*, 38.
45 Gareth Winter, 'Nation, William Charles', *Dictionary of New Zealand Biography*, first published in 1996, *Te Ara — the Encyclopedia of New Zealand*, https://teara.govt.nz/en/biographies/3n1/nation-william-charles
46 'Henry Anderson'.
47 Ellwood, *Islands of the Dawn*, 41; 'Henry Anderson'; Winter, 'Nation, William Charles'.
48 Angela Ballara and Mita Carter, 'Te Rangi-taka-i-waho, Te Mānihera', *Dictionary of New Zealand Biography*, first published in 1990, *Te Ara — the Encyclopedia of New Zealand*, https://teara.govt.nz/en/biographies/1t69/te-rangi-taka-i-waho-te-manihera
49 'Henry Anderson'.
50 Ellwood, *Islands of the Dawn*, 43; Winter, 'Nation, William Charles'.
51 Winter, 'Nation, William Charles'.
52 Ibid.
53 Ibid.
54 William Nation, *The Unseen World* (third edition) (Levin: self-published, 1920), 42–43.
55 C. J. B. Golder, *The fourth book of the King of Prophets: Being the author's last work arranged into small chapters, complete in themselves, to give separate glances into his life and works behind the veil* (Napier: R.C. Harding, 1886).
56 Matthew Stewart, '19th-century paper offers window on another time', *New Zealand Herald*, 16 October 2007, www.nzherald.co.nz/nz/19th-century-paper-offers-window-on-another-time/MQZ4HWCUF243WSMFXXHVHQWWHA
57 Don Farmer, '25 years on from bizarre ritualistic, satanic killing that stunned NZ', *New Zealand Herald*, 18 August 2017, www.nzherald.co.nz/nz/25-years-on-from-bizarre-ritualistic-satanic-killing-that-stunned-nz/OSATZFFSL4OXQDQVTQKYUTMNTI
58 Ellwood, *Islands of the Dawn*, 42.
59 'Spiritualism', *New Zealand Mail*, 13 June 1884.
60 Ellwood, *Islands of the Dawn*, 42.
61 It was reported in the *Evening Star*, the *Evening Post*, the *Auckland Star* and the Christchurch *Star* on 11 June 1886, with many other newspapers picking it up in the days following and into the following month.
62 James Cowan, *Fairy Folktales of the Maori* (Auckland: Whitcombe & Tombs, 1925), 149.
63 'Spiritualism', *New Zealand Mail*, 27 June 1884.
64 'A rhapsody of rapping', *New Zealand Mail*, 7 September 1888.
65 Untitled item, *New Zealand Mail*, 11 December 1891.
66 The story was reported on in nearly every issue of the *New Zealand Mail* throughout June 1894.
67 T. Shekleton Henry, *Spookland: A Record of Research* (Sydney: Maclardy, 1894).
68 Untitled item, *New Zealand Herald*, 20 September 1883; untitled item, 16 October 1883.
69 Edward A. Mackechnie, 'On the Influence of the Ideal', *Transactions and Proceedings of*

the Royal Society of New Zealand 30 (1897): 109–17; 'Auckland Institute', *New Zealand Herald*, 16 October 1883; 'Auckland Institute', *New Zealand Journal of Science* 1, no .4 (June 1882): 193.

70   Letter from Beverly to Bickerton, 20 September 1878, box 1, folder 1, item 3, Canterbury Museum Library; Bickerton, 'Partial Impact (Paper No. 4): On the General Problem of Stellar Collision', *TPNZI* 12 (1879): 184.

71   Broadley, 'Spirited Visions', 38–39; Hardwicke Knight and L. E. S. Amon, 'Beverly, Arthur', *Dictionary of New Zealand Biography*, first published in 1990. *Te Ara — the Encyclopedia of New Zealand*, https://teara.govt.nz/en/biographies/1b20/beverly-arthur

72   Broadley, 'Spirited Visions', 39.

73   Peebles, *Around the World*, 100.

74   'Memorandum to the Chancellor from Mr Justice Chapman', 4 December 1908, in material for a biography of Arthur Beverly, Sir Frederick Revans Chapman collection, MS-227, Hocken Collections, Letter, Robert Stout to Mr Burton, among papers relating to the Beverly Bequest, MS-287, University of Otago.

75   L. E. S. Amon, A. Beverly, J. N. Dodd, 'The Beverly Clock', *European Journal of Physics* 5, no. 4 (1984): 195–97.

76   Rev. Matthew Wood Green, *The Devil's Sword Blunted; or, Spiritualism Examined and Condemned Out of the Mouths of Its Own Advocates* (Dunedin: Geoffrey T. Clarke, 1879), 90–91, 104–11.

77   Theophilus Le Menant Des Chesnais, *Animal Magnetism and Spirit Mediums* (pamphlet) (Wellington, 1884), 14.

78   Broadley, 'Spirited Visions', 20; *Harbinger of Light* 28 (December 1872): 356–57; [Cunningham], *Crums [sic] of Thought* (pamphlet), n.d; *Echo*, 5 October 1872; *Tuapeka Times*, 20 February 1873; *Otago Daily Times*, 15 February 1873; *Harbinger of Light* 24 (August 1872): 294; ACLLA, *Prospectus of the Aurelia Co-operative Land and Labour Association* (Grahamstown, 1872).

79   Ellwood, *Islands of the Dawn*, 43; Nancy Swarbrick, 'Harris, Jane Elizabeth', *Dictionary of New Zealand Biography*, first published in 1993, *Te Ara — the Encyclopedia of New Zealand*, https://teara.govt.nz/en/biographies/2h16/harris-jane-elizabeth

80   'Jenny Wren', *Woman's Work and Destiny* (paper read before the Thames Mutual Improvement Association and published as a pamphlet) (Thames: *Evening Star* Office, 1884).

81   Betty Gilderdale, *The Seven Lives of Lady Barker: Author of* Station Life in New Zealand (Christchurch: Canterbury University Press, 2015), 18, 81.

82   'Melbourne', *Otago Witness*, 12 July 1873.

83   'Switzers', *Otago Witness*, 8 May 1869.

84   Susan Nugent-Wood, *Bush Flowers from Australia — By a Daughter of the Soil* (London: J. Nisbet, 1867), 55–57.

85   Thomas Bracken, *Lays of the Land of the Maori and Moa* (London: Sampson Low, Marston, Searle, & Rivington, 1884), 107.

86   Lectures Given by Mrs. T. Harris at the Opera House, Wellington (pamphlet) (Thames: Thames Star Office, 1897).

87   Swarbrick, 'Harris, Jane Elizabeth'.

88   Ellwood, *Islands of the Dawn*, 46.

89   Quoted in ibid., 211–12.

90   Swarbrick, 'Harris, Jane Elizabeth'; Ellwood, *Islands of the Dawn*, 46–49.

91   Ellwood, *Islands of the Dawn*, 49–50.

92   Ibid., 254 n.37.

93 'The Story of the Motor Ambulances', *The Pioneer* 1, no. 3 (2014): 70–71, cited in Owen Davies, *A Supernatural War: Magic, Divination, and Faith during the First World War* (Oxford: Oxford University Press, 2018), 81.
94 Arthur Conan Doyle, 'The Military Value of Spiritualism', *Light* 11 (May 1918): 147; cited in Davies, *A Supernatural War*, 81.
95 Geoffrey K. Nelson, *Spiritualism and Society* (London: Routledge and K. Paul, 1969), 154, cited in Davies, *A Supernatural War*, 81.
96 Reported in the *Liverpool Echo*, 21 September 1915, cited in Davies, *A Supernatural War*, 94.
97 M. C. de Vesme, 'Armées, flottes et combats phantomatiques', *Annales des Sciences Psychiques* (February 1916): 26.
98 *The Hamilton Advertiser*, 26 October 1918, cited in Davies, *A Supernatural War*, 146.
99 Susan King, *The People's King: The True Story of the Abdication* (London: Palgrave Macmillan, 2004), cited in Davies, *A Supernatural War*, 151.
100 'Tai Tokerau Hui – Service to Return Hone Tahitahi's Prayer Book' (audio file), 1986, Ngā Taonga Kōrero collection, Ngā Taonga Sound & Vision, Ref: 50377; 'Life saving prayer book returns to NZ', *New Zealand Herald*, 26 April 1999.
101 *Yorkshire Evening Post*, 4 August 1915, cietied in Davies, *A Supernatural War*, 182.
102 J. W. Graham, 'A Brief Resume of the Developmental History of Spiritualism in New Zealand', *New Zealand Psychic Gazette* 103 (July 1988): 12–13.
103 Section 28, subsection 4, NZ Police Offences Act 1884; *New Zealand Herald*, 12 September 1892; *Auckland Weekly News*, 17 September 1892, 35.
104 Ellwood, *Islands of the Dawn*, 52; 'Spiritualist Mediums and the Law', *New Zealand Psychic Gazette* 30 (January 1982): 1, 11.
105 Katherine Blakeley, 'Suffragist: Mrs M. Rough', https://nzhistory.govt.nz/suffragist/mrs-m-rough
106 E. Katherine Bates, *Seen and Unseen* (London: Greening, 1907), 49, 64.
107 Blakely, 'Suffragist: Mrs M. Rough'; William Rough, *Forty Years' Experiences of Occult Research* (Pahiatua: *Pahiatua Herald*, n.d. [c.1920]).
108 Blakely, 'Suffragist: Mrs M. Rough'; 'Inquest at Roslyn', *Evening Star*, 12 October 1900.
109 Robert Stout Pamphlet Collection, Vol. 86, Victoria University of Wellington Library; K.A. Coleridge, 'The Pamphlet Collection of Sir Robert Stout' (Wellington: Victoria University of Wellington Library, 1987); W. M. Bolt, *Land and Labour* (Dunedin: S. Lister, 1882), 15; Bolt biographical file, in Roth Papers, Ace 94-106-63/12, ATL; Claire Connell, 'Women in Politics 1893–1896: A Study of Women's Organisations and Their Interest in Social and Political Reform' (MA thesis, University of Otago, 1975), 17, 113.
110 Richard Hudelson, 'Popper's Critique of Marx', *Philosophical Studies* 37, no. 3 (1980): 259–70.
111 Leon Trotsky, 'Dialectical Materialism and Science' (1925), in *Problems of Everyday Life: Creating the Foundations for a New Society in Revolutionary Russia* (New York: Pathfinder, 1973), 217, 219.
112 'Agricultural and Pastoral News', *Otago Witness*, 17 August 1904; Alma Rutherford, *The Rutherford Story* (Dunedin: self-published, 1987), 6, 15–16; K. C. McDonald, *City of Dunedin: A Century of Civic Enterprise* (Dunedin: Dunedin City Corporation, 1965), 200–02; 'Social and general', *Otago Daily Times*, 21 January 1874.
113 'Tea meeting at Warrengate', *Otago Daily Times*, 1 May 1883.
114 'CHIPS', *Saturday Advertiser*, 29 December 1877.
115 William McLean, biographical file in Roth papers, MS 94-106-65119, items 88–98, Alexander Turnbull Library; 'Untitled', *New Zealand Times*, 7 November 1890, 'Funeral notice', 26 August 1914; Ellwood, *Islands of the Dawn*, 44, 52; Peebles, *Around the*

World, 56; Pam MacLean and Brian Joyce, *The Veteran Years of New Zealand Motoring* (Wellington: A.H. & A.W. Reed, 1971), 3–8; Darrell Latham, *The Golden Reefs: An Account of the Great Days of Quartz-Mining at Reefton, Waiuta and The Lyell*, 2nd ed. (Nelson: Nikau Press, 1992), 74, 105–06, 145, 148, 161, 284, 386–67.

116   *Hansard* 75 (1892): 281, 621–22; Timothy McIvor, *The Rainmaker: A Biography of John Ballance, Journalist and Politician 1839–1893* (Auckland: Heinemann Reed, 1989), 205.
117   *Hansard* 75 (1892): 622.
118   William McLean, *Spiritualism Vindicated, and Clerical Slanders Refuted* (Wellington: Printed at the New Zealand Times office for the Wellington Association of Spiritualists, 1887), 14–17, 24, 27, 47.
119   'A tragic affair', *New Zealand Times*, 12 August 1919.
120   'Sequel to suicide', *Ashburton Guardian*, 12 August 1919.
121   Clive Chapman (with G. A. W.), *The Blue Room: Being the Absorbing Story of the Development of Voice-to Voice Communication in BROAD LIGHT with Souls Who Have Passed into the GREAT BEYOND* (Auckland: Whitcombe & Tombs, 1927), 54.
122   Ibid., passim.
123   Harry Price, *Fifty Years of Psychical Research: A Critical Survey* (London: Longmans, Green & Co. Ltd, 1939), 81.
124   'The Blue Room', *Otago Daily Times*, 31 May 1927.
125   Matt Wingett, *Conan Doyle and the Mysterious World of Light, 1887–1920* (Portsmouth: Life Is Amazing, 2019), 19–32.
126   Ibid., 32–36.
127   Ibid., 43–44.
128   Peter Underwood, *The Ghost Club: A History* (Luton: Limbury Press, 2010), 9, 35.
129   Arthur Conan Doyle, *The Wanderings of a Spiritualist* (Berkeley: Ronin, 1988).
130   'Faith healing, past and present', *Otago Daily Times*, 20 December 1920; 'The Conan Doyle lectures', *Otago Daily Times*, 14 December 1920.
131   'The Conan Doyle lectures', *Otago Daily Times*, 18 December 1920.
132   Arthur Conan Doyle, 'Darkey of Christchurch', *The Times* (literary supplement), 29 September 1921.
133   Editorial, *Otago Daily Times*, 22 December 1920.
134   Ellwood, *Islands of the Dawn*, 55.
135   'News of the week', *Otago Witness*, 9 July 1870, 'News of the week', 16 July 1870, 16; Untitled item, Dunedin *Echo*, 27 May 1882; 'Practical Spiritualism', *Evening Star*, 10 June 1879, 'Practical Spriritualism', 16 June 1879, 'Practical Spiritualism', 27 June 1879, 2; McLean, *Spiritualism Vindicated*, 46.
136   Gareth Winter, 'Edward Wyllie', *New Zealand Journal of Photography* 26 (February 1997): 25–27.
137   Arthur Conan Doyle, *The Coming of the Fairies* (London: Hodder and Stoughton, 1922).
138   'Fairies, Phantoms, and Fantastic Photographs', *Arthur C. Clarke's World of Strange Powers* (Yorkshire Television, Episode 6, Season 1, first aired ITV, 2 May 1985).
139   Massimo Polidoro, 'Houdini's Impossible Demonstration', *Skeptical Inquirer*, 12 April 2017.
140   Cited in Ellwood, *Islands of the Dawn*, 57.
141   'In praise of New Zealand's charms', *The Press*, 25 January 1921.
142   'Into mountain wilds — spiritualists' strange pilgrimage — search for lost airmen', *Auckland Sun*, 13 March 1929.
143   Quoted in Ellwood, *Islands of the Dawn*, 60–61.
144   Ellwood, *Islands of the Dawn*, 62.

145 Charles Anderson, 'Lost in the long white cloud,' *Sunday Star-Times*, 14 July 2013.
146 Arthur Conan Doyle, *The Edge of the Unknown* (London: Murray, 1930), 147–49.
147 C. Joy Axford, 'Cottrell, Violet May', *Dictionary of New Zealand Biography*, first published in 1998. *Te Ara — the Encyclopedia of New Zealand*, https://teara.govt.nz/en/biographies/4c39/cottrell-violet-may
148 Ibid.
149 Ibid.
150 *Daily Telegraph* (Napier), 10 July 1930, cited in Ellwood, *Islands of the Dawn*, 63.
151 'Spiritualists sceptical. Napier claims doubted in Dunedin', *Daily Telegraph* (Napier), 13 July 1930, cited in Ellwood, *Islands of the Dawn*, 64.
152 Cited in Ellwood, *Islands of the Dawn*, 65.
153 Cited in Ellwood, *Islands of the Dawn*, 67.
154 Axford, 'Cottrell, Violet May'.
155 Ibid.
156 Scrapbook of the Christchurch Psychical Research Society Inc., Macmillan Brown Library, University of Canterbury Manuscript 165; Una Platts, *Nineteenth Century New Zealand Artists: A Guide and Handbook* (Christchurch: Avon Fine Prints, 1980), 155; see Margaret Lovell-Smith, *Plain Living High Thinking: The Family Story of Jennie and Will Lovell-Smith* (Christchurch: Pedmore Press, 1995); Julian Vesty and Joanna Cobley, 'Southern Spirits: The Case of the Psychical Research Society of Christchurch', *Records of the Canterbury Museum* 29 (2015): 51–60.
157 See Vesty and Cobley, 'Southern Spirits', 52; *Canterbury Society of Arts Catalogue* (1914): 85.
158 'Concert sketch', *Auckland Star*, 8 October 1935.
159 'The Archer Insurance Policy Case', Scrapbook of the Christchurch Psychical Research Institute Inc, 10–12.
160 Scrapbook of the Christchurch Psychical Research Institute Inc, 67.
161 Ibid., 150.
162 Vesty and Cobley, 'Southern Spirits', 52.
163 Scrapbook of the Christchurch Psychical Research Institute Inc, 30.
164 Ibid., 110–18.
165 Ibid., 18, 90, 102, 107–08, 110, 116, 126; Vesty and Cobley, 'Southern Spirits', 53–54.
166 See Barry Gustafson, *From the Cradle to the Grave: A Biography of Michael Joseph Savage* (Auckland: Reed Methuen, 1986), 20.
167 See Garth Carpenter, 'Spiritualism. With Liberty of Interpretation', *Thursday*, 3 September 1970, 30ff.
168 Rosemary Vincent, 'Mary lets the spirits guide her', *New Zealand Times*, 11 April 1984; 'Radio psychic switched OFF', *Dominion*, 24 September 1983; Mary Fry, *Mary Fry's Own Story* (Wellington: Grantham, 1987).
169 Ellwood, *Islands of the Dawn*, 70.
170 Email correspondence with Joanne Duncan, president of Spiritualism New Zealand, 3 February 2022.
171 'Police reject psychic advice', *Bay of Plenty Times*, 1 February 2006.
172 Philip Matthews, '*Sensing Murder*: Sleuths or scammers?', *The Press*, 9 March 2009.
173 Matt Nippert, 'TV psychic row breaks out as police search for missing girl', *New Zealand Herald*, 11 October 2009.
174 'TV psychics "exploited" Furlong — NZ Skeptics', *Newshub*, 25 June 2012, www.newshub.co.nz/nznews/tv-psychics-exploited-furlong--nz-skeptics-2012062514

Chapter 8. The women of the Beast

1. Richard Kaczynski, *Perdurabo: The Life of Aleister Crowley*, 2nd ed. (Berkeley: North Atlantic Books, 2010), 6.
2. Ibid., 126–29.
3. Nevill Drury, *Stealing Fire from Heaven: The Rise of Modern Western Magic* (Oxford: Oxford University Press, 2011), 86.
4. Ibid., 85.
5. Aleister Crowley, *The Book of the Law* (San Francisco: Red Wheel/Weiser, 1976), 9.
6. Fred Licht, 'The Vittoriale degli Italiani', *The Journal of the Society of Architectural Historians* 41, no. 4 (December 1982): 318–24, at 318.
7. See Henrik Bogdan and Martin P. Starr (eds), *Aleister Crowley and Western Esotericism* (Oxford and New York: Oxford University Press, 2012); Martin Booth, *A Magick Life: The Biography of Aleister Crowley* (London: Coronet Books, 2000); Tobias Churton, *Aleister Crowley: The Biography* (London: Watkins Books, 2011); Kaczynski, *Perdurabo*, passim; Gary Lachman, *Aleister Crowley: Magick, Rock and Roll, and the Wickedest Man in the World* (New York: Penguin Random House, 2014); John Moore, *Aleister Crowley: A Modern Master* (Oxford: Mandrake, 2009); Marco Pasi, 'The Neverendingly Told Story: Recent Biographies of Aleister Crowley', *Aries: Journal for the Study of Western Esotericism* 3, no. 2 (2003): 224–45.
8. Kaczynski, *Perdurabo*, 212.
9. Ibid., 224.
10. 'New religion', *Hawera and Normanby Star*, 15 December 1910.
11. Leila Waddell, 'Two Anzacs Meet in London', *Shadowlands: Expressing the Arts* 9, no. 2 (October 1923): 51, 72.
12. Toby Creswell, *Notorious Australians: The Mad, the Bad and the Dangerous* (Sydney: ABC Books, 2008), 57–60; 'Miss Leila Waddell, Obituary', *Sydney Herald*, 14 September 1932.
13. Creswell, *Notorious Australians*, 57–60.
14. Kaczynski, *Perdurabo*, 212.
15. Francis King, *The Magical World of Aleister Crowley* (Durrington Worthing: Littlehampton Book Services Ltd, 1977), 61. Thanks to Richard Kaczynski for drawing this to my attention.
16. Paul Ashford Harris, *Odd Boy Out: A Memoir* (Edgecliff: Venture Press, 2018), 191–92.
17. Richard Kaczynski, 'Frieda Lady Harris', United States Grand Lodge OTO, https://oto-usa.org/usgl/lion-eagle/frieda-lady-harris
18. Letter from Frieda Harris to Gerald Yorke, 16 November 1957, NS76 Yorke Collection, Warburg Institute, University of London.
19. Sir Jack Harris, *Memoirs of a Century* (Wellington: Steele Roberts, 2007), 22.
20. Harris and Colquhoun were both moving in surrealist circles in Paris at the same time, and both contributed works to the 1942 exhibition *Imaginative Art Since the War* at the Leicester Galleries, London. In a letter written in May 1940, Harris tells Crowley that Maxwell Armfield has suggested a possible venue in which to exhibit the Thoth tarot paintings, NS37 Yorke Collection, Warburg Institute, University of London. In a June 1947 letter to William Holt, Harris writes that she is sending him a book 'written by A.E. whom I knew & respected': Russell died in 1935. HO-62; General Correspondence, CC00628: William Holt, Author, Artist and Traveller of Todmorden, Papers, West Yorkshire Archives, Calderdale.
21. Sir Percy Harris, *Forty Years In and Out of Parliament* (London: A. Melrose, 1947), 26.
22. Ibid., 26–27.
23. Harris, *Odd Boy Out*, 192.

24 Harris, *Memoirs of a Century*, 76.
25 Harris, *Forty Years*, 30ff.
26 Harris, *Memoirs of a Century*, 23.
27 See Lon Milo Duquette, *Understanding Aleister Crowley's Thoth Tarot* (Newbury Port: Weiser Books, 2003); James Wasserman, *Instructions for Aleister Crowley's Thoth Tarot Deck*, booklet, 3rd edition (Stamford: US Games Systems, 2006); Aleister Crowley, *The Book of Thoth: A Short Essay on the Tarot of the Egyptians, Being the Equinox Volume III No. V* (New York: Samuel Weiser, 1974); Gerd Ziegler, *Tarot: Mirror of the Soul: Handbook for the Aleister Crowley Tarot* (Newbury Port: Weiser Books, 1988).
28 For a description of this system, see Olive Whicher, *Projective Geometry: Creative Polarities in Time and Space* (East Sussex: Rudolf Steiner Press, 2013); Claas Hoffmann, 'Projective Synthetic Geometry in Lady Frieda Harris' Tarot Paintings in A. Crowley's *Book of Thoth*', *Association for Tarot Studies Newsletter*, 15 March 2004.
29 'Correspondence between Aleister Crowley and Frieda Harris (mostly regarding Thoth Tarot designs)', Hermetic Library, https://hermetic.com/crowley/crowley-harris
30 Richard Kaczynski, 'Frieda Lady Harris', United States Grand Lodge OTO, https://oto-usa.org/usgl/lion-eagle/frieda-lady-harris
31 Harris, *Memoirs of a Century*, 22.
32 Kaczynski, *Perdurabo*, 501; Stephen Skinner (ed.), *The Magical Diaries of Aleister Crowley: Tunisia 1923* (Newbury Port: Weiser Books, 1996), 79.
33 Kaczynski, 'Frieda Lady Harris'; 'Correspondence between Aleister Crowley and Frieda Harris (mostly regarding Thoth Tarot designs)', Hermetic Library, https://hermetic.com/crowley/crowley-harris
34 Marco Pasi, 'Aleister Crowley in Cefalu: The Works from the Palermo Collection', in *The Nightmare Paintings: Aleister Crowley; Works from the Palermo Collection*, ed. Robert Buratti (Subiaco: Buratti Fine Art, 2012), 10–15, at 12.
35 Aleister Crowley, 'Introduction', in *The Book of Thoth: A Short Essay on the Tarot of the Egyptians* (Equinox III:5) (New York: S. Weiser, 1944).
36 Letter from Harris to Crowley, 29 December 1939, NS37, Yorke Collection, Warburg Institute, University of London. Emphasis in original text.
37 John Newton, *Hard Frost: Structures of Feeling in New Zealand Literature, 1908–1945* (Wellington: Victoria University Press, 2017), 69.
38 Gillian Boddy, 'Mansfield, Katherine', *Dictionary of New Zealand Biography*, first published in 1996, *Te Ara — the Encyclopedia of New Zealand*, https://teara.govt.nz/en/biographies/3m42/mansfield-katherine; Roberta Nicholls, 'Beauchamp, Harold', *Dictionary of New Zealand Biography*, first published in 1993, *Te Ara — the Encyclopedia of New Zealand*, https://teara.govt.nz/en/biographies/2b14/beauchamp-harold
39 For a discussion of Mansfield and *Rhythm*, see Angela Smith, 'Katherine Mansfield and Rhythm', *Journal of New Zealand Literature* 21 (2003): 102–21.
40 Kaczynski, *Perdurabo*, 258.
41 *Rhythm* 9 (October 1914).
42 Ida Baker, *Katherine Mansfield: Memories of LM* (London: Michael Joseph, 1971), 85–86.
43 Kathleen Jones, *Katherine Mansfield: The Story-Teller* (London: Penguin/Viking, 2010), 129.
44 Baker, *Katherine Mansfield*, 86.
45 James Moore, *Gurdjieff and Mansfield* (London: Routledge & Kegan Paul, 1980), 18; Claire Tomlin, *Mansfield: A Secret Life* (New York: Viking, 1987), 98–100.
46 Moore, *Gurdjieff and Mansfield*, 18.
47 Ibid., 18; Tomlin, *Mansfield*, 98–100.

48 See P. D. Ouspensky, *In Search of the Miraculous: Fragments of an Unknown Teaching* (New York: Harcourt, Brace, Jovanovich, 1977); C. S. Nott, *Teachings of Gurdjieff: A Pupil's Journal: An Account of some Years with G.I. Gurdjieff and A.R. Orage in New York and at Fontainebleau-Avon* (Abingdon-on-Thames: Routledge and Kegan Paul, 1961); John Shirley, *Gurdjieff: An Introduction to His Life and Ideas* (New York: J.P. Tarcher/Penguin, 2004).

49 For more on the relationship between Mansfield and Orage, see Jenny McDonnell, *Katherine Mansfield and the Modernist Marketplace: At the Mercy of the Public* (Basingstoke: Palgrave Macmillan, 2010), 15–45.

50 Gerri Kimber, 'Mansfield, *Rhythm* and the Émigré Connection', in *Katherine Mansfield and Literary Modernism: Historicizing Modernism*, eds Janet Wilson, Gerry Kimber and Susan Reid (London: Bloomsbury, 2013), 27.

51 A. R. Orage, 'Talks with Katherine Mansfield', *Century Magazine* 87 (November 1924): 36–40; Vincent O'Sullivan and Margaret Scott (eds), *The Collected Letters of Katherine Mansfield* (Oxford: Oxford University Press, 2008), 360.

52 Linda Lappin, 'Katherine Mansfield and D. H. Lawrence, A Parallel Quest', in *Katherine Mansfield Studies: The Journal of the Katherine Mansfield Society*, Vol. 2 (Edinburgh: Edinburgh University Press, 2010), 72–86.

53 Susan Kavaler-Adler, *The Creative Mystique: From Red Shoes Frenzy to Love and Creativity* (New York and London: Routledge, 1996), 113. For Mansfield and Gurdjieff in general, see also Pierce Butler, '"The Only Truth I Really Care About": Katherine Mansfield at the Gurdjieff Institute (for Jack Lamplough)', *Katherine Mansfield Studies* 9 (2007); Gerri Kimber, '"A child of the sun": Katherine Mansfield, Orientalism and Gurdjieff', in *Katherine Mansfield and Russia*, eds Galya Diment, Gerri Kimber and Martin W. Todd (Edinburgh: Edinburgh University Press, 2017); Jeffrey Meyers, 'Katherine Mansfield, Gurdjieff and Lawrence's "Mother and Daughter"', *Twentieth Century Literature* 22, no. 4 (December 1976); Carole Cusack, 'Gurdjieff and Katherine Mansfield Redux: Alma de Groen's "The Rivers of China"', *Australian Religion Studies Review* 27, no. 3 (2014); and 'Katherine Mansfield at Fontainebleau', www.gurdjieff-bibliography.com/Current/katherinemansfield.htm

54 Nevill Drury and Gregory Tillet, *Other Temples, Other Gods: The Occult in Australia* (Sydney: Coronet/Hodder and Stoughton, 1982), 85.

55 Ethan Doyle White, *Wicca: History, Belief, and Community in Modern Pagan Witchcraft* (Brighton: Sussex Academic Press, 2016), 39; Nevill Drury, *Pan's Daughter: The Strange World of Rosaleen Norton* (Sydney: Collins Australia, 1998), vii; Nevill Drury, *Homage to Pan: The Life, Art and Sex-Magic of Rosaleen Norton* (Telford: Creation Oneiros, 2009), 9–14.

56 Drury and Tillet, *Other Temples*, 85.

57 'Norton, Rosalind [sic] (1917–1979)', in *Encyclopedia of Occultism and Parapsychology*, 5th ed., Vol. 2, ed. J. Gordon Melton (Farmington Hills: Gale, 2001), 1125.

58 Drury, *Homage to Pan*, 15.

59 Doyle White, *Wicca*, 39.

60 Drury, *Homage to Pan*, 15–16.

61 Melton, 'Norton, Rosalind', 1125.

62 Drury, *Homage to Pan*, 19.

63 Ibid., 19–21.

64 'Art models show their own art', *Pix* 12, no. 1 (3 July 1943).

65 Drury, *Homage to Pan*, 21–24; Doyle White, *Wicca*, 39–40.

66 Doyle White, *Wicca*, 40.

67 Rosaleen Norton, *The Art of Rosaleen Norton* (Sydney: Wally Glover, 1952).

68   Drury, *Homage to Pan*, 26–38.
69   Ibid., 38–41.
70   Cited in David Salter, 'The Conservatorium director and the witch', *Sydney Morning Herald*, 2 July 2015.
71   'Sir Eugene Goossens: Sex, magic and the maestro' (Goossens interviewed by Michelle Arrow), *Rewind*, ABC-TV, 5 September 2004; Geoff Burton, *The Fall of the House* (documentary), Kurrajong Films, 2003.
72   Doyle White, *Wicca*, 40.
73   Anna Hoffman, *Tales of Anna Hoffman, Volume One* (Auckland: self-published, 2009), 124; although she doesn't appear in news reports or court transcripts, see Redmer Ysker, 'Scene-Stealer', *New Zealand Listener*, 8 January 2015.
74   Hoffman, *Tales*, 154.
75   Ibid., 254–57.
76   Ibid., 259.
77   'Hoffman, self-proclaimed witch, planned her exit well', *New Zealand Herald*, 15 December 2014.
78   Murray Edmond, *Time to Make a Song and Dance: Cultural Revolt in Auckland in the 1960s* (Pokeno: Atuanui Press, 2021), 56.
79   'Michele Hewitson interview: Anna Hoffman', *New Zealand Herald*, 23 June 2012.
80   Alan Brunton, *Years Ago Today* (Wellington: Bumper Books, 1997), 8.
81   Hewitson, 'Anna Hoffman'.

Chapter 9. In science's robe
1   Ficino, *De vita libri tres* (1489), 3.20.
2   John Maynard Keynes, 'Newton, The Man', in *Proceedings of the Royal Society Newton Tercentenary Celebrations, 15–19 July 1946* (Cambridge: Cambridge University Press, 1947).
3   Gottfried Leibniz, 'The Kingdom of Darkness: Leibniz, Correspondence with Samuel Clarke, 1 and 5', in *The Book of Magic: From Antiquity to the Enlightenment*, ed. and trans. Brian Copenhaver (London: Penguin, 2014), 571.
4   Jeff Hughes, 'Making Isotopes Matter: Francis Aston and the Mass-Spectrograph', *Dynamis* 29 (2009): 131–65, at 139.
5   Chris Gosden, *Magic, a History: From Alchemy to Witchcraft, from the Ice Age to the Present* (New York: Farrar, Straus and Giroux, 2020), 11, 29.
6   Keith Thomas, *Religion and the Decline of Magic* (Harmondsworth: Peregrine, 1971), 800.
7   Louisa S. Cook, *Geometrical Psychology, or, The science of representation: An abstract of the theories and diagrams of B. W. Betts* (London: George Redway, 1887).
8   E. R. and N. M. Brewster, *Welcome Queen Elizabeth II*, commemorative music score sheet (New Plymouth: Norian, c.1953). An inscription in the copy held by Puke Ariki, New Plymouth, confirms that it was performed for the Queen.
9   Roy Brewster, *Norian Thoughts* (Conical Hill: Stratford, c.1973), verses 36–37.
10 Rhonda Bartle, 'Roy Brewster: Heaven Could Be Shaped No Other Way', Puki Ariki, https://terangiaoaonunui.pukeariki.com/story-collections/taranaki-stories/roy-brewster-heaven-could-be-shaped-no-other-way
11 Roy Brewster was the subject of an exhibition, *A Different Angle*, at Puke Ariki, New Plymouth, in 2017; John Hales, 'Second Coming: Part 2', *Rolling Stone* (New Zealand), 24 May 1973; John Hales, 'Second Coming: Part 3', *Rolling Stone* (New Zealand), 7 June 1973.
12 'About the Seekers Trust', www.theseekerstrust.com/about-us
13 'The Seekers', in *Encyclopedia of Occultism and Parapsychology*, 5th ed., Vol. 2, ed. J. Gordon Melton (Farmington Hills: Gale, 2001), 1383.

14 'Peloha', Ministry for Culture and Heritage, updated 20 December 2012, https://nzhistory.govt.nz/culture/radiant-living/peloha
15 Mathew Wright, *Havelock North: The History of a Village* (Hastings: Hastings District Council, 1996), 169; 'Peloha'.
16 Lyman Tower Sargent, 'Herbert Sutcliffe and Radiant Living: Self-Help and New Thought in New Zealand', *Utopian Studies* 23, no. 1 (2012): 2–27, at 6.
17 Herbert Sutcliffe, *Radiant Living: Official Organ of the Sutcliffe Schools of Radiant Living* 13, no. 1 (February–March 1959): 7–9.
18 Herbert Sutcliffe, *Healing Rays and Consciousness* (Havelock North: Peloha International Headquarters, n.d.), 20–22.
19 Herbert Sutcliffe, *My Purpose: As Used by the International Sutcliffe Schools of Radiant Living* (Hastings: Hart Print, n.d.). Emphasis in the original.
20 Herbert Sutcliffe, *Radiant Living: The Vital Science and Philosophy Applied to Human Life by Co-operating with Physical, Mental, and Divine Laws,* 7th ed. (Havelock North: Peloha International Headquarters, 1952), 46.
21 Sutcliffe, *Healing Rays and Consciousness*, 6.
22 Sargent, 'Herbert Sutcliffe and Radiant Living', 18.
23 'Dominion Reconstruction Conference', *Northern Advocate*, 20 November 1941.
24 Michael Gill, *Edmund Hillary: A Biography* (Nelson: Potton and Burton, 2017), 56.
25 https://nzhistory.govt.nz/culture/radiant-living/edmund-hillary-radiant-liver
26 Sir Edmund Hillary Archive, Auckland War Memorial Museum Tāmaki Paenga Hira, PH-2010-4, box 6, folder 137.
27 Edmund Hillary, *Nothing Venture, Nothing Win* (London: Hodder and Stoughton, 1975), 27.
28 Robert Twigger, *White Mountain: Real and Imagined Journeys in the Himalayas* (London: Weidenfeld and Nicolson, 2016), 249.
29 Martin Doutré, *Ancient Celtic New Zealand* (Auckland: Dé Danann Publishers, 1999).
30 Blanche Baughan, *Snow Kings of the Southern Alps* (Christchurch: Whitcombe & Tombs, 1910), reprinted and collected in Blanche Baughan, *Studies in New Zealand Scenery* (Auckland: Whitcombe & Tombs, 1917), 59.
31 Baughan, *Studies in New Zealand Scenery*, 58.
32 https://nzhistory.govt.nz/culture/radiant-living/herbert-sutcliffe
33 www.wgtn.ac.nz/scholarships/current/herbert-sutcliffe-hardship-scholarships
34 Bruce Cathie, *Harmonic 33* (Wellington: A.H. & A.W. Reed, 1968); *Harmonic 695 — The UFO and Anti-Gravity* (Wellington: A.H. & A.W. Reed, 1971); *Harmonic 288 — The Pulse of the Universe* (Wellington: A.H. & A.W. Reed, 1977); *Harmonic 371244 — The Bridge to Infinity* (Sanger: America West Publishers, 1989); *The Energy Grid Harmonic 695 — The Pulse of the Universe* (Sanger: America West Publishers, 1990); *The Harmonic Conquest of Space* (Sanger: America West Publishers, 1994).
35 'UFO Australia', *In Search Of . . .*, Alan Landsburg Productions, Season 4, Episode 4, first aired 11 October 1979.
36 'The Ancient Architects', *Ancient Aliens*, Prometheus Entertainment, Season 12, Episode 4, first aired 19 May 2017.
37 R. Buckminster Fuller (with E. J. Applewhite), *Synergetics: Explorations in the Geometry of Thinking*, Vol. 1 (New York: Macmillan, 1971).
38 'Tesla Tower in Shoreham Long Island (1901–1917) meant to be the "World Wireless" Broadcasting system', Tesla Memorial Society of New York, www.teslasociety.com/teslatower.htm
39 Alfred Watkins, *The Old Straight Track: Its Mounds, Beacons, Moats, Sites and Mark Stones* (London: Methuen, 1945).

40   'Bruce Leonard Cathie' (obituary), *New Zealand Herald*, 3 June 2013.
41   www.magic.co.nz/Ken-Ring-predicted-Chch-Earthquake-and-the-current-terrible-weather/tabid/506/articleID/16322/Default.aspx
42   Ken Ring, 'Christchurch Earthquake Update', https://predictweather.co.nz/ArticleShow.aspx?ID=306
43   www.penguin.com.au/authors/Ken-Ring; https://web.archive.org/web/20100526220746/http://www.mathman.co.nz/author.html
44   Errol Kiong, 'Moon Man offers forecasts to help selectors', *New Zealand Herald*, 6 September 2007; Sarah Lang, 'Thinking outside the square', *New Zealand Herald*, 23 June 2008; Steve Mason, 'Running rings around the moon', *Marlborough Express*, 13 May 2011.
45   H. A. Marmer, 'The Problems of the Tide', *The Scientific Monthly* 14, no. 3 (March 1922): 209–22.
46   Harry Alcock, *Lunar Effect: Moon's Influence on Our Weather* (Wellington: Moana Press, 1989).
47   Ken Ring, 'An Inexact Science', https://predictweather.co.nz/ArticleShow.aspx?ID=194&type=home
48   Alison Campbell, 'Predicting Earthquakes, Hedging Your Bets', 'Bioblog', University of Waikato, 1 March 2011, https://blog.waikato.ac.nz/bioblog/2011/03/predicting-earthquakes-hedging; Andre Huber, 'Christchurch earthquake sceptics take aim at Ken Ring', *Herald on Sunday*, 13 March 2011; Alex Walls, 'Nick Smith: Ken Ring offensive; should be held to account', *National Business Review*, 15 March 2011; Lincoln Tan and Amelia Wade, '5.1 quake but Moon Man link ruled out', *New Zealand Herald*, 21 March 2011; Jimmy Ness, 'Moon Man predicts big quake by 2016', *Upper Hutt Leader*, 5 October 2011.
49   'Late Mr Joseph Taylor', *Nelson Evening Mail*, 28 July 1942; Taylor Family Papers, MS-Papers-11933-5, National Library of New Zealand, Wellington.
50   Joseph Taylor, 'Psycho-Radio-Cosmics', *Nelson Evening Mail*, 26 October 1909.
51   Eugen Weber, *Apocalypses: Prophecies, Cults, and Millennial Beliefs Through the Ages* (Cambridge, MA: Harvard University Press, 2000), 197.
52   'Astrology, mining, and the Upper House', *Nelson Evening Mail*, 22 June 1910.
53   'The Puponga mine charges', *Nelson Evening Mail*, 29 October 1902; 'The Joseph Taylor case', *Nelson Evening Mail*, 23 March 1903; Taylor Family Papers, MS-Papers-11933-5, National Library of New Zealand, Wellington.
54   'Astrology, mining, and the Upper House'.
55   'Advertisements', *Nelson Evening Mail*, 7 September 1907.
56   'Late Mr Joseph Taylor'.
57   'Death of Mr Joseph Taylor', *Nelson Evening Mail*, 24 July 1942.
58   'Late Mr Joseph Taylor'.

Chapter 10. The Age of Aquarius
1   An incredibly involved and complicated magical ritual found in the grimoire *The Book of Abramelin* (probably fifteenth century), most familiar from Mathers' nineteenth-century translation of seventeenth-century German versions with considerable elaborations. The rite, which exists in two versions taking six and 18 months to perform, respectively, is intended to put the magician in contact with their guardian angel. The film *A Dark Song* (2016) accurately conveys the sense of the thing while being wildly inaccurate in detail. Crowley notoriously moved on from Boleskine having failed to conclude the rite, to which a litany of subsequent fires and tragedies at the house have been attributed over the years.
2   See Gary Lachman, *Aleister Crowley: Magick, Rock and Roll, and the Wickedest Man in the World* (New York: TarcherPerigee, 2014).

3   Hermann Haupt, 'Der Begin des Wassermannzeitalters, eine astronomische Frage', *Anzeiger der Österreichische Akademie der Wissenschaften, Mathematisch-Naturwissenschaftliche Klasse* 129 (1992): 75–78.
4   Nicholas Campion, *The Book of World Horoscopes* (Swanage: The Wessex Astrologer, 1999), 489–95.
5   Mitch Horowitz, *Occult America: The Secret History of How Mysticism Shaped Our Nation* (New York: Random House, 2009), 256.
6   Larry Sloman, Michael Simmons and Jay Babcock, 'Out, Demons, Out! The 1967 Exorcism of the Pentagon and the Birth of Yippie!', *Arthur* 13 (November 2004), https://arthurmag.com/2011/04/13/out-demons-out-the-1967-exorcism-of-the-pentagon-and-the-birth-of-yippie-arthur-no-13nov-2004
7   'Beginnings', Ministry for Culture and Heritage, last updated 29 September 2015, https://nzhistory.govt.nz/culture/rock-music-festivals/beginnings
8   'The Vietnam War', Ministry for Culture and Heritage, last updated 8 December 2016, https://nzhistory.govt.nz/war/vietnam-war
9   Jock Phillips, 'The New Zealanders — Ordinary blokes and extraordinary sheilas', *Te Ara — the Encyclopedia of New Zealand*, published 8 February 2005, last updated 20 May 2015, www.TeAra.govt.nz/en/photograph/1982/demonstration-against-the-vietnam-war
10 Jock Phillips, 'Drugs — Cannabis use', *Te Ara — the Encyclopedia of New Zealand*, published 5 September 2013, www.TeAra.govt.nz/en/drugs/page-3
11 Caren Wilton, 'Communes and communities — Communes: 1960s and 1970s', *Te Ara — the Encyclopedia of New Zealand*, published 5 May 2011, reviewed and revised 4 April 2018, www.TeAra.govt.nz/en/communes-and-communities/page-2
12 Miro Bilbrough, *In the Time of the Manaroans* (Wellington: Victoria University Press, 2020).
13 John Newton, *The Double Rainbow: James K. Baxter, Ngāti Hau and the Jerusalem Commune* (Wellington: Victoria University Press, 2009), 23.
14 Ibid., passim.
15 Wilton, 'Communes and communities'.
16 *Ohu: Alternative Life Style Ccommunities* (Wellington: Published for the Ohu Advisory Committee by the Dept of Lands and Survey, 1975); Wilton, 'Communes and communities'.
17 Noel Street, *The Story of the Lotus Ashram* (Miami: Lotus Ashram, n.d.); *Karma: Your Whispering Wisdom* (Fabens: Lotus Ashram, 1978); *Reincarnation: One Life — Many Births* (Fabens: Lotus Ashram, 1978); *Healing with the Maori Indians in New Zealand* (Miami: Lotus Ashram, 1973).
18 David Herkt, 'Author Martin Edmond tells of unforgettable days of Red Mole — a theatre of danger', *Stuff*, 27 October 2020, www.stuff.co.nz/entertainment/books/123186229/author-martin-edmond-tells-of-unforgettable-days-of--red-mole--a-theatre-of-danger
19 Alan Brunton, 'The Rite of Winter: Study of Ritual and Dream in *The Tempest*' (BA thesis, Victoria University of Wellington, 1968).
20 Murray Edmond, 'From Cabaret to Apocalypse: Red Mole's *Cabaret Capital Strut* and *Ghost Rite*', ka mate ka ora 4 (September 2007), www.nzepc.auckland.ac.nz/kmko/04/ka_mate04_murrayedmond.asp
21 Ibid.
22 Ibid.
23 Alan Brunton, '1960–1969 Restoring the Commune' (Introduction), in *Big Smoke: New Zealand Poems 1960–1975*, eds Alan Brunton, Michele Leggott and Murray Edmond (Auckland: Auckland University Press, 2000).

24 Alan Brunton and John Geraets, 'Questions and Answers', *Brief* 19 (March 2001).
25 Alan Brunton, 'Remarks on "The Future of Poetry". Seeing Voices', Auckland, 23 August 1997, *A Brief Description of the Whole World* 7 (September 1997), www.nzepc.auckland.ac.nz/authors/brunton/future.asp
26 See Arthur Pickard-Cambridge, *The Dramatic Festivals of Athens* (Oxford: Clarendon Press, 1953).
27 Murray Edmond, *Then It Was Now Again: Selected Critical Writing* (Pokeno: Atuanui Press, 2014), 96.
28 Martin Edmond, *Bus Stops on the Moon: Red Mole Days 1974–1980* (Dunedin: Otago University Press, 2020).
29 Herkt, 'Author Martin Edmond'.
30 'Ancient Iwi', https://ngaitahu.maori.nz/ancient-iwi/; 'Notes and queries', *The Journal of the Polynesian Society* 34, no. 4 (1925): 385–87, at 386; Te Maire Tau, 'Ngāi Tahu — Ngāi Tahu and Waitaha', *Te Ara — the Encyclopedia of New Zealand*, published 8 February 2005, updated 1 March 2017, www.TeAra.govt.nz/en/ngai-tahu/page-4; Ministry of Justice, *The Ngāi Tahu Land Report* (Wellington: NZ Government, 1991), 179; Ian Hugh Kawharu, *Waitangi: Maori and Pakeha Perspectives of the Treaty of Waitangi* (Oxford: Oxford University Press, 1989), 236–37; Janet Stephenson, Heather Bauchop and Peter Petchey, *Bannockburn Heritage Landscape Study* (Wellington: Department of Conservation, 2004), 29; Te Taumutu Rūnanga, 'Our History', https://tetaumuturunanga.iwi.nz/our-history; George Graham, 'Te heke-o-nga-toko-toru (The migration of the three)', *The Journal of the Polynesian Society* 31, no. 4 (1922): 190–92, at 386; Āpirana Ngata, 'The Io Cult — Early Migration — Puzzle of the Canoes', *The Journal of the Polynesian Society* 59, no. 4 (1950): 335–46, at 338; Ashburton District Council, *Ashburton District Plan — 02 Takata Whenua Values* (Ashburton: Ashburton District Council, 2014), 3; Hilary Mitchell and John Mitchell, 'Te Tau Ihu tribes — Early traditions', *Te Ara — the Encyclopedia of New Zealand*, published 8 February 2005, updated 22 March 2017, www.TeAra.govt.nz/en/te-tau-ihu-tribes/page-1; Megan Ellison, 'Teparapara Continued', Te Rūnaka o Ōtākou, www.otakourunaka.co.nz/tauparapara-continued; W. A. Taylor, 'Murihiki', in *Lore and History of the South Island Maori* (Christchurch: Bascands Ltd, 1952), 148.
31 31 Barry Brailsford, *Song of the Waitaha: The Histories of a Nation* (Christchurch: Ngatapuwae Trust, 1989).
32 www.stoneprint.co.nz/about-barry-brailsford
33 Michael Goldsmith, 'Strange Whakapapa: Colliding and Colluding Claims to Ancestry and Indigeneity in Aotearoa', *Sites: New Series* 10, no. 1 (2013): 73–92, 75.
34 Barry Brailsford, *Song of the Stone*, 2nd ed. (Christchurch: StonePrint Press, 2008), 7.
35 Goldsmith, 'Strange Whakapapa', 77.
36 Brailsford, *Song of the Stone*, 10–11.
37 'New Zealand telegrams', *Taranaki Herald*, 19 November 1989.
38 'Sermons in stones', *Evening Post*, 7 March 1910; 'The stones of Kupe', *Evening Post*, 16 April 1910; 'The mystic Maori pillars', *Poverty Bay Herald*, 26 March 1910.
39 K. M. Ballantyne, 'Notes on Maori Art', *Art in New Zealand* (September 1930): 35–38.
40 Judith Hoch, *Prophecy on the River: My Journey to Waitaha* (Auckland: Attar Books, 2019).
41 K. R. Howe, 'Māori and Polynesian Origins and the "New Learning"', *The Journal of the Polynesian Society* 108, no. 3 (1999): 305–26; Barry Fell, 'Maoris from the Mediterranean', *New Zealand Listener*, 27 February 1975, 10–13; 'Maoris from the Mediterranean, Part Two: How Ancient Maori Was Written', *New Zealand Listener*, 1 March 1975, 20–21. Barry Fell (1917–1994) was a New Zealand zoologist who rose to the esteemed rank of professor of invertebrate zoology at the Harvard Museum

of Comparative Zoology and became infamous for his theories that centuries before Christopher Columbus, various Old World peoples including Celts, Basques, Phoenicians and Egyptians had commerce with the peoples of North America. He had similar theories about Old World cultures visiting the Pacific. Reuel Anson Lochore (1903–1991) was a New Zealand public servant, diplomat (New Zealand's first ambassador to West Germany), scholar and philologist, who likewise promoted the theory that Aotearoa had been visited by Old World peoples prior to Abel Tasman in 1642.

42 Kerry Bolton, *Lords of the Soil: The Story of the Turehu, the White Tangata Whenua*, 3rd rev. ed. (Waikanae: Spectrum Press, 2000); *Ngati Hotu: The White Warrior Tribe* (Paraparaumu Beach: Renaissance Press, 2003); *Legends of the Patupaiarehe: New Zealand's White Fey Folk* (Paraparaumu Beach: Renaissance Press, 2004).

43 Martin Doutré, *Ancient Celtic New Zealand* (Auckland: Dé Danaan Publishers, 1999); *The Littlewood Treaty: The True English Text of the Treaty of Waitangi* (Auckland: Dé Danaan Publishers, 2005).

44 'Don Brash — Ragging on Te Reo', *Radio New Zealand*, 2 December 2017.

45 Makere Harawira, 'Neo-imperialism and the (mis)appropriation of indigenousness', *Pacific World: An International Quarterly on Peace and Ecojustice* 54 (October 1999): 54–61.

46 Goldsmith, 'Strange Whakapapa', passim.

47 Jim Wilson, *Journey to the Centre of My Being* (Mumbai: Zen Publications, 2019), 166–68.

48 Amber Allott, '"A clear attack on the authority of Ngāi Tūāhuriri" — hapū slams occupation's claim of red zone ownership', *Stuff*, 7 April 2022, www.stuff.co.nz/pou-tiaki/128299190/a-clear-attack-on-the-authority-of-ngi-thuriri--hap-slams-occupations-claim-of-red-zone-ownership

49 I would not be the first to note that, prior to Strieber's book, purported close encounters described a diversity of extra-terrestrial beings, including Scandinavian *Übermenschen*, literal little green men, hairy dwarves and robots. Following publication these encounters mostly describe the so-called 'Gray' type, foetal-looking with a large head and big black eyes as described by Strieber and prominently depicted on the cover of his popular book.

50 Jani King, *The Gift* (Perth: Triad Publishers, 1996); *The P'taah Tapes: An Act of Faith* (Perth: Triad Publishers, 1991); *The P'taah Tapes: Transformation of the Species* (Mulgrave: Light Source Publishers, 1991); https://ptaah.com.au

51 Roy Wallis, 'Figuring Out Cult Receptivity', *Journal of the Scientific Study of Religion* 25, no. 4 (December 1986): 494–503.

52 Paul Morris, 'Diverse religions — Recent and new-age religious movements', *Te Ara — the Encyclopedia of New Zealand*, published 5 May 2011, reviewed and revised 12 July 2018, www.TeAra.govt.nz/en/diverse-religions/page-9

53 Paul Morris, 'Diverse religions — Recent and new-age religious movements', *Te Ara — the Encyclopedia of New Zealand*, published 5 May 2011, reviewed and revised 12 July 2018 [image], www.TeAra.govt.nz/en/photograph/32290/transcendental-meditation-teacher-1983

54 Paul Spoonley, *The Politics of Nostalgia: Racism and the Extreme Right in New Zealand* (Palmerston North: Dunmore Press, 1987), 82–87.

55 Spoonley, *The Politics of Nostalgia*, 87; Martin van Beynen, 'Zap's top three now key Canty figures', *The Press*, 26 August 2008; Martin van Beynen, 'Henderson assets in friends' hands', *The Press*, 24 January 2011.

56 Bruce Ansley, 'Change of Heart', *New Zealand Listener*, 18 November 2006.

57 Bruce Brown, 'New Zealand in the World Economy: Trade Negotiations and Diversification', in *New Zealand in World Affairs III 1972–1990*, ed. Bruce Brown (Wellington: Victoria University Press, 1993), 44.

58 Quoted in Spoonley, *The Politics of Nostalgia*, 87.
59 Van Beynen, 'Zap's top three now key Canty figures'.
60 Ibid.
61 'Zap house is out of this world', *New Zealand Herald*, 14 January 1982.
62 Ibid.
63 'Facing the critics' and 'Quantum leap or cult control', *Sunday Star-Times*, 11 April 1999.

Chapter 11. Witchcraft and neopaganism

1 See, for example, Alison M. Hight, '"What are ye, little mannie?" The Persistence of Fairy Culture in Scotland, 1572–1703 and 1811–1927' (MA thesis, Virginia Polytechnic Institute and State University, 2014).
2 William Inge, *Faith and Its Psychology* (New York: Charles Schribner's Sons, 1910), 44.
3 Thomas Waters, *Cursed Britain: A History of Witchcraft and Black Magic in Modern Times* (New Haven and London: Yale University Press, 2019), 9–18.
4 'Superstition of the Nineteenth Century', *Wellington Independent*, 26 December 1863.
5 *London Standard*, 9 June 1838; *Nairnshire Telegraph and General Advertiser*, 22 September 1858; James Augustus St. John, *The Education of the People* (London: Chapman and Hall, 1970), 29.
6 Waters, *Cursed Britain*, 78.
7 Ibid., 188.
8 Although there is anecdotal evidence for this in New Zealand, it is better documented in the Australian settler context. See Ian J. Evans, 'Touching Magic: Deliberately Concealed Objects in old Australian Houses and Buildings' (PhD thesis, University of Newcastle, NSW, 2010); *Seeking Ritual in Strange Places: Dead Cats, Old Shoes, and Ragged Clothing. Discovering Concealed Magic in the Antipodes* (Mullumbimby: self-published pamphlet, 2015); Susan Arthure and Cherrie de Leiuen, 'A Context for Concealment: The Historical Archaeology of Folk Ritual and Superstition in Australia', *International Journal of Historical Archaeology* 20, no. 1 (March 2016): 45–72.
9 James Bertram (ed.), *The New Zealand Letters of Thomas Arnold the Younger, with Further Letters from Van Diemen's Land and Letters of Arthur Hugh Clough 1847–1851* (Wellington: Wright and Carmen, 1966), 63–64.
10 'Police Court — This Day', *Auckland Star*, 19 January 1878.
11 Michael King, *The Penguin History of New Zealand* (Auckland: Penguin, 2003), Chapter 12, especially p. 193; Charles Terry, *New Zealand, its Advantages and Prospects as a British Colony: With a Full Account of the Land Claims, Sales of Crown Lands, Aborigines etc.* (London: T&W Boone, 1842), 172, 178–79; Elsdon Best, 'Maori Magic: Notes upon Witchcraft, Magic Rites, and Various Superstitions as Practised or Believed in by the Old-Time Maori', *Transactions and Proceedings of the Royal Society of New Zealand* 34 (1901): 69–98; W. H. Goldie, 'Maori Medical Lore: Notes on the Causes of Disease and Treatment of the Sick among the Maori People of New Zealand, as Believed and Practised in Former Times, Together with Some Account of Various Ancient Rites Connected with the Same', *Transactions and Proceedings of the Royal Society of New Zealand* 37 (1904): 1–120, at 3–4, 22, 31–45; D. E. Hanham, 'The Impact of Introduced Diseases in the Pre-Treaty Period: 1790–1840' (MA thesis, University of Canterbury, 2003), 13, 79–90; Lachy Paterson, 'Government, Church and Māori Responses to Mākutu (Sorcery) in New Zealand in the Nineteenth and Early Twentieth Centuries', *Cultural and Social History* 8 (2011): 175–94, at 177; Waters, *Cursed Britain*, 165–68.
12 Lawrence M. Rogers (ed.), *The Early Journals of Henry Williams* (Christchurch: Pegasus Press, 1961), 248, 261, 430.

13 Paterson, 'Government, Church and Māori Responses to Mākutu', 175; Vincent O'Malley, 'English Law and the Māori Response: A Case Study from the Runanga System in Northland, 1861–65', *Journal of the Polynesian Society* 116 (2007): 7–33, at 8–9; *New Zealand Herald*, 16 November 1877; Waters, *Cursed Britain*, op cit.
14 Rev. Thomas Buddle, *The Aborigines of New Zealand, Two Lectures* (Auckland: Williamson and Wilson, 1851), 28.
15 Paterson, 'Government, Church and Māori Responses to Mākutu', 186–88; Waters, *Cursed Britain*.
16 Malcom Voyce, 'Māori Healers in New Zealand: The Tohunga Suppression Act of 1907', *Oceania* 60 (1989): 99–123, at 103; Waters, *Cursed Britain*, op cit.
17 Derek A. Dow, '"Pruned of Its Dangers": The Tohunga Suppression Act 1907', *Health and History* 3 (2001): 41–64; Voyce, 'Māori Healers in New Zealand', 101; 'Revival of Tohungaism', *New Zealand Herald*, 20 September 1905; Waters, *Cursed Britain*, op cit.
18 Paterson, 'Government, Church and Māori Responses to Mākutu', 186; Waters, *Cursed Britain*, op cit.
19 'A White Tohunga', *Rangitikei Advocate and Manawatu Argus*, 11 October 1917; 'The Leader in Trouble', *Northern Advocate*, 11 October 1917.
20 'Tohungaism Discovered', *Thames Star*, 28 July 1914.
21 James Cowan, *The Adventures of Kimble Bent: A Story of Wild Life in the New Zealand Bush* (London, Melbourne and Christchurch: Whitcombe & Tombs, 1911), 327–29.
22 Anon. [Frederick Maning], *Old New Zealand, A Tale of the Good Old Times; and a History of the War in the North Against the Chief Heke, in the Year 1845. By a Pakeha Maori* (London: Bentley, 1876), 111.
23 Letter from the Rev. Thomas Kendall to the Rev. J. Eyre of Paramatta, 27 December 1822, in *New Zealand Notables Series Three*, Randal M. Burdon (Christchurch: Caxton Press, 1950), 49.
24 John Elder (ed.), *The Letters and Journals of Samuel Marsden* (Dunedin: Coulls Somerville Wilkie and A.H. Reed for the Otago University Council, 1932), 351.
25 'Waikato Past and Present', *Otago Witness*, 6 November 1901.
26 'Local gossip', *New Zealand Herald*, 12 January 1924; 'Superstitious settlers: "Makutus" in the North', *New Zealand Herald*, 7 January 1924; 'Abandoned farms', *New Zealand Herald*, 22 January 1924; Waters, *Cursed Britain*, op cit.
27 'Superstitious settlers'.
28 'Ideal motor road', *New Zealand Herald*, 24 April 1925.
29 'Local gossip', *New Zealand Herald*, 24 August 1929.
30 Johannes C. Andersen, 'Maori Words Incorporated into the English Language', *Journal of the Polynesian Society* 55 (1946): 141–62, at 141, 153.
31 'Taniwha halts work on highway', *New Zealand Herald*, 4 November 2002.
32 'Scottish fish farm rejected — after campaigners warn fishermen could be lured to their deaths by fairies', *The Scotsman*, 23 January 2020.
33 See Joseph S. Te Rito, 'Struggles to Protect Puketapu, a Sacred Hill in Aotearoa' (165–77), and Mere Roberts, 'Genealogy of the Sacred: Maori Beliefs Concerning Lizards' (249–64), both in *Sacred Species and Sites: Advances in Biocultural Conservation*, eds Gloria Pungetti, Gonzalo Oviedo and Della Hooke (Cambridge, UK: Cambridge University Press, 2012).
34 'The Waikato alligator story', *Evening Post*, 5 October 1886.
35 'The saurian', *Christchurch Star*, 4 November 1887.
36 See *Auckland Star*, 30 September 1886; 30 October 1886; 9 November 1886; 5 November 1886.
37 'The real story behind the wraith of Waihi', *New Zealand Truth*, 20 October 1927.

38   'Spooks provided the music and the furniture did a jazz', *New Zealand Truth*, 28 November 1929.
39   Pliny the Younger, 'LXXXIII. To Sura', in *Letters, by Pliny the Younger*, ed. Charles W. Eliot, trans. William Melmoth; rev. F. C. T. Bosanquet, *The Harvard Classics 9* (New York: P.F. Collier & Son, 1914).
40   J. M., 'Maori ghost', *Waikato Independent*, 4 April 1941.
41   'Live frogs entombed', *New Zealand Herald*, 12 December 1982.
42   Charles Hoy Fort (1874–1932) was an American journalist and author who made a career of collecting reports of anomalous phenomena from around the world and publishing them in a popular series of books. The terms 'Fortean' and 'Forteana' have come to refer to such phenomena, although one can't help but detect a sublimated tone of satirical scepticism in his writing.
43   Jerome Clark, *Unexplained! Strange Sightings, Incredible Occurrences, and Puzzling Physical Phenomena*, 3rd ed. (Detroit: Visible Ink Press, 1993), 257.
44   Nile Green, 'The Global Occult: An Introduction', *History of Religions* 54, no. 4 (May 2015): 383–93, at 383; cf. Michael Dodson and Brian Hatcher (eds), *Trans-Colonial Modernities in South Asia* (London: Routledge, 2012); Kris Manjapra and Sugata Bose (eds), *Cosmopolitan Thought Zones: South Asia and the Global Circulation of Ideas* (London: Palgrave, 2010).
45   James Cowan, 'An Isle of Ghosts', *Otago Daily Times*, 3 June 1913.
46   James Cowan, 'Land of the Kauri: Scenes and Stories in the North Country', *New Zealand Railways Magazine* 6, no. 5 (November 1931): 26–28, at 27–28.
47   See Michael Dunn, 'Frozen Flame & Slain Tree: The Dead Tree Theme in New Zealand Art of the Thirties and Forties', *Art New Zealand* 13 (Spring 1979): 40–45.
48   *New Zealand Official Yearbook 1899*, www3.stats.govt.nz/New_Zealand_Official_Yearbooks/1899/NZOYB_1899.html#idsect1_1_11276
49   'Witches in England', *Evening Post*, 28 December 1927; 'Witches in England', *Otago Daily Times*, 6 January 1928; 'Gypsy's witchcraft', *Manawatu Standard*, 3 January 1928.
50   'Witches spells evidence of fears', *Poverty Bay Herald*, 27 May 1935.
51   'Witchcraft, a lamentable superstition', *Otago Daily Times*, 25 October 1930.
52   Constant Reader, 'Airships and Broomsticks', *Otago Daily Times*, 11 September 1909.
53   Oliver Madox Heuffer, *The Book of Witches* (Skowhegan: Kellscraft Studio, 2016), passim.
54   For a detailed discussion, see Jill Trevelyan, *Rita Angus: An Artist's Life* (Wellington: Te Papa Press, 2008), Chapter 9.
55   'Rita Angus', *Year Book of the Arts in New Zealand* 3 (1947): 68.
56   Ron Brownson, 'Symbolism and the Generation of Meaning in Rita Angus's Painting', in *Rita Angus*, Janet Paul et al. (Wellington: National Art Gallery, 1982), 84.
57   Dick Dodds, *90 Years of History of the Association of Kindred Clubs of N.Z. (Inc) 1926–2016* (Timaru: self-published, 2016).
58   Mike Heaney, 'The Earliest Reference to the Morris Dance?', *Folk Music Journal* 8, no. 2 (2002): 513–15.
59   'Chris B.', 'New Zealand Morris Dancing', https://sites.google.com/site/nzmorrisdancing/history-in-nz
60   Mark Stocker, 'Shurrock, Francis Aubrey', *Dictionary of New Zealand Biography*, 1998. *Te Ara — the Encyclopedia of New Zealand*, https://teara.govt.nz/en/biographies/4s24/shurrock-francis-aubrey
61   See Clare Button, '"A Very Perfect Form of Discipline": Rolf Gardiner, Folk Dance and Occult Landscapes', in *The Occult Imagination in Britain, 1875–1947*, eds Christine Ferguson and Andrew Radford (London and New York: Routledge, 2018), 58–73.
62   Rolf Gardiner, 'Summer Tour in Germany, 1928', *North Sea and Baltic* 4 (1938): 75–76.

63 See Maureen Sharpe, 'Anzac Day in New Zealand: 1916 to 1939', *New Zealand Journal of History* 15, no. 2 (October 1981): 97–114.
64 'The war memorial', *Otago Daily Times*, 22 March 1923.
65 Ronald Hutton, *Blood and Mistletoe: The History of the Druids in Britain* (New Haven: Yale University Press, 2009), 125–32.
66 Ibid., 140–41.
67 M. Mosley, *Illustrated Guide to Christchurch and Neighbourhood* (Christchurch: T. Smith & Co, 1885), 94.
68 Jock Phillips, 'Men's clubs — Friendly societies and other fraternal organisations', *Te Ara — the Encyclopedia of New Zealand*, revised 2018, www.TeAra.govt.nz/en/photograph/31285/grey-lynn-druids-1909
69 Hutton, *Blood and Mistletoe*, 132.
70 www.groveofthesummerstars.nz/about; www.thewoolshedretreats.co.nz
71 https://druidry.org/about-us; Rosemary Guiley, *The Encyclopedia of Witches, Witchcraft and Wicca* (New York: Facts on File, 1989), 111, 410.
72 Margaret Murray, *The Witch-Cult in Western Europe: A Study in Anthropology* (Oxford: Oxford University Press, 1921).
73 In recent years these aspects have been actively deconstructed by some groups because they might exclude LGBTQIA+ practitioners, and also because the idea that women can only fit within the tripartite archetypes of Maiden-Mother-Crone is seen as needlessly restrictive and dependent on patriarchal gender roles.
74 See Aiden Kelly, *Crafting the Art of Magic: A History of Modern Witchcraft, 1939–1964* (Portland: Llewellyn, 1991); Philip Heselton, *Gerald Gardner and the Witchcraft Revival: The Significance of His Life and Works to the Story of Modern Witchcraft* (Taunton: Capall Bann Publishing, 2001).
75 Vivianne Crowely, 'Wicca as Nature Religion', in *Nature Religion Today: Paganism in the Modern World*, eds Joanne Pearson, Richard H. Roberts and Geoffrey Samuel (Edinburgh: Edinburgh University Press, 1998), 171.
76 'Witch's P.R.O.', *Sunday Telegraph*, 3 May 1964; Alan Spraggett, 'Mrs Bone, the Witch', *The Robesonian* (Lumberton, NC), 2 March 1975.
77 Julia Phillips, 'History of Wicca in England, 1939–Present Day', talk given at the Australian Wiccan Conference, Canberra, 1991.
78 www.oakgrove.nz/about-us.php
79 Diana has long been considered a goddess of witchcraft. See Carlo Ginzburg, *Ecstasies: Deciphering the Witches' Sabbath* (Chicago: University of Chicago Press, 2004), 90.
80 Kathryn Rountree, *Embracing the Witch and the Goddess: Feminist Ritual Makers in New Zealand* (Abingdon: Routledge, 2004), 7.
81 Kathryn Rountree, 'Spirituality and the Essentialism Debate', *Social Analysis: The International Journal of Anthropology* 43, no. 2 (1999): 138–65, at 142–43.
82 Ibid., 145.
83 Bron Taylor, 'Bioregionalism: An Ethics of Loyalty to Place', *Landscape Journal* 19, no. 1/2 (2000): 50–72.
84 See Juliet Batten, *Celebrating the Southern Seasons: Rituals for Aotearoa* (Auckland: Tandem, 1995).
85 Kathryn Rountree, *Embracing the Witch and the Goddess: Feminist Ritual-makers in New Zealand* (London and New York: Routledge, 2004), 151, cited in Paul Morris, 'Diverse religions — Recent and new-age religious movements', *Te Ara — the Encyclopedia of New Zealand*, published 2011.
86 Pete Jennings, *Pagan Paths: A Guide to Wicca, Druidry, Asatru, Shamanism and Other*

Pagan Practices (New York: Random House, 2002), 53–54; Andy Norfolk, 'Out of the Shadows: George Pickingill', *The Witchtower* (December 2008/January 2009): 6–7; Bill Liddell, *The Pickingill Papers: The Origin of the Gardnerian Craft* (Milverton: Capall Bann, 1994), passim.

87 Lauren Bernauer, 'Modern Germanic Heathenry and the Radical Traditionalists', in *Through a Glass Darkly: Reflections on the Sacred*, ed. Frances Di Lauro (Sydney: Sydney University Press, 2006), 265–74; Jenny Blain and Robert J. Wallis, 'Representing Spirit: Heathenry, New-Indigenes and the Imaged Past', in *Images, Representations and Heritage: Moving Beyond Modern Approaches to Archaeology*, ed. Ian Russell (Berlin: Springer, 2006), 89–108.

88 See Nitzan Lebovic, *The Philosophy of Life and Death: Ludwig Klages and the Rise of a Nazi Biopolitics* (London: Palgrave Macmillan, 2013).

89 See Julia Zernack, 'Nordische Mythen in der deutschen Literatur. Eddaspuren bei George und Wolfskehl', in *Intermedialität und Kulturaustausch: Beobachtungen im Spannungsfeld von Künsten und Medien*, ed. Annette Simonis (Bielefeld: transcript Verlag, 2009); Robert E. Norton, *Secret Germany: Stefan George and His Circle* (Ithaca, NY: Cornell University Press, 2002).

90 Karl Wolfskehl, *An die Deutschen / To the Germans* (chapbook), ed. and trans. Andrew Paul Wood and Friedrich Voit (Lyttelton: Cold Hub Press, 2013); Andrew Paul Wood and Friedrich Voit (ed. and trans.), *Karl Wolfskehl — Three Worlds / Drei Welten* (Lyttelton: Cold Hub Press, 2016); Friedrich Voit, *Karl Wolfskehl: A Poet in Exile* (Lyttelton: Cold Hub Press, 2019).

91 See Carl Jung, 'Wotan', *Neue Schweizer Rundschau* (March 1936).

92 Carrie B. Dohe, 'Wotan and the "Archetypal Ergriffenheit": Mystical Union, National Spiritual Rebirth and Culture-creating Capacity in C. G. Jung's "Wotan" Essay', *History of European Ideas* 37 (2011): 344–56, at 349 and n.64.

93 'Whites only for the Church of Odin', *Star Weekender*, 7 November 1981.

94 See Kathleen Harvill-Burton, *Le nazisme comme religion. Quatre théologiens déchiffrent le code religieux nazi (1932–1945)* (Québec: Les Presses de l'Université Laval, 2006); Richard Steigmann-Gall, *The Holy Reich: Nazi Conceptions of Christianity* (Cambridge, UK: Cambridge University Press, 2003).

95 A. Asbjørn Jøn, '"Skeggǫld, Skálmǫld; Vindǫld, Vergǫld": Alexander Rud Mills and the Ásatrú Faith in the New Age', *Australian Religion Studies Review* 12, no. 1 (1999): 77–83.

96 Matthias Gardell, *Gods of the Blood: The Pagan Revival and White Separatism* (Durham and London: Duke University Press, 2003), 165.

97 The *Æsir* being the primary Norse pantheon of gods, in contrast with the secondary pantheon of the *Vanir*.

98 Sigurdur A. Magnússon, *The Icelanders* (Reykjavik: Forskot, 1990), 198; 'Saga félagsins' (The History of the Fellowship), https://asatru.is/saga-felagsins

99 See Betty A. Dobratz and Stephanie L. Shanks-Meile, *The White Separatist Movement in the United States: 'White Power, White Pride!'* (Baltimore: Johns Hopkins University Press, 2000); Matthias Gardell, *Gods of the Blood: The Pagan Revival and White Separatism* (Durham and London: Duke University Press, 2003); Jeffrey Kaplan, 'The Reconstruction of the Ásatrú and Odinist Traditions', in *Magical Religion and Modern Witchcraft*, ed. James R. Lewis (New York: State University of New York, 1996), 193–236; Stephen McNallen, 'Three Decades of the Ásatrú Revival in America', in *Tyr: Myth, Culture, Tradition*, Vol. 2, eds Joshua Buckley and Michael Moynihan (Atlanta: Ultra, 2004), 203–19.

100 Jeffrey Kaplan, 'Else Christensen', in *Encyclopedia of White Power: A Sourcebook on the Radical Racist Right* (Lanham: AltaMira Press, 2000), 48; Gardell, *Gods of the Blood*, 176.

101 Fensalir ('fen hall') is, according to the thirteenth-century *Poetic Edda*, the dwelling place of Frigg, the wife of Odin and goddess of fertility and marriage.
102 Andrea Vance, 'NZ group committed to "the survival and welfare of the Ethnic European Folk as a cultural and biological group" ', *Stuff*, 30 March 2019, www.stuff.co.nz/national/christchurch-shooting/111537465/group-interested-survival-ethnic-european-folk; New Zealand Media Council, case 2777, www.mediacouncil.org.nz/rulings/cameron-mottus-and-others-against-stuff
103 Tharik Hussain, 'Why did Vikings have "Allah" embroidered into funeral clothes?', *BBC News*, 12 October 2017, www.bbc.com/news/world-europe-41567391

Chapter 12. The Rosy Cross and the OTO

1 Marsilio Ficino (1433–1499) was one of the most influential humanists and philosophers of the Italian Renaissance. Much of his writing was devoted to attempting to harmonise astrology, Hermeticism and neo-Platonism with Christian theology for the Medici. Another area of his interest was to bring Jewish writings on the Kabbalah into line with Christian beliefs.
2 Susanna Åkerman, 'Three phases of inventing Rosicrucian tradition in the seventeenth century', in *The Invention of Sacred Tradition*, eds James Lewis and Olav Hammer (Cambridge: Cambridge University Press. 2007), 158–76.
3 Hereward Tilton, 'Rosicrucianism (introduction)', in *The Cambridge Handbook of Western Mysticism and Esotericism*, ed. Glenn Alexander Magee (Cambridge: Cambridge University Press, 2016), 171–83.
4 Francis X. King, *Modern Ritual Magic: The Rise of Western Occultism*, 2nd ed. (Toronto: Prism, 1989), 28; Gordon J. Melton, *Encyclopedia of American Religions: A Comprehensive Study of the Major Religious Groups in the United States* (New York: Triumph Books, 1991), 179; Christopher McIntosh, *The Rosicrucians: The History, Mythology, and Rituals of an Esoteric Order* (York Beach: S. Weisser, 1997), 109; 'Robert Wentworth Little', Grand Lodge of British Columbia and Yukon, http://freemasonry.bcy.ca/biography/esoterica/little_r/little_r.html; Societas Rosicruciana in Anglia, https://sria.uk.com; H. Spencer Lewis, *Complete History of the Rosicrucian Order* (San Diego: Book Tree, 2006), 131.
5 Patrick Bentham, *The Avalonians* (Glastonbury: Gothic Image, 1993), 102. It is not entirely clear how Felkin came into contact with and adopted the Baha'i faith. Stella Matutina member Neville Gauntlett Tudor Meakin (c.1876–1912) was a Baha'i and had known Felkin since 1909. Abdu'l-Bahá, head of the Baha'i from 1892 to 1921, visited the United Kingdom in 1911, a visit Meakin appears to have facilitated. Felkin met Abdu'l-Bahá on this visit at the home of Lady Blomfield and was given two rings. The primary contact between Stella Matutina and Baha'i seems to have been Wellesley Tudor Pole (1884–1968), who had encountered the Baha'i in Constantinople in 1908.
6 Robert Felkin, 'The Rosicrucian Society in Europe: A Lecture given to the Study Group', General Assembly of the Metropolitan College of the SRIA, London, 14 February 1916.
7 Bentham, *The Avalonians*, 101.
8 Lil Osborn, 'The extraordinary life and work of Robert Felkin — Baha'i Mage' (2012), 6–7, https://bahai-library.com/pdf/o/osborn_life_robert_felkin.pdf
9 In 1885, the English physician, mystic and Avalonian John Goodchild (1851–1914) purchased a blue bowl while in Italy and 10 years later, compelled by a vision, buried it near the famous well at Glastonbury, where it was found by Pole and his Spiritualist circle in 1908. Steve Blamires, *The Little Book of the Great Enchantment* (Cheltenham: Skylight Press, 2013), 195; Gerry Fenge, *The Two Worlds of Wellesley Tudor Pole* (Sedona: Lorian Association, 2010), 8–14.

10 Osborn, 'The extraordinary life and work of Robert Felkin', 8.
11 www.mastermason.com/felkincollege/Contents%20%20d3-3.htm
12 The Martinists are an order of mystical esoteric Christianity that emerged from the eighteenth-century Rose+Croix group, with the mission of transcending the fall of humanity and reuniting it with the divine. See Bernd-Ulrich Hergemöller, *Mann für Mann: biographisches Lexikon zur Geschichte von Freundesliebe und mannmännlicher Sexualität im deutschen Sprachraum* (Hamburg: MännerschwarmSkript-Verlag, 1998), 911; T. Apiryon, 'Doctor (Albert Karl) Theodor Reuss, 33° 90° 96° X°', https://hermetic.com/sabazius/reuss; 'Theodor Reuss', *The Free Encyclopedia of Thelema*, https://web.archive.org/web/20071229121329/http://fet.egnu.org/wiki/Theodor_Reuss; Ellic Howe, 'Theodor Reuss: Irregular Freemasonry in Germany, 1900–23', in *Ars Quatuor Coronati* (February 1978), www.freemasonry.bcy.ca/aqc/reuss/reuss.html; Peter-Robert König; *Das OTO-Phänomen. 100 Jahre magische Geheimbünde und ihre Protagonisten von 1895–1994. Ein historisches Aufklärungswerk* (Munich: ARW, 1994); Helmut Möller and Ellic Howe, *Merlin Peregrinus, vom Untergrund des Abendlandes* (Würzburg: Königshausen & Neumann, 1986).
13 Richard Kaczynski, 'Carl Kellner's Esoteric Roots: Sex and Sex Magick in the Victorian Age', *Beauty and Strength: Proceedings of the Sixth Biennial National Ordo Templi Orientis Conference*, Salem (MA), 10–12 August 2007 (Riverside, CA: United States Grand Lodge, Ordo Templi Orientis, 2009); Josef Dvorak, 'Carl Kellner', *Flensburger Hefte* 63 (December 1998); Neil Powell, *Alchemy, the Ancient Science* (London: Aldus Books, 1976), 127.
14 Theodor Reuss, *Das Aufbau-Programm die Leitsätze der Gnosticschen Neo-Christian OTO* (Munich: Oriflamme, 1920).
15 Aleister Crowley, *The Confessions of Aleister Crowley* (London and Boston: Routledge and Kegan Paul, 1979 [1929]), Chapter 73.
16 Francis King, *The Magical World of Aleister Crowley* (New York: Coward, McCann & Geoghegan, 1978), 78–81.
17 Crowley, *The Confessions*, Chapter 73.
18 'IAO' is a traditional Gnostic transliteration of the Hebrew Tetragrammaton ✡✡✡✡, whence we derive both Jehovah and Yaweh, and hints at the Gnostic name of the Demiurge Yaldabaoth. Compare the Crowley formulation of IAO — Isis, Apophis, Osiris — with the Masonic JOB — 'Jehovah, Osiris, Baal'.
19 Likely some roundabout corruption of Mohammed.
20 For the full ceremony and various glosses on its meaning, see Aleister Crowley, *Liber XV: Ecclesiae Gnosticae Catholicae Canon Missae* (Berkeley: Horus Temple Edition/Thelema Lodge, OTO, n.d.); and the special 'Mysteries of the Gnostic Mass' issue of *The Journal of Thelemic Studies* 3, no. 1 (2015).
21 'Merlin Peregrinus' [Theodor Reuss]; *I.N.R.I., O.T.O., Ecclesiae Gnosticae Catholicae, Canon Missae, Die Gnostische Messe* (Munich: privately printed, 1918).
22 See Francis King, *The Secret Rituals of the O.T.O.* (Newburyport: Samuel Weiser, 1973); Richard Kaczynski, *Panic in Detroit: The Magician and the Motor City*, revised and expanded Blue Equinox Centennial Edition (Ellicott City: independently published, 2019); Martin P. Starr, 'Aleister Crowley—Freemason?!', in *Aleister Crowley and the Western Esoteric Tradition*, eds Henrik Bogdan and Martin P. Starr (Oxford: Oxford University Press, 2012), 227–40.
23 Kaczynski, 'Carl Kellner's Esoteric Roots', 332.
24 Peter-Robert Koenig, 'Kenneth Grant and the Typhonian Ordo Templi Orientis', in *The Ordo Templi Orientis Phenomenon*, ed. and annotated James M. Martin (1991), www.parareligion.ch/k_grant.htm
25 The irony is surely not lost on the reader that the supposedly ancient 'Wiccan Rede' of

'Do as thou wilt though harm it none' is a rather prissy plagiarism of Crowley's 'Do as thou wilt be the whole of the law'.

26   Rodney Orpheus, 'Gerald Gardner & Ordo Templi Orientis', *Pentacle Magazine* 30 (2009): 14–18.
27   Peter Koenig, 'All We Want Is a "Caliph"', *The Ordo Templi Orientis Phenomenon*, www.parareligion.ch/minutes/minutes.htm
28   This influence on Browning can be seen in his early works, such as the esoteric elements in his book-length epic poem *Paracelsus* (1835) and the neoplatonic and Hermetic themes in his 'Saul' (1845–1855). See Paula Alexandra Guimarães, 'Esoteric Victorians: The Hermetic and the Arcane in the Poetry of Browning, Rossetti and Swinburne', *O Imaginário Esotérico. Literatura, Cinema, Banda Desenhada*, org. C. Álvares et al. (Coleção Hespérides, Literatura 35, Edição do Centro de Estudos Humanísticos da Universidade do Minho e Húmus), 189–203.
29   Paul V. Young, 'A Link in the Golden Chain: The Life & Times of Vyvyan Deacon, Australia's Pioneer Metaphysical Teacher', *New Dawn* 161 (March–April 2017), www.newdawnmagazine.com/articles/a-link-in-the-golden-chain-the-life-times-of-vyvyan-deacon-australias-pioneer-metaphysical-teacher
30   Norman Lindsay (1879–1969) was one of the most prolific and popular Australian artists of the mid-twentieth century, notable for canvases rejecting modernism and populating the Australian landscape with voluptuous nudes, and for his generally anti-Christian, libertine sentiments. His public popularity came mainly through his cartoons published in the Australian *Bulletin* magazine and for writing and illustrating the children's novel *The Magic Pudding* (1918). In the loosely biographical movie *Sirens* (1994) he was played by New Zealand actor Sam Neill.
31   Young, 'A Link in the Golden Chain'.
32   Keith Richmond, *Progradior and the Beast: Frank Bennett & Aleister Crowley* (Geelong: Neptune Press, 2004), 118.
33   Vivienne Browning, *The Uncommon Medium* (London: Skoob Books Publishing, 1993), 77.
34   Aleister Crowley to Frank Bennett, 23 February 1923, cited in Keith Richmond, *The Progradior Correspondence, Letters by Aleister Crowley, C. S. Jones, & Others* (Cape Neddick: Titian Press/Weiser Antiquarian Books, 2009), 98.
35   Gregory Tillett, 'Ordo Templi Orientis: Self-Definition of an Australian Version, A.O.T.O, A Statement Regarding the History of the Ordo Templi Orientis in Australia', www.parareligion.ch/dplanet/html/oto_au.htm
36   Young, 'A Link in the Golden Chain'.
37   'Soror Egeria', 'New Zealand: Land of Contrast', https://oceanialodgeoto.wordpress.com/part-two-new-zealand
38   The Typhonian Order, previously known as the Typhonian Ordo Templi Orientis (TOTO), is a self-initiatory Thelemic sex-magickal Luciferian left-hand path organisation based in the United Kingdom. It was originally led by British occultist Kenneth Grant (1924–2011) and his partner Steffi Grant, and is now believed to be led by Michael Staley.
39   'Soror Egeria', 'New Zealand: Land of Contrast', https://oceanialodgeoto.wordpress.com/part-two-new-zealand
40   'Soror Egeria', 'Kephra Abbey 1983', https://oceanialodgeoto.wordpress.com/kephra-abbey
41   Christian Rebisse, *Rosicrucian History and Mysteries* (San Jose: Rosicrucian Order, AMORC, 2015), 161–63.
42   H. Spencer Lewis, *Rosicrucian Principles for Home and Business* (San Jose: Rosicrucian Order, AMORC, 1953), 15.
43   E. Dale Odam, untitled review of Keith L. Bryant Jr, *Arthur F. Stilwell: Promoter with a*

Hunch (Nashville: Vanderbilt University Press, 1971); *The Business History Review* 46, no. 2 (Summer 1972): 248.
44   Erik Davis, *The Visionary State: A Journey Through California's Spiritual Landscape* (San Francisco: Chronicle Books, 2006), 112.
45   Raquel Tibol, 'Apareció la serpiente: Diego Rivera y los rosacruces', *Proceso* 701 (9 April 1990): 50–53; Diego Rivera, *Arte y política* (Mexico City: Grijalbo, 1979), 354.
46   Incomplete runs held by the Alexander Turnbull Library, Wellington.
47   *Evening Post*, 13 January 1940.
48   Antoine Faivre, 'Courants ésotériques et le rapport. Les exemples de Nouvelle Acropole et de la Rose-Croix d'Or (Lectorium Rosicrucianum)', *Annuaires de l'École pratique des hautes études* 104 (1995): 427–37; Antonin Gadal, *Der Triumph der Universellen Gnosis* (Amsterdam: In de Pelikaan, 2006), 46; Jean-Pierre Chantin, *Dictionnaire du monde religieux dans la France contemporaine: 'Sectes', dissidences, ésotérisme* (Paris: Editions Beauchesne, 2001), 103.
49   Linda Edwards, *A Brief Guide to Beliefs: Ideas, Theologies, Mysteries, and Movements* (Westminster: John Knox Press, 2001), 454.
50   Jan van Rijckenborgh, *The Chinese Gnosis* (Haarlem: Rozekruis Pers, 1996); *Dei Gloria Intacta* (Haarlem: Rozekruis Pers, 1962); *The Elementary Philosophy of the Modern Rosycross*, 3rd ed. (Haarlem: Rosycross Press, 1986); Jan van Rijckenborgh and Catharose de Petri, *The Universal Gnosis* (Haarlem: Rosycross Press, 1980); Jan van Rijckenborgh and Catharose de Petri, *The New Caduceus* (Haarlem: Rozekruis Pers, 1999).
51   Harald Lamprecht, *Neue Rosenkreuzer: Ein Handbuch* (Göttingen: Vandenhoeck & Ruprecht, 2004), 350.
52   Faivre, 'Courants ésotériques et le rapport', 247.
53   Robert S. Ellwood, *Islands of the Dawn: The Story of Alternative Spirituality in New Zealand* (Honolulu: University of Hawai'i Press, 1993), 226.

Chapter 13. The Devil rides out
1   Qur'an, 36.60.
2   See Eugen Weber, *Satan franc-maçon: La mystification de Léo Taxil* (Paris: René Julliard, 1964).
3   Multiple reports, *New Zealand Tablet*, 1882–97.
4   Young Richard Kim, *Epiphanius of Cyprus: Imagining an Orthodox World* (Ann Arbor: University of Michigan Press, 2015), 37–39; Wouter Hanegraaff and Jeffrey Kripal, *Hidden Intercourse: Eros and Sexuality in the History of Western Esotericism* (New York: Fordham University Press, 2011), 11–12.
5   See Elliot Rose, *A Razor for a Goat: A Discussion of Certain Problems in the History of Witchcraft and Diabolism* (Toronto: University of Toronto Press, 1962).
6   François Ravaisson Mollien, *Archives de la Bastille*, vols IV, V, VI, VII (Paris: G. Perdone-Lauriel, 1866–1884); for a complete history, see H. T. F. Rhodes' popular-market but highly readable *The Satanic Mass* (London: Rider & Company, 1954).
7   See Stephen Flowers, *Lords of the Left Hand Path: A History of Spiritual Dissent* (Smithville: Rûna-Raven Press, 1997); Don Webb and Stephen Flowers, *Uncle Setnakt's Essential Guide to the Left Hand Path* (Smithville: Rûna-Raven Press, 1999); Richard Sutcliffe, 'Left-Hand Path Ritual Magick: An Historical and Philosophical Overview', in *Paganism Today: Wiccans, Druids, the Goddess and Ancient Earth Traditions for the Twenty-First Century*, eds Graham Harvey and Charlotte Hardman (London: Thorsons/HarperCollins, 1996), 109–37.
8   Rachel Barrowman, 'Desmond, Arthur', *Dictionary of New Zealand Biography*, first

published in 1993, *Te Ara — the Encyclopedia of New Zealand*, https://teara.govt.nz/en/biographies/2d9/desmond-arthur; Chris Cunneen, 'Desmond, Arthur (c. 1859–1929)', *Australian Dictionary of Biography*, National Centre of Biography, Australian National University, published first in hardcopy 1981, https://adb.anu.edu.au/biography/desmond-arthur-5963/text10175; 'The Hawke's Bay Election', *Hawke's Bay Herald*, 16–19 July 1884; Ragnar Redbeard (Arthur Desmond), *Might Is Right; or, The Survival of the Fittest* (London: W.J. Robins, 1910).

9 Joe Abrams and Kelly Wyman, 'Modern Satanism', 'Satanism: An Introduction', The Religious Movements Homepage Project, University of Virginia, https://web.archive.org/web/20060829152745/http://religiousmovements.lib.virginia.edu/nrms/satanism/intro.html#atheistic/theistic

10 Nick Redfern, 'Order of Nine Angles', *Secret Societies: The Complete Guide to Histories, Rites, and Rituals* (Canton: Visible Ink Press, 2017), 227–28.

11 Graham Harvey, 'Satanism in Britain Today', *Journal of Contemporary Religion* 10, no. 3 (1995): 283–96, at 293.

12 Jeffrey Kaplan, 'Order of Nine Angles', in *Encyclopedia of White Power: A Sourcebook on the Radical Racist Right* (Lanham: AltaMira Press, 2000), 235–38; Jacob C. Senholt, 'The Sinister Tradition: Political Esotericism and the Convergence of Radical Islam, Satanism, and National Socialism in the Order of the Nine Angles', paper presented at the *Satanism in the Modern World* conference, Trondheim, 19–20 November 2009.

13 Anonymous, 'Getting Beyond Ritual Abuse: Thoughts for Counsellors and Clients from a Survivor', *Broadsheet* (Autumn 1994): 44–45.

14 'Christchurch, New Zealand Ritual Abuse Cases', www.religioustolerance.org/ra_newze.htm

15 See Sylvia Jean Pack, 'New Zealand Counsellors Talk About Ritual Abuse: A Discourse Analysis' (MA thesis, Massey University, Palmerston North, 2009).

16 Ross Francis, 'New Evidence in Peter Ellis Case', *New Zealand Law Journal* (November 2007): 399–444.

17 Lynley Hood, *A City Possessed: The Christchurch Civic Crèche Case* (Dunedin: Longacre Press, 2001).

18 Francis, 'New Evidence in Peter Ellis Case'; David McLoughlan, 'Second Thoughts on the Christchurch Creche Case: Has Justice Failed Peter Ellis', *North & South*, August 1996, 54–69.

19 McLoughlan, 'Second Thoughts'.

20 Ontario Consultants for Religious Tolerance, www.religioustolerance.org/satanism.htm

21 John Latham, 'The Darker Side of the Moon: Satanic Traditions in New Zealand as Magick Systems' (MA thesis, Victoria University of Wellington, 2001), 8–13.

22 This is hardly surprising. Dunedin Lawyer and politician William Larnach (1833–1898), builder of the famous castle on Otago Peninsula, had an unhappy end, a tragic, dysfunctional family, and committed suicide. Allegedly he still haunts the Parliamentary Library in Wellington. His tomb is a delightful gothic chapel designed by R. A. Lawson, after the spire of Dunedin's First Church, lending itself to such things. An editorial in the *Otago Daily Times* from 18 January 1972 describes a Black Mass being held there 20 years earlier, and all manner of nefarious parties and vandalisms have occurred there since the 1950s. The legend that Larnach's skull was stolen from there in 1972 and never recovered doesn't hurt either. Charmian Smith, 'Laying Larnach to rest', *Otago Daily Times*, 8 July 2009.

23 Margaret 'Maggie' Burke (1849–1871) was the Irish maid of Canterbury runholder and member of the New Zealand Legislative Council William 'Ready Money' Robinson (1814–1889), and was brutally murdered by Robinson's butler Simon Cedeno. Robinson had her buried in the Barbadoes Street Cemetery with a headstone of Halswell Quarry

sandstone. When wet, iron impurities in the stone would give the impression of mysterious bloodstains. This attracted an unsavoury element, and the headstone was eventually vandalised in 1962 and removed by Christchurch City Council.

24 Witch Hill or Te Upoko o Kurī likely gained this reputation because of its settler name, which seems to derive from the area being regarded as tapu by Ngāi Tahu, and its resemblance, as author James Cowan (1870–1943) put it, to 'a fanciful fairy fort' (https://nzhistory.govt.nz/keyword/witch-hill). The war memorial placed there in 1917 does look like some kind of rustic altar. Legend states that the Māori explorer and chief Tamatea and his companions were caught in a freezing storm on the hill. Tamatea called out a karakia asking for fire from the North Island's volcanoes, which was duly delivered (https://my.christchurchcitylibraries.com/ti-kouka-whenua/te-upoko-o-kuri). In 1883 two young boys were caught in a similar change in the weather and died, further adding to the legend of the place.

25 Craig Hayes, 'Sinistrous Diabolus — Total Doom//Desecration', metalbandcamp.com, 3 May 2013, http://metalbandcamp.com/2013/05/sinistrous-diabolus-total-doom-desecration.html

26 Robert S. Ellwood, *Islands of the Dawn: The Story of Alternative Spirituality in New Zealand* (Honolulu: University of Hawai'i Press, 1993), 245.

27 Latham, 'The Darker Side of the Moon', 14.

28 Norman Cohen, *Europe's Inner Demons: The Demonization of Christians in Medieval Christendom* (London: Pimlico, 1993), 78.

29 Lawrence M. Rogers (ed.), *The Early Journals of Henry Williams* (Christchurch: Pegasus Press, 1961), 265.

30 Reverend Ruawai D. Rakena, 'The Maori Response to the Gospel', *Wesley Historical Society (NZ)* 25, no. 1–4 (1971): 20.

31 Sometimes referred to as 'Hauhau' in older texts though this designation is now regarded as offensive.

32 Folder MS-1196, National Library of New Zealand, Wellington.

33 James Belich, *Making Peoples: A History of the New Zealanders* (Auckland: Penguin, 1996), 221.

34 'Mr J.J. Croft's Lecture at Oamaru', *New Zealand Tablet* 7, no. 388 (17 September 1880): 15.

35 Latham, 'The Darker Side of the Moon', 23.

36 W. R. van Leeuwen, 'Dreamers of the Dark: Kerry Bolton and the Order of the Left Hand Path, a Case-study of a Satanic/Neo-Nazi Synthesis' (MA thesis, University of Waikato, 2008), 29–30. This thesis is somewhat controversial and should be taken with caution.

37 K. Thomson, *Satanism in New Zealand: The Shocking Tale of Sinister Conspiracy* (1998); Latham, 'The Darker Side of the Moon', 24.

38 Massimo Introvigne, *The Origins of Contemporary Satanism, 1952–1980* (Leiden: Brill, 2016), 365.

39 Nicholas Goodrick-Clarke, *Black Sun: Aryan Cults, Esoteric Nazism, and the Politics of Identity* (New York: New York University Press, 2002), 226–31; 'Case Number 696 — K. Bolton against the *Dominion*', New Zealand Press Council, July 1998; K. R. Bolton, 'NZ National Front Responds to Anarchist PR' (press release), New Zealand National Front, 10 June 2004; Tony Wall, 'A picture of white supremacy', *Sunday Star-Times*, 9 May 2004; 'Case Number 985 — K.R. Bolton against *Sunday Star-Times*', New Zealand Press Council, August 2004; John McCrone, 'A right muddle', *The Press*, 5 December 2009.

40 Gavin Baddeley and Paul Woods (eds), *Lucifer Rising: A Book of Sin, Devil Worship and Rock 'n' Roll* (Medford: Plexus Publishing, 2000), 221.

41   Roald E. Kristiansen, 'Satan in Cyberspace: A Study of Satanism on the Internet in the 1990s', *Syzygy: Journal of Alternative Religion and Culture* 11 (2002): 23–26.
42   See Raymond Klibansky, Erwin Panofsky and Fritz Saxl, *Saturn and Melancholy: Studies in the History of Natural Philosophy, Religion, and Art* (Montreal: McGill-Queen's University Press, 2009), Part II.
43   Latham, 'The Darker Side of the Moon', 25–26.
44   Introvigne, *The Origins of Contemporary Satanism*, 367.
45   Gilbert Wong, 'Dogma of the dark deities', *New Zealand Herald*, 30 November 1996.
46   Ibid.
47   Ibid.
48   Ibid.
49   Ibid.
50   Thomson, *Satanism in New Zealand*.
51   Wong, 'Dogma of the dark deities'.
52   Latham, 'The Darker Side of the Moon', 24.
53   Wong, 'Dogma of the dark deities'.
54   Susan Teodoro, 'Manawatu "Satanic attack" re-enacted for docu-drama', *Stuff*, 20 August 2015, www.stuff.co.nz/entertainment/tv-radio/71277744/manawatu-satanic-attack-re-enacted-for-docu-drama; 'TV show recalls crime that shocked NZ', *New Zealand Herald*, 9 August 2015; Theresa Garner, 'Disgraced ex-detective found dead', *New Zealand Herald*, 17 October 2003.
55   Latham, 'The Darker Side of the Moon', 29–30.
56   Goodrick-Clarke, *Black Sun*, 226–31.
57   Van Leeuwen, 'Dreamers of the Dark', 33–34.
58   Ibid., 34.
59   Ibid., 34–35.
60   Ibid., 35.
61   Kerry Raymond Bolton, *Phoenix Rising: The Epic Saga of James H. Madole*, rev. ed. (Paraparaumu: Renaissance Press, 2006).
62   See Jeffery DeBoo, 'Nazism, Racism and Satanism', *The Burning Ground* 1, no. 1 (1994).
63   Frank Meyer (1909–1972) was an American philosopher and political activist, a founding editor of the *American National Review*, and a close friend of conservative US intellectual William F. Buckley, Jr. His main contribution to philosophy was his attempt to combine libertarianism with political conservatism into a theory he called 'fusionsim'. Hans-Hermann Hoppe (b.1949) is a libertarian/anarcho-capitalist Austrian School economist, Professor Emeritus of Economics at the University of Nevada, Las Vegas (UNLV), Senior Fellow of the Ludwig von Mises Institute, and a vocal, socially conservative critic of the principles of democracy.
64   George Orwell, 'W. B. Yeats', in *Critical Essays*, George Orwell (London: Secker and Warburg, 1946), 114–19, at 118.
65   David Neiwert, 'What the Kek: Explaining the Alt-Right "Deity" Behind Their "Meme Magic"', Southern Poverty Law Centre, 9 May 2017, www.splcenter.org/hatewatch/2017/05/08/what-kek-explaining-alt-right-deity-behind-their-meme-magic; Warwick's YouTube and BitChute handle is Styxhexenhammer666.
66   Chaos Magic emerged in the United Kingdom in the 1970s from the occult ideas of Austin Osman Spare and applied postmodernism. It is the magical equivalent of the 'prosperity gospel' of the Evangelical churches, labelling itself as results orientated with a cynical, libertarian — or at least anarchistic — undertone, eschewing absolute truths in favour of eclecticism, individualism and a DIY approach. Anything goes.

67 See Christopher Faraone, 'Hermes but No Marrow: Another Look at a Puzzling Magical Spell', *Zeitschrift für Papyrologie und Epigraphik* 72 (1988): 279–86; David Frankfurter, 'Narrating Power: The Theory and Practice of the Magical Historiola in Ritual Spells', in *Ancient Magic and Ritual Power,* eds Marvin Meyer and Paul Mirecki (Leiden: Brill, 1995), 455–76.
68 See Paul Furlong, *The Social and Political Thought of Julius Evola* (London: Routledge, 2011).
69 Franco Ferraresi, *Threats to Democracy: The Radical Right in Italy after the War* (Princeton: Princeton University Press, 2012), 44.
70 Stephen E. Atkins, *The Encyclopedia of Modern Worldwide Extremists and Extremist Groups* (Westport: Greenwood Press, 2002), 89.
71 See Nicholas Goodrick-Clarke, *The Occult Roots of Nazism: Secret Aryan Cults and Their Influence on Nazi Ideology: The Ariosophists of Austria and Germany, 1890–1935* (Wellingborough: Aquarian Press, 1985).
72 See Jörg Lanz von Liebenfels, *Theozoologie, oder Die Kunde von den Sodomsäfflingen und dem Götter-Elektron eine Einführung in die älteste und neueste Weltanschauung und eine Rechtfertigung des Fürstentums und des Adels* (Vienna: Moderner Verlag, 1905).
73 Ian Kershaw, *Hitler, 1889–1936: Hubris* (New York: W. W. Norton & Company, 1998), 138–39.
74 Giosuè Carducci (1835–1907) was a prominent Italian poet and literary critic of the late nineteenth century. He was the first Italian to win the Nobel Prize for Literature, in 1906. In his youth, he was a fiercely anti-clerical atheist, and like many Italian leftists of the time adopted Satan as a symbol of liberation, rebellion and free-thinking. Later in life he reconciled with his Roman Catholic faith.
75 Mikhail Bakunin (1814–1876) was a Russian revolutionary anarchist and socialist and is widely regarded as one of the most influential radicals in the philosophical development and international spread of the anarchist movement.
76 Howard Phillips Lovecraft (1819–1937) was an American pulp author of horror, fantasy and weird fiction, best known for his stories involving the eldritch abomination Cthulhu and other god-like ancient beings who regard people as less than insects interloping on their planet, for his histrionic xenophobia, and for his philosophy of 'cosmicism' — a kind of nihilism emphasising the near total irrelevance of humanity in the vastness of an uncaring and arbitrary universe.
77 John Lewis, 'Satanic group saving souls', *Otago Daily Times*, 29 March 2017; Andre Chumko, 'Devil in its detail: Inside the world of New Zealand's Satanists', *Otago Daily Times*, 5 January 2019.

Epilogue
1 Monica Black, *A Demon-Haunted Land: Witches, Wonder Doctors, and the Ghosts of the Past in Post-WWII Germany* (New York: Macmillan, 2020).
2 Michael E. Bell, 'Vampires and Death in New England, 1784 to 1892', *Anthropology and Humanism* 31, no. 2 (2008): 124–40.

About the author

For nearly two decades cultural mercenary Andrew Paul Wood has been one of Aotearoa New Zealand's leading writers on matters art-historical and aesthetic. His work has appeared in publications in New Zealand, Australia, the UK, Europe and the US. His range runs the gamut from critically acclaimed translations of the poetry of German-Jewish author Karl Wolfskehl with Friedrich Voit to teasing out the history of the pavlova to international media interest with Annabelle Utrecht. He is art editor for *takahē* magazine. Mostly harmless.

Acknowledgements

I would like to acknowledge and thank the many people who directly and indirectly made this book possible.

First, my muse, Fiona Pardington, who created the amazing and inspiring cover. Nicola Legat, Anna Bowbyes and everyone else at Massey University Press for letting me do it. The maestro himself, Robert Ellwood, whose *Islands of the Dawn* was an important starting place, for his kind words of encouragement. Preeminent folklorist Owen Davies for being an inspiration and showing some interest. The wonderful people who scanned everything that goes into the Papers Past website. John Latham for helpful advice on dealing with the subject in the New Zealand context. Occult historian and Aleister Crowley expert Richard Kaczynski for going above and beyond to help with sources and clarifications. The very busy television producer Rob Tapert for providing such a great anecdote — and thanks to my industry contact who made that happen, you know who you are. Penelope Jackson for information on Daisy Osborn. Hilary Stace for expert help on Radiant Living. OTO New Zealand and Spiritualism New Zealand for being very helpful. Barney Brewster and the Brewster family for information and images of Roy and Nettie Brewster and their Beehive House, Norian. Archivists and librarians everywhere who kindly helped me find things and imparted their wisdom. Everyone I have forgotten to mention.

I'd also like to give special thanks to everyone who answered their emails, even if they weren't able to help.

Index

Page numbers in **bold** refer to images

A

A City Possessed 348–49
A Goddess of Mercy 308
À rebours 19
'A Wayfaring Man' 93–95
Abaaner Incendium 358
Abbey of Thelema *see* Thelema
Aboriginal Australians 68, 178
Abraham, Larry 291
Abrams, Albert 126
Absolutism 269
abuse, ritual 292–93, 348–49
  see also paedophilia
An Act of Faith 288
Adams, F. B. 307–8
Addey, John 273
Adorno, Theodor 21
Age of Aquarius 273–93
Age of Reason 249
Ager, Raymond 241
Albertus Magnus 249
Alcock, Harry 266
aliens & encounters 264, 274, 288
Allan, Frank 60
Allen, Gary 291
Alpers, O. T. J. 145, 149, 152
Alpha et Omega Order 86, 117, 122
alt-right 290, 317–18, 354, 358–60
The American Boys' Book of Signs, Signals, and Symbols 112–13
An die Deutschen 317
Ancient Aliens 264
Ancient Celtic New Zealand 259
Andreae, Johann Valentin 323
Anglican Church 18, 19, 42, 64–65, 297

Angus, Rita 308
animal welfare 47, 73
Animals Protection Act 1960 73
anthropology 16–17, 307, 312, 352
Anthroposophy 74–75, 103, 120, 130–39, 233, 325, 360
Antiquus Mysticusque Ordo Rosæ Crucis 336–37
anti-Semitism 290, 316
Anzac Day commemorations 310
Aotearoa, monoplane 205–8
Archer Insurance Policy Case 214–16
Argenteum Astrum 86, 225, 233
Ariosophy 360
Armfield, Maxwell 231
Arnold, Edwin 230
Arnold, Thomas, the Younger 298–300
Arnold, Tom 187
The Art of Rosaleen Norton 240, 241
Arthur C. Clarke's World of Strange Powers 203
The Aryan Maori 39–40
Asatru & Asatrú 318–19
Asatrú Folk Assembly 319
Asatru Free Assembly 318–19
Ásatrúarfélagið 318
Aston, Francis 249–50
astral spirits 249
astral travel 100, 103
astrology 191, 228, 249, 273, 298
'At the End of the Passage' 18
Atkinson, Alison Yvonne 58
Atkinson, Hal 138
Atkinson, Harry & Annie 39
Atlantis: The Antediluvian World 190

Aurelia Co-operative Land and Labour Association 182
Australia and New Zealand: The Home of a New Sub-Race 68
automatic writing 171

B

Bachofen, Johann Jakob 316
Baden-Powell, Robert 109–11
Baker, Ida 236
Bakunin, Mikhail 361
Ball, Hugo 281
Ballantyne, K. M. 286
Ballantyne, Tony 38
Banks, Harry H. 49
Barker, Mary Anne 183
Barrett, Samuel 305
Bastiat, Frédéric 291
Bates, Katherine 190
Batt, Leon 238
Batten, Juliet 314
Baudelaire, Charles 345
Baughan, Blanche 262
Bavarian Illuminati 84
Bax, Clifford 232–33
Baxter, James K. 56, 276
Beard, Daniel Carter 109, 112–13
Beardsley, Aubrey 234
Beauchamp, Harold 234–35
Beeby, Clarence 73
Beeville 71–73
Behind the Tomb and Other Poems 184
Beinteinsson, Sveinbjörn 318
Belich, James 353
Bennett, Allan 98
Bennett, Frank 332–33
Bent, Kimble 302
Bergier, Jacques 274
Besant, Annie 38, 58, 63, 65–67, **66**, 176, 250

Besoldus, Christopher 323
Betts, Benjamin 250–52, **251**
Beverly, Arthur 179–80
Beyond the Looking Glass 297
Bhagavad Gita 39
Bickerton, Alexander 134, 179
Big Smoke 281
Bilbrough, Miro 276
Billing, Roy 245
Bing, Adolf 231
biodynamic agriculture 103, 131, 139
bio-regionalism 314
Bismarck Weekly Tribune 145
Black Masses 343–45
Black Order of Pan-Europa 358
Blavatsky, Helena Petrovna 31–37, **32**, 40, 46, 54, 56–58, 250
Blerta 277, **278**
Blood for Satan 361
Bloomsbury set 235
Bloxam, John Astley 230
Blue Peter 212
The Blue Room 196–200, 197
The Blue Room 196–98, **197**
Bodin, Jean 345
Böhme, Jakob 24, 324
Bolt, William Mouat 190–91
Bolton, Kerry 286, 317, 354–55, 358
Bone, Eleanor 'Ray' 313, 315
The Book of Life 283
The Book of Thoth 232–34
The Book of Tokens 125–26
The Book of Witches 308
Boole, Mary Everest & George 252
Borborites 343
Boughton, Rutland 90
'The Bowmen' 187
Bracken, Thomas 184
Bradlaugh, Charles 176
Bragdon, Claude 117
Brailsford, Barry 284–88
Braithwaite, Joseph 191
Brassington, Claudius 56
Brewster, Edgar Roy 'Chook' & Nettie 252–54, **253**
Broadley, Shaun 158–59, 163
Broadsheet 348
Broome, Frederick 183

Browning, Robert & family 156, 158, 177, 331
Brownson, Ron 308
Brunton, Alan 245, 279–83, **280**
Buckminster Fuller, R. 264
Budapest, Zsuzsanna 313
Buddhism 33–34, 40, 55, 98, 230–31
Buddle, Thomas 301
Builders of Adytum 104, 117–23, 124–25
Bulwer-Lytton, Edward & Robert 34, 82, 235
Burbury, Ethel Edwina (Edna) 136, 138–39
Burdon, Philip 291
Burke, Pearl 194–96
Burn, David William Murray 64, 71
Burrell, Truda 61
Burton brothers, photographers 203
Bus Stops on the Moon: Red Mole Days 1974–1980 283
Butler, Brian 139
Butler, Samuel 159

C

Campbell, A. E. 73
Campbell, William D. 178–79
Carducci, Giosuè 361
Carey, William Reynolds 137
Carpenter, W. B. 159
Case, Paul Foster 117–18, **119**, 122–24, 125
Cathie, Bruce 263–64
Catholic Church 23, 93, 180–82
The Cauldron 315
Chambers, Hugh 139
Chambers, John & Mason 94
Chaos magic 240, 359
Chaos Magick 331
'Chapel Perilous' 26
Chapman, Clive 196–200
Chapman, Kyle 287
Chapman, Vera 312
Chapman-Taylor, James 94–95
Chariots of the Gods? 274
Charles Theodore, Elector of Bavaria 326
Chesterman, William 104, 122, 124
Child, Janee (Jane Thompson, Jane Ball, Yasmine Child) 292–93

Chinese, belief systems 23
Chippenham 276
Christ, Carol 313
Christchurch Civic Crèche case 348–49
Christchurch Society for Psychical Research, scrapbook 213–17, **215**
Christensen, Else 318, 319
Christian Astrology 298
Christian Mystics of the Rosy Cross 332
Christian Outlook 59
Christian Science 143
Church of England *see* Anglican Church
Church of Odin 317–18
Church of Satan 346–47
Churchill, Winston 310
'Cipher Manuscripts' 82
Clarkson, W. A. P. 145
C'mon 274
Cohen, Norman 352
Collegium Satanas 355
Collins, William Whitehouse 149–51
colonialism, in NZ 18, 38, 70, 95, 159, 167–70, 178, 301, 353
colour therapy 103, 258
Colquhoun, Ithell 231
The Coming of the Fairies 203
communal living 18, 45, 71–73, 276–77
Communion 288
Community of the Resurrection 88, 91
Complete Herbal 298
Comte de Paris 23
Conan Doyle, Arthur 187, 198, **199**, 200–205, 211, 303, 332
Concerning the Spiritual in Art 235
Condel, Thomas de Renzy 38
Confessions 328
Conjurors, Cardsharps and Conmen 14
Conrad, Joseph 18
Conroy, Beresford Lionel 238
Cook, Gary 287
Cook, Louisa S. 252
Cooper-Mathieson, Veni 332
Cooper-Oakley, Isabel 38
Cosmic Circle 316–17
Cossgrove, David & Selina 109–13, **110**

Cott, Jonathan 297
Cottingley Fairy hoax 47, 203–5
Cottrell, Horace Spence 210–13
Cottrell, Violet May 208–13, **209**
Council of Combined Animal Welfare Organisations of New Zealand 47
Covid-19 287
Cowan, James 176, 306
Coward, Noel 214
Cox, Mr & Mrs James 38–39
Crawford, David 317
Creswell, Toby 229
Croft, J. J. 353–54
Crompton-Smith, Rachel & Bernard 135
Crookes, William 163
Crowley, Abraham 223
Crowley, Aleister 48, 64, 223–29, **224**, 232–36, 238, 273
   & rituals 104, 122, 327–30, 332–33
   Argenteum Astrum 86
Crowley, Rose 223, 225
Cruickshank, George Craig 139
Cruickshank, Kelvin 218
Crusade for Social Justice 258
Culpeper, Nicholas 298
Curry, Mary 'Saint' Elizabeth 302
curses 307–8 *see also* mākutu

D

Dalhoff, John (John Ultimate) 289–92
Dalton, David 297
D'Annunzio, Gabriele 226
Davidson, Allan 169
Davies, Ann 118–22, **123**
Davis, Alice Marie 230
Davis, Andrew Jackson 182
Davis, Charles Oliver Bond 170
de Groot, Ethan 14
De la démonomanie des sorciers 345
de Montespan, Madame 345
de Petri, Catharose 338
De vita libri tres 249
Deacon, Elizabeth 331–33
Deacon, Vivian (Vyvyan) 186, 331–33

Deakin, Alfred 167
Deane, Ada 216
Dee, John 80, 112, 122
'The Demon Lover' 194
A Demon-Haunted Land 364
Des Chesnais, Theophilus Le Menant 182
Desmond, Arthur 346–47
Devil worship 343–61
The Devil's Sword Blunted 180
Diabolus 351
Dionysos 282–83
'*Discorso Sul Flusso E Il Reflusso Del Mare*' 266
Disney, Walt 336
Donald, Rod 276
Donnelly, Ignatius 190
Dougan, Abdullah Isa Neil 24
Doutré, Martin 259, 286
Dowie, John Alexander 203
Dowse, Percy 122
dowsing 264
Draffin, William Henry & Sarah 43, 45
Drayson, Alfred Wilks 200
Dreaver, Mary Manson 217
drugs 236, 249, 275–76, 279
Druids 312 *see* United Ancient Order of Druids
Dunedin Freethought Association 190
Dunedin Mutual Improvement Association 190
Dunedin Society for Investigating Spiritualism 180
Dunn, Elisha 163–65, **166**
Dunningham, Brian 48, 73
Dürer, Albrecht **299**
Dyer, Joseph Frank & Phoebe 235

E

Eating Media Lunch 218
Echo 161
ectoplasm 157, 203
Eddles, Mrs 216
Eddy, Mary Baker 143
Eddy, William & Horatio 34
The Edge of the Unknown 208
Edger, Kate Milligan 43
Edger, Margaret Lilian 43–45, **44**
Edmond, Martin 281, 283
Edmonds, Beatrice & Jane 52–54

Edmonds, John 158
Edmonds, Thomas **52**, 52–54
education 73–74, 133–39
Edward VIII 188
Egypt 38
Einstein, Albert 250
Ellis, Peter 348–49
Ellwood, Robert 31, 118, 339, 351
   & Spiritualism 170, 175, 178, 185, 186, 207
   & Theosophy 43–44, 58, 65–67, 71, 73, 159
Elsmore, Bronwyn 169
Eminent Victorians 18–19
Empire Sentinels **110**, 111–13
Encausse, Gérard 'Papus' 33, 327
Englefield Rock Festival 275
Ensor, Beatrice 74
Epiphanius of Salamis 343
The Equinox 122
Equipus Spiritae 357
Erridge, Mary Jane 189–90
Esoteric Buddhism 40
Espérance Club 309
Etts, Carrie 165
Evola, Julius 360

F

fairies 26, 47, 93, 203, 297–98, 364
Fairy Scouts 112
faith healing *see* spiritual healing
Fama Fraternitatis Rosae Crucis 84, 323
Fantl, Peter 279
Farnell, Billy 244, 245
Farquhar, Grant 59–60
Farr, Florence 85–86, 98
Farrell, Nick 96, 98, 104, 120–22
far-right beliefs 290, 317–18, 354, 358–60
fascism & neo-fascism 318, 346–47, 354, 358–60
Faustus Scorpius 354–55
Fawcett, Edward Douglas 48
Felkin, Ethelwyn 91–93, 103
Felkin, Harriot 91–95, **92**, 103–4
Felkin, Mary 88
Felkin, Robert William 86–89, **87**, 91–103, 324–26
Felkin, Samuel & Laurence 103

Fell, Barry 286
Fellowship of the Rosy Cross 86
Fensalir Kindred 319
Ferguson, Christine 22
Ferguson, Margret 174
Ficino, Marsilio 23, 249, 323
Finkel, Irving 157
First Anglecyn Church of Odin 318
Fitzgerald, Father 88, 91
Fitzgerald, Noel 331
The Flaming Sword 358
Fleetham, Eliza Jane 208
The Forerunner 90
Forster, E. M. 235
Fortean phenomenon 305–6
Fortune, Dion 90
Forty Years' Experiences of Occult Research 190
Foster, Frederick 244
Foster, Norah 216
'Fourth Way' 237
Fox, Margaret & Kate 157–58
Franklin, Benjamin 84
Fraser, Peter 262
Frazer, James George 17, 250
Freemasonry 23, 58, 80, 85, 111–12, 327, 330
Friends of the Eilean Fhlodaigearraidh Faeries 304
Fry, Mary & Warwick 217
Fullerton, Alex 67
Furlong, Jane 219

G

Gadal, Antonin 338
Galileo 266
Gallipoli: The Scale of Our War exhibition 188
gardening *see* biodynamic agriculture
Gardiner, Reginald & Ruth 89, 94, 103
Gardiner, Rolf 309
Gardner, Gerald 26, 312–15, 331
Garner, Brent 357
Gellner, Ernest 16
genius loci 306
Geometrical Psychology 250–51, **251**
George, Stefan 316
Germer, Karl 330–31
'Getting Beyond Ritual Abuse' 348
Ghost Club 201

Ghost Rite 281
ghosts 157, 161, 176, 300, 305 *see also* mediums & mediumship
Gibb, Robin 274–75
Gibson, Wilfred William 235–36
Giles, Joseph 189
Gillie, J. L. 162
Girl Guides 109
Glover, Walter 240
Gnostic Mass 328–30
Gnostic Society 24
Gnosticism 24–25, 323–25
Goethe, Johann Wolfgang von 133
Goetheanum 131–33
The Goetia 104
The Golden Bough 17
Golden Dawn 25–26, 79–105, 86, 112, 117, 120–22, 126–27 *see also* Stella Matutina; Whare Rā
Golder, Charles Joseph Bonaventure 174
Goldsmith, Michael 285
Gonne, Maude 80
Good, Roy 274
Goodric-Clarke, Nicholas 360
Goodyear, Frederick 235
Goossens, Eugene 241–44
Gopal, Ram 234
Gordon, Charles 88
Gosden, Chris 17
Gowland, William Percy 198
Grainger, George William 208
Grant, Kenneth 331
Grant, S. W. 99
Great Ngāruawāhia Music Festival 275
Greeley, Horace 158
Green, Matthew Wood 180
Green, Nile 306
Greenlees, Gavin 240–43
Greenstone Trails: The Maori and Pounamu 284
Greer, Mary 82
Grey, George 179, 183
Griffiths, Frances 47, 203–5
Grote, George 16
Grove of Summer Stars 312
Gudjónsson, Thorsteinn 318
Guild of Spiritual Healing 255
Gurdjieff, George 33, 237

H

Habermas, Jürgen 22
Hackett, James & Priscilla 178
Haereticarum Fabularum Compendium 343
Hahn, Peter von 34
Halley's Comet 267
Hansen, Dan & Edith 71–72
Hansen, Jörmundur Ingi 318
Hansen, Olive 71–73
Hansen, Ray 71–73
The Happy Colony 18
The Harbinger of Light 176, 184, 210
Hard Frost 234
Hardinge Britten, Emma 161, 167–68, **204**
Hargrave, John 112
Harmonic 33 263–64
The Harmonic Code — The Harmonics of Reality 264
The Harmonic Conquest of Space 263
Harmony Prayer Circles 255
Harris, Jack 231, 232
Harris, Jane Elizabeth & Thomas 182–86
Harris, John Chantry 170, 175
Harris, Marguerite Frieda & Percy 230–34
Harris, Susannah 186
Harris, Thomas 189
Harris, Woolf (Wolf) 231
Havelock Work 89–93
Hayek, Friedrich 359
Hayward, Henry 226
Healing Rays and Consciousness 257
health & healing 52, 137, 263, 298, 302 *see also* spiritual healing
Heart of Darkness 18
Heartwood Community 276
heathenry 315–19
Hedged with Divinities 40
Heidegger, Martin 15
Heindel, Max 338
Hemus, Charles & Gertrude Evangeline 45
Henry, T. Shekleton 178
The Heretic 355, 358
Herkt, David 283
Hermes Trismegistus 23, 85
Hermetic Order of the Golden Dawn *see* Golden Dawn
Hermetic Society of the Morgenröthe 86

Hermeticism 23, 85, 323
Hess, Tobias 323
Heuffer, Oliver Madox 308
Higher Thought New Zealand 122, 124
Hill, Mary Ann 302
Hillary, Edmund 47–48, 259–62, **261**
Hillary family 259
Himmler, Heinrich 361
Hinduism 34, 36
Hinzenburg, Olgivanna Lazovitch 237
Hipparchus 273
Hirsig, Leah 225, 229
Hobbs, Marion 276
Hobsbawm, Eric 23
Hobson's Pledge movement 286
Hoch, Judith 286
Hockley, Frederick 82
Hodge, Mabel 136
Hodgkins, Frances 65
Hodson, Geoffrey 47, 73
Hodson, Jane 47
Hoff, Rayner 238
Hoffman, Anna Karina 240–45
Holdsworth, John and Maggie 256
The Holy Book of Women's Mysteries 313
Home, Daniel Dunglas 163, 177
homosexuality 68, 358
Honer, Francis 241
Hood, George 205–8
Hood, Lynley 348–49
Hope, Lily 214, 216–17
Hoppe, Hans-Hermann 359
Horos, Theo 84
Horowitz, Mitch 118, 273–74
Hosking, John 149–51
Houdini, Harry 158, 205
How to Live a Century and Grow Old Gracefully 163
Hugo, Victor 84
Hunt, Emma 40
Huysmans, Joris-Karl 19, 345
'Hymn to Satan' 361
Hypatia 59

I

Illuminati 326
Imiaslavie sect 33
'In Defence of Science' 20
In the Time of the Manaroans 276
Independent and Rectified Rite of the Golden Dawn 86
Inglis, Agnes & family 61
International Astronomical Union 273
Io-Ana temple 120
Iopata, Wallace 174–75
Irwin, Tim 289
Isis Unveiled 40
Islands of the Dawn 31

J

'J. Habakuk Jephson's Statement' 200
Jam Factory 275
Jellicoe, John Rushworth 98–99
Jenks, Lorna Ann 240–45
Jerusalem, Whanganui River 276
Jones, Betty 96, 105
Jones, George Cecil 225
Jones, Kathleen 236
Jordan, Evelyn Maud 152–53
Joseph, M. K. 24–25
Journal for the Scientific Study of Religion 288–89
Judaism & Jews, in NZ 39, 230–31, 317–18
Judd, Pearl 196–200
Jugendbewegung 109
Jung, Carl 317, 323–24
The Jungle Book 111
Juveny, Miranda May de la 152–53

K

Kabbalah 38, 100, 148
Kaczynski, Richard 229
Kandinsky, Wassily 235
Kant, Immanuel 15
karma 36, 37, 131, 218
Katherine Mansfield: The Story-Teller 236
Kellner, Carl 327
Kēnana, Rua 302
Kendall, Thomas 303
Kershaw, Ian 360–61
The Key to Theosophy 40
Keynes, John Maynard 249
Khlysty sect 33
Kibbo Kift 112
Kieckhefer, Richard 343
Killen, J. M. 194
King, Augustine 38
King, Francis 229
King, Jani 288
Kipling, Rudyard 18, 111, 117
Kirk, Norman 277
Kollerstrom, Gustav & Oscar 70
Krishnamurti, Jiddu 63–67, 70, 72
Kurlander, Eric 21–22

L

Là-Bas 19, 345
Lada cars 291
The Lantern 93, 105
'Lanterne magique' 19
Larnarch's mausoleum **350**
Latham, John 122, 349–52, 354
Laver, James 236
LaVey, Anton 25, 346
The Law 291
Lawson, John & Stella 205–8
Le Calvaire **344**
Leadbeater, Charles 40, 63–70, **69**, 250, 332
Leary, Timothy 276
Lectorium Rosicrucianum 338–39
Lectorium Rosicrucianum 324
Leene, Henk & Zwier Willem 338–39
Lehmann, Rosamond & Rudy 230
Leibniz, Gottfried 249
Les Fleurs du Mal 345
Lestrange, Bridget 300
Letters on Demonology and Witchcraft 297
Lévi, Éliphas 34
Lewis, C. S. 98
Lewis, Harvey Spencer 336
ley lines 264
Liber AL vel Legis 223
Liberal Catholic Church 40, 42, 68, 332
Liddell, E. W. 'Bill' 315
Life and Work at the Great Pyramid 179
The Life of Gargantua and of Pantagruel 225
Light 187, 200
The Light of Asia 230
Lilly, William 298
The Lion, the Witch, and the Wardrobe 98

Little, Robert Wentworth 80, 324
The Lives of Alcyone 67
Livingstone, Ray 355–57
Lo, These Are Parts of His Ways 55–58, **57**
Lobachevsky, Nikolai 33
Lochore, R. A. 286
Locke, Elsie 276
Logan, John & family 165–67
London Dialectical Society 163
Lorrain, Jean 19
Lotus Ashram 279
Louisson, Charles 152
Lovecraft, H. P. 361
Loveday, Raoul & Betty May 225
Lovell-Smith, Edgar & family 213–14
Lovelock, Olive 139
Lucifer 79
Lunar Effect: Moon's Influence on Our Weather 266
Lutyens, Mary 68
Lux, Anna 21
Lye, Len 65

M

Macandrew, James 162–63
Machen, Arthur 85–86, 187
Mackechnie, Edward Augustus 178–79
Mackenzie, Kenneth 82
MacKinnell, Terry 273
Madole, James H. 358
The Magical World of Aleister Crowley 229
The Magician's Nephew 98
Mahupuku, Hāmuera Tamahau 171
mākutu 300–305 *see also* curses
Malden, Henry 136, 137, 139
Maning, Frederick 303
Mansfield, Katherine 229, 234–37
Manson, Charles 274
Māori 20, 39–40, 68, 95, 262, 283–88, 314
 belief systems 14, 22–23, 37–38, 167–72, 176, 300–307, 352–54
 marriage rites, legal & spiritual 71, 143, 146–48, 218
Mars and Venus 357
Marsden, Samuel 303

Marshman, John 159
Marx, Karl & Marxism 191, 274
Mason, Dulcia 49–51
Mason, Henry Greathead 'Rex' 48–51, **50**
Mass of Vain Observance 343–45
Massey, Gerald 37–38
Mathers, Samuel Liddell MacGregor 79–86, **81**, 96, 103, 104, 112, 117, 223
'A Matin Song' 183
Maurais, Augustus William 59–60
McIntosh, Christopher 79
McLean, Donald 353
McLean, William 186, 192, **193**
McMurty, Grady 331, 333
McNallen, Stephen 318–19
Meakin, Neville Gauntlett Tudor 324–25
Mechanics' institutes 179
mediums & mediumship 25, 34, 103, 156–219 *see also* ghosts
Meebold, Alfred 103, 139
Meers, William Denne 50
Mellinger, Frederick 331
memes 359–60
mental health 103, 180
mermaids 304
Message of Life 173
metagenetics 318–19
Methodist Church 297, 352
Meyer, Frank 359
Middleton, Sue 73–74
Might Is Right; or The Survival of the Fittest 346
'The Military Value of Spiritualism' 187
Mills, Alexander Rud 318
Ministry of Fog 245
miracles, religious 14, 167, 249, 297
modernity 15–16
Mokoia Island 306
Moncrieff, J. R. 205–8
Montessori, Maria 74
moon, effect of 265–66
Moore, Alan 26
Moore, Josephine Ericsson 143
Moral, Spiritual and Social Advancement Movement of New Zealand 258

More Light 172–73
The Morning of the Magicians 274
Morris, Joe 243
Morris dancing 309
Mortadello, or The Angel of Venice 235–36
Mottus, Cameron 319
Mr Asia 275
'Mr. Sludge, "The Medium"' 158
Muller, Selina 238–40
Mumler, William 202
Murphy, Ellen 194
Murray, John Middleton 235, 237
Murray, Margaret 312
music festivals 274–75
Mysteria Mystica Maxima 229

N

Nairn, Barbara 104
Nathan, Elizabeth 231
Nation, William Charles & family 170–74, 186
National Association of Spiritualist Churches in New Zealand 186, 188
National Association of Spiritualists of New Zealand 186
Natural History 265–66
natural magic 23, 26, 80, 249–67
Nazism & neo-Nazism 20–21, 258, 316–18, 358, 359–60
Neil, James 59
Neill, J. S. 184
Nelson, Ruth & Gwen 136, 138–39
Nemesis 357
Neuburg, Victor 235
New Age 105, 273–93
The New Age 237
New Education Fellowship 73–74
New Force 317
'The New Thelema' 235
New Thought churches 118, 210
New York Conference of Spiritualists 34
New Zealand Labour Party 49
New Zealand Media Council 319

New Zealand Vegetarian Society 47
New Zealand's 1899 Customs Tariff 307
Newman, John Henry 19
Newton, Isaac 249
Newton, John 234
The Nexus 358
Ngāi Tahu 283–85
Ngāi Tūāhuriri 287
Ngāpuhi 352
Ngāti Māmoe 287
Nicholas II & Tsarina Alexandra 33
Nichols, Ross 312
Nicholson, Sue 218
Niers, Peter 345
Nietzsche, Friedrich 15
Nimoy, Leonard 264
Nineteenth Century Miracles 167
nirvana 37
None Dare Call it Conspiracy 291
Norcliff, Lord 208, 210
Nordic paganism 315–19
Norian philosophy 252–54
Norian Thoughts 254
Norton, Rosaleen 'Roie' 237–44, **239**, **242**
Notorious Australians 229
nuclear bombs 263

O

Oak Grove coven 313
Occult Chemistry 250
'Occult Memetics' 359
The Occult Roots of Nazism 360
occultures 15–27
Oddie, John 60
Odin worship 316–17
Odyssey 157
ohu 277
Olcott, Henry Steel 34, **35**, 38–39, 43–45, 50–51, 58
Old Diary Leaves 43–44
Ontario Consultants for Religious Tolerance 348
Orage, A. R. 237
Orden des Gold- und Rosenkreutz 324
Order of Bards, Ovates & Druids 312
Order of Nine Angles 347–48
Order of the Deorc Fyre 356
Order of the Golden Dawn 25
Order of the King's Daughters 146
Order of the Left Hand Path 354
Order of the Round Table 61
Order of the Star in the East 63–65
Order of the Sword of Damocles 357
Order of the Table Round 102–3, 121, 324–26
Ordo Sinistra Vivendi 354–58
Ordo Templi Orientis 186, 225, 229, 233, 323–34
O'Regan, Tipene 285
Orwell, George 359
Osborn, Daisy 55, 56, **57**, 58
Otter, Gwen 236
Otto, Rudolf 16
Ouija boards 14, 157, 158
Ouspensky, P. D. 33, 237
Owenite sect 18
Oxford Movement 18

P

pacifism 50, 71, 73, 134
paedophilia 63–64, 67–70 *see also* abuse, ritual
paganism 14, 281, 352–53, 360
  neopaganism 24–25, 297–319, 351–52, 356, 358, 364, 366–67
Page, Jimmy 273
Pai Mārire 353
Pairman, Robert & Susannah 60
Pānapa, Wiremu Nētana 96
Panarion 343
'Pania of the Reef: A Maori Legend' 212–13
Papahurihia (Te Atua Wera) 169, 352
Paracelsus 22–23, 324
Parris, Robert 135
Parsons, Jack 330
Partridge, Christopher 15
Pascal, Blaise 21
Pauwels, Louis 274
Pawmistry 265
Peebles, James Martin 163–65, **164**, 179–80
Peloha 256
Pemberton, Robert 18
'The People's Plan' 259
Perdurabo: The Life of Aleister Crowley 229
performing arts 277, **278**, 279–83, 309
Pertinent 238, 240
Peter the Great 34
Petone Spiritualist church 217
Pew Research Forum 14
Phillips, Julia 313
photography, spirit 202–3, 216
Pickingill, George 314–15
Pickingill Papers 314–15
Pjeturss, Helgi 318
Plaskow, Judith 313
Pliny the Elder 249, 265–66
Plunkett, Mary 143–46, **150**, 151
Podmore, Frank 200
Pole, Wellesley Tudor 325
Police Offences Act 1884 189
politics & the occult 33, 49, 88, 103, 133–34, 185, 190–91, 358–61 *see also* specific political parties
Pollard, Sarah Rosetta, Rose & Cecilia 61
Poltergeist phenomenon 170–71, 200, 305
Popper, Karl 191
Popular Mechanics 252
Porleifsson, Dagur 318
P-Orridge, Genesis 15
Porter, Jessie 231
Potts, Fred 194–95
Predicting the Weather by the Moon 266
Presbyterian Church 58–59, 161
Price, Harry 198
Priestly, J. B. 90
Princess Mary's Gift Book 47
prison reform 134, 135, 177
Progradior and the Beast 332
'Psychological Investigations' 178
Psycho-Radio-Cosmics 267
'public sphere' 22
pyramids & pyramidology 152, 179–80, 274
Pytheas of Massalia 265–66

Q

Quantum Dynamics 292–93
Quayle, Dan 27

R

Rabelais, François 225
Radford, Andrew 22
Radiant Health movement 52
Radiant Living movement 48, 255–60
Radio Liberty 291
Radionics 126
Rainbow Network 287
Rais, Gilles de 345
Raison, Ron 121
Rakena, Ruawai 352
Ramanda, Azena 288
Randolph, Paschal Beverly 327
Rasputin, Grigori 27, 33
Rātana, Tahupōtiki Wiremu 201
Rātana church 14, 49, 207–8
Rationalism 58
Red Mole company 279–83
Red Mole on the Road 282
Redbeard, Ragnar 346–47
Redwood 70 festival 274–75
Regardie, Israel 126–27
Reid, Bernard 14
reincarnation 36, 37, 61, 91, 100, 131, 279, 288, 293
Reizenstein, Ernst 138
religion 14, 15–27 *see also* specific religions
Religion and the Decline of Magic 250
Remarkable Experiences in the Phenomena of Spiritualism in New Zealand 173
Reuss, Theodor 326–27, 330, 333
Rhythm 235
Richmond, Emma Jane, Henry & family 48, 134–35
Richmond, Keith 332–33
Riedel, Albert Richard (Frater Albertus) 120
Rig Veda 54
Rijckenborgh, Jan van 338
Riley, Bridget 274
Ring, Ken 265–66
Ringatū 14
'Rites of Eleusis' 228–29
Ritual Action Group 348–49
Riviera, Diego 336
Roberts, Charles Nathaniel 185
Robinson, Henry F. 46, 124
Roddenberry, Gene 336
Rodwell, Sally 279–83

Rops, Félicien **344**
Rosaline, Kay 348
Rosenkreuz, Christian 84–85, 93, 323
Rosicrucianism 80, 82–86, **83**, 93, 323–39
Ross, Thomas 60
Rough, William 60, 189–90
'Rules to be Observed When Forming Spiritual Circles' 161
The Runestone 318
Ruskin, John 252
Russell, Andrew Hamilton 99
Russell, Geoffrey 292
Russell, George 231
Russia & Russian Orthodox Church 31–34
Rutherford, Robert 191
Rutu 308

S

Sadler, Michael T. H. 235
Salt, Francis 'Frank' 99–100, 105
Samhain 310
Sanders, Anne 71–72
Sanders, Charles W. 43, 45
Sandwich Factories 289–90
Sankaran, Jay 175
Sargeson, Frank 234
Satanic New Zealand 361
Satanic Reds 361
The Satanic Temple 361
Satanism 343–61
Satanism in New Zealand 354
Satan's Slaves 351
Savage, Michael Joseph 49, 258
Savage Club 309
Scandinavian paganism 315–19
School of Ageless Wisdom 117, 120
School of Radiant Living 255–60
Schopenhauer, Arthur 15, 26, 39
science 15–27, 249–67
Scientology 24, 289–90
Scott, Sidney 200
Scott, Walter 297
Scott-Moncrieff, C. W. 64
Scout movement 109–13
The Secret Doctrine 36–37, 46, 56–58

Secret Inner Order Rituals of the Golden Dawn 121
Seddon, Richard 216
Seekers Centre & Seekers Trust 255
Seen and Unseen 190
Sensing Murder 218–19
Seton, Ernest Thompson 109
sex magic 122–24, 223–25, 237–38, 327, 334
Shadbolt, Tim 276
Shadowland 229
Shaw, Archie 104–5
Shaw, George Bernard 65
Sheringham, Hugh Tempest 325
Shrubsall, Vera 244
Shurrock, Francis 309
Simpson, Charles A. & Florence 254–55
Simpson, Grace 254–55
Sinclair, Peter 274
Singh, Gobind 187
Sinnett, Alfred Percy 38, 40
Sisters of the Silver Star 334
Sivas Esoteric Community 338–39
Skiffington, Sharon 244
Smaragdum Thalassa *see* Stella Matutina order; Whare Rā
Smith, James 162–63
Smyth, C. Piazzi 179
Smythe, Robert Sparrow 201
Snow Kings of the Southern Alps 262
Social Credit 50, 71
social imaginary 21–22
Societas Rosicruciana in Anglia 80–85, 324–26
Societas Rosicruciana in Scotia 324
Society for Spiritual Progress 185
Society of the Blue Veil 146
Society of the Southern Cross 90–93
Soles for Satan 361
Soljak, Miriam 20
Solomons, Brother 310
Somerset, Crawford 73
Song of the Stone 284–85, 287
Song of Waitaha 284, 287
Sons of Daniel Boone 109
'Soror (Sister) Egeria' 333–34, **335**

Spare, Austin Osman 240, 359
'The Spell of the Supernatural' 178–79
The Spiral Dance 313
spirit photography 202–3, 216
spirit writing 171
spiritual healing 96, 143, 149, 180, 201, 254–58 *see also* health & healing
& Spiritualism 207–8, 218, 279
Spiritualism 25, 31, 34, 50, 58, 60, 157–219
Spiritualism and Theosophy: Twain Brothers of the Anti-Christ 59
Spiritualism New Zealand 218
Spiritualist Church 186
Spiritualist Church of New Zealand 188–89
Spiritualist Investigation Society 161
Spiritualist Motor Ambulance Fund 187
Spookland 178
Sprengel, Anna 82–85
St John, Theodore & Theodora 68
Stacey, May Banks 336
Starhawk 313
Station Life in New Zealand 183
Staveren, Herman van & Miriam 39
Steiner, Rudolf 74, 93, 130–39, **132**, 324
Steiner schools 74–75, 136, 137–39
Stella Matutina order 18, 86, 93–105, 118–20, 126–27 *see also* Golden Dawn
Stewart-Harawira, Makere 286–87
Stilwell, Arthur 336
Stone, John 60
Stone, Louisa 60
Stopes, Marie 210
Storm, Jason Josephson 16
Stout, Anna 167
Stout, Robert **160**, 161, 180
Stowell, Henry Matthew 39
Strachey, Lytton 18–19, 235
Street, Noel & Coleen 277–79
Strieber, Whitley 288
Stuart, Samuel 43, 45

Stuart-Menteath, Jean 139
Stumpp, Peter 345
Sturdy, Edward Toronto 39
Summer of Love 25, 274
sun, rising 54
Sun Goddess 308
supernatural imaginary 21–22
Sutcliffe, Herbert 48, 255–60, **261**
Sutcliffe, Phyllis 256, 263
Swaby, Beatrice 217
Symbolist movement 33
Symes, Aisling 219
Symes, William Henry 286
Symonds, Lily Loder 200
synergetics 264

T

Tahitahi, Hone 188
Talbott, Garth 133
Tales of Anna Hoffman 243–44
Talisman 355–57
Talmage, Thomas de Witt 180
taniwha 304–5
Tapert, Rob 125–26
Tarawera eruption 176
tarot 82, 117–18, 125–26, 232–34
The Tattooed Land 284
Tau, Te Maire 287–88
Tawhai, Huia & Lou 174–75
Tax Reduction Integrity Movement 289, 292
Taxil, Léo 343
Taylor, Charles 21–22
Taylor, Jack 104–5, 120, 121, 126
Taylor, Joseph 266–69, **268**
Taylor, Richard 167
Te Ika A Maui 167
Te Mata Peak 96, 256
Te Pani 284–85
Te Rangi-taka-i-waho, Te Mānihera 171–72
Te Rau, Kereopa 353
Teenage Satanism 349
The Tempest 279
Temple of Set 355
Temple of Truth 25, 50, 143–53, **147**
Tennyson, Alfred 30
Tenzing Norgay 259
Terry, W. H. 39, 184
Tesla, Nikola 264

The Brescians 226–27
The Old Straight Track 264
Thelema faith 225–26, 235, 324, 328–31
Theodoret of Cyrrhus 343
'Theosophy and Imperialism' 71
Theosophy in New Zealand 71
Theosophy & the Theosophical Society 24, 25, 31–75, 134–35
Auckland lodges 43, 45–46
Christchurch Lodge 50–55
Dunedin Lodge 58–63, **62**
H.P.B. Lodge 45–46, 48
New Zealand Section 38, 40, 45–46, 47, 70–71
NZ lodges (branches) 39, 40–43, 45–46
Theosophical Order of Service 73
Theosophical Women's Association 50
Wellington Lodge 39, 40, 48–49
Thomas, Keith 250
Thomson, K. 354, 357
Thoth-Hermes Temples 117, 126–27
Three Witches **242**
Thule Society 360–61
Tibet 31, 33–34
Tillett, Gregory 333
The Time of Achamoth 24–25
Titokowaru 302
Tohunga Suppression Act 1907 301–2
Tong, Eunice Mary Lew 332–33
Tractarianism 18
Transcendental Meditation 289
Tregear, Edward Robert 39–40, **41**
The Triumph of Pan 235
Troilus and Cressida 265
Trotsky 191
'Two Anzacs Meet in London' 229
Two Worlds 187
Twyneham, Ron 136–37
Tylor, Edward Burnett 17
Typhonian Order 331

U

UFOs 263–64, 306
United Ancient Order of Druids 310–12, **311**
Universal Church of the Master 279
University of Auckland 20
Uruaokapuarangi waka 283

V

Valentine, Greta 233
Valiente, Doreen 26
Vāmācāra 345–46
Vance, Andrea 319
Vasanta School 74
Vedanta 39
Vegas, Frankie 361
vegvísir 14
Vietnam War & protests 275
Viking Brotherhood 318–19
Vis, Margaret van der 63
visual arts 307, 308–9
The Vital Message 200
Vögtle, Berta 307
Völkner, Carl 353
von Dadelszen, John 89, 103–5
von Däniken, Erich 274
von Liebenfels, Jörg Lanz 360

W

Wachtmeister, Constance 38, 59
Waddell, Leila Ida Nerissa Bathurst (Laylah) 226–30, **227**
Waddell, Rutherford 59
Waihi 305
Waikato Expressway 303–4
Waikato saurian 304–5
Waitaha 283–88
Waite, Arthur E. 82, 86, 98, 324, 325
Wallace, Alastair 121–22
Wallace, Alfred R. 159
Wallis, Roy 288–89
The Wanderings of a Spiritualist 201, 205
Warren, Phil 274–75
Warwick, Tarl 359
The Watcher 355
Watkins, Alfred 264
Watson, Elizabeth 206–7
Weatherwise 214
Webber, Deb 218
Weber, Max 15–16, 250
Webley, Sarah Ann 170
Wedgwood, James Ingall 331–32
Weishaupt, Adam 326
Weleda 136, 263
Wellington Association of Spiritualists 175–77
Wellington Spiritualist Investigation Society 175–76
Wells, Ada, Chris & family **132**, 133–34, 136–37
West, Jessie 194–96
West, T. J. & West Pictures 226–27
West, William Robert 194
Westcott, William Wynn 79, 82, **83**, 85, 88, 326–27
Westra, Ans 73
Whare Rā 93–99, **97**, 102–5, 120–22 *see also* Golden Dawn
Whiro-te-tipua 352
White Order of Thule 358
white supremacism 34, 288, 315, 348, 355, 358–60
Wicca 14, 26, 312–15
The Wiccan 315
Williams, Charles 98
Williams, Henry 300–301, 352
Wilson, Hilda Gertrude 255–56
Wilson, John Cracroft 51
Wilson, Robert Anton 26
The Witch **299**
witchcraft 14, 237–45, 297–319
Witchcraft Act 1735 189
Witchcraft Today 313
The Witch-Cult in Western Europe 312
Wolfe, Jane 225
Wolfskehl, Karl 316–17
'Woman's Work and Destiny' 183
Womanspirit Rising 313
Wong, Gilbert 355, 357
Wood, Cecil 54
Wood, Robert 59
Wood, Susan Nugent & John 183
Woodcraft Indians 109
Woodman, William Robert 79–80, 85
Woodstock festival 274
Woodstock: Music from the Original Soundtrack and More 274
Woolf, Virginia 235
World 177
The World as Will and Idea 26, 39
World War I 40, 90, 94, 186–89, 210
World War II 137, 216, 308, 330
Worrad, Timothy 95
Worthington, Arthur Bently 50, 135, 143–53, **144**
Wotan worship 316–17
Wragge, Clement 286
Wright, Elsie 47, 203–5
Wright, Matthew 91
Wyllie, Edward 203

X

Xena: Warrior Princess 125–26

Y

Yeats, W.B. 86, 331
Young Theosophist 72–73
Youth International Party 274

Z

Zach, Franz Xaver von 326–27
Zalewski, Chris 126, 334
Zalewski, Patrick 'Pat' 102, 121, 126–27, 334
Zenith Applied Philosophy 289–92
Zenobia, Madame 189

First published in 2023 by Massey University Press
Private Bag 102904, North Shore Mail Centre
Auckland 0745, New Zealand
www.masseypress.ac.nz

Text copyright © Andrew Paul Wood, 2023
Images copyright © as credited, 2023

Design by Megan van Staden
Cover photograph by Fiona Pardington

The moral right of the author has been asserted

All rights reserved. Except as provided by the Copyright Act 1994, no part of this book may be reproduced, stored in or introduced into a retrieval system or transmitted in any form or by any means (electronic, mechanical, photocopying, recording or otherwise) without the prior written permission of both the copyright owner(s) and the publisher.

A catalogue record for this book is available from
the National Library of New Zealand

Printed and bound in China by Everbest Investment Ltd

ISBN: 978-1-99-101637-9
eISBN: 978-1-99-101651-5